I Didn't Get Where I Am Today

I Didn't Get Where I Am Today

An Autobiography

David Nobbs

WILLIAM HEINEMANN : LONDON

Published by William Heinemann in 2003

1 3 5 7 9 10 8 6 4 2

Copyright © David Nobbs 2003

Photograph of Leonard Rossiter and David Nobbs
and
Extract from *Leonard Rossiter*, compiled by Robert Tanitch and published in 1985 by Robert Royce

The author and publishers have made all reasonable efforts to contact copyright holders for permission, and apologise for any omissions or errors in the form of credit given.
Corrections may be made in future printings

First published in the United Kingdom in 2003 by William Heinemann

The Random House Group Limited
20 Vauxhall Bridge Road, London, SW1V 2SA

Random House Australia (Pty) Limited
20 Alfred Street, Milsons Point, Sydney, New South Wales 2061, Australia

Random House New Zealand Limited
18 Poland Road, Glenfield
Auckland 10, New Zealand

Random House (Pty) Limited
Endulini, 5a Jubilee Road, Parktown 2193, South Africa

The Random House Group Limited Reg. No. 954009

www.randomhouse.co.uk

A CIP catalogue record for this book is available from the British Library

Papers used by Random House are natural, recyclable products made from wood grown in sustainable forests. The manufacturing processes conform to the environmental regulations of the country of origin

Typeset in 12/15pt Garamond by SX Composing DTP, Rayleigh, Essex
Printed and bound in the United Kingdom by Mackays of Chatham Plc, Chatham, Kent

ISBN 0 434 00897 4

CONTENTS

1 My War

On 13 March, 1935, Hitler achieved air parity with Britain, Golden Miller won the Cheltenham Gold Cup for the fourth time, the Duke of Norfolk shot a rhino, and I reluctantly exchanged the comfort of my mother's womb for the uncertainty of life in Orpington.

When I did consent to appear, slowly, painfully, several days late, my birth was so awkward and prolonged that it almost killed my poor dear mother. She was told afterwards that she couldn't have any more children. I doubt if this was much of a blow to her after what she'd been through, or, to be more precise, after what I'd been through with such difficulty. As an only child I spent long hours alone with my imagination. I wonder if I'd have developed into a writer if I'd had brothers and sisters. I don't recall ever wanting them. I don't think I was very childlike as a child, though I would become much more so as an adult.

I was born in a maternity home in the trim South London suburb of Petts Wood, where the most exciting thing that ever happened was the invention of Daylight Saving. My father was senior maths master and deputy headmaster at the City of London School, and caught the 8.02 to Cannon Street every morning. Both my grandfathers taught maths and were headmasters. My mother taught maths before her marriage. Both my grandmothers taught maths before their marriages. What went wrong with me?

We lived in a neat, neo-Georgian, 1920s detached red brick house in Sevenoaks Road, Orpington. It was number 47. Later, when more houses were built, it became number 55. There is no plaque.

It wasn't a large house. It had three bedrooms, two reception rooms, a small dark room called The Box Room, although there were never any boxes in it, and another small, less dark room called The Breakfast Room, although nobody ever breakfasted in it. The only extraordinary feature of the house was the glass case full of bells in the kitchen, one bell for each room, so that the servants would know to which room they were being summoned. I could understand that at Blenheim Palace, but at 47, Sevenoaks Road? Even to me, at three, it was a potent symbol of a vanishing world.

The main feature of number 47/55 was the huge horse chestnut tree in the front garden. Glory lay in wait for me when the conker craze began. Also, my father had built a wonderful model railway which ran in and out of the garage and round the back garden. I can't remember whether I remember seeing it or whether I just remember imagining it from what my father told me during the war.

I have just four memories of my life before the outbreak of the Second World War. In one I am standing at the dining-room window with Beryl, our maid, waiting to see my parents return from the Congregational Church in St Mary Cray. They'd been gone for two hours, or half a lifetime. There was no certainty, in my tiny mind, that I would ever see them again.

In another, I am standing at that same window and looking out over our neat front lawn to the wide road beyond, and trying to catch a glimpse of a Colmans' lorry. My father had told me that Colmans made their fortune from the mustard left on people's plates. I took this literally, and imagined the mustard men in their mustard-yellow caps walking along the pavement crying 'Any mustard today?' and scooping the left-over mustard into their great mustard vats. I believed in the mustard men long after I'd learnt the terrible truth about Father Christmas.

I distinctly recall Len Hutton beating Don Bradman's record test score of 334 in the Oval Test Match of 1938, when I was three. We all had to be very quiet in the dark, dusty, dining room of High House in Sible Hedingham in Essex. My father's father, retired now but still headmasterly, insisted on total silence as Hutton approached the record. I didn't realise what was going on – I've deduced it since – but I can still feel the tension, and smell the dust and my grandfather's smoky moustache and his over-ripe Gorgonzola cheese, runny and bubbly with advanced decay. I wasn't able to enjoy cheese, after the smell of my grandfather's Gorgonzola, until I was twenty-three.

My next memory is the clearest. My father and I were sitting in the breakfast room – we weren't breakfasting, of course – and he was being very solemn, in his patient, kindly way. He told me that we might have to move to the countryside 'for the duration'. I didn't know what a duration was and why we couldn't have one in Orpington, and then he talked, obliquely, about the war. I remember sensing, from his tones, that dreadful things would happen in the world.

Then he showed me a big round wooden clock that he'd bought. It was painted bright blue, and I loved it instantly. He told me that, if we did have to move, he would teach me how to tell the time. With one masterly stroke, he reconciled me to evacuation.

We moved to Marlborough, in Wiltshire. The Headmaster of Marlborough College, Mr F.M. Heywood, invited the City of London School to share their premises 'for the duration'. It was a big change for a small boy. Orpington is a sprawling suburb. Marlborough is a compact market town, surrounded by glorious, empty countryside.

At first we lived a mile or so out of the town, on the Pewsey Road, in hilly, well-wooded country. We lodged in a pleasant Georgian house – not neo-Georgian but the real thing – called Granham House, which had a rather grand drive . . . well, it seemed grand to me. The house was owned by a severe spinster called Miss Jeans, and she had a rather fluffy-brained assistant called Miss Avery. Miss Avery was terrified of Miss Jeans. Maybe we all were. She was very strict, and lost no opportunity to remind us how kind she was being. We were not the only family from the school living there. There were the Hendersons, and very possibly another family as well.

Behind the house there was a farm, and on the farm there was a farm-hand. I believe his name was Frederick, and he was a sadistic beast who terrified me. More than once he grabbed me, held me over the cattle pens and threatened to drop me in. I don't think it was a well-kept farm. I recall the floor of the pens as covered in thick, sticky, foetid liquid. I was frightened that he would drop me in among the hooves of the confused beasts. Frederick swore me to secrecy, on pain of doing something worse, and I've honoured that secrecy until today.

'Hendy' Henderson and his wife Barbara had two boys, Timothy and David. Timothy and I got on well enough, without ever becoming friends, but David was faulty, and he frightened me. He couldn't walk and lay in his cot long after he'd passed the age of cots. His face made strange twisted movements, and he cried terribly. I just didn't understand what was wrong with him. I later learned that he was what in those days was called a spastic. He made me feel extremely uncomfortable.

That first winter of the war was fearsomely cold. I had a china wash basin in my bedroom, and I would often have to break the ice in my water jug before pouring the water, complete with miniature ice floes, into the bowl. I don't recall complaining, but then I don't recall washing much either. An insect without a wanderlust could have lived very happily behind my ears. There was no central heating, of course. There was a tiny fireplace in each bedroom, but you only had a fire if you were ill, and the fire was so small that it wouldn't melt the ice on the inside of the windows.

Great drifts of snow lay at the side of the road to Marlborough. I remember skating on little ponds deep in the magical white woods. We drove through Savernake Forest, the trees rigid with frost, the birds silent, in our green Morris 8, HMM642, to the Kennet and Avon Canal, a frozen thread winding through the stiff, still countryside. We skated, gloriously, on its sparkling surface. What days. I've never skated since. It would be an anti-climax.

I remember crying when it thawed. What a disgusting thing is a thaw to a small child. The woods became like a million dripping noses. The mud was drear. I put away my sledge and my toboggan and my red mittens and I knew that things would never be quite as good again.

The summer of 1940 seems to me now to have gone on for ever. I recall it so vividly: the front garden with the hens roaming, the grown-ups having afternoon tea in the sunshine, Miss Jeans being sternly gracious.

The great joy of my life at Granham House was helping Harry collect the hens' eggs of a morning. It was exhilarating to find those perfect eggs gleaming in the straw. The smell of those huts, that strangely healthy, mealy, rotting smell, is in my nostrils still. Every morning I would write down the number of eggs laid. Yes, I'd learnt to write and count even though I hadn't started school yet. I assume that my mother had taught me.

Harry was Miss Jeans's odd job man. He was retarded, and I knew why: his birthday was on 29 February. If he only had a birthday every four years, it was natural that his mental age would be four times less than other people's. I was deeply upset when I discovered that my deduction was wrong.

Harry was kind and gentle, and I loved him, but suddenly I wasn't allowed to collect the eggs with him any more. I wasn't told why, and Harry couldn't understand why I wasn't friendly to him any more. I deduced, not unnaturally, that there was something wrong with him, something mysterious and unhealthy, something unsafe.

The truth was quite different and outside a five-year-old's comprehension. I only learnt it many years later. Miss Jeans, self-righteous little black-shawled Miss Jeans, sold her eggs on the black market and was frightened that my little black book would incriminate her. I suppose it's quite an honour for an author to have a book banned at the age of five, but my thoughts were for poor bewildered Harry.

The Battle of Britain passed me by. There were no aerial dog fights over Wiltshire. I only recall one incident whose intensity may perhaps have been caused by the tension of the times, and that was the dreadful affair of the runner beans.

Miss Jeans sent a parcel of runner beans to a relative. Miss Avery packed it in an old used envelope and forgot to cover up the address of

Granham House. The beans travelled across England – and back. When the parcel was opened, the beans were shrivelled and black. I cowered, but not as much as Miss Avery, as Miss Jeans vented her mighty wrath. Her thesis was, I seem to recall, that with invasion imminent and the population under-nourished Miss Avery's stupidity had made Hitler's task much easier. His troops would overwhelm the bean-starved populace.

Towards the end of the summer of 1940, the Nobbses and the Hendersons moved to Marlborough itself, into a spacious, rambling 1920s house called The White House. It was rented and shared, but I'm sure the adults were pleased to have escaped the eagle eye of Miss Jeans, who always managed to give the impression that these metropolitan folk weren't quite up to the standards expected by the county.

I, of course, didn't want to move – it was the womb syndrome again – but I had to admit that The White House was lovely and had a big and beautiful garden.

Opposite us was a house so huge it had a little baby house at the gate. Gordon Richards, the jockey, lived there, but I never once saw him. Jockeys are, of course, notoriously small and difficult to spot.

That autumn I started school. Naturally I dreaded it, but my mother painted such rosy pictures of what fun it would be that in the end I went quite eagerly and was very disappointed that we had to learn things. Another boy was surprised to have to go on the second day. 'I went yesterday,' he complained indignantly. I had no idea why I was going to school, or what it was for.

My school was at the end of our quiet, prosperous road so, even for the first day, I could go on my own. It was called a kindergarten and it was run by a tall lady called Miss Kinder. Being reasonably bright, I deduced that it was called a kindergarten because it was run by Miss Kinder, and I had a furious row with a girl who told me she went to a kindergarten run by a Miss Brown. I told her, with fine scorn, that a school run by a Miss Brown was a browngarten.

I felt humiliated when I discovered that I was wrong and this incident, coming so soon after the February 29th debacle, caused me to mistrust intellectual speculation. My chance of becoming a distinguished philosopher may well have disappeared at that moment of disillusion. I may already have been doomed, had I but known it, to write for Dick Emery and Jimmy Tarbuck.

I endured two moments of even greater humiliation at Miss Kinder's. I don't wish to introduce a sordid note so early in the book – there'll be all too many opportunities for that later – but honesty compels me to admit that these humiliations were bound up with those necessary bodily functions which countless classical authors from Shakespeare to Jane Austen have managed to ignore completely. I refer, of course, to what were known then as number ones and number twos.

The first incident occurred on my first day. I'm often asked how autobiographical my work is, particularly my seventh novel, *Second From Last In The Sack Race*, the rites of passage one. I'll deal with this in more detail later, but I have to admit that Henry Pratt's first day at school was based on mine. I quote:

> The pressure on his bladder grew rapidly, and he was far too shy to be able to ask to be permitted to relieve it . . .

And

> There was no sign of Belinda Boyce-Uppingham. Henry was glad of that as he made his puddle.
>
> 'You'll have to go to the utility room, Ezra,' said Miss Candy. 'Take your trousers and pants off, wash them in the sink, and hang them on the pipes to dry. Show him the way, Henry, and bring me the bucket, the mop and the disinfectant.'
>
> Cyril/Henry led Henry/Ezra to the utility room/locker room/boiler room, and there he spent his first morning at school.

And

Henry took off his trousers and pants and washed them with a bar of green carbolic. He had never washed clothes before. The soap didn't produce lather, just a greeny-white slime. The world of rinsing was also an unexplored continent to him and, despite his best efforts, much of the soap proved impossible to remove. He gave up, and put the long, baggy shorts and thick yellowing pants on the pipes to dry. Time passes slowly when you're five years old and have nothing to do except stand and watch your clothes drying. That morning was an eternity of misery to Henry, standing with his fat legs bare, and his shirt not even covering his cowering little willie, in the hot little room with the noisy boiler and the frosted-glass window.

And

Suddenly children were pouring into the utility room and looking at him and giggling as they collected their coats if they were going home to dinner or their sandwiches if they weren't. One older boy said, 'Look at his little willie,' and Patrick Eckington said, 'I can't. I forgot me magnifying glass,' and there was laughter, and then Miss Candy was there, saying, 'Your clothes are dry. Why haven't you put them on?' and he mumbled, 'Didn't tell me to,' and Miss Candy, who had a bottomless supply of minatory saws of her own invention, said, 'Mr Mumble shouted "fire" and nobody heard,' and he put his pants and shorts on with difficulty because the soap had caked hard, and the afternoon was a blur, and that was his first day at school, and it was to be the first of many, and they would all be like that, and life was awful.

There was still no sign of Belinda Boyce-Uppingham.

Well, ladies and gentlemen, there you have it. My first day at school. How astonished I would have been if I'd known that one day I would put the incident in a novel.

Right at the beginning of his first day at school, Henry had been told that there were so many Henrys that he would have to be known as Ezra. This also was based on fact. My father's name was Cyril Gordon Nobbs, though he was always known as Gordon. My name was David Gordon Nobbs, and now there were so many Davids in the school that I too would be known as Gordon. I hated the name. I hated my sudden Davidlessness. One is one's name as a small child, and now I wasn't entirely me any more.

The second incident involved the other major area of bodily waste. You think that coy? Well, my mother had taught me to be coy. One day I was late for school, my excuse being that I was sitting on the lavatory at the time. This seems to me to be a splendidly hygienic reason for lateness, but the authorities tend to disagree. No rollcall ever went 'here' 'here' 'he's having a crap, sir'. 'Excellent'. Anyway, I asked my mother how I should explain my lateness. 'Be honest,' she said. 'Tell them nature called.'

'Why are you late, Gordon?' asked Miss Kinder's assistant, who had a moustache and a motorbike.

'Nature called, miss.'

The assembled school burst into laughter. Belinda Boyce-Uppingham laughed. Even Miss Kinder smiled. Humiliation dripped from my every pore.

But wait, I hear you cry, Belinda Boyce-Uppingham is fictional.

Not so, I fear. There was a tall girl with a posh voice at Miss Kinder's. I don't know her surname but her Christian name was Belinda and I loved her with a fervour that cannot be described as other than sexual. I never told her. I never even spoke to her. She was too posh. My love was as secret as Doris Day's.

Back at The White House that other David grew more and more faulty and died, and nothing was ever said about it to me. It was terrible. I felt a great burden because of it. I felt that I needed to behave well because I was lucky enough to be the David who survived. I couldn't handle the feeling of guilt and so behaved badly, and the silence would say, 'You have so much, he had so little, so be grateful.'

On the whole, though, my early childhood was not an unhappy one.

I had loving parents. I don't think I ever thought about the fact that my parents were loving. I was lucky enough to live in a society where parents *were* loving. I loved my parents, but I don't think that at this stage I thought much about the fact that I loved them. I don't imagine that I told them. My parents were reticent about emotion. My mother, though Welsh, often told me, 'I can't gush. I'm just not a gusher.' My father's terms of endearment were 'old sausage' and 'funny ossity'. I realised that he meant 'darling' but he said 'old sausage', and that suited me. None of us were tactile. It would be many years before I hugged.

I had a friend now. He had the splendidly banal name of Michael Ferguson. There were other children with whom I got on all right, including Timothy Henderson and Furze Swann, the vicar's son, whose magical garden ran right down to the river, and whose rock cakes were too hard to eat. Precocious child. I couldn't make rock cakes. I couldn't make anything. There were some freckled children too, but I didn't much like freckled children. Besides they gave me a book of the flags of all the nations for my birthday, a present so boring I wanted to burst into tears.

Only with Michael Ferguson was I totally at ease. I don't think I felt that a chap needed more than one friend. Michael and I roamed freely over the downs and along the great valley of the huge River Kennet, the Mississippi of Wiltshire. There were lapwings everywhere. Kingfishers flashed exotically along the mighty waterway. I tamed a hedge sparrow till it would eat out of my hand. I became expert at identifying newts. I collected tadpoles. I observed my tadpoles. I came to a conclusion about tadpoles. One tadpole is very like another.

I was seven before I saw my first film, in Marlborough's little flea pit. It was *Bambi*. The excitement, in those days before television and video, was intense. In the film Bambi's mother tells Bambi, 'If you can't say anything nice about somebody, don't say anything.' My mother must have repeated this to me at least thirty times. It's a shame that I'll have to ignore it, but it might be a bit of a damper on an autobiography.

For our holidays we went to my father's family at Sible Hedingham or my mother's family in Swansea. My English grandfather, James

Alfred Nobbs, read J.B. Priestley and listened to *The Saturday Play* so I thought him intellectual. Granny Nobbs always seemed stiff and stern, but I think now that she had a heart of gold. High House was a little dark, and they weren't on the electric, so there was a great deal of lighting of lamps, and the house was full of shadows, and my grandfather teased me. I didn't like being teased. People who tease think they're proving that they have a sense of humour. I think they're usually proving that they haven't.

My father's sister, my Auntie Kathleen, had married a farmer, and they lived a few miles from my grandparents, in Little Yeldham. Uncle Charlie was much older than Auntie Kathleen. He was small and wrinkled and sunburnt and wore very baggy trousers and his eyes always twinkled. I liked him enormously, but I was in awe of him and could never think of anything interesting to say in his presence. 'How are you, chap?' he'd say, and I'd mumble, 'All right, thank you,' and feel feeble.

Auntie Kathleen was full of fun, and produced the best scrambled eggs in the world. She also produced John.

My cousin John was three years and five months younger than me. My excitement at his birth was enormous. I couldn't wait to go to Little Yeldham to see him. I rushed into the house, yelling, 'Where is he? Where is he?' He was fast asleep in his pram, or he had been until I rushed in yelling, 'Where is he?' He woke up, cried, drank some milk and went back to sleep. I was bitterly disappointed, heartbroken even. 'Is that all he does?' I asked, in a voice dripping with disgust and disillusionment.

Later he became like a younger brother to me. Our closeness, and the joy our friendship brought, suggest that I might have missed having brothers or sisters more than I'd realised – but of course they might have been older brothers and sisters, and I don't think I'd have coped very well with that.

When we visited High House, John was only four miles away, but in those days of petrol rationing and infrequent buses there were times when we felt as if we were separated by the Andes.

Mealtimes with my English grandparents were sombre affairs. My granny wasn't the world's best cook; she overcooked everything in the manner of the times – 'Very tough, granny,' I said of a piece of cod that had been steamed to the consistency of flannel. However, it was the silence, rather than the food, that unnerved me. I longed to chatter. The only time I ever heard my grandfather swear was when he called me 'a bloody babbling Welsh brook'.

A bloody babbling Welsh brook I may have been, but I couldn't get a word in, in Wales. If you wanted to make a remark in my Welsh grandparents' home, you had to book it in advance.

They lived at 16, Eaton Crescent, Swansea, just off the Uplands. It was Dylan Thomas country, and my mother had taught him in Sunday School, where he looked deceptively like an angel. We didn't lead a Dylan Thomas life. My grandfather, David Williams, retired head-master of Landore School, was a deeply religious man, but as kind as he was strict. I presume that I was named after him. His house was strictly teetotal and I recall his referring to a man called D.H.I.P., who was a journalist and probably an editor, as if he was the incarnation of everything loose and evil, and therefore not fit to be mentioned by anything more personal than his initials. Yet this three-storey town house was full of laughter and fun, except on Sundays when everyone went to chapel three times. My grandfather and grandmother – a twinkly woman of immense kindness – went to a Welsh-speaking chapel called Ebeneser, as did my Auntie Louie, who wasn't a real auntie but was very interesting because she had a goitre and a postcard of a Swiss funicular railway in her bedroom. The rest of us, my Auntie Dilys, a spinster schoolteacher, and my Uncles Kenneth and Glandon, went to Walter Road Congregational Chapel. Halfway through the service the children went out to their separate service. I was too shy to join them, even though it meant I had to listen to the Reverend Maurice Charles's thunderous and lengthy condemnations of Sin.

Uncle Kenneth was an accountant with Price Waterhouse, and deeply interested in politics. Whenever he made a challenging state-ment, whenever he felt he was on risky ground, he gave the show away inadvertently by saying 'I beg your pardon?' 'The war'll be over by Christmas, I beg your pardon?'

Uncle Glandon was handsome and glamorous. He was a surgeon in

Shrewsbury, and had played for Wales at hockey and croquet. It was impossible to believe that his wife had died, with her child, in childbirth. Such things couldn't happen to the Uncle Glandons of this world. They were untouchable.

I spent a lot of time in the top storey of the Swansea house, running a bus service with empty sweet tins to all corners of the carpets. I loved it when traffic delays caused buses to bunch, and three sweet tins came at once. I'd never heard of London Transport, yet I acted out their worst nightmares every day in that austere yet vibrant town house.

I must have been about seven when I discovered my first truly great writer. His name was Captain W.E. Johns, and he wrote about a character called Major James Bigglesworth, 'better known to all his friends as Biggles'. Sometimes he wrote about another character called Gimlet, whom I didn't like as much, although on reflection I'm sure that Gimlet was virtually the same as Biggles. I liked his books about Worrals even less. Worrals, you see, was a girl, albeit a girl with a remarkable resemblance to Biggles and Gimlet.

Biggles was called upon, along with his chums Bertie, Ginger and Algie, to fight evil threats from nasty men in obscure corners of the globe. All these men were foreigners, and many of them were deformed. Political correctness had not yet laid a finger on children's literature. Stunted mulattos abounded. Pock-marked Lascar seamen were everywhere.

I can remember writing *my* first story. I was in the play-room at The White House so I couldn't have been older than nine. Much later I came upon a list of titles for books I never wrote. They were 'Badger Flies North', 'Badger Flies South', 'Badger Flies East', 'Badger Flies West', 'Badger Flies In', 'Badger Flies Out', 'Badger Sweeps The Desert' and, more mysteriously, 'What Is Happiness?' Yes, I'd crossed Biggles with a badger. It's a pity that the most commercial idea I ever had came at the age of eight.

There was no trace of humour in these books, and not much in my reading. I read *Winnie-The-Pooh* and *Alice in Wonderland* and *The Wind In The Willows*, but I took them absolutely literally and saw nothing funny in them at all.

My only real-life contact with the literary world was with Kingsley Amis. He was one of my father's pupils. He came to tea at The White House. We stood in the same room. I didn't speak to him.

My parents and their friends must have had a difficult social life at Marlborough. I think the City of London School was well and truly frozen out by the county. I imagine there was a lot of bridge and a lot of reading. I know there were musical evenings. I used to creep downstairs from my bed and perch on the steps, listening. If I'd been forced to attend I'd have been bored beyond belief. As an uninvited guest I was enthralled.

Towards the end of our time in Marlborough I went for a walk with the boy next door. He opened his heart to me. The other boys were cruel to him. One boy dug his nails into him so hard that it left marks. Something about this boy irritated me beyond measure. I expressed great sympathy and then, at the furthest point of our walk, I dug my nails into him with all the force I could muster, and ran off. Why do I tell you this? Because if I'm going to ignore Bambi's Mother's advice I'm going to have to be hard on myself as well.

The shadow of peace was beginning to fall across my innocent little world. Soon the lights would be going on all over Europe, and we'd have to move back to London, and another new start.

How much had I been conscious of the war? Very little, in truth. In 1940, while we were at my Welsh grandparents' home in Eaton Crescent, the Luftwaffe ripped the heart out of old Swansea, Dylan Thomas's 'ugly, lovely town'. I can just recall the sense of shock that silenced the laughter in that lovely house. I didn't understand its cause.

I remember mysterious gas cylinders fixed behind the 74 buses in Swansea. Our Morris 8 gradually ceased to be available. Woolworths in Marlborough ran out of toilet paper and Mrs Field, the French wife of the French master, thundered 'I vill do vithout', thus confirming to half Wiltshire that the land of the bidet was basically dirty.

I remember, too, my father being taken short. As we rushed to the Gentlemen's at the station we met one of my father's colleagues, Geoffrey 'Jimmy' Riddle. He quoted a poster of the period and asked,

'Is Your Journey Really Necessary?' 'Yes,' gasped my father before speeding off in desperation.

A bomb fell on the railway line between Ingatestone and Shenfield, and when John and I were taken to London for the day we had to transfer, thrillingly, to a bus. I loved buses. I loved my first taste of the vibrancy and immensity of London, but I didn't want to go and look at anything in particular. I just wanted to see the whole vastness of it from the top of a bus.

Once or twice we went into the dark, dank cellar of High House during air raids, and I recall gawping at Italian prisoners-of-war being marched along the A642.

On the whole, though, I had a quiet war – until 1944.

In 1944 the City of London School decided that the risk of bombing was over, and returned to London, ending its uneasy partnership with Marlborough College. The county, who had never accepted these London folk, breathed a collective sigh of relief.

Our return to Orpington was hardly a voyage into the unknown – we were going back to our old house, which had been rented out – but I dreaded it. Suddenly I loved Miss Kinder and her moustachioed assistant. I knew how deeply I would miss the newts. I dreaded my new school.

What carrot did my dear parents dangle before me, in order to reconcile me to the move? They dangled Orpington Library! I would have access to books galore.

Then the doodlebugs began. They were pilotless planes, which were aimed towards targets in London. Their engines would cut out, and they would begin to lose height, and eventually they would crash and explode.

I heard my first doodlebug as I was walking back from my first visit to Orpington Library. I was clutching a pile of books in my hot little hands, and I heard this droning hum, and then it stopped.

We all lay, rather self-consciously, face down on the pavement of Sevenoaks Road, and waited. There was an eerie silence, then, after several minutes, a distant explosion, and we all stood up again and walked on. It was a rather surreal experience. To my surprise I didn't find it frightening. I wished the explosion had been nearer so that I'd have a better story to tell.

The doodlebugs grew more frequent. One destroyed the swimming pool of my new school, and my parents sent me to Swansea for several weeks. It was the warmest March in living memory. I spent my tenth birthday on Swansea beach in the sunshine.

Eventually I went back to Orpington and the very last doodlebug, the last bomb to fall in Britain during the Second World War, landed on an inoffensive house in the next street, Charterhouse Road. It brought down most of my bedroom ceiling on top of me. It hurt one of my thumbs.

At last my war had begun. The following week it ended, and so, I'm glad to say, did the rest of Europe's.

2 CALL THOSE BANANAS!

I FELT A huge smack on my right ear, and an explosion of pain in the inner ear. I saw red stars and revolving black holes.

'That'll teach you to stand up in future when I come into a room,' said Mr Bernie Farnfield, Headmaster of Bickley Hall Preparatory School.

All the other boys were standing, as smug as statues. I'd been concentrating on my work so hard that I'd been completely unaware of the headmaster's arrival. I was ten years old, and convinced of the shattering unfairness of life.

I didn't run home to my parents and complain. I certainly didn't suggest they sued for undetectable mastoids and psychological damage that might lead me to consume vast quantities of red wine in later life. I didn't even argue with Mr Farnfield. I said, 'I'm sorry, sir,' and put it down to experience. I probably thought then – I certainly think now – that the incident was a splendid preparation for the brutality and injustice of adult life.

I spent four years as a day-boy at Bickley Hall, a substantial stone mansion set in large grounds between the prosperous London suburb of Bickley and the even more prosperous suburb of Chislehurst. Strangely,

I remember nothing at all of my first day. Perhaps it was such a nightmare that memory has blotted it out.

I remember Mr Farnfield only as a threat on legs, but I remember our Latin master – the sharp-featured, long-nosed, sad-eyed Mr Selwyn – as vividly as if I'd met him yesterday. He was as dry as a stone wall, yet he taught me so much that many years later I wrote to thank him.

Our maths master, Mr Astbury, had a sandy moustache and threw text books at us, but always missed. Our French teacher, an attractive lady called Miss, or possibly Mrs, Miles, talked to us so graphically – in English – about an eye operation that I passed spark out, discovering one of my great talents – for fainting.

On Sports Day I gave my parents their first proud moment. It came in the 440 yards race and didn't last long. I went off like a train. 'Nobbs has a huge lead,' thundered Mr Astbury through his loud hailer. 'They're catching Nobbs up.' 'Nobbs is dying (a technical athletics term, I later learnt. It was a bit of a shock at the time).' 'Crameri and Webber are passing Nobbs.' 'Penfold and Edwards are passing Nobbs.' Everybody passed Nobbs, even Norton.

I also gave my poor parents what must have been one of the worst moments of their lives. I made my first public appearance in an inter-school quiz, on the stage of the assembly hall. My mother and father were in the audience, bursting with expectant pride. I had stage fright, and was unable to answer even the first question. It was in a round about nursery rhymes, and it wasn't deeply taxing: 'Who had three bags full?'

I still hear, on disturbed nights, a distant contemptuous voice saying, 'The answer is, of course, Baa Baa Blacksheep.' Perhaps for this reason, perhaps for other better reasons, I never watch *The Weakest Link*.

It's the smells that I remember best. A long corridor ran from the front entrance past all the classrooms to the Headmaster's Study, and it always smelt of cabbage and rissoles. We ate at long cheap wooden tables in an elegant panelled reminder of the days when this had been a fine home. That room too smelt of cabbage and rissoles, regardless of what was on the menu that day. The food was pretty awful. There was greasy toad in an equally greasy hole, and a bacon and egg pie so dry and powdery that it was like eating a crumbling seventeenth-century wattle and daub cottage. I realise now that it would have been made with powdered egg. We had to eat every bit, of course. There'd been a war.

Below the classrooms there were extensive cellars which we used as changing rooms, and in the middle of them there was a large stone footbath. It smelt of earth and damp and stone and the unripe cheesiness of pre-pubescent boys. I hated it and I hated the changing rooms. I was embarrassed by my extreme skinniness. I didn't like being called Belsen Boy, even though I didn't know what it meant.

A major scare occurred when I found myself at the bottom of the rebuilt swimming pool, possibly propelled there by one or two of the larger boys. I thrashed around in panic, thus preventing the natural process of floating to the surface. I was quickly rescued, and didn't have time to think about dying . . . I didn't yet have much past life to flash by . . . but the experience left its mark. I've been distinctly uneasy about water ever since. I drink very little of it.

I certainly had my fair share of humiliations and disasters at Bickley Hall, and it was here that I began to develop humour as a pre-emptive device: to make them laugh with me before they laughed at me.

I used to stand on my chair and do my party piece, pretending, for some obscure reason, to be a greengrocer from Abergavenny. I only had the one act. Ask me to be a draper from Abergavenny, or a greengrocer from Kirkcaldy, and I was lost. 'Do the greengrocer from Abergavenny, Nobbsey. Do do do,' would come the cry, just before the master entered the classroom.

Flattered, I would launch forth. 'Carrots I do have, indeed to goodness yes, Mrs Price-Evans, but parsnips I do not have, indeed to goodness, isn't it?'

'What exactly do you think you're doing, Nobbs?' the master would ask, catching me literally in the act.

'Nothing, sir.'

'Well you shouldn't be doing nothing. You should be revising. Take fifty lines.'

I realise now that the boys were deliberately getting me into trouble, but I'd like to think, for all that, that they found the greengrocer from Abergavenny at least mildly amusing.

My biggest laugh in the Bickley years was inadvertent, though. I tripped over a cat while playing football, and apologised to it instinctively. Even the referee laughed. How I blushed.

I did have minor triumphs. I once saved a penalty in a football match, and I top scored at cricket with three in an innings totalling nine. Uncle Kenneth took me to the Oval in 1946, to see Surrey play Yorkshire. Surrey were all out for 115. At stumps Yorkshire were 150 for 5. Hutton was 91 not out, and I had my hero. All the other boys were for Compton and Edrich. I clung resolutely to my Len. Perhaps I wasn't a *complete* wimp.

There were boarders at Bickley, and the day-boys, or day-bugs as we were known, were considered an inferior species. I didn't mind. I loved the journey to school. In the morning I caught the 8.14 to Chislehurst. My father still caught the 8.02 to Cannon Street. The trains were full of pin-striped men with bowler hats and rolled umbrellas. It would be almost thirty years before I created Reginald Iolanthe Perrin, but the seed must have been planted during those four years of commuting to school.

Our trains were boring little electric things, redeemed only by such curiosities as 'Ladies Only' compartments and long rectangular compartments where people sat on all four sides as if at an invisible dinner party. However, the expresses, bound for exotic places like Hastings or Dover, had steam engines. Some of us would hang around the railway lines, collecting numbers. A little shunting engine arrived at Orpington late every afternoon, to construct and deconstruct goods trains in the sidings. The cry of 'The shunter's coming' would cause a ripple of excitement that seems incomprehensible now.

The weather caused a great deal of disruption to our train travel. There was a lot more weather in those days. In the winter of 1947 there was an enormous amount of snow. My father and I walked along country lanes past banks of snow twice my height. I would struggle up to Orpington Station, along Sevenoaks Road, up The Avenue (unadopted and full of potholes – I didn't know why it was unadopted or who would have adopted it if it had been adopted, certain subjects stirred absolutely no intellectual curiosity in my little mind) only to find that the 8.14 hadn't even left Sevenoaks yet. Sometimes we waited three or four hours for a train. We'd get to school just in time to be sent home early because of the weather.

Then there were the London fogs, those real pea-soupers. It's good to realise that there are some ways in which our environment has actually improved. We stood on the platform, surrounded by thick white walls, and *heard* our train come in. We held our hands in front of us and moved slowly forward till we felt the train. The train proceeded through the whiteness at a very reasonable pace, probably fifteen miles an hour. Signalling was done by means of detonators, so the journey was punctuated by little explosions. When we got to Chislehurst we opened the doors very slowly, lest we hit a merchant banker full in the face. We were, most of the time, very well behaved children indeed.

Not quite always, you'll be relieved to hear. One memorable afternoon a few of us went up to the great terminus of Waterloo, from which King Arthur class engines steamed to the West Country. We got so excited by this cornucopia of train spotting that we became completely out of hand. We ran and we shouted and we bumped into passengers and our conduct was reported to Mr Farnfield. He lectured us in school assembly on the inferior manners and morals of day-bugs. He didn't like us. Our parents paid less. Poor Mr Farnfield. With every word of rebuke our status grew. With every recital of our heinous crimes, the envy of the boarders increased.

There was further trouble in store when we acted out episodes of *Dick Barton* in the huge gardens of the prosperous people of Chislehurst. *Dick Barton, Special Agent* was a radio programme listened to by every child in Britain. It would have been the apogee of youth culture had such a term existed then, but the snobs of Chislehurst were unmoved by the exploits of Dick, Jock and Snowy. What mattered the odd geranium? we argued, when national security was at stake. We argued in vain. What is the point of a shrubbery if you can't hide in it from pock-marked master criminals? we asked. Our question was ignored with disdain. We were in further trouble. The boarders were even more jealous. Yes, there were some happy days even at long-gone Bickley Hall, which was replaced by a housing estate many years ago. Imagine it! The footbath gone! Trim, herbaceous borders where once the grocer from Abergavenny reigned supreme! Some people have no sense of heritage.

At home I led a very quiet life. Our house was calm and cosy, with a coal fire in the sitting room in winter, and a glass-paned blue stove crackling in the dining room. It made a fine womb. I did my homework reasonably diligently and my father helped me a little, but only in the way that any other parent would. He was such a fair-minded man that he refused to use his expertise as a schoolmaster to give me an advantage over the other boys!

I read a lot. While not entirely abandoning the works of Captain W.E. Johns, I had realised that I had been mistaken in thinking him the best author in the world. That honour now went to Arthur Ransome. I read and re-read *Swallows and Amazons* and its sequels time and time again. I lived the lives of these other children whose holidays were so much more exciting than mine. The books had illustrations and the jackets featured all these illustrations, in miniature, on a white background. It was exquisite torture to receive one of these volumes, to long to tear into the story and gobble it up, but also to want to just look at these pictures and not open the book at all, because, after you had read one page, there was already one less page to read.

I've re-read these books more than once in my adult life. They enable me to become a child again. They were very well written and supremely well constructed. The man was a master story-teller, and it can't have done me any harm as a writer to have allowed books as near perfect as *Winter Holiday*, *Pigeon Post* and *The Big Six* to soak into my subconscious.

How innocent the world was then, when a whole series of books could feature a girl called Titty and nobody would see anything odd about it.

By the time I was ten or eleven my sense of humour seemed suddenly to have come to life. My parents loved to laugh, and we were a very close-knit family as we listened to a whole succession of radio shows. We never mentioned love and affection. Our shared laughter round the snug coal fire spoke of these things for us. I particularly liked *Itma* with

Tommy Handley and Jack Train and *Much Binding In The Marsh* with Kenneth Horne, Richard 'Stinker' Murdoch and Sam Costa. Catchphrases abounded, and I waited for them eagerly. Programmes like *Monday Night At Eight* and *Variety Bandbox* were a constant delight, apart from the boring musical bits. I had no interest in music. Many children didn't. It's hard to imagine it today, but there was no pop, there were no groups, there were no charts. Gwen Catley, the Welsh Nightingale, was as zippy as it got.

I don't think that at any stage of my childhood I had any thought of becoming a writer. I wrote my little stories in Marlborough as a hobby, and I don't recall writing anything during the Bickley years. However, I did develop what I suppose was my first situation comedy. It was called 'Muggins'. Muggins was utterly and completely useless at everything he did. The plot development was simplicity itself: Muggins got into worse and worse scrapes. Think it unsophisticated if you must, but I was only eleven at the time, and I don't think it was that much less sophisticated than *Mr Bean* or *Some Mothers Do 'Ave 'Em*.

Muggins had no scripts. It was all improvised. I played all the parts, although there was really only one part. Anyway, it always went down a hoot with the studio audience, which consisted of my cousin John, and to my amazement he remembers it with affection.

However, it was all just for fun. I had no precocious ambition. The only definite response I can remember making to the inevitable question, 'And what are you going to do when you grow up?' was 'Be retired, like my grampa.'

The other question I hated was 'Haven't you grown?' I could never think of an interesting answer to that one.

So there I was, seeing Reginald Perrins by day, soaking up catchphrases at night – it's not hard to see where it all came from.

In general, despite the occasional humiliations, these were happy years. My father converted the box room where no boxes were kept into a railway paradise for me. He built embankments and tunnels and bridges and stations and sidings. On my own I soon got bored with all this and preferred peeping out at the spotted flycatchers' nest in the trellis. It was an enormous thrill to think that these birds came all the way back to number 55 each summer. The railway, I'm afraid, was a classic case of the father enjoying the toy more than the son. I preferred to play cricket against myself, bouncing a tennis ball off the wall of the house and dispatching it to all parts of Lords and the Oval as I hammered the mighty Australians, or to watch the real trains thundering along the high embankment that bordered my world to the south. The highlight was the restoration of the Golden Arrow, the *Flèche d'Or*, to Paris. Paris! It was an unattainable dream. There was no such thing as a school trip in those years after the war, and my parents would never have taken me anywhere so exotic. I'd never even been to a hotel. My father was a quiet man and not a very confident one. He didn't feel at ease in hotels, thinking they were for toffs. He was also quite solitary. Often in the evenings he would go into the breakfast room and work. He wrote maths text books, and later a book on navigation, which was very close to his heart.

Sailing was his great love. Every August he went off to Fambridge on the River Crouch, and sailed for a month. My mother was a bad sailor and only tried it once. She and I would go to Swansea for August. I loved it and was devastated every year when the month was over. The beaches of the Gower Peninsula were paradise for a child, and cricket at St Helen's was a bonus. I didn't sleep a wink before the match between Glamorgan and the Australians of 1948. It rained remorselessly all the first day, that warm soft relentless Welsh rain that the massed hydrangeas of the Swansea suburbs love so much.

As petrol rationing loosened its grip, my mother began to take the car to Swansea. There would be at least one puncture on every trip in those days. We would go for 'runs' over the Black Mountains or even to Tenby. As we drove up the stark valley roads my grandfather would point out modest houses where great rugby players had been born, and stern, square chapels that my ancestors had built. 'Your great great uncle built that,' he would say of some monstrosity, and I would feign enthusiasm.

Auntie Louie, who wasn't a real auntie, would sit paralysed by fear and try to curb my mother's imagined driving excesses by means of a running commentary to me. 'Mummy's coming to a steep hill, David. Watch her change gear.' 'Mummy's approaching a sharp bend, David. See how she slows down.' Uncle Kenneth, visiting from London, would say, 'The electorate made a surprisingly sophisticated choice when they rejected Churchill in 1945, I beg your pardon?' and it all went in one ear and came out of the other hand fifty years later.

The house was always awash with talk, and words I wasn't supposed to hear would be said in Welsh, which aroused my interest in what would otherwise have been boring gossip. We ate well in Swansea, laverbread and sausage meat for breakfast, lovely soups, kippers from the market. One day we had melon as a starter. 'Melon!' said Auntie Louie with a loud sniff. 'Putting on airs!' Let that be the epitaph for those innocent times.

When my father came back from his yacht we would spend a few more days in Swansea and then go to Yeldham where John and I would ride in the harvest wagons from breakfast to bedtime and think it great fun. Auntie Kathleen made marvellous teas with drop scones and crunchy little cakes made of cornflakes and chocolate. We were in heaven.

There were endless games of cricket, of course, and when my cousin Elizabeth came down from Edinburgh she had to play cricket too. She would be bowled out second ball, and then would have to bowl at John and me for hours. She coped manfully. Well, girlfully. She was yet another only child, and my only other cousin. The responsibility for carrying on the name of Nobbs in our declining family therefore rested entirely on my shoulders. I failed utterly.

Elizabeth's father, my Uncle Mac, was very like my father – tall, gentle, serious yet humorous. He lectured at Edinburgh University and he also wrote books, including one on Dutch history. So there was writing in my genes.

At the end of the harvest we would go, by bus, to Westcliff or Southend to watch Essex's last cricket match of the season. On one of the bus rides I saw a bull mounting a cow and convulsed the top deck by yelling 'John! John! Quick! Look at those cows. You may never see anything like that again.'

*

Michael Ferguson's widowed mother lived in South London so I continued to see him after the war. Then something happened. I think my parents found us in bed together, playing at mothers and fathers or doctors and patients. It was decided that the friendship was too close, and soon we didn't see each other any more. Was it too close? I can't speak for him, but, yes, I think I did feel pre-pubertal stirrings.

My father began to spend more and more time in the breakfast room, writing his maths text books and emerging only for his very favourite comedians. My mother and I took to playing game after game of bezique. I adored cards. At Christmas time my father relaxed and we played canasta for hours.

My father was a great walker, and we would trek together round the dimly-lit suburban streets in companionable silence, like two old men, or, on Sunday afternoons, venture into the Kentish countryside. Our favourite walk was 'up to Downe', a neighbouring village. This simple joke amused us hugely.

Our walks often took us through the straggly village of Green Street Green, which was much less lovely than its name. We would pass a corner café called The Oven Door. Many years later, when the world had gone posh, this became a bistro called The Oven D'Or. I didn't go in to ask if the name was ironic or post-modern or merely naff.

The peace and quiet of suburban life at number 55 was soon to be shattered. The unwitting cause of it was Uncle Kenneth. He used to drive to Orpington for lunch almost every Sunday, bringing with him a touch of topicality. 'The Attlee government will go down as one of the few truly radical governments in British history, I beg your pardon?'

Outside, between the gardens and the road, there was a wide pavement, and Uncle Kenneth only went and parked on the pavement with the front ten inches of his car protruding into the territory in front of number 57, didn't he? Mr Smith, our neighbour, called to complain about this outrage. Uncle Kenneth moved his car, but the damage had been done. From that day on, every time we went into the garden the Smiths lit a bonfire. Since our garden was situated to the north-east of theirs, you don't have to be a geographical genius to deduce that the prevailing south-westerlies carried a great deal of smoke across our futile attempts at afternoon tea. Since the Smiths never went away we had to endure this every weekend for the next decade.

Mr Smith was a member of the rolled umbrella brigade, and his stifling, stifled suburban life may just have contributed a bit, unwittingly, to the germination of the Reginald Perrin idea.

No child's view of the immediate post-war world would be complete without mentioning the return of the banana. I was too young to remember pre-war bananas, and my excitement was intense. I was only allowed one a day. I loved them mashed, with milk and sugar. They stood proudly in a fruit bowl in our dark hall, in celebration of our world's gradual return to normality. Our other neighbour, Mrs Orpen, who was South African and beautiful, saw them and exclaimed, with rare insensitivity, 'Call those bananas!'

I knew that I couldn't stay at Bickley Hall for ever, and it was entirely characteristic of me that I grew to like the place and feel happy and secure there about a month before I had to leave it. I assumed that I would go to the City of London School, in its elegant building on the Embankment near Blackfriars Bridge. My father, though, had other ideas. He believed that I might be in a difficult position as a pupil in the school where he taught. His choice was Marlborough College, whose qualities he had seen at first hand during the war. Many people at the City of London thought he was being snobbish and superior, but he did it from the best of motives. He wasn't a rich man, and it involved considerable sacrifice.

I responded to his generosity, on being told the news, by bursting into tears.

3 An Unlucky Backside

I WALKED UP the hill towards Granham, looking down over the cluster of school buildings that had become my new home, and over the River Kennet, which turned out not to be mighty at all, but just a small, lazy trout stream. I was an innocent fourteen-year-old, almost as innocent as I'd been when I'd lived at Granham House. After that afternoon, I would never feel truly innocent again.

As I reached the bottom of the long drive that led up to the unpretentious old brick house where I'd collected the eggs with Harry, I felt a great longing to be five again. Ten minutes later, I felt about twenty-three.

I turned left down the track opposite Granham House, and passed through a deep arch under the disused railway, and there he was, standing at the edge of a ploughed field, as if he was waiting for me, which he can't have been, as even I hadn't known what direction my walk would take. It was a dank, damp day. Behind him the land rose towards the forest.

I walked towards him, innocently, to go past him towards the trees, and was utterly astonished when he grabbed me and began pulling my trousers down. I writhed like an angry cat, but I was fourteen and skinny and he was eighteen and burly. He forced my buttocks apart and shoved his erect penis up my anal passage, and I thought, 'This isn't happening. Lord, tell me it isn't happening', but it was.

It was over very quickly, and then he said, 'I'm sorry. I hate this great purple thing.' That made two of us.

I don't know whether he intended to make me feel better by telling me of his regret. I do know that he didn't succeed. The fact that nobody had enjoyed it made it all the more wretched and outrageous. All that for nowt, as we say in Yorkshire.

No rape is pleasant, but I was distressed rather than traumatised. One learns something from every experience, I hope, and that ordeal has enabled me to imagine what a horrendous experience rape is for a woman. There's no comparison. The rape of a man is so much less invasive, there's no interference with the sexual organs, the risk of infection and injury is much less, there is no risk of a ghastly unwanted and resented pregnancy, and the attack is from the rear, so one is spared the gleam in a rapist's eye and the nausea of a rapist's breath. Nevertheless, it's not to be recommended on a sensitive fourteen-year-old's Sunday stroll. As I walked down the hill I felt wretched and dirty and wet. I was considering if I should tell anyone, who I should tell, what I should tell, how I should tell. Of course I couldn't tell anyone and, if I had, I didn't know who the boy was and could only describe accurately a part of his anatomy that wouldn't have enabled many people to identify him.

What I dreaded most was that I might come face to face with him again. I never did. It was a large school.

Did this event contribute to the sexual confusion that I was soon to experience? Was the shock of it part of the cause of my being such a late developer? Very probably. On the whole, though, it seems to me that I took it pretty calmly. I certainly didn't feel that I needed a psychiatrist. I'm glad of that. The first psychiatrist I ever knew, many years later, invited me to dinner and answered the door on all fours going 'woof woof'. She was trying to see what it felt like to be a dog. I thought she was literally barking mad.

*

I'd been at Marlborough quite a while when this unhappy stroll occurred. My mother had driven me down. We'd stopped for tea at a hotel full of stuffed animals in Hungerford. I'd wished I was a stuffed animal. I'd have described my behaviour as wimpish except that would suggest a degree of resolution that I didn't possess. How my mother managed to leave me I don't know. She must have felt awful on the long drive back to Orpington.

I was in a junior house, called Upcot, away from the main school, along the Bath Road. My school number was 208. I couldn't forget that any more than I could forget that the registration number of our Morris 8 was HMM642.

That first night I spent so long washing myself – psychological! – that I was still in the washroom when lights out came. I crept along a corridor, into the dark dormitory, felt my way to the second bed on the left, got in. My feet touched something soft. I screamed. It was a boy. I was in the wrong dormitory.

At last I reached my own bed and clambered in. My feet touched something soft again. This time I didn't scream, and this time it wasn't a boy. It was a dead song thrush.

That night I lay in bed and listened to the traffic thundering along the Bath Road and imagined I was playing bezique with my mother in front of a nice coal fire. I fell asleep, eventually, just before it was time to wake up.

I think I managed to hide most of my misery from the world, and I wasn't miserable all the time. In fact I really enjoyed most of the lessons. What an admission!

My feeling, had I been clever enough to express it, was that Marlborough would be a fine place if there hadn't been any boys there. Having begun this chapter with such unpleasant events, I should perhaps say that I think that Marlborough College was a very good school and I became proud to be there. It was, I felt, at least reasonably enlightened. Fagging had been abolished many years before I went there. So had compulsory games. Boys who hated games were allowed to do other outdoor activities like nature study, as long as they provided proof of what they'd been doing, and as long as it was considered wholesome.

I didn't hate games, although I had my reservations about rugger. There seemed to me to be pleasanter ways of spending one's life than catching a muddy slippery oval ball in freezing drizzle on November afternoons, on playing fields utterly unprotected from the prevailing winds, just as eight burly forwards flung you to the ground underneath them. Bezique with my mother springs to mind. I played at fly half, centre, wing, full back and in the scrum. Peter Ustinov said, memorably, that people reach the top of the ladder because they have none of the talents that might have detained them on the rungs. I reached the scrum because I had none of the talents that might have detained me outside it. I did score a try once, but I fell about eight inches short of the line and squirmed over illegally.

I adored cricket and hockey but was moderate at both, although I did take six wickets for one run on the day I pitched my leg breaks right. Cricket provided my very first appearance in print. There it was, in the *Marlborough Times*, my name. Well, almost. The entry reads, 'Hobbs not out o'.

I played squash and fives with enormous enthusiasm. Fives is a little known game in which you hit the ball with your gloved hand. My *Compendium of Games* states, 'Fives will be played wherever there are balls and walls, and enjoyed wherever there are walls and balls.' I must have inherited some of the teaching ability of my ancestors. I taught fives and squash so well that everyone I taught could beat me after three lessons.

I have no recollection of the inside of Upcot House, but at fifteen I moved to my senior house, Cotton House, a little nearer the main school along the Bath Road, and I can remember every corner of that – the showers, the dormitories, the baths, the dining hall which doubled as the room where we did our prep in the evenings, the calm of the small library with its big central table and its shelves of books including *The Loom of Youth* by Alec Waugh, which fell open at a particularly juicy description of homosexual activity. These pages were discoloured by the grubby fingers of generations of salacious youths. The rest of the book was crisp, clean and unread.

Bullying was rife in Cotton House at that time. There was a set of about eight boys who threw their weight around. Our housemaster, Mr E.H. 'Spud' Dowdell, may have been too unworldly to know about it. He was a humane man and I don't think he would have countenanced it.

Bullying requires not only bullies but people ripe for bullying. There was a boy with a goofy expression, so he was known as Goofy and teased mercilessly. Few weeks passed without his head making involuntary acquaintance with the inside of a lavatory bowl. Another boy had a sheen of sweat on his face all day, so frightened was he. He might as well have worn a placard saying, 'Bully me'.

I regret to say that I too must have had an aura of bullyability, because on one dark and cold Wiltshire winter night this group of boys grabbed me, took me outside, tied me to a tree and began to beat me with a doubled-over rope. I think there were eight boys who each beat me eight times. Marlborough was not a lucky venue for my backside. The pain grew greater with each stroke, then for a while I could feel nothing, and then suddenly the pain became excruciating. It was a mental battle. I determined to show no reaction whatever. They went about their work in grim silence. They became uneasy. I remained utterly passive. The silence was deafening. Even the owls were awed.

When they'd finished they untied me, again in silence, and we all went back into the changing room, in sombre mood. I'd spoilt their fun and they hadn't done much for my evening.

They took my trousers down – my backside had at least not been bare during this ordeal – and examined my buttocks, which were bleeding and horrible. Nothing was said. They filed out and left me on my own. I said nothing to anyone. I was never bullied again, and I knew I wouldn't be. I was able to settle to some degree of normality, even, very gradually, to start to enjoy my schooldays.

They say things come in threes. It was perhaps inevitable, therefore, that my unfortunate rear should be assailed for the third time. It received six of the best from the soft-spoken, round-faced, rose-cheeked Mr E.H. 'Spud' Dowdell.

What did I do to deserve this extreme punishment? I bit Brownlow. I can't recall now why I bit him. I've never bitten anyone else, and I don't remember disliking him particularly. Maybe he had that air of a boy just waiting to be bitten.

No doubt you'd like to know exactly where I bit Brownlow. Nowhere very exciting, I'm afraid. I bit him in the changing room.

Further pain was inflicted on my lower body, but at the front this time, due to my carelessness. One day I was late for a cricket net, so didn't have time to find my box, the genital protector so memorably described by Rachel Heyhoe-Flint on *Test Match Special* as a man-hole cover. I was batting quite well until I misjudged a rather vicious delivery and there was a collision between three balls, only two of which were mine. I reeled. I saw stars. I crawled back into the house, grabbed a glass of water, struggled to the study that I shared with a boy named Henry Ormerod, who later became a vicar, and collapsed into a chair. The sweat streamed off me. Henry entered with an older, slightly stooping version of himself and a very posh, glamorous lady, and said, 'David, I'd like you to meet my parents.' I struggled to my feet, shook hands, groaned, croaked 'How do you do?' and collapsed back into the chair. Henry's father said, 'Are you all right? I'm a doctor,' and I said, 'Fine. I feel terrific,' and passed out. This was not the first impression I would have chosen.

I wasn't an exceptional student, but I worked hard. I wasn't stupid, but I didn't set the world on fire. In fact at maths I suddenly sank from the top of the class to near the bottom, and there was the school equivalent of a stewards' enquiry. Was I not trying? The answer was that I'd come upon a series of subjects that I had no power to understand. I had a tremendous facility with figures, which would make me a useful man to have in a darts team, but I was no mathematician. Algebra and calculus were closed books to me. Trigonometry was meaningless.

I was only average at history and geography. I didn't quite grasp their relevance, and it wasn't entirely my fault. We learnt a section of French history. Need to know about Richelieu? I'm your man. Interested in French history before Richelieu? Forget it. Not my period. The tyranny of the syllabus is not an entirely modern phenomenon.

If I'd been told that history is the riveting story of the human world and how it became what it is, and that geography is the riveting story of the physical world and how it became what it is, I might have been . . . well . . . riveted.

I was weak on science, but languages were my forte. My favourites were English, because I knew it already, and Latin and Greek, because there was never any risk of meeting anyone who spoke them and realising how primitive one's grasp was.

I wasn't so keen on French, because I thought I might make a fool of myself if I ever met a Frenchman. Lots of the boys did meet Frenchmen, of course, regularly. They were sophisticated. We had a master called Mr Audemars, and his nickname was Pont. I had no idea why. I was well into my twenties before I passed through Pont-Audemer on my way south from Le Havre. Lots of the chaps passed it every year on their way to their ripping holidays. Thank goodness I never plucked up the courage to admit my ignorance. How those blighters would have chortled at my expense.

I recall three English masters. Mr Fogden was known as Foggy F and with reason – he set us the wrong book for an exam and only realised his mistake a week before it took place. He was once overheard at Marlborough Station asking for a third person singular to London. Mr Davis was tall and thin and sallow and had very black hair. He was most encouraging and led me to believe that I had a certain talent with words.

I wrote an essay for him on 'The Happiest Day Of My Holidays'. Yes, we really did have to write about that. I described a day's sailing with my cousin John and my father in his yacht 'Fairy' (the world was still innocent) in the salty muddy estuary of the River Crouch in Essex. I began by describing a night of bad sleep and upset stomachs as the wind was blowing against the tide and the little 20-footer was shuddering and yawing on her mooring. Only later did everything become worthwhile. This intrigued Mr Davis and made him read on. He rewarded me by asking me to stay in after class and write the whole essay out again, so that he might keep it and show it to future generations as an example of good writing. I thought that unjust, but he told me that it was a privilege which I would come to value, and I suppose I did, because it made me feel good about my writing.

My growing self-confidence was knocked out of me by my next English master, Mr Spreckley. He would read out essays, particularly mine with their tendency towards purple passages. He hated purple passages. '"I set off *on my bicycle down the lane*,"' he would read. 'We are astonished, Nobbs. You have amazed us. We quite thought that you set off *under your bicycle along the hedge*.' Quite soon I found it impossible to put words to paper at all. ('"To paper", Nobbs. You astound us. We quite believed you wrote on chocolate.')

My main love at Marlborough, however, was the study of the ancient languages of Greece and Rome, especially Greece. What a liquid, limpid language.

I particularly recall three classics masters, all rather splendid. First, and fearsome, was Mr Shaw, a brisk, pink, scrubbed young man. He used to rap our knuckles very hard with his ruler if we got things wrong. Once a term, though, he ordered us to rebel, and we had to rap his knuckles and answer back. For one of these rebellions he hid up the chimney and descended like Father Christmas to our great astonishment. When we got older Mr Shaw sometimes saw us in smaller groups in his study and proved not to be fearsome at all.

Mr Knight was large but it was all muscle. He played cricket for Wiltshire, and used his bulk to score runs at a prodigious rate. He had a lovely, shy, slightly twisted smile that lit up his face. He built on the foundations drummed in by Mr Shaw, and began to bring the ancient world to life. He once told us that I was the first boy he had come across in his whole career to argue the side of Sparta against Athens in an essay on their wars. This reveals my burgeoning perversity. Sparta gave the world the word 'spartan' and Athens gave the world the word 'democracy'. Nobody but a blinkered right-wing commander of a private army could prefer Sparta.

Mr Knight's main contribution to my life, however, was that he always read Damon Runyan to us on the last day of term. I'd discovered humorous writing by this time. My father was a huge fan of P.G. Wodehouse and had introduced me to him and Stephen Leacock, and I was beginning to read and admire the diamond sharp dialogue of Evelyn Waugh. Now here was this great comic writer, the most individual of all, one of the few men to create his own world, not by distorting everyone else's world, but by describing everyone else's world in such a unique and inimitable way that it became his own world. I'm not claiming that Runyan was as great a comic writer as Waugh – I don't think he was, he was so much more limited in scope and ambition – but he was a supreme stylist, like Orton, and there are others, including my closest friend, Peter Tinniswood. But I anticipate.

Back to Classics. I ended my time at Marlborough as a very middling member of the Classical Upper Sixth. Our form master was Mr A.D. Whitehorn. He was bald and dapper and had a trim moustache and twinkly eyes. He must have been about sixty, but he still opened the batting for Savernake Cricket Club. He came to school one day with a plaster on the top of his bald head. He had ducked to avoid a bouncer, and he had not avoided it. He told us with delight that the ball had sailed on over the boundary on the full, so he scored six leg byes off the top of his head.

Every Monday morning he came into class a few minutes late and said, 'Sorry I'm late. I didn't sleep well at the weekend. Those Christians were ringing their bells again.' He was scholarly without being dogmatic, interesting without being populist, strict without being fearsome. He taught, as he batted, with economic elegance. Many years later I had the pleasure of meeting his daughter, Katharine Whitehorn, the distinguished journalist, and telling her how much I had admired him.

Mr Whitehorn once invited me to tea, in his small, neat, elegant terrace house, and there I met his wife, who was blind. I think there were a few other boys there. Mr Whitehorn hadn't told us that his wife was blind and he never referred to it then or afterwards. Neither did she and neither did we. In those days, when disabled people were kept away from one much more than they are now, people were embarrassed by disability in a way that they aren't today, and that is something to remember when we fulminate, as I do, against the absurdities of political correctness. That afternoon there was no embarrassment whatever. It was a lesson in manners.

Poor Henry Ormerod, my study-mate. Soon I will reveal a great embarrassment that I brought upon myself at his home in Bristol. I hope, therefore, that he'll forgive me for mentioning a minor embarrassment that he suffered in the Classical Upper Sixth.

Henry was somewhat strait-laced, as befitted a future vicar, and had been embarrassed by a passage – of Horace, perhaps – in which our old friend, the copulation of cattle, is described. When we had to translate this passage for an exam, the reference was removed from our tender gaze. 'You were obviously very taken with the description of the bull mounting the cow, Ormerod,' twinkled Mr Whitehorn. 'You translated it most vividly, even though it was no longer there.'

I found Greek tragedy and its strict rules absolutely fascinating. We went to see a performance, in Greek, at Bradfield College, between Newbury and Reading. It was a stunning experience, but an intellectual one, and it's hard now to relate this austere and earnest event to the excitement and betting and prize-giving and carousing of a dramatic festival in ancient Athens.

I felt a strange excitement as we studied the comedies of Aristophanes. They're astonishing works, ebullient, experimental and viciously satirical. They were hugely topical and yet still work after 2,500 years. They seem utterly modern, yet that thought is an insult to history. Why should Greek drama have been old-fashioned just because it was written five hundred years before Christ? Sometimes I think that we think that we are the only people who were ever modern.

My excitement was the first inchoate stirring of my ambition, but I wasn't ready to recognise that yet.

I was inspired by Roman writers too, by Pliny and his magnificent description of the eruption of Vesuvius, by Catullus and his splendid cynicism and sexuality and emotion and tenderness and respect for the trivial. When you read something that was written two thousand years ago and brings to immortality a dead sparrow, a long-gone girl friend (a long-gone boy friend, too, but we won't go into that, though Catullus did), you can't fail to grow excited by the power and wonder of words. Why should we study dead languages? For the sake of our souls.

Our headmaster, Mr F.R. Heywood, was a good scholar and a good teacher. He shocked the parents one speech day by attacking the public school system and the privileges it bestows, and he moved on to become headmaster of a much less prestigious school for handicapped children.

He was succeeded by Mr Garnett, who struggled to win the same respect. He professed himself shocked at the laxity of our morals, and came to Cotton House one evening to lecture us on the subject. Unfortunately he had a speech defect, and he was accompanied by Mr Dowdell, who was carrying a rubber ring as he was recovering from an operation for piles. The scene that followed was the funniest thing that I had ever experienced, but it was impossible to laugh. It was torture.

I don't remember Mr Garnett's exact words, but I used the experience shamelessly in *Second From Last In The Sack Race* and those words will have to do.

> 'I want to schpeak to you today on a very sherioush schubject. Sheksh. In particular, the shin of homoschekshuality. Because it is a shin. Oh yesh.'

It goes on a bit in the book. I do get carried away. One more sentence will suffice here.

> 'As I shee you shitting there, sho sholemn, sho shad, your expressions shuffused with shame, yesh, the shame shame that I myshelf felt at my shschool, I confesh that my schpirits shag.'

Of course that is exaggerated, but in real life there was an amazing tag to the scene, which I couldn't use in the book because it would have taken the passage away from the theme that it was illustrating.

In real life Mr Garnett ended, 'Finally, on a different schubject, I am determined to find the identity of the boy who is trying to teach my dog to schmoke.'

I had never felt very excited about going to church. I'd gone because it was expected of me. Now, at Marlborough, I began to enjoy it. In the early days, the miserable days when I was still being bullied, chapel was a safe haven, and the singing, with seven hundred boys, was on a scale that proved very moving, even addictive. The lusty singing of a popular hymn is very powerful and I found I got very emotional. I was part of a great team, God's worshippers. I decided to train for Confirmation, and it was an enormous joy and privilege to become accepted into the Church of England. I found it truly exhilarating to walk along the Bath Road on a cold, grey, winter's dawn to partake of the body and blood of Christ.

I can't recall any great philosophical process behind my religious feelings, but when I look back I realise that there was a great battle going on at school between good and evil. I was firmly on the good side because the evil side was so frightening. The naughty boys were so dangerous, and you needed a good reason for standing apart from them. Godliness was the best reason of all. It was cast-iron. I do think now that the rape must have played some part in all this. I felt a deep, private stain. I needed to wash myself clean.

There was talk of boys consorting with prostitutes in the town (how many prostitutes can there have been in Marlborough?), and one or two boys claimed to have visited a brothel in Swindon on a cultural cycling trip, but most sexual activity revolved around homosexuality. There just weren't any girls around. Here were all these horny boys, their sexuality aroused and not yet in control, and the only easily available soft yielding flesh was that of younger boys. On one occasion our dormitory was declared out of bounds by a group of rather sophisticated boys. A homosexual orgy was to take place there. Did it really? It must have. There were damp patches on my sheets that night.

I can't leave the subject of my dormitory without telling you a little statistical curiosity about it. When I tell people this they say, 'That's just the sort of thing that would happen to you', as if it's part of the scenario that is bound to surround a writer of comedy. The curiosity is that there were six boys in our dormitory and we had a total of twelve testicles. Nothing odd about that, but two + two + two + two + one + three? Unlikely, but true. As you will remember from the cricket ball incident, I was one of the normal ones.

*

When Cotton House's social cricket team played against the pretty downland village of Aldbourne, we stopped at a village pub on the way back. I refused to go in. Friends will find that hard to believe, but at that time I thought all alcohol except communion wine was evil. I braved ridicule. Actually, I didn't get ridicule. I got respect.

On the question of religion I have a curious feeling that I'm writing somebody else's biography, and I can't quite get beneath the surface of his motives, so I'm casting around for explanations. What is clear is that his faith . . . sorry, *my* faith . . . began to fall away relatively soon.

Within eighteen months of my Confirmation I went to the tiny church in Little Yeldham at the crack of dawn on Christmas morning, 1952. I was seventeen. Uncle Charlie and Auntie Kathleen had invited a lonely spinster from the village for Christmas dinner. She was a vegan and a teetotaller. She refused an alcoholic drink so vehemently that I heard myself saying, 'Well, you had a big enough swig of the communion wine this morning.' It was true. It had been noticeable. Total silence fell. A livid red spot appeared in the centre of both her cheeks and she stormed out. I was appalled. Uncle Charlie put an arm on my shoulder and said, 'Don't worry, chap. She got angry because it was true, and it'd have ruined my Christmas dinner, watching her toying with a sprout.'

Little Yeldham church played a part in my loss of faith. Worshipping there was so very far removed from the heady adolescent fervour of our flamboyant school chapel. One summer Sunday I went with Granny Nobbs to church and there was only one other person there, a villager who had only twice been beyond Great Yeldham. 'What do we think . . .' the Reverend Cann enquired of us '. . . as we emerge from the theatre, having seen Mr T.S. Eliot's *The Cocktail Party*?' A few days later I found his sermon, word for word, in the religious paper *The British Weekly*. Mr Cann had lifted it lock, stock and inappropriate reference. Granny Nobbs went very silent when I told her. I suppose I should have kept it to myself, but I was very angry. I was putting so much into my faith. The Reverend Cann seemed to be putting so little into his.

Had I not become so deeply religious I might have drifted on as a social believer, but my faith was important enough to me to need testing at every point. I found myself asking awkward questions in religious education. Boys with no faith asked nothing, showed no interest. I asked out of deep need, and was unable to get the proof I sought. Back to *Second From Last In The Sack Race* and Henry Pratt . . .

> He went through all the arguments over and over again. Cosmological. Teleological. Ontological. There must be a God because there is no other explanation of why the world began, or indeed how it began. But what is the explanation of why there is a God and how God began? There are so many signs of order and purpose in Nature that it is inconceivable that there is not an over-all creative Mind controlling it. There are so many signs of disorder and chaos in Nature that it is inconceivable that there is an over-all creative Mind controlling it. There must be a God, otherwise how would we be able to have the idea of God? Well there must be nuclear bombs because how else would we be able to have the idea of them? By inventing them. Have we not invented God? . . . In the end either you plump for a God out of need or temperamental inclination, and that is grotesque, or God is Revealed to you.

Not often in our lives are we as deeply deluded as when we wrestle with the problems of religion. They are so personal and so important that we believe that our wrestling with them is brilliant and unique. It's galling to find that millions of people have the same thoughts all over those parts of the world where freedom of thought is not too frightening.

Anyway, God was not Revealed to Henry Pratt, or to me. In the summer of 1953 we again went to Aldbourne to play cricket. This time I led the way into the pub. They say that beer is an acquired taste. It took me twelve seconds to acquire it.

In my next cricket match after the visit to the pub I was struck by lightning. It wasn't a direct hit or I wouldn't be where I am today. The sky was darkening. I was fielding close to the wicket. It began to rain. There was a peal of thunder and, simultaneously, a great flash of lightning. An electric current surged through my body. My feet were rooted to the ground. I looked at the two other boys who were fielding close to the wicket. Their faces had gone white, utterly white, ghostly white. Their hair was standing on end. Then their hair returned to normal, and I could move my feet again, and we ran to a tiny pavilion, little more than a hut, and stood there shivering and shaking till the storm passed.

Did I for one moment believe that it was a thunderbolt from an angry God? No. It was lightning.

And so his religion just stopped, drifted away. He . . . sorry, I . . . stopped taking Holy Communion, stopped going to church except for weddings, funerals and an occasional duty visit to please the family. I hadn't wanted to stop believing, any more than I had wanted to start.

In my early years at Marlborough I lived for the holidays. Granny and Grandpa Nobbs had moved to Northend, a hamlet of Little Yeldham, to be near Auntie Kathleen and Uncle Charlie. They'd bought a rather ugly, square house called The Pines, though there were no pines anywhere near it. It had none of the charm of High House. It was stern and unloving, brick-built, dusty, and full of my grandfather's books. My happiest memories of it are of reclining in the morning sunshine on a lovely green chaise longue in the dining-room window, and devouring the cricket reports in the *News Chronicle*.

Above the dining room, another memorable event occurred. I was sharing a twin-bedded room with my father. It was a sunny morning and I'd just awoken and was day dreaming pleasantly about this, that and the other, especially the other, whatever that was, when, in the words yet again of *Second From Last In The Sack Race* . . .

The slumbering giant awoke, leapt up, and spat. It was brief, burning, terrifying, amazing, wonderful.

It was also disconcerting. Nobody had prepared me for this. I had to work everything out for myself. I also had to wait till my father got up so that he wouldn't see my wet pyjamas. I can't recall how old I was when this happened, but it was before the real onset of my religious phase.

During my teenage years I had several crushes and fantasies – among those I yearned for were Doris Day, Tess of the D'Urbevilles and Sheila Bridgeland, who lived opposite – but during my last year at school I actually fell a little in love for the first time. He played in the same cricket team as me at Cotton House and, although I think he knew what I felt, it didn't get any further than a major outbreak of foolish smiles and general soppiness. I won't embarrass him by revealing his name. He probably became a captain of industry.

Does it surprise you that after all this lusting after unattainable women in the steamy sterility of my bedroom I should fall for a boy? It didn't surprise me or shock me. I had been shocked by homosexuality during my self-righteous phase. No longer. He wasn't the first boy I'd felt attracted to, but he was the first one I'd had a crush on. That was all it was, I suppose. An adolescent crush.

I've been moving backwards and forwards in time a bit in this chapter, and also between religion and sexuality, in an attempt to capture something of the confusion of the whole thing, the way in which different bits of my personality matured at different rates, the way in which thoughts can be so much at odds with feelings as the hormones kick in.

Something that added to my adolescent confusion was that towards the end of my time at Marlborough I began to enjoy the terms more than the holidays. This was very disconcerting.

I had begun to feel very discontented at home. My behaviour must have been very difficult for my parents. I began to kick doors and skirting boards. When Uncle Kenneth told me, at the bridge table, that something I didn't understand was a convention, I said, 'I don't believe in convention,' and chucked my cards on to the fire. Insufferable prig! Once I got so angry with my parents that I stepped out of the car – no longer HMM642 – on a dual carriageway, when it was doing at least forty miles an hour. I was dragged along the A11, ruining my trousers, grazing my thighs and hips, and being a great deal luckier than I deserved.

This was my teenage rebellion, late like everything else. What was I rebelling against? Our lack of sophistication! I was ashamed of the cosy unpretentious simplicity of my parents' lives, ashamed that we had tea instead of dinner, ashamed that we never went abroad. I'm more ashamed of this than of anything else in my life – well, almost. Oh, not ashamed that we weren't sophisticated. That doesn't matter a hoot. Ashamed that I was ashamed of it. Ashamed how much I must have hurt my dear parents.

It was all because I'd gone to Marlborough College. I can't blame the school. It tried so hard to stop us feeling superior, but the boys were having none of that. One of our masters didn't speak quite poshly enough. He became known as Oiky K. The faintest hint of failure to match up to the highest standards of the upper middle classes was frowned upon.

My holidays still consisted of visits to Swansea and to Yeldham to stay with my grandparents, but from the late 1940s we also went for a week to Frinton. Frinton prided itself on being posh. You searched for a fish and chip shop or a pub in vain. Of candy floss was there none. A wide swathe of grass separated the town from the sea-front. Woe betide you if you called this anything but the greensward, and woe betide any dog that fouled the greensward. (I once heard a woman yell at a chihuahua that seemed likely to be naughty, 'Come on, Kenneth.' Why do I find Kenneth such a hilarious name for a chihuahua?)

There were posh houses on all sides, but we lodged in modest digs with Mrs Walker. There was my mother and me, and Auntie Kathleen and John, and sometimes Auntie Dot and Elizabeth. Mrs Walker did us very nicely. To borrow an immortal phrase from the great Tinniswood's description of Uncle Mort's honeymoon: 'she only burst the sausages once'.

Our evening entertainment consisted of walking round Frinton and looking at the large houses. How unbelievably tedious that sounds now, but in my teens, believe me, it was even more tedious.

Tedium, however, was not the problem. Lusty was the problem. Lusty was in Cotton House, and he lived in Frinton and he was well-off, he was a Lusty of Lusty's Soups, and I'd have been in the soup if Lusty had seen me gawping admiringly at his house. Oh, the feeling of inferiority. Once you have it, it takes decades to wash it away.

The days on the beach were fine, except for the fact that we had a beach hut, and in front of the beach hut ran the prom, and who was to say that Lusty might not wander along insouciantly with a pretty girl on each arm? It never occurred to me that Lusty wouldn't be seen dead anywhere near Frinton prom, that he'd be sporting himself in St Tropez or Cannes. I can't buy his lobster bisque without shuddering.

Then there were the Ormerods. What torture, and I brought it on myself. Henry had told me a story at school about a very odd burglar who only stole . . . I can't remember exactly what, but something like a wireless, a ball of string and a pound of tomatoes. I went to stay with his family in Bristol. They had a large town house near Clifton Downs, and had dinner in the evening, not tea, and his mother was elegant and I was over-awed and couldn't think of anything to say at dinner, and dredged a story from my memory, and said, 'We had a very odd burglar at home. All he stole was a wireless, a ball of string and a pound of tomatoes.' Henry went pink and glared at me, and I remembered. His father said, 'Well, that's amazing. We had the same burglar. He must have moved from Bristol to Orpington. This could be a vital clue for the police.' I can't recall how I managed to prevent him from ringing for the police, but I can still feel the sweat running down my back.

Uncle Charlie was something of a gourmet – he ate raw broad beans for breakfast – and Auntie Kathleen was a very good cook and remained so almost until her death at the age of ninety-two. Once, when they took me to the George Hotel in Colchester, I saw an elderly woman – she was at least thirty-three – dining happily on her own on a rare fillet steak with a green salad. I remember thinking, 'That's sophistication.'

Uncle Charlie took us to sophisticated restaurants in London – L'Ecu de France in Jermyn Street, Le Jardin des Gourmets in Soho. I have only the vaguest memories of these restaurants, but I can recall in vivid detail the Bertram Mills circuses, and the spectacular ice shows at Olympia, and our meetings with Thelma, John's aunt, who drank and smoked and dressed rather like a man and had elegant friends who used lots of scent and wore dresses that swirled and seemed very exotic to me, and our annual visit to Hamley's in Regent Street, to stare at toys beyond belief.

London in the dark was an exciting swirl of lights and taxis and scent and cigarettes, and each year after the war the lights grew a little brighter. London in summer seemed stale and spent to me then. There were no pavement cafés. Nothing spilt out on to those dull hot pavements. The whole city hid from the sun behind closed doors, like a vast gentleman's club. It was a winter city in those days.

Uncle Glandon was a sophisticated figure too. He took me to see the Canada Cup golf at Wentworth. He told my parents that we'd have to leave early, because the car parks got very full. It was a lie. A relative lying! How thrilling. We left early because friends of his ran a pub at the side of the Thames and we went there for sherry before the golf. This was living. Uncle Glandon always got tickets for Wimbledon too. He took me there once, and I saw a magnificent final between Hoad and Rosewall.

Uncle Kenneth's bachelor life held a touch of glamour for me as well. He lived between Kensington and Chelsea, played bridge, ate at Schmidts in Charlotte Street, went on motoring holidays to Spain and Austria, went to concerts in Vienna and had three teeth extracted in Madrid. He took me to a major athletic event at the White City. I saw the great Arthur Wint win the 440 on his incredibly long silky black legs where now accountants sit in rows saving the BBC money.

But we didn't have dinner in the evening and we didn't go to restaurants and we didn't have foreign holidays. Probably my father couldn't afford them because he was paying for my education, which makes the memory of my discontent all the more distressing to me now.

When I see children's bedrooms today, and I think of my bedroom at the back of the house in Sevenoaks Road, I'm appalled at its starkness and lack of personality. I made no attempt to decorate it. There weren't yet posters of pop stars, of course, and probably not of footballers either. My life in my bedroom revolved entirely around books. My bed was a womb where I read and read and read. 'Look at him with his nose buried in a book,' said Auntie Louie. 'There hasn't been a truly great English writer since Dickens, I beg your pardon?' said Uncle Kenneth. Auntie Dilys – prudish spinster Auntie Dilys – gave me *The Rainbow* by D.H. Lawrence! She was highbrow, so literature was on a plane elevated from life. Lesbian bathing was inconceivable in Swansea, but in literature it was fine.

I devoured Lawrence and Aldous Huxley – every serious developing reader went through an Aldous Huxley phase – but my great love now was Thomas Hardy. Arthur Ransome put Captain W.E. Johns in his place. Now Thomas Hardy routed Arthur Ransome. All his books were great, their misery was addictive, but Tess! Oh Tess of the Tosterones, how often I rewrote the ending and married you and made you happy and you were so grateful – oh, the things you did to me in your gratitude, in my stark bedroom. Sometimes I felt quite guilty about being unfaithful to Sheila Bridgeland, who didn't know that I was being unfaithful because she didn't know how I ached for her and what things she'd done to me in my bedroom, before I'd met Tess.

I think the lack of external stimuli, and the complete absence of pop culture, ensured that I developed an inner imagination, a private individual culture of my own. I do fear that an excess of pop culture can make the external so stimulating to children that the internal life is neglected. It seems like a great burst of freedom that has come upon the world since I was a lad, but it can also burden young people with far more peer pressure to conform than we faced in our day.

Towards the end of my time at school I achieved the very modest success of being elected a House Prefect. The Head of House was a boy called Chris Hogg, and he did become a captain of industry. He became Sir Christopher Hogg of Courtaulds. He sits on the board of the National Theatre. Under his enlightened prefectship Cotton House became very different. There was hardly any bullying any more. The house prefects ruled through respect, not fear, and the memory of this has led me to realise that all the people in the world who rule through fear do so because they know that they will never win respect.

Chris and I became good friends. We would get up at six to swot for our 'A' Levels and would make coffee for the other voluntary early risers, and there were many. The coffee was thick with condensed milk, and everybody loved it.

By now I had learnt to be sociable. I wasn't a loner. I was reasonably popular. And yet . . . Something must have been missing still. I didn't keep up with Chris Hogg. I haven't seen my old study mate Henry Ormerod for more than forty years, though we still send cards and occasional letters. I've never been to a school reunion. It's as if in my late development the person I really am had not yet emerged. I have just one good friend from all my schooldays, Tony Robinson, and we were little more than acquaintances at school. Friendship came later, fuelled by cricket, beer and, at last, a touch of maturity.

I had gone through all the sexual uncertainties, all the processes of religious argument, all the crises about my identity, from the comparatively rare 'I don't know who I am' to the much more common 'I know who I am only too well, and don't like it'. All this seemed so individual in its pain but was actually humiliatingly universal. I had begun, though, to realise that there were two things about me that were perhaps a bit individual. They were my writing and my sense of humour. I didn't think they had any merit. I just thought they were different.

I began to take my writing more seriously. I had my first piece published, in the school magazine. It was a review of the cadet corps's exercise day. It's a busy piece. In the course of three hundred words it mentions Solomon, Queen Elizabeth the First, the Ancient Mariner and Mau Mau terrorists, and quotes from two poems. It's too full of incomprehensible local and topical references to quote in full, but it did contain my first joke in print: 'As he hurried back through the Highstreet (reputed by many experts to be the widest in Marlborough) . . .'

I must have written a few more pieces as well, because my name was given to Mr Murray. Mr Murray was the PT teacher and I recall him as a bad example, even as slightly bent (in physique, not habit), but he ran the school literary society. I don't think I even knew there was a literary society. Anyway, he took some of my pieces, and I think he must have read them to the literary society. He was hugely supportive and encouraging. To my shame, I never wrote to thank him.

Chris Hogg and I ended our last term at school by doing a little show for Cotton House. It consisted of no more than two or three sketches and I think we did them sitting in chairs rather than acting them out, but at least I got through it without stage fright, and the laughter was a joy to my ears. I knew then that laughter would be the most important thing in my life.

As a House Prefect I was permitted a radio. It was huge, oblong, bright red and shiny, and out of it came something massive. It was called *In All Directions*, a comedy show, written by and starring Peter Ustinov and Peter Jones. It featured an endless search not for the meaning of life, but for something far more important – Copthorne Avenue! It had a riotously funny parody of the Coronation (we still hadn't a television, we'd had to watch it at Mrs Dakin's at number 51) called 'Taking The Biscuit' in which a series of BBC commentators – brilliant parodies of Richard Dimbleby, Audrey Russell and others – spoke in hushed tones about a ceremony centred on an enormous biscuit. There was also a sketch in which all the passengers on the *Queen Elizabeth* had to be brought off on stretchers in the service of a scam of some description. I can't remember enough to bring it to life, but it went into my funny bone like a powerful drug and I felt a most enormous excitement. I played it to the chaps in the dorm and they laughed and I felt absurdly proud, as if I had written it.

I knew that I wanted to write stuff as funny as *In All Directions*. I might even have left school eagerly if National Service hadn't been coming up next.

On our last night, Mr E.H. 'Spud' Dowdell invited the house prefects to his study for the last time, for strawberries and cream, and then asked us, shyly, quietly, if we'd like to watch him putting his hens to bed. A strange treat. A strange man. I would guess that he was a kind man and a lonely one. (One of his colleagues claimed to have come upon him sitting on the floor surrounded by long chains of unrolled toilet paper.

In his capacity as bursar he was counting the number of sheets in order to calculate which was the best buy.)

Later, bottles of wine were removed from under floor boards and a late-night party was held. I didn't get drunk. There wasn't enough wine. Nevertheless, it was singularly delightful and even a bit intoxicating, this sense of comradeship.

I had longed for my schooldays to end. I left them behind me with deep regret.

4 YOUR COUNTRY REALLY DOESN'T NEED YOU ALL THAT MUCH, ACTUALLY, TO BE HONEST

CATTERICK CAMP IS a large, straggling community built on the side of a windswept hill in a singularly nondescript corner of the otherwise beautiful county of Yorkshire.

It was 3 September, 1953, and I was to join the Royal Corps of Signals. A few months previously I'd been for a medical. My testicles had been held in an iron grip and I had coughed. The soles of my feet had been banged with an iron spoon and I had felt disturbingly little. My puny chest expansion had been measured in grim silence. My urine had been comprehensively tested. It didn't look too good to me. My stools, which I had brought with me on the train at no extra cost, had received the same rigorous examination. My throat and eyes had been examined with a powerful torch. My congenital psoriasis had been noted. I had been tested for colour blindness. I've always had difficulty with blues and greens and hoped that this might stand me in bad stead. There was no possibility of failing the rudimentary intelligence test, but by and large I felt confident that I'd done pretty wretchedly. Imagine my consternation when Her Majesty decided that I was fit to serve her. It was early in her reign and it was clear that her judgement had not yet fully matured.

So there I was, along with hundreds of other stick-out ears and bad complexions, crossing the station forecourt in freezing Richmond and unathletically clambering up on to the first of many ten-ton trucks.

We were allocated to our respective spiders. A spider's body is the ablutions block, and the legs are the huts that fan out from it. The huts contained two rows of beds and a narrow space in the middle. Right in the middle of the hut there was a stove, fuelled by coke.

We were kitted out at the Quartermaster's Stores. Khaki, gun-metal and drab green. Just not my colours. At some stage we must have been given a meal, but the human mind has an amazing capacity for blotting out serious traumas.

Eventually, we were all assembled in our hut, looking ill at ease in our khaki uniforms, and were introduced to Sergeant 'You play ball with me, I'll play ball with you, you mess me around I'll have your bollocks on toast for my tea with piccalilli' Pollard. He showed us how to stow our kit, and how to make bed-packs, those neat parcels of blankets and sheets that would make the hut look so inspiringly neat each morning. He made a bed-pack – the show bed-pack – and then we made ours. Ours were shapeless parodies of his. We made them again. By this time it was dark and rain was splatting against the glass. Sergeant Pollard cast a cold eye over our bed-packs, condemned them all as disgraceful, and threw every single one out of the windows. They landed on the damp earth of the flowerless flower-beds. Then he announced that it was bedtime and lights out. We had to grope our way out in the dark, retrieve our bedding in the dark, grope our way back and make our beds in the dark, get undressed in the dark, clamber into the damp, muddy bed in the dark and struggle to get to sleep in our misery, only to be woken at 5.30. Two years of this!

We were kept working all day every day. It was at least six weeks before we got a Naafi break that lasted long enough for us to be served before it ended.

Every morning, before breakfast, we had to draw a line, with black boot polish, along the hut, and then line our beds up exactly on it. We then had to wash off all traces of the boot polish. We were being paid four shillings a day, and we had to provide our own boot polish. It probably only cost about threepence, but that would have been more than 6 per cent of the day's wage, and one tin didn't go far.

The centre of every military unit is the square – that great empty windswept space across which the hoarse, rancid shouts of innumerable sergeants sailed away into the ether. Our early days were spent almost entirely in various kinds of square bashing – learning to about turn, about wheel, mark time, halt, stand to attention, stand easy, slope arms, order arms, present arms, fix bayonets, unfix bayonets, and do the first and second IA (Immediate Action) on the bren guns which, due to a cock-up in supplies, we did not yet have.

On that very first day I was lined up next to a young man who seemed immensely old at twenty-one, having elected to go to university before National Service, a ruse which simply hadn't occurred to me.

The drill sergeant, who always used an aitch when there wasn't one, and never used an aitch when there was one, said to this individual, 'Never, hin my twenty-six years hin the British harmy, 'ave hi seen hanythink has 'ideous, has 'orrible, has hidle, has hugly has you.' He put him on a charge: filthy hand hidle hon parade.

He looked at me rather sadly, and said, quite softly, 'My God, you run 'im ha bloody close second.'

I was put on several charges in those early days. One of them was for hinsolence. The sergeant said to me, after some more than average piece of incompetence on my part, 'You, you 'orrible little man, what's your name?'

'Nobbs, sarge.'

'Don't you speak to me like that. You're hon ha charge. Hinsolence.'

'But it's my name, sarge.'

'Don't you hargue with me, laddie, hor you'll be hon two charges. Hinsolence hand hinsubordination.'

Hafter the . . . sorry . . . after the day's work, exhausted though we were, we would have to spoon our boots. Our boots were rough, their surface uneven. We had to heat up a spoon and work it across the surface of the boot until you could see your face in it. When you did see your face, it looked so pale and drawn and knackered that you wished you couldn't see it.

One young squaddie proved much better than the rest of us at spooning his boots. 'Well done,' said Sergeant Pollard. 'You ain't got nothing to do now, have you? Shame. Well, you'd better do it again, then, 'adn't you?' and he got out a penknife and dug great scratches in the boots.

One day our drill sergeant got it in for a member of our squad, called Green. He issued the strange order, 'Squad will laugh hat Signalman Green by number, squad hat Signalman Green, laugh.' Later this command was extended and we actually had to chant, 'Signalman Green smells two three ha two three, ha two three ha.' We didn't do it with enough enthusiasm, we were sorry for the wretched fellow. It was made clear to us that if we didn't throw ourselves into it we'd be back for extra drill. We told Signalman Green that we didn't mean it, but it wore him down and he had a nervous breakdown. No doubt the drill sergeant felt pleased with himself. He was rooting out the weedy. The nation could sleep safely in its beds.

One of our tasks was to go round the trees that bordered the parade ground, test every leaf and pull off any that were loose, so that no autumn leaves would flutter untidily to the ground during the CO's inspection.

Another job was painting the coal in the coal store white, so that nobody would mistake it for darkness and fall over it.

One day we found our ablutions block out of bounds. We had to go to an ablutions block in a different spider. Later we found out why. A man had hanged himself in one of the toilets. We were told that two out of our intake of a thousand committed suicide, and I know that there were rumblings in the newspapers on the issue.

These figures are not typical and in discussions with contemporaries I've never found anybody who discovered conditions as bad as I've described, but this is my story not theirs and I'm not exaggerating. There will be other things in this chapter that you'll be tempted to doubt. Please don't. I think my career proves that I can make up things that amuse. There's no need of that here. I'm giving the unvarnished truth.

One of the worst experiences of our army life was washing up fatigues. Compared to washing up fatigues, square bashing was a perfectly timed orgasm with Catharine Deneuve on a private nudists' beach on the sheltered side of Cap Ferrat with a bottle of nicely chilled Menetou-Salon at one's side. The tins are many, and they are vast, the grease is thick, the water is cold. The grease gets on everything. How can you wash a vast greasy tin with a vast greasy sponge held in a frozen greasy hand?

It was while I was doing washing up fatigues that Rennie entered. Rennie had been head boy at Marlborough and now he was Second-Lieutenant Rennie, orderly officer of the day. He was a year older than I, but in National Service a year was a century. I have no quibble with Rennie. He seemed a decent sort and may well have gone on to be a captain of industry. It's the system I'm complaining about. It was the system that made Second-Lieutenant Rennie ask me one of the most stupid of the many stupid questions I've been asked. 'Are you enjoying the army, Nobbs?' he enquired. It was the system that made me give the even more stupid reply of, 'Very much, sir.'

A day or two later the sergeant looked me up and down and said, 'You're going hoff tomorrow. You hare ha potential hofficer.'

'I don't want to be an officer, sir,' I said.

'Shut up,' shouted the sergeant. 'You've been to ha boarding school, 'aven't you? Then you hare ha potential hofficer, heven though you know hand hi know that you haren't fit to be ha potential fucking sanitary hinspector.'

We were marched, the potential hofficers, with our kit bags and rifles, up stark streets, past stark parade grounds and stark barracks, to an even windier location right on the edge of the camp.

A young officer, barely older than us, approached us.

'All those who haven't been circumcised proceed through the gate on your right,' he shouted. 'Cross the field, climb over the style into the next field, go into the small, stone barn and wait for the surgeon.'

I'd been circumcised, as foreskins were deemed dirty in chapel circles, but I felt no relief as I watched those stricken figures stumbling towards their doom. It seemed that we were stepping into an even more barbaric world. It turned out that the senior potential officers, soon to take their WOSB (War Office Selection Board) were permitted to play a jolly jape against the new-bugs. This was their jolly jape.

Life in our new regiment was still hard – in some ways harder still – but we were being trained to command men and so we could at least see the point of it. Also, we did at last get some time to ourselves. A few of us went to Richmond and saw Charlie Chaplin's *Limelight*, starring Claire Bloom. I've heard it criticised. You wouldn't have criticised it if you'd seen it on your first evening out in National Service.

We even had a weekend's leave. I came back from London on the night train and met a doctor's son called Colin Macandrews on Darlington Station at 6.30 a.m. He had a bottle of his father's claret and we made a fine breakfast in that unlikely setting.

The only truly dreadful thing about this second regiment was the assault course. It was no fun at all to swing over wires, clamber up poles, hurl oneself over walls, crawl through tunnels, all in helmet, battledress and heavy boots and carrying your rifle.

Just as we were about to embark on this torture, a lad was brought off the assault course on a stretcher with a bone sticking out of his thigh at a horrendous angle. 'Don't look,' screamed our sergeant. 'Carry on.'

I just went for it, hurled myself at it, quite soon it would be over, nearly finished, done.

'Well done, Nobbs,' said the sergeant. I found myself resenting the surprise in his voice. 'You've won. You're in the next round.'

I hadn't even known there was a next round.

When it came to our turn to play a jape on the new arrivals, we were much kinder. We simply lined them up, one of our number gave the order to 'quick march' and then we left them to it. They marched for four and a half miles before they dared turn round, and found there was nobody with them.

*

Our two-day WOSB took place near Aldershot. I felt rather tense about it. It was vital that I should fail and I found the first day difficult. I needed to do badly, but not so badly that people might deduce that I was failing deliberately. It was hard going.

Why was I so anxious not to be an officer? I suppose it was from a mixture of good and bad reasons, like most things in this life. I lacked self-confidence, I hated the army, I had a deep desire for obscurity, I had no talent for responsibility. I could survive as a signalman. I would have loathed being the junior sprog in the officers' mess.

These were reasons born of weakness. On the credit side, I had a genuine abhorrence for the uses and abuses of power, and I just didn't believe that I belonged to a superior class that had a divine right to order inferior classes around.

After the first day of our WOSB, a group of us went into Aldershot and saw *Roman Holiday,* starring Gregory Peck and Audrey Hepburn. Some critics thought the film slight. They should have seen it half way through their WOSB. I was now madly in love with Claire Bloom and Audrey Hepburn – and I wouldn't have said 'no' to Gregory Peck.

On the second day I felt more relaxed. Failure was in the bag. I could happily do my best. Disturbingly, my results when I was doing my best were worse than when I was trying to fail. I had to organise the carriage of some heavy material over a hypothetical, fast-flowing river. All my men fell into the hypothetical river and were hypothetically drowned.

Anyway, the important thing was that I had succeeded. I had failed.

My next posting was to Garats Hey Camp, in the little village of Woodhouse Eaves, near Loughborough, in Leicestershire. Here, through the winter of 1953–4, I learnt to receive morse, under the benevolent instruction of Sergeant 'Windy' Gale. There was square bashing too, of course, but with nothing like the ferocious intensity of those early days in Catterick. Reveille was still far too early, though, and our nostrils were still full of the acrid fumes from our coke stove, and some mornings were perishing cold. On one such morning, Corporal Isaacs, who was tiny, said to a very tall signalman, 'Bit cold up there, is it?' The signalman replied, 'Yes. Touch of ground frost is there down there, Corporal?' and was on a charge for insolence.

We had a certain amount of time off now – evenings and most weekends. I found that I was making close friends more easily. There was John Medcalf, John Bowden . . . oh dear. If this was a novel I wouldn't call them both John. How can I help you remember them? By what they became. So . . . there was John 'Catholic Priest' Medcalf, John 'Editor, SCM (Student Christian Movement) Press' Bowden (did I choose my drinking companions because there was something religious about them, or was it my friendship that drove them to religion?) and Ken 'Music Teacher' Hewlings, who was from Tenby and had been part of a musical accompaniment to Dylan Thomas when he read his poems and got roaring drunk and didn't behave like the angel he resembled.

One evening I too got roaring drunk, for the first time. It was on dark rum, an unwise choice, in Loughborough, another unwise choice. Loughborough was a dull, drab place in those days, though I'm told it's deteriorated since. I was very sick in a blackthorn hedge, felt ill for three days, didn't drink for three weeks, and didn't drink dark rum for three decades.

Our pleasures were often much more civilised, though. John, John, Ken and I made several happy visits to Nottingham. It was a fine city, noted for its pretty girls. We ran the gamut from ice hockey with the legendary Chick Zamick to a concert with the legendary Kathleen Ferrier making the purest sounds you could imagine. Nottingham Playhouse provided a very moving production of *The Master Builder*, with the not quite legendary Marius Goring in the lead. I've never agreed with those who find Ibsen dull, and this visit filled me with longing, longing to begin life, longing to leave the army, longing for this period of what seemed like waste to be over. I was perhaps dimly aware that this longing had something to do with wanting to write, because I decided that I would be a journalist when I grew up, and I enrolled in a correspondence course on the subject.

The nearest I came to action was in a large scale exercise in which we had to prevent hostile forces – Russian, I believe – from invading somewhere – Canada, I think. Our Maginot line was the Leicestershire-Nottinghamshire border. I was regimental runner and was given the sergeant-major's daughter's bicycle, which was far too small for me. I cycled around for about eight hours of a long winter's night, hoping to be given a message. At last I was, at about 6.30 in the morning. I had to find a Canadian sergeant who was manning a border post (actually a hedge near Barrow-on-Soar) and tell him that three brown cows had flown past the green fox. A grey dawn was breaking, I was cold and tired and hungry and unshaven, but I was equal to the task. I found the sergeant fast asleep. I shook him gently. He moaned and fell back into sleep. I shook him quite violently. Well, I had to give him the good news. Or bad news. There was no way of telling. At last he woke up.

'What?' he said, rather gracelessly, I thought, to be honest, when I'd ridden so far and so fast to tell him, on a bicycle several sizes too small.

'Three brown cows have flown past the green fox.'

'What??'

'It's a message.'

'I know it's a message, you idiot. I didn't think it was nature notes. But what the fuck does it mean?' No charm, this fellow.

'I don't know. I'm only the runner. You're supposed to know.'

'Well I don't. So fuck off.'

I did. Fast. Well, as fast as I could on my little bike.

By this time we got a 48-hour pass once a month, and I'd rattle down to St Pancras on the train. Every other week we had a 36-hour pass, and I would hitch-hike to London. Often I didn't get home till seven in the evening, just in time to eat and then sleep till Sunday lunchtime. I realise in retrospect that I needed the army to knock all that cobblers about sophistication out of me before I went to Cambridge. Now I could really love my parents and my home, though I still couldn't tell them, of course.

One weekend my mother repaired a tear in my battledress trousers, which had got ripped when I climbed on to a motorbike while hitch-hiking home.

'Who darned those trousers?' bawled Corporal Purkiss on Monday's drill.

'My mother, corporal.' (Laughter)

'Shurrup. It's not funny,' said Corporal Purkiss to the platoon. To me he said, 'Tell your mother she's on a fucking fizzer. I've never seen such sloppy work.'

I did tell my mother (leaving out the f word, of course) and she was hugely amused.

Towards the end of May, our course was finished. Sergeant 'Windy' Gale had taught us all there was to know about receiving morse code. We were craftsmen now, and posted to various places to carry out our craft.

After a fortnight's embarkation leave, my departure for the Depot Regiment at Denbury Camp, near Newton Abbot in Devon, was a bit of a first. My parents were more upset than I was. They would miss me deeply, but I was setting off on an adventure.

I knew that Cyprus might be dangerous. The Enosis crisis was at its height. The majority, the Greek Cypriots, wanted the island to be united with Greece. The minority, the Turkish Cypriots, wanted partition. The Greek Cypriot activists made the British a prime target for terrorism. However, I'd never been abroad, and I was looking forward to the sun and the sea. My best friends were going elsewhere, John 'Editor, SCM Press' Bowden to Germany, John 'Catholic Priest' Medcalf and Ken 'Music Teacher' Hewlings to Austria, but the lads of XOX draft got on well and we were all excited about going abroad together.

What I didn't know was that at the Depot Regiment my national service would ascend into farce (I say 'ascend' deliberately. I'm fed up with the automatic use of 'descended into farce'. Farce is more difficult to write than tragedy.)

We were allocated to a hut, rather more pleasant than we had experienced so far. We stowed our kit, and we waited. And waited. And waited. Nothing happened. Nobody told us where to go. Nobody gave us anything to do. Days passed. We ate and slept and slept and ate and lolled on our pits (beds). We read books. We did crosswords. We amused ourselves. We abused ourselves.

Suddenly the door of our hut burst open, and an officer stood there. We jumped off our beds.

'Who are you?'

'XOX, sir.'

'Ah!'

He left us in peace.

A day or two later, the door opened again. Another officer.

'Just what do you all think you're doing?'

'We're XOX, sir.'

'Ah!'

He left us in peace.

It was sheer luck – what I'd call serendipity when I became a writer. The name of our draft, XOX, sounded important, like SOS or SAS. People thought they ought to know what it signified and wouldn't let on that they didn't.

Eventually, our existence could be hidden no longer. Nobody seemed very angry with us, but I feared the worst when I was summoned to Lieutenant Brooke's office.

'You're pretty sensible, aren't you, Nobbs?' he said.

'I suppose I am, sir,' I admitted cautiously. I wasn't sure what I was letting myself in for.

'Your chaps are pretty sensible, aren't they?'

'I suppose they are, sir.'

'There are far too many people in this camp. More than we're allowed.'

'I see, sir.' That's always a good reply when you have no idea what's going on.

'It would help me if a few people I could rely on went spare, as it were. Supposing I asked you chaps to walk out of camp every morning, get a bus to Torquay, spend a nice day on the beach, get a bus back in the evening. Could you do it?'

'We'd have a damned good crack at it, sir.'

'Good man. Can I rely on you chaps not to do anything silly and to keep out of all sorts of trouble?'

'Definitely, sir.'

What a rash promise. But we managed it. We were on sunbathing fatigues for at least a week, and all went well.

Only one of our number, Hodge, from Jersey Marine, Swansea, broke ranks. He was studying for something and wanted to stay all day in the camp library. Hodge was laid back before the concept existed. He moved into an unoccupied corporal's room – there were too many signalmen, but not enough corporals – and legitimised the move by advertising it. He put a notice on the door – 'Signalman Hodge'. Once there was a notice on the door, nobody queried it.

A good example of quick military thinking occurred while I was on sunbathing fatigues. The CO's inspection found Hodge in the library at a time when it was out of bounds.

'What are you doing in the library?' thundered the CO.

'I'm the assistant librarian, sir,' said Hodge blithely.

'Ah.' The CO turned to the librarian. 'Is this man proving satisfactory?'

'He's a good worker, sir,' said the librarian.

When the CO had gone, Hodge's eyes met the librarian's. The librarian's eyes had a gleam in them.

'I've been needing an assistant,' he said. 'I'll be taking the day off tomorrow. You'll manage, won't you?'

Not long after our week on the beach, the blow fell. I wasn't going to Cyprus with my mates. I would need a home posting, because of my psoriasis. XOX draft departed without me. I was devastated. I went to the MO and asked how my psoriasis could be cured.

'Lots of sun. Lots of sea bathing.'

'Then why can't I go to Cyprus?'

'Because this is the army.'

I told the MO that if I wasn't going to Cyprus with my muckers I wanted the psoriasis to be cleared up. He was very obliging and sent me by military ambulance to the Royal Naval Hospital in Plymouth, where I spent a pleasant seven weeks of the summer of 1954. I had coal tar baths and was covered in coal tar ointment and my psoriasis disappeared, soon to return after the treatment ended. In the afternoons I walked on the Hoe and listened to the band. I tried to drink my daily tot of free rum but just couldn't get the stuff down. The only excitement was when I went to get the dinners for the ward and got stuck in the lift for three hours. The ward went hungry, while I had a rare opportunity to eat fourteen hospital dinners.

Back at Denbury, in our picturesquely situated camp in the rich South Devon countryside, with the stern sweep of Dartmoor as our backcloth, I spent the rest of the summer most pleasantly. Time and my life stood still. I went for long walks with a friend called Pete Willis. I drank in the local pub and tried to put the glow-worms out on the way back by peeing on them. I asked everybody to send me really long letters, and I'd spend my mornings taking them very slowly, a page at a time, to the incinerator at the top of the camp.

'What are you doing, laddie?'

'Keeping the camp tidy, sir. Going to the incinerator.'

'Well done, that man.'

Eventually I was put to work in an office which now had three clerks when it should only have had two. Every week, on the day of the CO's inspection, I had to cease to exist. I had to walk to the top of the camp, past the incinerator and the cricket pavilion, and go over a style into a field behind. On my first visit I was amazed to find about forty people in the field, including several officers, all surplus to requirements and forced to hide for several hours.

Then, suddenly, I was posted to Germany, to Munster, the capital of Westphalia. I was excited as I walked from the troop train to the troop ship at Harwich. I'd never been abroad before. I'd never been to sea before. I'd never been on a big ship before.

There were three drafts on the ship – the Irish Greys, the Green Howards and me. Due to an administrative error, each draft was given one deck to sleep in. I don't know how crowded the Irish Greys and the Green Howards were, but I had two hundred bunks. It was a rough crossing. By the end of the night the Irish Greys were as green as the Green Howards, the Green Howards were as grey as the Irish Greys, and I'd slept like a log.

When we disembarked at the Hook of Holland we were ushered towards a long, low shed. The entrance had been divided by tape into three – one for the Green Howards, one for the Irish Greys, one for me. I sauntered up the middle, trying not to look too smug. A huge and very surprised Dutch chef offered me 160 boiled eggs, 320 slices of toast, and an urn of tea or coffee.

The Hook of Holland is not a pretty place. In fact it's the arsehole of Europe. The road, rail and river links end up there. The electricity and gas supplies end up there. It's a mass of roads and railways and pylons and storage tanks and sub-stations. But it was abroad, and it fascinated me. Even the silly colours of the Dutch trains fascinated me. We hadn't taken to silly colours in those days.

Indeed, everything fascinated me as I rolled along in splendid isolation, in the three carriages reserved for me. We crossed busy canals and I caught glimpses of picturesque towns. It was such a busy, crowded little country. Then we were crossing the flat plains of Northern Germany and suddenly the countryside was almost empty. There were huge farms and moated manor houses and small towns with stern Romanesque churches and giant water towers. I wished that journey could go on for ever.

The Hauptbahnhof at Munster was thrillingly crowded and bustling. I was relieved to find that at last my singularity was no surprise. I was met and driven to Nelson Barracks on a long straight road that led towards Osnabruck and the East.

My home for the cold continental winter of 1954–5 was very different from my English camps. Gone were the single-storey huts. Two long heavy three-storey blocks ran the length of a huge parade ground. In these blocks the corridors were endless and rang with the clatter of army boots all day and half the night.

I was found a bed and told to report to the Lecture Theatre for a talk from the Regimental Sergeant-Major.

'Sexual diseases,' began that worthy. 'Do you know how to avoid them? I'll tell you how to avoid them. You avoid them by avoiding the frauleins. Not all of them is as clean as what our women is. You can catch things off of them.

'Now the red light district of Munster is out of bounds, so don't go there. How will you know where not to go? Easy. Don't get on the

number eleven tram. If by any chance you do find yourself on the
number eleven tram, don't get off at the second stop beyond the railway
bridge. If you find you have got off at the second stop beyond the
railway bridge, don't whatever you do go into the third house on the left.
If you catch crabs or the clap or something worse, report to the MO.
You'll be in trouble, but you'll be in far worse trouble if you don't.

'Urges. You may feel urges. We all feels urges. I feels urges. Even the
officers feels urges. What do we do when we feels urges? We go running.
We have a very fine athletics track here. If you feel an urge, run the 880.
If it's a severe urge, run the mile. Corporal, dismiss the man.'

'Man, dismiss.'

Did I feel urges? You bet I did. Did I run the 880? You bet I didn't.
The Onanism crisis followed the Enosis crisis as night follows day. Did
I get off the number eleven tram at the second stop beyond the railway
bridge? I did catch a number eleven tram, to see what a red light district
looked like – tatty and disappointing – but, no, all sorts of reasons, good
and bad, prevented me from going anywhere near the third house on the
left. Morality, timidity, fear of the clap . . .

The final ten months of my national service fell into a pattern and
became not at all unpleasant. Our job was to listen to morse. We worked
a four-day shift cycle which gave us one complete night shift every four
days, and an evening off followed by a whole day off every four days.

I can't tell you why we were listening to morse, because I signed the
Official Secrets Act. Germans on buses used to ask us why all our aerials
faced East, and we would say, 'Do they really? I hadn't noticed.'

Gradually I became quite good at the job and became one of the crack
operators, entrusted with listening to a high-speed unit that transmitted
in excess of thirty words a minute. A word was a technical term meaning
five letters, as everything was in code. Letters in morse have an average
of at least three dots or dashes, so I was listening to morse at about four
hundred and fifty dots and dashes a minute and writing it down.

On our evenings off, we got late passes till 2 a.m., and we went out
on the town and got smashed. Mind you, we did it in a pretty civilised
way. We found a wonderful bar called Pinkus Muller, full of atmosphere

and good beer, and there was a nice restaurant called Emil Pinte, where we ate oxenschwansuppe followed by wienerschnitzel mit paprikakartoffeln and a side salad, and thought it the height of sophistication, and indeed it was compared to most English food of the period.

Moselwein succeeded the beer and after the meal we drank liqueurs. I developed a party piece of ordering six different liqueurs at the same time. How could we afford all this? Germany was still technically an occupied country, which was why it qualified as a home posting and all right for the psoriatic. We paid in British army monopoly money called Baffs. I think the exchange rate must have been extremely favourable.

We'd arrive back in camp just before two in the morning. I can't speak for the others, but I would barely be able to stand or sign myself back in. Among our group was not only John 'Editor, SCM Press' Bowden but, keeping up the religious theme, another young man, David Pink, who would become a vicar.

I don't think any of us had a drink problem. We didn't drink at all on the other three days of our shift cycle. We had an employment problem. We didn't want to be in the army, and we drank to forget that we were.

On days off we often slept late and I usually had a thick head. We went for long walks around Munster, which had many charms, some lovely old arcaded streets, a beautiful medieval town hall, a splendid Gothic church, a heavily damaged cathedral against which the older men used to urinate, and a splendid wooded walk round what must have been the old town walls. It also had the world's least impressive river, the aptly named River Aa, which flowed from a lake, the Aasee, right under the town in a conduit, to emerge just beyond a lovely half-timbered hotel called the Uberwasserhof and dribble away between its ugly cemented banks into the great plain of Westphalia.

John Bowden and I went to several charming light operettas that winter, and I ventured to the wrong side of the tracks, perilously close to the red light district, to see a circus which included the legendary Grock, who was just about the world's most famous clown. I don't remember his act in any detail. I just have an impression of a strange, sad, slow man, with elements perhaps of Chaplin and Max Wall, moving as if under water. I don't think I laughed, but then I rarely did at clowns.

During this winter I fell into a kind of love. I wandered around all soppy and moony, and then, just as I was on the verge of doing something about it, he was posted to Braunschweig, near the East German border.

I call it a kind of love because I think I must have always known deep down that I wasn't really homosexual. However, there were absolutely no women available to us, except with the crabs and the clap in the third house on the left. I was young and healthy and, in the absence of women, I found myself desiring a man.

And then he was gone.

Spring came suddenly to Westphalia and lifted all our spirits. There were now only 200 days to demob. We were on the run in. I attacked my London School of Journalism correspondence course with a little more enthusiasm, but not much. It was an uninspiring course, and I was an uninspired pupil.

Some time early that year West Germany ceased to be an occupied country and was given back her status as an independent nation. It didn't make much difference to us. I never had the feeling that it was anything else. I certainly didn't have any impression, nine years after the war, in Munster, of a depressed or defeated land.

In April the regiment moved from Munster to a camp in the countryside a few hundred yards from the Dutch border. I think everyone was sorry to leave Munster. I've been back twice and feel a great affection for my first foreign city.

Our new camp consisted of small two-storey blocks. It was light and airy, if flimsily built. The countryside was pleasant, gently rolling, very open and heavily wooded. There were pretty walks through the sandy woods, but on one such walk a few of us ended up in a Dutch bar by mistake. We bought two bottles of cherry brandy to bribe the Dutch and German border guards to let us return to Germany without passports. It worked, but at a cost. The guards made us share the cherry brandy. I'd never been so drunk. I woke up the next day at half past eleven to find one of our number, Mick Baker, a probation officer, lying naked on top of his bed with a three-foot-high sunflower in his mouth.

As the months passed, our platoon became a more and more integrated and happy unit. Two of our number, Gus Johnson, a London barrow boy, and 'Neavo' Neaves from Maidstone, orchestrated a way of marching in which the first ranks of the platoon took enormous steps and the last ranks took tiny ones and the others were graduated from big to small so that as we marched the squad elongated like a concertina. Even our amiable Sergeant Milne was furious, but the manoeuvre was perfectly executed and no one person could be blamed – and we couldn't be punished since nobody else could do our job. This leads me to believe that our work might actually have had some real importance, though I'll never know what it was.

We made happy trips to Cologne and Dusseldorf and Aachen. One night, on the last bus from Munchen Gladbach (which doesn't quite sound like a song) I had a golden opportunity to chat up a very pretty young lady. I was in the front seat on the left. She was in the front seat on the right. Even I couldn't throw up an opportunity like that. We chatted, and things went well.

'May I take you out next Tuesday?' I asked, astounded at my confidence and sangfroid.

'Sadly that will not be possible,' replied this vision, in perfect English. 'Tomorrow my mother here – I should have introduced my mother, most remiss of me – will escort me to the convent where I am taking up my calling as a nun.'

John Bowden and I had a week's leave and enjoyed a wonderful trip down the Rhine. This was my very first holiday without my family, and I was twenty!

I also went on a day trip to Amsterdam with a friend called Potter, who was going to become a vet. Amsterdam was an explosion of beauty and opportunity, but the only firm offer, 'Englishman, you want ficky-fucky with black woman?' found me going all English and saying, 'Not just now, thanks very much all the same. I'm just going for lunch.' I had lobster for the first time that day. How could we afford it all?

The arrival of Second-Lieutenant Bagnall showed me what my

military career might have been like if I hadn't failed my WOSB. He was an unimpressive, anxious young man, and no match for Gus Johnson and 'Neavo' Neaves, who always called him Mr Bogroll, because that was what his signature looked like.

Gus was a good impressionist and this man was easy meat. One balmy summer's evening – I can still smell the resin from the pines on the heath behind the camp – Mr Bogroll was taking the evening parade of Guard, Fire Picket and Defaulters.

'Guard, Fire Picket and Defaulters, left wheel,' he squeaked unimpressively.

'Guard, Fire Picket and Defaulters, right wheel,' squeaked Gus from an upstairs window.

Within two minutes there were Guards, members of Fire Pickets and Defaulters marching in about nine different directions at once, all over the square, narrowly missing each other in a manner that would have done credit to the Keystone Cops. We were all cheering and laughing, and Mr Bagnall was imploring 'Stop! Halt! No, chaps, men, stop, halt, please!'

Comedy is cruel. I learnt more about comedy in five minutes that evening than I learnt about journalism from the whole of my correspondence course.

I can't remember exactly when the young man I cared so much about returned from Braunschweig, but it can't have been very long before our demob, as I only recall going out with him once.

We went to a restaurant in a small town called Heinsberg. It had become a favourite haunt, even though it involved a walk of at least four miles in each direction. We always ordered the same thing – a plain omelette followed by wienerschnitzel. However many of you there were, they brought one big, extremely fluffy omelette and cut it into portions at the table. If there were eight of us it would be a twenty-four-egg omelette and still as light as a feather. And, of course, there'd be lots of beer and moselwein, and I still hadn't grown out of my six liqueur routine.

But this night, of course, it was *à deux* – my first intimate dinner with a loved one, two squaddies in an obscure German restaurant. We got drunk, of course, and as we walked back on a soft summer's night we fell into a clinch and then into a haystack. It was exciting and yet tender to be with one's lover in a haystack at midnight as a crescent moon rose and the many creatures of the German night snuffled softly in the background. I felt full of love and sexuality and booze.

My memories are hazy and alcoholic, but I don't think we actually went all that far. A bit of a hand to hand engagement as befitted military men, but we certainly didn't strip. The continental nights are cool at the end of summer, and hay is prickly at any time.

Still, it was not the kind of thing that we wanted to tell the military police. At some moment right in the middle of our stubbly tryst, in a snoring village less than two kilometres away, an English soldier, full of beer and hatred, chopped the head off a statute of the Virgin Mary. This was the only truly serious incident between soldiers and natives that I came across in my time in Germany. It was serious indeed. The local people were in uproar. The military police had to be seen to be doing their best to catch the culprit. What more natural than to ask us all to account for our every movement at the exact time of the incident?

Some of my movements had been things I couldn't possibly tell the military police. We told as much of the truth as we could, with the physical contact and the haystack removed. They seemed to think we'd taken a long time over our walk. I'm sure they must have had their suspicions about us, but I think they were only really interested in the outrage, and I don't think they suspected us of that. It was a pretty horrible grilling, though, and it proved a complete damper on our liaison. We didn't risk anything again.

Two or three days before our return to England, Sergeant Milne informed me that he was recommending my promotion to Lance-Corporal if I'd sign on for another three years. I scorned this deeply unappetising carrot.

Nevertheless, the recurring pattern of my life to date was operating again. I'd longed for demob. Sometimes it had seemed so far away that

I didn't believe it would ever come. Now that it was approaching I could feel none of the exultation I'd expected. I felt nostalgia for my new friends and for the comradeship. I dreaded having to make my own decisions. I had become institutionalised.

What did I think of National Service? What would I say to good old Disgusted of Tunbridge Wells, who wants to bring it back?

Yes, Disgusted, National Service did give us discipline, but it didn't give us respect for authority. It taught us to say, 'Yes, sir' while thinking, 'You stupid bastard', and that is no kind of discipline worth having. I daresay that for those who had worthwhile jobs to do it had some value, but they were few and far between. A generation of young men learnt every four-letter word except 'work'. To skive was to survive. We all became brilliant at it, and many people went on to put that talent to great use in British industry.

5 MATCH-BOXES AND PICKLED ONIONS

SEPTEMBER IS THE month of beginning. Kindergarden, prep school, boarding school, national service and now Cambridge. Even nowadays, every September, when the first chills lie sweetly on the misty morning air, I feel an exquisite mixture of fear and excitement.

The beauty of Cambridge is awesome. At times, along the backs, by the peaceful Cam, it threatens to break one's heart. It isn't easy to live up to all that mellow stone and brick, all that history, all those manicured lawns. I felt clumsy, lumpish, unworthy.

I expected everyone at Cambridge to be brilliantly clever. Some were. William Ragg certainly was. My first memory of him is the abiding one. There was a meeting of the entrants for the classical tripos, and we were set our first task – a piece of Latin translation. I suggested that we all do it together, so rusty had I become in the twenty-six months since I'd last looked a piece of Latin in the eye. William's irredeemably boyish face was awash with incredulity. There was no indication that we would soon become close friends.

William, of course, had come straight from school. I had forgotten most of what I knew. That wasn't too serious. What was serious was that I knew, that morning, that I no longer wanted to be a scholar. I no longer wanted to study dead languages. I was twenty, and I wanted to live.

There had never been any question of my not going to St John's College. My father had been there and, as I recall it, these were the last moments when that counted for something. I'd tried for a scholarship, and failed, but that had only had financial implications. My 'A' Level results had been good enough. I hadn't even had to go for an interview.

In those days you applied for a grant from your local authority, which examined your parents' means. I think the authorities proceeded in different ways, but Kent's way was to assess your needs, estimate your costs, tell your parents what they should pay, and give you the rest. My parents, of course, obliged with their share as instructed. Not all parents could or did. I had just about enough to live on. I didn't enter 'the real world' burdened with student debt. It shocks me profoundly that it is not so now.

However, at this moment I was beholden to my local authority and to my parents. For my parents, education was almost everything. It was inconceivable that I should let them down, leave college, even change subject. I was a classics student, and I was stuck with that for my first two years at least.

I had a large, high-ceilinged room in a forbidding stone block in First Court, overlooking the bulky, undistinguished chapel. First Court lacked the charm of the next two older brick courts.

I decided immediately that I needed some style in my life. My rooms needed the personal touch, an individual statement. The message of my statement was a bit confused. I bought a Matisse print, a Vlaminck print, and vast numbers of match-boxes of different sizes, which I balanced in various patterns (but not very various) all along the picture rails. I regard this now as an aesthetic gaffe.

I wouldn't want you to think that match-boxes were my only stylistic statement. There were the pickled onions as well. I forget now why I thought that the occasional insouciant consumption of a pickled onion beneath my match-boxes might give me a faintly Bohemian air. Unfortunately I got the scale rather badly wrong. I bought the most enormous jar. I ate two pickled onions a day for six weeks and still hadn't got through a fiftieth of them. I even suspected that the lady who 'did' for me – my 'bedder', to use the technical term – was restocking the jar out of spite.

Does it seem extraordinary to you that I was given a cleaner, who made my bed every morning? Are they provided still? Do red-brick universities and upgraded polytechnics have bedders?

Nobody can live on match-boxes and pickled onions alone. There had to be more to my life than that, and there was. The liver sausage rolls at the Volunteer, where I played darts most lunchtimes, were excellent. Barely had I left Cambridge, incidentally, before Len and Pip, mine hosts, denied my custom, retired, and the place became a typewriter shop.

There was a vast array of societies at Cambridge, all vying for one's attention. I joined the Union, went to a few debates, drifted away. I joined the sailing club, because I'd enjoyed sailing in my father's boat. I discovered that dinghy racing wasn't for me. All rivers are wet, but the Ouse at St Ives is wetter than most.

I think it's true to say that in part I found my life-style through my friends, and in part I found my friends through my life-style. At each stage of my life I was finding it a little easier to make real friends, friends for life.

William was the first of my Cambridge friends for life. His scorn (rapidly hidden) at my wanting to do a communal translation hadn't lasted. Soon he was introducing me to Barry Slater, a gingery and freckled youth from a modest background in Keighley, as clever as William but as blunt as a barnacle. Although I had a room to myself during my first year, I recall that William and Barry shared. They were not at all alike. William had great natural charm, though I think he believed that he had none. Barry had no natural charm, though I think he believed that he had lots. I came to love them both (I suppose in view of the last chapter I must emphasise that I am speaking platonically here).

William introduced me to the third great friend for life of my Cambridge days, Charles Barham. William's father had been a publisher. His mother Mollie had married another publisher and they lived in a house in Hampstead that oozed charm and culture. Charles, a schoolfriend of William, had charm and culture too. He was strikingly good-looking and very well spoken. He carried himself very erect and had a lovely dry, wry gleam in his eyes (he still does). We used to go to his rooms in Caius College to listen to *The Goon Show*. I enjoyed it without becoming a true fan. The concepts were inspired, but I always felt it would have been even funnier if there had been fewer silly voices.

Charles introduced me to the works of John Cowper Powys and William introduced me to the novels of Sartre and Wyndham Lewis, while with Barry it was the novels of Samuel Beckett. We used to sit in William and Barry's rooms and read his novels out loud. *Malone Dies*, *Molloy* and *Watt* were our bibles, our religion. Verbose, almost entirely lacking in plot or even incident, often scatological, always hilarious and elegant, they were triumphs of style over substance. I've always seen Beckett as an optimist. There are things worth arguing over, things worth being emotional over, things worth remembering, even if you live in a dustbin or are trapped under a mountain of sand.

I haven't dared go back to *Malone Dies* and *Molloy* and *Watt* for fear I would no longer enjoy them.

Before I'd been at Cambridge very long I'd turned my back on university politics. I thought the politically active students drab souls sailing through the storms of life on their inflatable egos. For me the world of politics has no charm and not much fun. Real politics are fascinating because they matter, my God, how they matter, but pretend politics are dreary. I still don't like political debate round the dinner table. It's pointless, whereas the real thing is exciting.

I refused to take things seriously at this stage of my life. I was a student. Let's have fun. Somebody asked me to give one and six (one and a half shillings, old money) for War on Want, and have a miserable lunch of bread and cheese while thinking about the world's poor. I gave him three shillings and said I'd rather go to the Volunteer, so my three shillings were all profit, but this miserable character didn't appreciate my gesture – it was the symbolic suffering he wanted from me even more than my money.

My first trip away from Cambridge was to visit my erstwhile companion of the haystack, and stay at his home in the Wirral Peninsula in Cheshire. I'd looked forward to the visit keenly, so I must have felt that our relationship was more than a flash in the haystack. I'd talked about it freely to my friends, so I couldn't have felt any sense of shame about it. Rather the reverse, in fact. I felt it gave me a touch of worldliness and disrepute. It was my one tiny bit of street cred – or at least of haystack cred.

He lived with his mother and I don't imagine that she had any inkling that he had homosexual tendencies. We explored Chester, went to a very lively pub beside the Dee – discovering why it was so lively when the tide surrounded it and trapped us till well after closing time – and sailed round the hills of North Wales on his motorbike. Later I crept to his bedroom and there were some rather irresolute fumblings, but the presence of his mother on the other side of a thin wall was a deeply inhibiting factor. Besides, I began to get a very strong feeling that, acceptable though this was in the absence of anything better, a woman would have been a great improvement. I suspect that he felt the same. I left the next day without either of us referring to the events of the night. I never saw him again, and I never again felt any sexual attraction for a male.

But where to find a woman? There was an open day at a ladies' college and I went along to take tea with two young ladies there. They were charming hostesses but I couldn't cope with the artificial nature of the event, was overcome by nerves, and fled in embarrassment as soon as was decently possible.

Don't condemn me too harshly. I'd been in all-male schools, the all-male Royal Corps of Signals and now I was in an all-male college. Sheila Bridgeland had been the only girl I'd ever got within talking distance of, and, perhaps not surprisingly, I'd been too terrified to talk.

So, on my twenty-first birthday, it was an all-male gathering in my rooms. There was no food whatsoever – I don't recall there ever being food at Cambridge parties – but there was booze in wild profusion. The lights were dim, and I at least enjoyed myself enormously. I recall that Colin Macandrews (he with the wine on Darlington Station) was there and I also remember that he once invited me round to his rooms in St Catharine's College because he had some very good wine and didn't know anybody else with sophisticated enough tastes to enjoy it. This is wildly at variance with my picture of myself, but I can only present things as I remember them.

I don't recall being too worried about the absence of sex from my life. There was always me to fall back on, unless of course I was playing hard to get. A man has some pride. I didn't want to be serious about anything. I was free to play this amazing game called Life.

I went to lectures, but very few on Latin or Greek. I preferred Professor Pevsner on architecture, the aptly-named Professor Wisdom on philosophy, the legendary Dr F.R. Leavis, who knew that he was legendary, on literary criticism. The fact that they weren't the lectures that I should be going to added to the pleasure.

We went to London to see plays. We saw *Look Back In Anger* in which John Osborne introduced real life to the English theatre and caused a revolution. We saw Beckett, who made philosophy exciting. Ionesco and N.F. Simpson brought us the Theatre of the Absurd and almost blew my mind. They are almost forgotten now but I might not be where I am today if they hadn't existed.

We saw films. We drank films. Everything from *The Battleship Potemkin* to *Calamity Jane*. We went to the film society on Sunday afternoons, often under the influence of sherry. Sunday sherry parties were all the rage.

Nothing excited me more than the first two films of Jacques Tati – *Jour de Fête* and *Monsieur Hulot's Holiday*. They were entirely visual, utterly innocent and stunningly funny. They were pure. They had no pretensions. Tati seemed to know that humour is enough in itself. Sadly, in his later films it became clear that he didn't. The comedy became more and more buried beneath his statements about the modern world. What a lesson the decline of Tati is to a comedy writer.

I never bothered about my clothes. Duffel-coats were universal. We didn't bother about popular music either. It still hardly seemed to exist before Bill Haley. The Top Twenty had only just begun, and Eve Boswell picking a chicken was as groovy as it got.

We weren't allowed to see *Rock Around The Clock*, with Bill Haley and the Comets, in Cambridge. The city authorities decided that something as revolutionary as Rock and Roll would cause riots twixt town and gown. However, it was showing in Soham, a small town with a magnificent church, in nearby Suffolk. William, Barry and I took a train there. Arriving too soon for the film, we visited the church. We really did love old churches. I still do. I'm glad other people believe, or there would be no churches for me.

The vicar entered as we wandered around, and asked us what we were doing in Soham. We didn't dare tell him the truth. William said that we were on a tour of East Anglian churches. The vicar said it restored his faith in British youth and spent half an hour showing us round with enormous enthusiasm. Luckily, a few minutes before the film was due to begin, he excused himself.

'Alas,' he said, 'I can linger no longer. I have to attend a parish meeting.'

We found the film pleasant enough but disappointingly mild fare. I don't know what the vicar thought. We didn't like to ask him, even though he was sitting next to us.

At lunchtimes we would sometimes go to a restaurant called Lucy's in the passageway opposite John's. I shouldn't have been spending my grant or my parents' contribution in this way. It must have been a very strange restaurant because I used to alternate between my two favourite dishes at that time – wienerschnitzel and dhansak. Then back to my rooms for crumpets toasted on the gas fire beneath the match-boxes. A quick pickled onion, a bit of work, a beer in the Buttery and dinner in the college's great dining hall. Not a bad life.

Of course I didn't reject the sporting side of things. Another great friend, Anthony Lynch, had been to school in Marlborough, but at the village school at the other end of the wide high-street of my youthful joke. Under Ant's tutelage I soon became quite good at rolling marbles across a carpet and up a ramp into an empty Shredded Wheat packet.

*

On my first long vacation, in August, 1956, I sailed to Denmark with my father in a 30-foot yawl called *Charm* II. Our skipper was a friend and former colleague of my father, Dr A.J. Eley. My father was navigator and I was radio officer because of my morse. The fourth member of the crew, an architect named Rex, was seasickness officer. He threw up every time it was windy but loved sailing so much that he accepted it as a minor inconvenience.

Eley, as my father called him in the manner of those surname days, announced straight away that he'd been the very first person to walk out of *Waiting For Godot.* 'I think it's the greatest play I've ever seen,' I exaggerated frostily – a great start, as we slipped silently past the Essex mud banks.

August 1956 was a horrendous month. We lay hove-to off Denmark in a force 7 on the way over and were twice hove-to in a full gale in the German Bight on the way home. The waves seemed as high as the boat was long, and again and again it seemed inconceivable that she would breast them. I really did expect to die, and I felt so ill that I was quite calm about the prospect.

The importance of this trip for me was that it was the longest time I ever spent with my father. We had a delightful day exploring the pleasant town of Aalborg, and an idyllic day cycling round the gloriously pastoral island of Samso. At these times I felt the peaceful companionship, a togetherness beyond words, that had been hinted at in our walks. At other times, however, I felt that I disappointed him. I am not a competent sailor. I sail as a comedy writer should. I'm very bad at knots. (Since I'm also hopeless at erecting flagpoles and a complete duffer at jacket potatoes I've drawn a veil over the torrid time I had in the Scouts.)

I felt that my father wanted Eley to be impressed by me, and that this was extremely unlikely to happen. Now, however, fate handed me a chance to impress. We'd been so battered by storms that we opted to return through the Dutch canals. Accordingly we needed to enter the estuary of the Elbe (scene of my father's favourite novel, *The Riddle of the Sands,* by Erskine Childers). As radio officer I had to take bearings on the morse transmissions of lightships every half hour. Where these bearings met was where we were. Are you with me?

It was easy, except that it wasn't working. Where were the banks of the Elbe? Eley insisted that we were going the wrong way. The unspoken sub-text was that anyone who didn't walk out of *Waiting For Godot* must be an idiot.

My father said that it was the discipline of the ship that the radio officer be trusted, but I knew he didn't really trust me either. Hours passed. No Elbe appeared. Eley clearly thought that the next land we saw would be the North Pole. It was silly, but this had become important. I felt that I was in a definitive moment of my life with my father. If I failed him in this, I would have failed him in everything.

And then there they were, the flat banks of the Elbe, just where I'd thought they'd be. Oh, the relief. I was only to experience relief on that scale twice in my life, once in the River Cele in France and once in a lavatory in the Outer Hebrides. Read on!

At some stage during that summer William, Barry and I went down to William's family's sweet little cottage in Aldeburgh, on the Suffolk coast. We had a wonderful time, sailing their dinghy on the Alde (much lovelier than the Ouse in October – warmer, prettier, not nearly as wet), cycling through the lonely lanes, exploring old churches, making our own meals, fetching beer in a large milk can from the jug and bottle entrance to the Black Swan, and drinking in that crowded, raffish, delightfully down-market pub long after closing time. (Don't look for it. It's Black Horse Antiques now. How the world is being gentrified.) I noticed how much more relaxed William seemed than he was at Cambridge, but I didn't think much about it. I remember his talking, very wistfully, about cricket, a game he couldn't play because of, I think, a congenital back defect. All this was to come back to me later.

In my second year I shared what I think was called 'a set' in New Court, the so-called Wedding Cake, across the river at the back of the college. It's an ornate stone building in execrable taste which looks much better than it deserves. We had a small sitting room and a bedroom. I shared with a young man called Jack Billington, and rightly so. He was a Jack Billington if ever I saw one – a Lancashire lad, straightforward and hard-working. I believe he was reading maths but it might have been something scientific. Jack went to bed early and got up early, so he was always asleep when I went to bed and had always disappeared when I got up. We got on extremely well as a result. I didn't see him after Cambridge, but I hope that he's had, and is still having, a happy and wonderful life.

My second year was really very like the first, though perhaps slightly more subdued because I knew that I had to get through my part one exam. By this time I knew that I wanted to be a writer, not a job for which a degree is required, but I needed to pass for my parents, who had invested so much in me, and for myself, so that I could enjoy my third year. I'd already decided to switch to English for my final year. I might be able to busk my way through that without too much hard work, which would leave time and energy for learning to write.

I suppose that in my social life I tripped tentatively towards being an aesthete. We would wander along the exquisite 'backs', my friends and I, punt on the River Cam, stroll idly through the more beautiful of the colleges, read comic literature out loud, go to plays, films and art exhibitions, and play a great deal of croquet.

I read all twelve volumes of Proust's great novel, ending up with a marathon session of two days and a whole night. I devoured the flamboyant comic novels of Thomas Love Peacock. Another great comic hero was the American *New Yorker* writer James Thurber, almost forgotten today.

I don't think I drank a vast amount, except at parties. I was still too shy not to drink at parties. In fact I used to have to drink before the parties as well, in order to gain the confidence to go to the party in the first place.

I had an awkward, perverse streak. One evening I was enjoying a pre-dinner beer in the College Buttery when I became incensed at the need to wear a gown and tie for dinner in Hall. I went back to my rooms and dressed from head to foot in yellow oilskins (a relic of my sailing club days), topping them with gown and tie, and entered Hall. I was refused admission. I argued that nowhere in the college's regulations was it stated that one could not dine in yellow oilskins. I won the day. How the chaps cheered, but it was a pyrrhic victory. The sweat ran down me in rivulets throughout that steamy dinner, and I learnt that one cannot be a hero without suffering.

I can't let my two years as a classics student pass without mentioning my tutor, John Crook. Oh no! Even my tutor was a John. He was quite short, solidly-built, with a slightly baggy face beneath very black hair. It was a pleasure to sit in his civilised rooms by his warm gas fire and have one's fumbling efforts treated with more respect than they deserved. One afternoon he gave a few of us a most delightful tea of crumpets and cakes, of which he participated fully. Then he sighed, told us he was on a diet, got out his slimming foods and ate those too. He claims that this story is apocryphal. I seem to remember it distinctly. Who is right? I honestly have no idea. What a tease is Memory.

I scraped through part one, and set off, on my second long vacation, on my little version of the Grand Tour. To earn money for this I picked strawberries in Kent. Also picking strawberries were two BOAC pilots on holiday. After cruising at vast speeds high above the ground, they found that to proceed at a snail's pace with one's nose sniffing the earth fulfilled a need. Mind you, they only worked till lunchtime and then they went to the pub. They wanted me to go too, but I said I couldn't afford to, so they paid for all my drinks and for the wages I would have received in the afternoon. Maybe I wasn't such bad company after all.

My companions on the grand tour were Chris Rudd and Sally Williams. I've no recollection of how I met Chris, but it was through him that I met Sally, a very pretty young lady whom half the men in Cambridge desired. She was the Zuleika Dobson of her day. Chris already knew Sally well. Did I really want to be a wallflower in Tuscany? Yes. Anything was better than not going. Anyway, we both ended up as wallflowers. Two wallflowers and a rose.

Chris and I hitch-hiked from southern Germany to Milan, spending three days in the car of a German doctor and his newly-wed wife. They were delightful. I was sorry not to spend the rest of their honeymoon with them. Sally flew out to Milan to join us, and we hitched to Genoa, Pisa, Florence, Arezzo, Perugia, Siena, San Gimignano, Florence again,

Bologna, Ferrara, Venice and over the Grossglockner Pass towards Munich and home.

We lived for days on dry Italian bread. We feasted on frescoes and drank architecture. The glory of Italy swept us off our feet and made it possible to forget that we were two randy young men with a beautiful woman who didn't want either of us. The ordered flamboyance of Italian architecture thrilled me. It was all straight lines and circles and inspired asymmetry. And we have the gall to call the Italians inadequate custodians of their treasures, we who drop litter in fountains and have dotted our great cities with the poxy, boxy horrors of the sixties, as dull as they are ugly.

We argued and laughed and haggled. We stayed in youth hostels and B&Bs and universities. In Florence we actually took a hotel room and washed all our spare clothes. We hung our disgusting smalls to dry on the sixth-floor balcony. A wind got up and sent them plunging to the floors below. Elegant Italians kept knocking on our door with greying moth-eaten underpants and saying, 'These are yours, I think,' with scrupulously polite contempt.

In Florence we met up with another college friend, John Dowden. Oh dear, yet another John, and only one letter different from John Bowden. If I'd realised I was going to write my autobiography I'd have chosen my friends more carefully. John Dowden is a lovely man whose words tumble out faster than he can manage in his enthusiasm. He grew light-headed, we noticed, every time he had ice cream. Let him be known as John 'Excited by ice cream' Dowden.

In Bologna we got all our drinks free in a bar because the landlady admired Sally's 'bella architectura'. There are moments, in Italy, when the thought of going back to England is too painful to bear.

There were moments, too, that you had to laugh about, like the occasion when a van driver gave us a lift, took us three hundred yards, turned right into a housing estate and rang his chimes. We hadn't noticed that it was an icecream van.

Less funny was the lorry driver who stopped on a deserted road, and told Chris and me to get out. He wanted Sally. He was extremely big, but we shouted at him loudly, and he shrugged and let the three of us out.

In Ludwigshafen kindly police officers let us sleep in an old Nazi bunker under the town. In Mainz students smuggled us into the university to sleep on their floors. In a village in Holland, there was no food in the youth hostel and the only café was closed for a wedding. No problem. We were invited to the wedding, where we were made very welcome. All the young girls danced with each other and all the boys lurked in corners and watched and giggled.

I've described this trip at some length because it had a simply enormous impact on me – my first real foreign holiday, at twenty-two. I returned a happier, more confident person, excited about the world I lived in, a lover of beautiful landscapes and cities, and bursting to write.

Back at Cambridge, I had a dreadful shock. William had tried to kill himself. Why? Why? Why? Had I been a good enough friend to him? Had I missed signs? Why? Why? Why?

He had deep, dark eyes. What demons lurked in them? I never saw him with a girlfriend – or a boyfriend, for that matter. That wasn't exceptional in those days, when so many of us were late developers, but even now I can't imagine him ever having a girlfriend. He would laugh and make jokes – very good jokes – but he was under-pinned by a great seriousness. Did he feel dreadfully lonely and isolated?

I recalled how happy and relaxed he'd been at Aldeburgh. I knew how much he wanted to play sports. There was a sense, I sometimes thought, of his shrinking away from something. There was a slightly withdrawn, uncomfortable look about his mouth. Was he shrinking from his own cleverness, from being set apart by it, from being trapped in it?

At some stage, too, Chris Rudd tried to kill himself and had a complete breakdown. I visited them both in different mental hospitals. Later I lost touch with Chris, but William will return to this tale.

For my third year I had dreary lodgings in a northern suburb of the town. I'd left my match-boxes behind me, but I still had three-quarters of a jar of pickled onions.

When I met Peter Cook for the first time a few years later, at the Establishment Club in Soho, he astonished me by saying that I had been his hero at Cambridge. This from my hero! I thought him the funniest man alive. I still would, if only he were still alive.

When I was on top form, with the wind behind me and a few drinks inside me, among people I knew well, I could be very funny for whole minutes on end. Peter could be funny for hours on end, in any place at any time, with anyone whether drunk, stoned or sober.

Still, he was younger than I, and maybe he was impressionable. Certainly I had a few articles in *Varsity*, the university newspaper, and in the more arty and intellectual magazine, *Granta*.

I'd started bombarding these publications with articles during my second year. I never worked for them as a journalist, never promised them anything, just sent things whenever I thought them funny enough. Once I sent a serious piece to *Granta*. I heard nothing, so went to see them. 'It's just the kind of writing we can't stand,' the editor told me with all the ruthlessness of youth.

In my third year, my articles did begin to amuse a few people. Do they seem funny now? Let's see. They might be interesting to you anyway, as examples of early immature Nobbs.

But what to choose? It could be something I wrote for *Granta* – like my transcript of a tape-recorded discussion on 'the vexed question of reredos dumping' or a mock-tribute to a great artist, Schneiderstein, who threw himself into the Thames with the words, 'I do not exist. The Thames does not exist. The tide is out.' – but I've chosen a parody of a diary column, which appeared in *Varsity* under the title, 'The Senate House and Under'.

Algernon's party was a success, after all. We all know whose success it was too, don't we? I chatted to Sir Stanmore Cockfosters, an underground hero of two world wars. I found that I was up against a keen modern brain. Angela Pwippet, star of John Van Heusen's fiery religious drama, *Hot Dog Collar* at the Arts this week, came along afterwards. She has made a niche for herself in this play. 'I was always handy about the house,' she confided. 'I like houses.' Her latest escort? Titus Oates, a director of Scots Porridge Ltd. Tall and cold-shouldered, he had some interesting things to say about recent trends in Scots porridge.

'Mozart sonata stopped in full swing. Orchestra stalls.' Behind the animated chatter in the Chinese restaurants this week lies a tale of an orchestra stalling, a Mozart sonata being stopped in full swing, and a sick moocow swinging among the branches of a condemned larch in a spinney above 'twelve-acres'. It all happened at the Cherry Trumpington male-voice chambermaids' ninth annual concert of out-door chamber music in the last six years. 'We've never tried Mozart in full swing before, and it was a very cold night,' explained attractive part-time trumpet voluntary Thelma Clench. Three tables have been questioned about the incident. 'There was no looting,' was one comment I heard freely exchanged.

The Russian minister for cultural sewage paid an unexpected visit to Cambridge this week-end. 'I am here to study your cultural sewage,' he volunteered. He said that in Russia drains were an integral part of culture. 'Drainage is the natural concomitant of healthy,' he added, handing a crate of Ukrainian sweetballs to an elderly worker. 'We have the same name, George,' he explained, shaking the shy professor of thermocompulsives by the hand. Also on the agenda was a tour of the Chinese restaurants and a visit to a silage farm in Cherry-Linton.

A strange new haircut has been observed in Cambridge. It has become the main topic of conversation in the Chinese restaurants. Variously described as 'a male bun', 'the lunatic fringe' and 'Hairy growth', it consists of a side-step systematically reduced, then boarded and waved on a bit into a double-crested waft-end, brought down and woven. Ken Barnard, often overtaken by bicycles, was wearing one. 'I'll be there on the great day,' said the maestro, rubbing his back vigorously with a towel.

This doesn't seem too bad to me, for a 22-year-old, and I don't think it's difficult to detect the influence of the surrealist flavour of the times. I wrote with complete confidence. If I thought it was funny, it was. This confidence has still not been entirely destroyed by age, critics, script editors, producers, channel controllers and the occasional silence of audiences.

I had become friendly with a very clever young man named John (oh no!!) Aarons, who spoke at the Union, where he said that he was born with a silver spoon in his cornflakes. John and I actually managed to write a revue which was performed by the St John's College revue and cabaret society, the Unicorns. It was called *Feet Up* and had a marvellous cast, including John himself and quite a few people who weren't called John, including Bill Wallis and Freda Dowie, who both went on to fine professional acting careers; Hugh Brogan, son of the distinguished historian Sir Denis Brogan; and Fred Emery, who became a presenter on *Panorama*. It was produced by a very talented man called Eric Willcocks, and Jim McManus wrote some splendid music.

The show was a hit. As I sat there and listened to the laughter I knew beyond all doubt that comedy was my game. This isn't the first time I've written that, but survival kept getting in the way, and would continue to do so.

Back in Orpington for my last Christmas vacation, I did temporary postal work to earn myself a bit of spending money, and it was through this that I met Ann.

I found the postal work quite sad, involving as it did delivering vast numbers of Christmas cards to the poncy houses with signs like 'No hawkers or circulars' and almost no cards to little bungalows where lonely ladies would have loved the arrival of a hawker or a circular.

Then, at the end of one day's work, there was this face, which just seemed to be the face for me. It lit up the sorting office. Even the face of Helen of Troy, so good at launching ships, would have struggled to light up a sorting office. A touch of the gamine, a deliciously delicate nose, a sublime dimple on the chin. It's forty years since I saw that face. Time has taken its toll of my memory.

All shyness departed. I invited her for a drink. She demurred, being under age. What would her family say if it got back to them? Such things were important, in Orpington, in 1957. I made sure I got her address and telephone number, and went to the pub anyway.

I felt so happy in the pub that night, as if I already knew that Ann and I would become lovers. Several pints went down in no time, and then I remembered that my parents didn't know I drank. They weren't teetotal, but they hardly touched alcohol. I don't think there was drink on the table even at Christmas, although everybody got very excited by the brandy in the mince pies. I tried to be extremely sober when I got home that evening but I think my parents must have known. I could sense their disappointment. All their thoughts about drink were negative ones. The perils of drink. People who 'took to drink'. 'He drank' was, in two words, explanation, condemnation and obituary.

Shortly after Christmas I took Ann to London for the day. By now I had realised that she was still a boarder at Christ's Hospital School. We saw *Around The World in Eighty Days* and I took her for a meal of which I have no recollection. I kissed her lovely face properly for the first time in the drizzle on the Embankment. I told her she was very sweet and she got upset as she found the word patronising. By the time we got to Orpington I was forgiven, but she wouldn't let me walk her up her cul-de-sac lest her parents discovered she'd been out with a man.

Back at Cambridge, five of the sketches from *Feet Up* were performed at a Cambridge University Footlights Dramatic Club Smoking Concert in the Oak Room of the Dorothy Café. John Aarons and I were fêted. Michael Frayn bought me a gin and tonic. I felt that I'd arrived!

One of the actors in our sketches that night was Timothy Birdsall, a man of huge talent and even greater charm, who went on to do brilliant cartoons on *That Was The Week, That Was*. His obscenely early death from leukaemia was one of those, like that of Lilian Board the runner, which sent the whole nation into deep shock.

I had a couple of sketches in the *Footlights Revue* at the Arts Theatre that summer. 'Association Word Game' made it all the way from *Feet Up* via the smoking concert. It was a surreal sketch in which people ran around the stage like footballers but shouting sequences of words which occasionally ended in disappointment and sometimes in goals. They even changed ends at half time. It was a bit like a visual version of 'Mornington Crescent' in the wonderful radio classic, *I'm Sorry, I Haven't a Clue*.

The stars of the show that year were Joe Melia and Michael Collings. Great things were predicted for them both. They went on to do fine work, but the great things didn't happen. We all rode around Cambridge on our bicycles. Joe used to make his rear up like a horse while he emitted brilliant neighs of alarm. He would also shout, mysteriously, at the top of his voice, 'What about the crispy bacon we used to get before the war?' I liked that so much that I borrowed/stole it as a chapter title for *Second From Last In The Sack Race*.

By this time I was finding myself in the unaccustomed position of being a bit of a celebrity. I was invited to more and more parties and I found I didn't need to get so drunk before them. For a while I was consorting with people who would become famous. I don't like it when autobiographies descend into lists of well-known people. I said so to Martin Amis and Tony Blair only yesterday. However, the next chapter will see me return to what seemed to be my natural obscurity, so there is some dramatic point in describing my brief social glory. I would sit in the Arts Theatre Bar with the likes of those fine comic performers, John Bird and Eleanor Bron. I was friendly with John Tusa, later to find fame at the BBC and the Barbican. Michael Frayn and Bamber 'Never Known as Gazza' Gascoigne, both famous in Cambridge and already beginning to be famous outside Cambridge, took me out to lunch to give me advice about 'showbiz'. They even found me an agent, the amiable David Conyers.

I must mention the amazing Victor Spurber. I lost contact with him many years ago, but he was a bit special, was Victor, and he was an inspiration for a character in a book more than forty years later.

He was a pale, rather frail looking young man with a long, serious nose and sparkling eyes. He wore a yarmulke jauntily, as if it was a yachting cap, and when he walked he bounced. He looked like a cross between Mendelssohn and Piglet. He was a man of sudden enthusiasms. One day at Cambridge he knocked on my door and said, 'Come to Paris.' 'When?' I asked. 'Now!' I, a prisoner of my diary, turned him down. He went anyway.

On another occasion he came to say goodbye, very solemnly. He was disillusioned with academia. He was a simple man, a man of the people. And so he left Cambridge, and went to Grimsby to become a deep-sea fisherman. Two days later he was back. 'The sea looked so rough,' he explained cheerfully, without any sense of shame or defeat.

There were other good friends, such as Rogan Maclellan (we've lost touch, so I can't check the spelling) and Geoffrey Strachan. Rogan suggested that we go to the local spiritualist church for a laugh. I regret to say that we did laugh, heartless youths that we could sometimes be, especially when the minister said, 'I know a lot of people whose lives have been ruined by death', and when Rogan named his family's dog as someone he wished to contact on the other side. Geoffrey was a prominent member of the St Catharine's College revue and cabaret society, the Midnight Howlers (the college's nickname being Cats). Revue brought us together. Geoffrey is one of the most civilised people I know, and he will play a large part in my literary life.

Occasionally we played at being grown-up and hired a private room for a dinner party. The menu was always the same – whitebait, porterhouse steak and crème brûlée, which we were told had been invented by the college. We were served by our regular waiters, two very nice men with whom we went on drinking sprees more than once. Barry Slater would be there, and John 'Feet Up' Aarons, and John 'Excited by icecream' Dowden, and a man called Campbell Page, who was so cool that you never knew whether he was thinking great thoughts or absolutely nothing. He later became the *Guardian*'s correspondent in Athens.

A first glimpse of our hero.

First steps with Uncle Kenneth and my mother, Gwen, in
the back garden of Sevenoaks Road.

My first vehicle – in the garden of Sevenoaks Road.

Granham House, outside Marlborough, our shared home for
the first year of the war.

The three cousins on the steps of
The Pines – John, Elizabeth
and me.

What a picture of respectability. In my school
uniform in 1953.

My mother's family in Swansea – circa 1910. From left to right: Aunt Dilys, Uncle Glandon (Oliver in *Going Gently*), Uncle Kenneth (Bernard in *Going Gently*), Enyd (soon to die while nursing in the great flu epidemic), Granny Williams with my mother in front of her, and Grandpa Williams.

A gathering of two families for my parents' wedding – Eaton Crescent, 1928.
Back row: Uncle Kenneth, an unidentified Welsh relative, Grandpa Nobbs,
my father Gordon, Auntie Louie ('Mummy's approaching a sharp bend,
David. See her slow down'), Uncle Mac and Grandpa Williams.
Front row: Auntie Kathleen, Granny Williams, my mother, Granny Nobbs.

My Mother's parents in the back garden at Eaton Crescent.

In my last year I captained the college's social cricket team, 'The Willows', who played against the local villages. After the cricket we would eat in a splendidly eccentric Indian restaurant, where the waiter shouted everything down the dumb waiter in English breakfast talk – 'bacon, two eggs, sausage, tomatoes and bubble' and up came the chicken dopiaza, lamb dhansak, bhindi bhagi and pulao rice that we'd ordered. Just occasionally I would cycle back to my dull digs four sheets to the wind at midnight.

I still shudder at the memory of one morning. I heard my poor landlady talking to herself, as I struggled to wake up. 'He's been sick on the stairs!' A bit of grumbled muttering, then she was outside. 'He's been sick on the lawn!' Then a final, indignant cry of despair. 'He's been sick on the coal!' I don't know how I found the courage to face her. My tongue was stuck to the roof of my mouth. I managed to mutter a heartfelt apology and she was really very nice about it. I lodged with this woman for nine months and I have no other recollection of her – of her appearance, her character, even her name.

The college was always locked at midnight, so during my first two years at Cambridge there had been occasions when I'd had to climb in, a dangerous activity when sober, but perilous when drunk. I had thought, with relief, that this activity was over – Mrs Whatsername didn't mind what time I got in – but what I hadn't reckoned on was that there would now be occasions when I'd have to climb *out* of the college. Once, I met the Dean, a formidable drinker, on the Bridge of Sighs at three in the morning.

'Shouldn't you be in your lodgings?' he thundered.

'Yes,' I admitted.

'Leave,' he cried. 'Depart this university on the milk train. You are expelled. You are rusticated. You are sent down. Your education is terminated. Your prospects are ruined, feckless youth.'

'Yes, sir,' I replied. There was no need to do otherwise. He had always forgotten in the morning.

One student, however, did find himself sent down by the Dean. In his fury he managed to get hold of a lawnmower and mowed quite a stretch of the college lawns, though in a rather mysterious manner. The explanation came later, long after he'd left. He'd put some venomous concoction on the machine, and it poisoned the grass. 'Fuck the Dean' appeared in large, yellow letters on that very English lawn.

Unreal days. Delightful days. And then panic. Suddenly the exams were upon us. I knew that I hadn't done enough work. My tutor that year was a distinguished and delightful man called Hugh Sykes-Davis, on the rotund side and easy-going to a fault. He was rumoured to take opium. There was certainly a slight aura of the exotic about him. He didn't push me any harder than I wanted to be pushed.

I have a vivid memory of getting up at four o'clock one early summer morning and standing on the dewy grass on the minimal lawn in the tiny, tidy, lifeless garden of my lodgings with a book of poetry by a nature poet named Francis Thompson. My task was to learn a few quotes which I would regurgitate into one of my answers, irrespective of what the question was. Some sarcastic chap had written in the margin of the book. Where Thompson wrote 'feathered folk' this man had scrawled 'birds!' Alongside 'The scaly denizens of the deep' he had put 'Fish!' I have to admit I preferred the rewrites.

Well, the exams finished and I did pass with a modest two-two. Now we could spend hours and hours on the river, we could play croquet match after croquet match, we could drink beer till all hours, but the truth was that it wasn't quite so much fun when you weren't supposed to be doing something else.

It was the time of May Balls. In other words, this being Cambridge, it was flaming June. I had nobody to take to a ball. Sally had seventy-three invitations, and Ann was still at school. I regret to inform you that some of us donned dinner jackets, stole a punt, and poled ourselves up the river on a balmy summer night, gate-crashing several balls and somehow managing to stay up and about until morning so that we could sit in a little café called The Whim and have breakfast in our evening dress, and have one last crack at being wild before we entered 'the real world'.

All my life, from the age of five, I had been in institutions. Now, at twenty-three, I would be on my own.

Was I ready?

6 NOBBS OF THE STAR

TOWARDS THE END of my time at Cambridge I decided that I'd rent a garret in Vienna and become a real writer – exiled, starving, desperate, inspired, perhaps even tubercular. Why Vienna? Hard though it is to believe, it was the cheapest capital in Europe at the time.

The only drawback was that I couldn't do it without telling my parents, and I knew that I couldn't bear to witness their suffering and worry. They had no faith in my ability. Why should they have? I thought of just going, and sending a postcard: 'Saw the Lippizaner horses yesterday. Schoenbrunn tomorrow. From which you'll gather I'm in Vienna. Yes, it isn't "Goodnight, Vienna". It's "Goodnight, Orpington".' It would have been cowardly.

My next thought was that I would apply for a job as a radio officer on a liner . . . or even a coaster . . . let's face it, I'd have settled for a dredger. I gave this serious thought. True, I would have needed to learn to send morse as well as to receive it, but there couldn't have been many Cambridge graduates capable of receiving morse at thirty words a minute and eager for a life on the ocean wave, and I felt sure that I'd have plenty of time to write my great novel as we steamed through the Dardanelles.

I soon realised that as a career move for their beloved son this would rank only marginally above the Viennese garret in my parents' eyes. I also suspected that in those romantic surroundings I would never write a word. Instinct told me that I needed the opposite of romantic surroundings.

I don't recall now how I came to apply to Kemsley Newspapers for a job as a reporter. It was the only job I did apply for. I think it possible that a careers adviser at Cambridge told me that Kemsley's were looking for graduate entrants. Anyway, I persuaded myself that I wasn't selling out. Journalism was writing, after all.

The man who interviewed me was very friendly, chatted about my hobbies, put me at my ease, and said, 'How would you like to be drama critic for the *Sunday Times*?'

'Well, if I was lucky enough to be offered that position one day, I'd be thrilled,' I said.

'The last Oxbridge man I said that to thought I was offering him the job,' he said.

There were no further questions. I'd avoided his little trap and I was offered a post as a general reporter. He asked me if I was prepared to go to any of their newspapers. I said I didn't want to go to Aberdeen – too far away from my beloved family – or to Cardiff – too near my beloved Welsh family. He raised his eyebrows and sent me to Sheffield's evening paper, the *Star*. I said with disarming (I hoped) frankness that I didn't want to start until September. I fancied a last summer off. Even this didn't alert him to my deep lack of excitement at the prospect of a job.

Never mind Vienna or the radio officer idea, my parents were disappointed enough about the journalism. I think everyone in the family had hoped that I'd become a barrister. I had the gift of the gab, I loved an argument, I would take up a position in a discussion purely for dramatic effect with no regard for the truth, I'd have been perfect.

My Welsh grandfather was particularly upset about my choice of career. 'Journalists drink,' he said. 'Look at D.H.I.P.'

So what did I do during that last summer of freedom? I played cricket, I saw Ann, I sailed, and I waited for life to begin.

Immediately after the end of term I'd gone on a cricket tour of the West Country with the St John's College team. This was proper cricket, including an all day match against a naval establishment in Devonport. I surprised myself, with the aid of several not outs, by coming second in the batting averages.

Through my old schoolfriend Tony Robinson I now found myself playing for a club called The Cricket Society. I remember having three pints in a pub in Rottingdean before going out to bat, and advancing several yards down the wicket to almost every ball bowled by the spinners. 'I've never seen footwork like it,' enthused our skipper, Geoffrey Coppinger. Tony and I began to play for Geoffrey's works team. I don't want to brag, bragging's not my line, but I do believe that I'm probably the best comic novelist ever to play cricket for the National Bank of Belgium.

Tony and I graduated from acquaintanceship to friendship and have seen each other from time to time ever since. The Cricket Society was good fun, if at times rather patronising to our more rural opponents. Another skipper, after a match against a village near Sandwich, urged us to chat to our opponents with the memorably awful instruction, 'Bags of frat, chaps.' Frat, in case you didn't realise it, was short for fraternisation. Oh dear.

I don't think I did a vast amount of drinking that summer, but quite a lot was usually consumed after cricket. After one game I could no longer pretend to my parents that I was a moderate drinker. I don't recall how I got into the quarry in the North Downs and why I was lying full length on the chalk. I rang the doorbell of number 55 at 3 a.m., having lost my doorkey, and stood there, swaying in the moonlight, covered from head to foot in chalk, grinning furiously. My poor father almost passed out on the spot. After that summer of 1958 I only played cricket twice more in my life. It was one of the many sacrifices I made for my art.

I saw Ann quite often. Sometimes we would go to Richmond, where there were acres of parkland on which we could lie and do everything except make love. Once we went to Brighton for the day. We wandered slowly along the Regency terraces, had a good lunch, wandered even more slowly. By the time we'd finished our wanderings I was almost bent double, so intense was the pain in my balls. Bow windows and bow legs in Brighton. Oh, the joyous desperation of frustration.

There was simply nothing to be done about it. I couldn't go to her home or she to mine. Her parents would never have let her go away with a man, at her tender age, and she wasn't prepared to endure the tension and run the risk of telling elaborate lies.

The sailing was round the Isle of Wight with Victor Spurber, and his jaunty yarmulke now came into its own as a yachting cap. We picked up the hired boat in Gosport, and for the first two days we were joined by a friend of Victor's, Izzy Cohen, and his girlfriend, whose name escapes me.

We almost collided with another boat before we had even left Gosport Harbour. This boat had a tannoy and the yell of 'You! Little sailing boat! Get out of the bloody way!' could be heard from Southampton to Bognor Regis. Heads popped up from companionways on hundreds of moored boats. Snoggers on benches at the water's edge disentangled themselves to peep. Frankly I'd have expected an officer of an aircraft carrier to be more polite.

Somehow we managed to avoid the proud monster of the British Navy, but it was unnerving to have 900 ratings staring down at one in disbelief. I wasn't to be so embarrassed by ratings again until my sit-com *The Sun Trap* twenty years later.

By the end of the week we had destroyed the engine, made a large dent in the hull, and lost a rope and an oar. I haven't sailed since.

My parents drove their retired sailor son to Sheffield, and deposited me in my digs in Burngreave Road, then a pleasant gentle hill lined with late Victorian and Edwardian dark red brick houses. This was the golden age of digs and I spent a happy year and a half there. The place was run by a very nice married couple, Mr Turner and his wife, *Mrs Yardley*. Were they really married? If so, why did they have different names? I never dared ask. They were kindly and protective. She was rather big, with folds of flesh everywhere. He was neat and dapper.

I had a drab but not unpleasant room on the ground floor. The settee unfolded into a bed at night. The bathroom and toilets were communal. A narrow staircase led to a small basement room where two armchairs were pulled close to a coal stove. This was the living room of Mr Turner and Mrs Yardley, but it was also our dining room.

There were three other residents: a red-faced Irishman who rarely spoke, always smiled and never went anywhere; a bulky man from the Midlands who was heavily into the local operatic society, so that extracts from *The Desert Song* sung in a Walsall accent would waft round the house with the smell of the water from the greens; and a tall, thin sombre man who had a respectable, dull job by day and worked as a comedian in the clubs of an evening. His name was Al Oldcastle, but he needed something more exotic for the evenings, so he called himself Al Vernon. Or was it the other way round?

Every morning we had a cooked breakfast, every evening we had tea at six – meat and two veg and a proper pud. Every night we had supper at half past ten, and this was unvarying. It was cow heel, pigs' trotters and brawn. On Sundays, breakfast was at ten and Sunday dinner was at three when Mr Turner returned from his club, a little pinker and a little less dapper than usual. Sunday dinner consisted of herbal Yorkshire pudding with gravy, followed by roast beef and two veg and a proper pud. There was no tea at six on Sundays, but there was no escape from the cow heel, pigs' trotters and brawn. My pay was eight pounds a week, and the charge for room, meals and laundry would take a quarter of it.

And so my first day as a reporter dawned. I presented myself in my usual state of trepidation. The newsroom was large and grimy. There were rows of desks at which fierce-looking men were attacking elderly type-writers as if to finish them off. Facing these men, like a schoolmaster before his class, was a short stocky man with a ferocious snarl. This was Ernest Taylor, the news editor.

Beyond Ernest Taylor was a huge table strewn with paper and surrounded by chairs occupied by large men with sallow complexions and their sleeves rolled up. This was the sub-editors' desk, where the headlines were written and our copy was cut to fit the space available on the page.

The room throbbed with urgency. Everything was a race against time. Drama and cigarette smoke swirled in the stale air.

On every desk, at the side of every typewriter, there was paper: paper about to be used, paper being used, paper that had been used. The subs' desk was strewn with paper. Ernest Taylor's desk was sinking under paper.

It was all extremely cheap paper.

I walked forward. To my right was a row of grimy windows. I could dimly see, through the yellow fog in the newsroom, the even yellower fog outside. Those sulphurous fogs of Sheffield, like London's, are long gone.

Ernest Taylor looked at me as if I was a pile of dogs' doings and he was a pooper-scooper. He seemed to have about seven ways of showing scorn. He could raise half an eyebrow and it would say, unmistakably, 'Wanker'.

'Now what are we going to do with you?' he asked wearily. 'Calls, I suppose, or is that beneath a graduate entrant? Right. These are your calls. Infirmary . . .'

'Sorry. What are "calls"?'

'"What are 'calls'?". He asks, "What are 'calls'?". You go to the hospitals and the police stations and you ask for details of incidents. "Calls".'

And so, for what seemed like months, largely because it was months, I traipsed the streets of Sheffield, come rain, hail, snow, sleet, smog and fog, asking for details from police officers and hospital receptionists who all had far more important things to do. I wrote endless stories about injured welders and petty thefts.

There was a grimy Victorian splendour, a proud self-confident dignity, about much of Sheffield's city centre in those days, but Cambridge it wasn't. 'We aren't fancy folk here,' said the offices and shops. Only the Town Hall was allowed any grandeur, quite dwarfing the cathedral in this land where cutlery reigned supreme.

My travels took me not to these grand buildings, but to dingy corners, hospitals streaked with dirty rainwater, cramped police stations built on strict budgets. I did wonder, as I trudged the streets of this windy city, what I was doing there. I remembered those Footlights Smokers, Eleanor Bron being witty, Michael Frayn buying me a gin and tonic. There were moments when I felt deeply depressed, when I asked myself whether all this was a dreadful mistake.

The answer was 'No, it wasn't.' I needed to find my own perspective, my own way. I needed experience of life. As national service had been a balance to Marlborough, so my days as a reporter in South Yorkshire would serve as a balance to Cambridge. Also, there was that novel to be written, and I did write it, in my modest friendly digs in Burngreave Road, and I sometimes wonder if I would have written it if I'd opted for some more glamorous life in London.

But all that was still in the future. In the meantime, I had to learn my craft as a reporter.

You can imagine how proud I was when I saw my first word in print, the very first word of my professional career. Wrong! I wasn't proud at all. I was upset. It was 'Thives' – 'Thives who broke into the home of Mrs Emily Braithwaite stole . . .'

I was dogged my misprints. There was a man who went to hospital with a perforated dung. There was a young lady whose hubby was underwater swimming. A promotional piece about the Hippodrome Cinema was not enhanced by the information that it had opened in 1882 as a threat.

I contributed one gem. It was a one paragraph 'filler', taken from a news agency report. It was minimalist and meaningless and it ran as follows – 'The on-off, on-off separation between Frank Sinatra and Ava Gardner was today authoritatively stated to be "ow".'

I've already mentioned my psoriasis. Now I had warts as well. (Writers and skin diseases seem to go together. I was once asked what a quorum was for the Writers' Guild of Great Britain, and I replied, 'Four psoriasis, three eczema, two dermatitis and a ringworm.')

My warts had appeared during the summer of 1958, on my hands only, and Orpington Hospital had attempted to burn them off. It had been a fiasco. A doctor had now prescribed ointment, which had to be kept on all day, so it was necessary to cover the warts with sticking plaster. The ends of the plasters would come loose and wave in the Yorkshire wind.

Another problem was that my nose would run, due to going in and out between over-heated offices and the raw air of a Northern winter.

A third problem was that most people spoke in a thick South Yorkshire accent which I still found almost entirely impenetrable.

I like to think that, apart from plasters blowing in the wind, a streaming nose and the fact that I had to ask people to repeat everything at least three times, I cut quite an impressive figure.

Often we didn't have time to return to the office to file our copy, and would phone it through to a copy taker, one of whom was a splendid lady called Mrs Cooke.

The ritual was that you gave your name, and a catchword for your story, and then launched into your matchless prose. One day my conversation with Mrs Cooke went as follows:

'Nobbs. Lasso. An Eccleshall man . . .'

'About your warts, Mr Nobbs.'

'This is urgent, Mrs Cooke. An Eccleshall man was fighting for his life in Sheffield General Infirmary today . . .'

'I hope you don't mind my mentioning your warts, Mr Nobbs, but they're not exactly hidden, are they?'

'No . . . General Infirmary, after a loose rope on a lorry snaked across a road and . . .'

'I know what'll cure them.'

'. . . snaked across a road and lassoed him. Paragraph. You are taking this down, aren't you, Mrs Cooke?'

'Yes. It's called Harraps Wart Cure and I can tell you where you can get it.'

'A spokesman for the transport firm, the Attercliffe Haulage Company . . . where, Mrs Cooke?'

'Harraps Herbal Cures.'

'. . . Haulage Company said that it was a one in a . . . thank you very much, Mrs Cooke. It's very kind of you . . . in a million chance and the lorry driver, Mr Kirk Stannidge, of Sheffield Lane Top, was distraught.'

I soon found Harraps Herbal Cures. Within two weeks all my warts had gone. Within four weeks, so had Harraps Herbal Cures. Redevelopment.

Occasionally, in the evenings, we had to review plays, most of them performed by amateurs. I wrote that one woman, playing Helen of Troy, wouldn't have been able to launch a Hull dredger, let alone a thousand ships. There were letters of complaint, and my apology was as genuine as it was profuse. I was never wantonly cruel in print again.

My evenings in Sheffield fell into two main categories – working evenings and drinking evenings. I tried to spend two evenings a week writing that novel. I don't recall how I got the idea or how I began, but it gradually began to take shape. It was a surreal vision of the world I was living in, the story of a man moving from lodgings to lodgings in a Northern city. His landlady, Mrs Pollard, was a sort of version of dear Mrs Yardley. My hero had a rather fragile sense of identity. He began the book as Wilson. Chapter one ended:

> A face flattened itself against the frosted glass, and the door was slowly opened. Mrs Pollard stood before him.
> 'You'll be Mr Barnes,' she said.

The second chapter began:

> The house was filled with the aura of impending stew. Mrs Pollard led Barnes to his room and pointed out the sofa which it would be his task to convert into a bed each night.

Later he became Fletcher, Lewis, Simpson, Baker and Cooper. The book ends:

> The door was opened. Mrs Wills stood before him.
> 'You'll be Mr Smith,' she said.

Whatever his name, he's always searching for the universal panacea for all mankind. One of his schemes, drawn from my experience, was his invention of a points system so that everyone could get equal mail.

I called the book *The Itinerant Lodger*. When I dip into it now, it's as if it was written by someone else.

The drinking evenings began the moment we finished work. Our favourite pub was also the nearest. The Dove and Rainbow was a somewhat racy watering hole in those days. It was frequented in the early evening by policemen and lawyers as well as journalists. Everybody drank half-pints, which surprised me until I realised that beer goes a bit flat in the second half of a pint. When you drink halves it remains in mint condition, and you drink more.

I've referred to the fact that Kemsley Newspapers took graduate entrants. The arrangement was that we would have a trial six-month period, and at the end of it, if the newspaper wanted us to stay and we wanted to stay, we would sign indentures committing us to remain there for two more years.

I was not the only graduate entrant that autumn. There was Peter Tinniswood also. Peter was even thinner than me and has remained so as I have fattened. He is the 'emaciated vileness' of his fictional character in his hilarious Brigadier books about cricket in the village of Witney Scrotum.

Peter and I soon became great friends. It was stunningly exciting to find someone who shared almost all my enthusiasms and all my sense of humour. Oh, the laughs we've had over the years. Oh, the serendipity of my being sent to Sheffield.

We were thrown together all the more quickly because the other reporters resented the graduate entry system and were distinctly cool to us for a time. They'd learnt their craft the hard way on the *Rotherham Advertiser* and the *Jump and Wombwell Gazette*. They soon thawed, however, in view of our charm, the beers we bought them, and their innate good sense and decency.

Peter had been to Manchester University and had then done what I had only dreamt of – he'd gone to live in Vienna. The only thing he hadn't managed to do was write that novel.

The phrase 'street cred' had not yet been inflicted upon us, but I always felt that Peter had a lot more of it than me. Len Doherty, however, had twice as much as both of us put together. It was the most important thing in his life. He was street cred made flesh.

Peter and I were just starting to write. Len had done it. He was born in Maryhill, a tough area of Glasgow, and he lived in Thurcroft, a mining village near Rotherham. He had read profoundly, including all the Greek tragedians and, bizarrely, Arthur Ransome. He had written three novels while still a miner, and they had all been published. They were good, raunchy, sinewy books, full of realism and action. The *Star* welcomed him as the new D.H. Lawrence, an exaggeration that did his considerable ability no favours. All the publicity surrounding him upset some of the journalists. When somebody told Peter Cook that he was writing a novel, Peter replied, 'Really? Neither am I.' It was very like that on the *Star*. I think eighteen people were writing novels, or said they were. We all envied Len, but some envied him bitterly.

Len had a wife and children, but he never went home till late in the evening. Dark, tough-looking, combative, warm, tactile, wearing the gap between his teeth like a badge, clasping coins tightly in his hand in case there was trouble, showing off to us, taking us under his wing, leading us into rough pubs, where he would imagine trouble in order to save us from it, Len captivated us from the start. He would borrow money from us on a Monday, pay it back on the Friday and borrow it again the following Monday.

It dawned on Peter and me very gradually that, while we were genuinely starting to write, Len was stopping. He wrote features for the paper but I don't believe he ever wrote another word of a novel in the rest of his life. Perhaps he'd been inspired by being a lonely intellectual down the pit. Perhaps he felt too insecure in his new environment. Perhaps Peter and I with our university degrees and our silly conversation were no good for him. Perhaps he needed to be among the working classes to write about them. Whatever the cause, his muse was dying before our eyes. Later, but much too soon, he would accompany it.

Our drinking sessions had a very male feel to them. Only Pat Roberts among the women reporters braved our company with any regularity, and she and her husband, Les Nutbrown, are the only two people from the paper that I still see at all, except of course for Tinniswood. Jean Rook, later the star of the *Express*, was already too lordly for us, though she once gave me something to suck in Goole. It was a toffee. It's strange what you remember.

Letters from Ann at her boarding school caused me increasing excitement. I felt that I had never seen such beautiful handwriting. I had great confidence in our relationship and didn't need to look for other women, though I do remember chatting up, at our Friday night jazz club, a woman who had won the title 'Miss Venezuelan Legs'. I didn't get to know her well enough to judge whether she deserved her award.

The formidable Ernest Taylor retired, and was succeeded as the news editor by the far less formidable Ron Hankinson, whom we knew as Hank. We wouldn't have dared to shorten Ernest Taylor's name. Kemsley Newspapers became Thompson Newspapers, and I had the privilege of being introduced to Lord Thompson in the newsroom.

'This is David Nobbs, one of our general reporters, Lord Thompson.'

'I'm delighted to meet you, David. Always regard me as a friend rather than your employer.'

'Thank you, your lordship.'

We shook hands fervently.

A few minutes later, I needed to leave the newsroom to do a bit of research in the library. Who should come in but Lord Thompson?

'This is David Nobbs, one of your general reporters, Lord Thompson.'

'I'm delighted to meet you, David. Please think of me not as a boss but as a colleague.'

'I certainly will, your lordship.'

We shook hands fervently.

A few minutes later I needed to leave the library to do something great men and humble men have to do. As I stood there, in came Lord Thompson to stand beside me.

'This is David Nobbs, Lord Thompson, one of our general reporters.'

'I'm delighted to meet you, David. Please look on me as a friend rather than as your boss.'

'Thank you, your lordship.'

Thankfully, hygienic considerations prevented a third fervent handshake.

My friendships with Peter and Len continued to grow, and Peter and I were both busy at our real love – writing our novels. Peter, however, did have something of the journalist in him, and I most definitely didn't. On my way home one evening, after a long session in the pub, I saw four police cars parked outside a little pub called the Vine. I decided that I'd better go nowhere near it in my inebriated state and drifted home to convert my sofa into a bed. In the morning the headline in the *Daily Express* was 'Four Shot Dead in Sheffield Pub Harlem.' I would have been the first journalist on the scene. I kept very silent about that.

Allan Kassell, now a good friend in these my mature Yorkshire days, tells me that I was a very wild young man at that time. Allan ran a news agency with a man named Colin Gordon. Shortly before Christmas in 1958 I reeled out of the Dove and Rainbow, staggered up the street, and removed the red warning light from a hole in the road. Naturally, at this inept stage of my life, I did this in full view of a policeman, who approached me in a northerly direction and a threatening manner. I gave my name as Colin Gordon. When I had to show him my wallet, full of David Nobbs's documents, I claimed that I'd taken the wrong jacket from the pub. Pathetic.

Seven weeks later I received a letter from the Chief Constable, telling me that I wilfully and without authority did extinguish a red danger lamp contrary to the Towns Improvement Clauses Act, 1847, Sec 79. No action would be taken.

Allan also tells me that, as I suspected at the time, parties were arranged in great secret so that I wouldn't know of them. That was because, at two successive parties, I made my way upstairs to the hosts' bedroom and came down dressed, respectively, in my host's uniform of a lieutenant in the British army, and in a slinky black number belonging to my very attractive hostess.

*

During that long cold Yorkshire winter the editor, Gordon Linacre, moved me to the Rotherham office, which was much smaller, consisting of only four journalists. He assured me that it was therefore a promotion. I wasn't fooled.

The Rotherham office was run by a lovely man called John 'not another one!' Piper, a journalist to his fingertips. Nothing happened in the Rotherham area without John the Journalist knowing about it. When he was in the office, excitement transformed our dusty little room on the first floor of a sombre building in Frederick Street. When he left, we plodded on with the work at our own pace.

The other two reporters were Tom Geeson and Colin Parsons. When I asked Tom if he'd ever been to London he said, 'Not above ground.' It turned out that he'd regularly caught the tube from King's Cross to Waterloo, en route for holidays in the West Country, but hadn't ever dared to go above ground. Tom was a rather slow, very kindly man. Colin was a little more wary of this effete southerner, but one day he went slightly pink and said, 'I don't know if you ever go to the Co-op, David, but if you do you can use my divvy,' and I knew that I'd been accepted.

On my very first day in Rotherham, I had to go into the street, with a photographer, and stop passers-by for a vox pop feature. There was a raw wind and a penetrating drizzle in Frederick Street. Nobody would want to stop to be asked an idiotic question by a raw and foolish youth.

The first person I tried eyed me suspiciously.

'Excuse me,' I said. 'I'm from the *Sheffield Star.*'

'Oh aye?' he said.

'We do a feature each week in which we ask people their opinion on a topical issue.' God, how Cambridge I was sounding.

He took a while to digest my sentence. Then he said, 'Oh aye.'

'And we take a photo and put that in the paper over your comments.'

'Oh aye.'

'May I ask you the question we're asking people this week?'

'Oh.' He thought long, if not hard. 'Aye.'

'Do you think Britain is being too lenient to Archbishop Makarios?'

There was a very long pause.

'I don't know,' he said. 'I'm a stranger here.'

There was worse to come. One week the question was, 'Do you think it possible to get a fair deal in the used car market?' I approached a man I certainly wouldn't have bought a used car from. I should have guessed. On the page opposite his comment of, 'I honestly believe the used car market, in this area at least, is very honest, and prices are reasonable' was a story in which he was sent down for two years for used car fraud in his garage. He'd actually been on his way to court when I'd stopped him.

Slowly I began to get a grip on the South Yorkshire accent. I had one very sharp lesson on it in a pub in the Firth Park area of Sheffield. Peter Tinniswood and I were chatting to a rather gloomy man whose wife was very attractive. We told him we thought her so. He looked at us mournfully and said, 'Aye, tha might think so now. Tha should see her on t'po early doors.' Oh, the courtly, romantic nature of the male sex.

In Rotherham I began to cover court cases, and this gave me great insight into how life was lived in Britain at the end of the fifties.

At first I was mainly in the juvenile courts, and here I witnessed many sad examples of child abuse. There were usually three or four reporters from various local papers in the press box. The court would be grimly silent as terrified children gave their ghastly evidence in little more than a whisper. We didn't report any of it in those days, but we had to stay for the cases that were coming up later. Even battle-scarred old reporters were embarrassed as the children whispered their ghastly euphemisms. 'He put his Peter in my Mary.' The bulk of the cases involved fathers and daughters. One father had actually slapped his penis on the kitchen table and said to his daughter, 'There, lass. That's the biggest in Rotherham.' We sat, and listened, and learnt, and shuddered, and wrote not a word.

I just hope, rather desperately, that the vast increase in publicity about child abuse these days is because someone is tackling the problem at last, and it is no longer being ignored by society, rather than because it's increasing. I suspect, though, that it's a bit of both.

I was upset with the newspaper when I reported the comment of a magistrate as he sentenced three boys for stealing apples: 'You should have thought of the farmer who belonged to those apples.' This appeared in the paper as: 'You should have thought of the farmer whose apples those were.' I complained about the change and was told that the words I'd written made the magistrate sound ignorant. By a thousand such little strokes is the undeserved dignity of authority preserved.

A similar incident, but worse, happened in the adult court. A man stole lead off a church roof, and was chased by police and arrested after he'd driven his lorry at great speed. The chairman of that day's bench was a nice enough man, but deaf and vain. We all knew that he heard at most half of what was said in court, and his speech in sentencing this felon was brief and unfortunate: 'If you are going to continue to be a road user, you are going to have to drive a lot more carefully than that.' I reported his words. They were omitted. I complained. 'It made it sound as if he thought it was a traffic offence,' explained the chief sub.

'He did,' I said. No, we couldn't have that. Mustn't rock the boat. Must preserve the status quo.

No, my time in Rotherham didn't fill me with admiration for the workings of the magistrates' courts. In fact we reporters used to write down the verdict when we saw how the defendant was dressed. The neat, tidy, respectable, respectful usually got off. The unkempt rarely did.

I covered one murder, that of an elderly man named Thomas Crapper whose head was bashed against his draining board with enormous force. Much of the debate was about the content of his stomach, the degree of digestion being pertinent to the time of the murder. Some of the details caused the reporter from the *Daily Herald* to throw up, but your hero stayed at his post.

Sometimes I covered inquests. One was of a very respectable citizen who died of asphyxiation while entirely encased in armour and suspended from a beam in an exotic brothel. This was a brothel without women, just with mechanical aids to solitary orgasm. Most of the methods of getting thrills were through reduction of the supply of oxygen to the brain. A favourite method was imprisonment in a dustbin. Clearly one needed to have great confidence that the staff would remember to release one. This was a world that I in my innocence could never have imagined.

Every morning I took a smooth cream Sheffield bus or a rattling blue Rotherham one from the Wicker in Sheffield to Rotherham. At night, from the bus home, on winter evenings, I saw a sky lit up by the flashes from the great furnaces. I suppose I ought to point out that I had no car. We had one reporter with a car. Most of us couldn't afford one, and we didn't need one. Those were the halcyon days of public transport. Sheffield still had trams and trolley buses.

I was hungry all the time. In Rotherham there were two places to eat lunch. One was a Chinese restaurant cum coffee bar called the Rickshaw, which served thin, acrid curries and things with beansprouts. The other was an English café, so steamy and sticky that you could never see through the windows. I dined there in solitary splendour on meat pie and chips. The radio was permanently on in this cheery sauna. At 1.45 it was *Listen With Mother*. Many a time I saw weary travelling salesmen eating their lunch slowly so as not to miss the happy ending to the tale of Percy, the Porcupine whose prickles were so unprickly that he was ashamed of them.

In Sheffield I either went back for my tea and did some more work on the book, or I wandered into the Dove and Rainbow and drank the night away. Then I would go back to my digs to eat meat and two veg that had been kept warm for four and a half hours, or I had another thin, acrid, timid curry at the Sheffield branch of the Rickshaw. Indian restaurants had not yet reached the centre of Sheffield. There was a rumour of one in a distant suburb, but this was no use without a car.

Peter Tinniswood and I sometimes went to the theatre. The Sheffield Playhouse was run by a splendid man called Geoffrey Ost. Most of the plays had to be somewhat conventional, but he did mount a beautiful production of N.F. Simpson's surreal masterpiece, *One Way Pendulum*. It was played to a large house in total silence. Not one titter from beginning to end. Eerie.

Luckily I didn't realise at the time that my novel was a child of this movement of surrealism and absurdity. Even the title, *The Itinerant*

Lodger attempts to encapsulate a contradiction – rather less successfully than *One Way Pendulum*. Had I realised, the play's reception might have discouraged me.

On another occasion, at the Playhouse, two elderly ladies put their hats and coats on at the end of the second act of an Agatha Christie. As they set off for home I heard one of them say, 'What did you think of it, dear?' and the other one said, 'I thought it was quite good, but she did rather leave you up in the air this time.' I couldn't bring myself to tell them that there was a third act still to come.

I was so moved by a young Keith Barron in *Epitaph For George Dillon* that I wrote my first fan letter, and got a lovely reply. At the Empire I saw Ken Dodd. He was hilarious. I little thought that one day I would be writing for him.

Booze, however, was still the main activity. I shudder at the memory of one evening when, egged on by several colleagues led by Len Doherty, I somehow found myself posing as a representative of Hughie Green. I sat at a table in the corner of an upstairs room, in a rather rough city centre pub called the Lord Nelson, and auditioned vain hopefuls for *Opportunity Knocks*. 'We'll let you know,' I lied. I didn't dare set foot in the centre of Sheffield for at least a month afterwards.

I don't think I drank any more than most of my colleagues – a bit less than one or two of them. Why did we drink so much? Well, we were in a profession with a drink tradition, we enjoyed drinking, we were in a city not then noted for the variety of its restaurants or its entertainments, and very few of us were at ease with the opposite sex. I remember being envied because I'd managed to find a girlfriend, even though she was away at school. Everything came more slowly to us post-war boys than it does today – puberty, bananas, sex, cars, money, Indian restaurants, maturity.

Len took us to Thurcroft Working Men's Club, and I went to several similar clubs with Al Vernon in his glamorous incarnation as Al Oldcastle, or was it Al Oldcastle in his glamorous incarnation as Al Vernon? I noted how much better the manners were than in posh pubs in the south. In posh pubs the regulars occupy the whole of the bar counter and look at you as if you're a piece of pond life if you try to get through to buy a drink. In the clubs people were friendly and helped an outsider find his way.

In the endless beautiful summer of 1959 there was a printers' strike, and we had a lot of time off. Peter and I took long walks over the hazy, hot moors, stopping to read each other excerpts from work in progress. Peter's was a novel called *Joseph K.* It was beautifully written, tense, terse and immaculate, but I felt that it was too like Kafka to be viable. I suggested that he should write a humorous novel, since he was so wonderfully funny. He would have reached this conclusion himself, of course, but it is good to feel that I perhaps enabled *A Touch of Daniel* to hit the nation earlier than might otherwise have been the case.

During that lovely, gentle summer I had my first small break as a professional writer. I had two sketches accepted for a revue called *One To Another*, at the Lyric Theatre, Hammersmith. I can't recall how this came about. I'm not aware that I was writing anything except my novel. Anyway, there I was, and in wonderful company. The writers included Harold Pinter, John Mortimer, N.F. Simpson, Dorothy Parker, John Cranko, William Sansom and Robert Benchley. The cast included Beryl Reid, Patrick Wymark, Sheila Hancock 'and introducing' Joe Melia. It was directed by Eleanor Fazan and designed by Disley Jones, who said, 'You're a very clever young man, aren't you?' to which there is no possible reply, since 'yes' would be conceited and 'no' would be stupid.

One of my sketches, performed by Patrick Wymark and Joe Melia, didn't work quite well enough and was dropped, but the other, a monologue for Beryl Reid, was quite a success. As it was my very first professional success I think it would be interesting to quote from it. Beryl Reid came on in football gear:

> The doctor says I've got to hang up my boots. Do you know what I am? I'm injury prone. I get fatigued. I'm 57, you know. Still, you never want to give up. I'm sure I can still hold my own. Only last week – after we'd lost 19–0, after extra time, to Tranmere Amazons – Mr Toleado came up to me, and he

put his arm round my waist, as if he was a bandage and I was a slipped disc, and he smiled. He's awfully nice, is Mr Toleado. He's a gentleman. He said, 'Never mind, Maisie, you did your best' and then he said, 'I'll tell you what you've got, Maisie,' and I went all breathless in the knees, and I said: 'Tell me, Mr Toleado, what have I got?' and he said, 'You've got good distribution, Maisie.'

Simple stuff. Probably the most old-fashioned sketch in the revue, written by its youngest writer, but one thing does impress me about it, I left a lot of room for acting. Beryl Reid skirted round the double meanings deliciously, hinting at the depth of her unfulfilled passion for Mr Toleado. It was actually quite moving as well as funny.

Geoffrey Strachan and I went to the first night in evening dress, and in his typically generous way he was thrilled for me. But that Sunday night saw me back on the grimy train from St Pancras to Sheffield, never one of the great railway journeys of the world even in the heyday of steam. As I walked slowly along aptly-named Blonk Street and through the shabby Wicker towards my digs I realised that my brief incursion into showbiz had changed nothing.

The reviews for *One To Another* were typically mixed. W.A. Darlington in the *Daily Telegraph* said, 'What a dreary evening.' Cecil Wilson in the *Daily Mail* said, 'Won't somebody tell me the joke?' Harold Hobson, in the *Sunday Times*, said, 'It is the most original, the most profound, the most intellectually active and emotionally searching revue that London has ever seen.'

I continued with my novel, and eventually finished it. Unfortunately, my agent, David Conyers, had a nervous breakdown, not connected with my book, and I moved on to the books of a large agency, London Management. I'm not sure how this came about, but I think all David's clients were smoothly moved to other agents. At some stage, I can't remember exactly when, my precious novel began its rounds of the publishers, one publisher at a time, a lengthy process if you don't get accepted pretty soon.

*

What should have been a memorable event occurred during the golden summer of 1959. At last Ann and I managed to spend a whole night together, in a small private hotel near Earls Court. Its name escapes me, and so do all details of that night. How frustrating and perverse my memory is. Here I was, losing my virginity at an age when Georges Simenon would already have been approaching the thousand mark, and I can recall nothing of it. It's strange. I remember certain moments of sexual joy in my bed-sit in West Hampstead as if they happened yesterday, but on this and later nights in hotels on the continent I draw a blank.

It must have been a good experience because in the morning my heart was bathed in sunshine, as indeed was the hotel. I felt so wonderfully happy, so deeply in love. The sun streamed into the little breakfast room, but, as we ate, a rather large masculine lady of very stern aspect gave us several fierce glances. Ann was still very young, and it must have been quite obvious that we weren't married, and those things were so much more important then.

The masculine lady folded her napkin, rose stiffly from her chair, and approached us like a stream of lava. She looked judgemental and contemptuous. Our hearts beat faster. Were we to be publicly denounced as sinners.

'You look like sporting types,' she barked at us. 'I've got a red-hot tip for the 4.30 at Redcar.'

There's a comedy writer for you. Forgets all the wonderful sexual explorations with his lover, remembers only one absurd detail.

During that summer there was a trial for murder in Sheffield. A lecturer at Rotherham College, a sufferer from polio, was accused of murdering his ex-lover's boyfriend on the steps of the college. The paper sent some of us to the press box to witness the final stages of the judge's summing up and the verdict, even though, due to the strike, we couldn't report a word.

The judge told the court that he himself had suffered from polio. The verdict of 'guilty' was unanimous. I couldn't take my eyes off the defendant's face. It remained utterly without expression, as if there was nobody living in it. The judge put his black cap on very slowly. It was a stunning but indulgent piece of theatre.

Afterwards we went to Davy's for tea and toasted tea cake. We could hardly hold our cups, we were shaking so much.

The strike ended, and my life in Rotherham resumed. I reported on a court case involving two feuding neighbours who would crawl into each other's gardens with secateurs to cut down their favourite plants. One man saw a bush suddenly disappear while he was eating his Yorkshire pudding. I made a nice little story out of that. It was my kind of thing.

One of the men called in to complain that I'd made him look silly. I told him that he hadn't needed any help from me. He began to get angry and denied saying any of the things attributed to him in the story, so I opened a drawer which contained page after page of shorthand. (I had never learnt shorthand because Peter and I had always got detained in a pub on our way to night school.)

I took out a sheet of shorthand and said, 'There. That's what you said.'

'Oh, well, I may have done,' he admitted.

What I'd shown him was the availability and price of fish in Doncaster Market.

Far less welcome was the occasion when I visited a family to interview them about the death of their son in a motorcycle accident, only to discover that they didn't yet know. That was most definitely not my kind of thing. I can see that house still, the tiny front garden, the park opposite, the shock within.

That autumn Ann, who was keen to become a potter, went to Vallauris in southern France to work at Picasso's studios, and I chose to meet her at Trier in Germany, for reasons which escape me now. It was wonderful to have a few days together, although, with different names on our passports, I hadn't dared book us into a double room in a foreign hotel.

Later, in the beautiful city of Bruges, it was Ann, who spoke good French, who booked us into a hotel. The proprietress insisted that we have a double room and mocked us for being English and coy, but when we got back that evening we found that Ann had been moved to a single room in the annexe because she was under age. What age can she have been under? Is it possible that she was still only seventeen? I just can't remember.

Despite the fact that nothing ever seemed to be simple, those few days were very precious to us.

Peter Tinniswood joined us in Bruges and then Ann had to leave to begin her term at Reading University, where she was reading history. I felt like a man with one leg after she'd gone, but Peter was so funny that I couldn't remain desperate for long.

One day, in Liège, with the city bathed in the pale sunshine of that spectacular autumn and the smell of chips and mayonnaise and mown grass, Peter and I were wandering up a steep hill of eighteenth-century houses, when we realised that a baby was crying inside every one of them. Peter said, 'You know why those babies are all crying? They've just realised that they're Belgian.'

Peter and I both loved Belgium and still do. He has had very happy experiences there with Belgian productions of his work. It's a land of friendly people, beautiful cities, wonderful food and magnificent beer – but humour doesn't always have anything to do with truth, I'm afraid, and I laughed till I cried at Peter's remark.

Shortly before I left Sheffield, Ann came up to visit, so I went to a shop in the Wicker to buy Durex. I tried to be suave about this. 'I bet you get a run on them in Doncaster Race Week,' I said. The assistant was outraged. It was bad manners not to be furtive about such things.

Ann was given a room upstairs but she came to my room just before dawn. Nothing was ever said, but I could tell that Mrs Yardley and Mr Turner knew and felt that I had abused their hospitality, and I don't think things were ever quite the same between us after that.

Thompson Newspapers had continued Kemsley's indenture system and I should have signed my indentures in March, but I'd employed endless ruses for delay, and now it was December. I could avoid decision time no longer. The editor summoned me and told me that I must sign or leave.

It was no contest. I would never be a good journalist. I had a novel under my belt. Two of my sketches had been performed in a revue at the Lyric, Hammersmith, a revue which had transferred to the West End, although it had only done modestly there. I was a writer. I must at last brave my parents' displeasure and follow my muse.

I told Mr Linacre that I wouldn't sign. He showed no distress. He even smiled.

'I think you're doing the right thing,' he said.

That just about shows the calibre of the man. It was no surprise to me when he was knighted.

7 Love In The Afternoon

On that ill-fated Isle of Wight sailing trip, Izzy Cohen as Ship's Engineer had managed to over-heat the engine till it began to melt and seized up for ever. Now he made amends. He found me a cheap room in the house where he lived – 16, Lymington Road, in West Hampstead. It was a tiny bed-sit. The bed bit was small and hard, and the sit bit was smaller and harder. I had a desk and a hard chair and an easy chair and a table and an old portable Belling with two rings and no oven. To boil a kettle I had to go to a tiny kitchen across the corridor. I had found my garret, even if it was on the ground floor.

Izzy lived on the other side of the front door, in a much larger room, and the back room was shared by two young ladies from Leeds, Anne and Rita. They had a sitting room and a bedroom.

On the first floor there was Miss Quass, who figured in a *Guardian* article about 'Women of Today', though I can't remember why, and Dr Pappenheim. I didn't know what kind of doctor he was, but he had a central European accent and I once took a call for him on the communal phone. 'Please give him a message,' said a sinister voice. 'Amsterdam is off. It's Hamburg.' It was probably a gathering of philatelists, but in my imagination it was all much more sinister.

On the top floor lived Mr Walters, who told me that there was a bath in the middle of his room. No pipes, no taps, just a bath.

Everyone except me was Jewish, and the landlord was a diminutive Viennese Jew called Joe Hirsch. He also owned number 20, where Victor Spurber lived.

Ann often visited from Reading. Joe saw us once as we slipped out of my room. Next time I met him, he said, 'You have love in the afternoon?'

'Yes,' I said. There was no point in denying it.

'Is good,' he said. 'I am Viennese. For Viennese, love in the afternoon is good. Love in the evening is good. Love at night is good. Love in the morning is good. But love in the afternoon, with the world at work and the curtains drawn and the room palely lit by the sun through the curtains, that is best.'

A thought struck him.

'You think Anne and Rita have love in the afternoons?'

'I don't know.'

He lowered his voice. 'It is my fear, David, that one day one of my tenants will kill themselves.'

'It won't be me.'

'Good. That is good. Love in the afternoon tomorrow?'

'Not tomorrow, no. Sorry.'

It was in that environment that I began my career as a writer, though 'career' is putting it a bit strongly. I didn't begin it with my parents' blessing. I had told them, over our usual family Christmas in Essex, that I was leaving my job to seek fame and fortune. They were quietly upset, worried sick. It wasn't only that they didn't have faith in me, they couldn't accept the philosophy behind it. 'We've lived through the depression.' How often had I heard that. They'd never take risks, and they were far too worried about the risk I was taking to be objective.

Uncle Charlie and Auntie Kathleen took me to one side and said that they did have faith in me, they thought I was doing the right thing, they admired my courage and they wished me well. They expressed their regret that my parents didn't have faith in me, though they didn't make it sound like a criticism of my parents.

It is, of course, much easier to be an uncle and an aunt than to be a parent.

For a long time events seemed to bear out my parents' judgement. I wrote play after play, and they were all rejected.

Why did I choose plays? I think it must have been because I was getting rejections for *The Itinerant Lodger*, and so despaired of novels.

The reason given in one of these rejections was that 'There is no market for the detective story at present.' There was a huge market, and it wasn't a detective story, but apart from that it was a very intelligent comment.

My plays were all for the theatre. I knew nothing of television. I didn't even have a set. They were mixtures of the surreal and the unreal, these early plays of mine. They drew not at all on my varied experiences of life in Britain. You find this extraordinary? Not as extraordinary as I do – but I was under the influence of N.F. Simpson, and Ionesco, and Pinter, and Beckett. You shouldn't drive under the influence. Perhaps you shouldn't write under it either.

I gave up a great deal to become a writer. I've already said that I gave up the great, the supreme, the incomparable game of cricket. It was too expensive to keep the kit, to get to matches, to buy my round. I gave up almost all drinking, without any difficulty at all. Since I no longer went anywhere, I no longer required Dutch courage. I also gave up good food. Night after night I heated up a tin of ravioli on my Belling. Most weeks I went once with Anne and Rita to the Calcutta Restaurant, on Finchley Road. Anne was dark and curvy and cheery. Rita was tall and pale and quieter. They weren't unattractive, but I wasn't attracted. I was in love. At the Calcutta I almost always chose dhansak. Rita always buttered her chapatis. One week, when she didn't come, the waiter said, 'Buttered chapati not with you today?' and she became Buttered Chapati.

I gave up luxury, all hope of carpets, of my own bathroom, let alone a car. I gave them up without a moment's regret. I was utterly single-minded.

I was living in London, but I might as well have been on the North

Pole, for all the use I was able to make of the capital's attractions. I couldn't afford theatre, but I did manage to get to the cinema. I got enormous pleasure from American film comedies during the next few years. British film comedy left me cold after the decline of the Ealing Comedies. I found the *Carry On* films deeply unfunny, and the *Doctor* films pallid. I didn't need to lust after Muriel Pavlow now I had Ann. The Doris Day/Rock Hudson comedies, on the other hand, were brilliantly professional, very tightly scripted by Stanley Shapiro and others, and featured the irresistible Tony Randall. The two stars weren't bad either. Doris Day playing a virgin and Rock Hudson playing a macho heterosexual – that was acting.

But Billy Wilder was the king, especially when he wrote with I.A.L. Diamond. *Some Like It Hot* is the most successful comedy film of all time. One of its many virtues is the time and care it takes to establish that Jack Lemmon and Tony Curtis are in real danger, so that their disguise as women becomes necessary and not silly.

My main friends in London at this time were my old Cambridge companions – William Ragg, Charles Barham, Barry Slater and Anthony Lynch. I saw Charles the most frequently – mostly to see films, our senses of humour were so similar – but it was with Barry and William that I went to see *The Apartment*, the next Wilder/Diamond film. It was deeper, more sombre, but barely less funny than *Some Like It Hot*. Lemmon was masterly as always, Shirley MacLaine was exquisite and Fred MacMurray gave his very best performance. William, however, left the cinema halfway through. Later he explained that he'd been upset by a line to the effect that people who try to commit suicide and fail always try again. I didn't take that seriously enough.

I don't recall talking to William about his suicide attempt on any other occasion. I don't think I was brave enough to ask him why he had done it. I went to stay at his mother's elegant narrow three-storey house in Upper Terrace in the heart of old intellectual Hampstead. We were on our own. We got very drunk. When Mollie returned I was still in bed at noon, with a most inelegant hangover which clashed horribly with the surroundings. I'd promised to look after her son and she must have felt that I had let her down. I think I had. He was lonely. He was drifting. I gave him friendship, but not a friendship that was deep enough. My friendship didn't venture into the dangerous places.

The friendship of 'Ant' Lynch and his wife Paula was of great value to me during the years of struggle. Ant had been a conscientious objector when he went for National Service after our days of marbles and Shredded Wheat packets in Cambridge. He'd been put to work in a mental home in South London. When I'd gone to meet him there he had put me in the padded cell for five minutes. It was a weird experience to be utterly alone in a soft, silent, featureless world. Ant's two years had been so traumatic that he had rushed into industry to make money. He worked for a firm called Dexion Slotted Angles. They made . . . well, slotted angles. Ant would pick me up from time to time and drive me around southern England as he made his customer calls. That was such a pleasure for me in my trapped state, in my unpadded cell. I never really found out what slotted angles were. I just wasn't interested enough in the real world at this time. No wonder nobody bought my plays.

My life in Lymington Road really revolved around Ann. She would usually arrive from Reading early on a Saturday afternoon. We would spend the afternoon in bed. It was the least we could do to keep Joe Hirsch happy. A man has some responsibilities. What joyous moments we had in that cramped single bed in that tiny, cluttered, inelegant room. I couldn't believe that I had found such love at the very first time of asking.

When we got up we would go to the Calcutta, and with Ann I was more adventurous. One evening we discovered the delights of methi ghost, that dry curry with the pungent flavour of fenugreek. Izzy Cohen and his new girlfriend Vivienne entered, and asked if it was nice. Ann said it was delicious. Izzy said he would order it and if he didn't like it he would bang on our window later. He banged at the exact moment of climax.

My happiest memory of 16, Lymington Road is of a Sunday morning. I put on my dressing gown and picked up my key, to unlock my door, and a box of matches, to light the gas across the way for a cup of tea. I approached the door blearily, lit the match, held it to the keyhole, and looked mystified when the door wouldn't open. I looked back to see my beloved, beautiful and slender and naked and writhing with laughter. I didn't mind making a fool of myself if it gave such enormous pleasure.

Victor went off to live in Israel, as he believed that all Jews must assert their Jewishness. His place down the road at number 20 was taken by Emmanuel Plotsky, a small, shambling, dirty, bearded misfit with a fund of wonderful stories, a burning love of curries, and an important role to play in my life.

At Christmas time I did temporary postal work again, this time at the West Hampstead sorting office. One night I was running late and posted all the remaining mail back into a letter box. On Christmas Eve a kind lady offered me a drink and told me how good I'd been. 'Not like the one in the next street. My friend saw him posting all the mail back into the letter box.' 'There are people like that,' I said.

Christmas Day was very different in those days. There was a mail delivery, and I was plied with sherries and mince pies. Then I hurried to Liverpool Street Station, which was busy with cheery people rushing to catch trains to their celebrations.

The one thing I dreaded about Christmas at Yeldham was standing for the Queen's speech. I found this embarrassing in a farmhouse in the middle of the countryside. I always managed to slope off and miss it, and I never aroused suspicion.

In 1959, to my astonishment, Uncle Charlie had led me off to the Court Room, as the dining room was called, having served as a court in the fifteenth century. There we had shared a bottle of very old port, and he had told me that I was the only person in the family who would appreciate it. When I look back on what seems a pretty clueless adolescence I find it odd that on at least three occasions I was singled out as the only person who would appreciate fine wine. It was also odd to be drinking this wonderful stuff in what had previously been very nearly an alcohol-free zone.

Now, in 1960, Uncle Charlie and I were a year older, and this time the port was ten years older. He opened it, sniffed it, said that it had gone, poured it down the sink, and that was that.

*

The Easter holiday of 1960 was the highlight of my life in my first West Hampstead phase. Ann's family were away, and she suggested that I came to stay with her in Orpington. The only snag was that the neighbours had promised her parents to pop in from time to time to see if everything was all right. I would have to stay upstairs in her bedroom throughout. I assured her that I would be able to cope with that.

I told my parents that I was far too busy to visit them, so the journey on the Orpington train was somewhat perilous. Supposing somebody who knew my parents saw me. What on earth would I say?

I hurried out of the station, head down, heart racing, and hurtled off by a roundabout route, along boring streets where I knew nobody. I'd waited till it was dark, so that her neighbours were unlikely to be looking out, and all went well.

I suppose I must have stayed in bed for three whole days, apart from ablutions. From time to time we made love. From time to time Ann brought me bacon and eggs in a sweet little skillet. No food ever tasted so good. From time to time the neighbours called and I held my breath. It would have been lovely at any time, but to be so near my own suburban home turned this cramped idyll in Ann's single bed into a cry of victory over narrow suburban propriety. It was also a perfect way for an agnostic to celebrate Easter.

I left on the evening of Easter Monday, with a heavy heart and a light tread, through the back garden.

Peter Tinniswood came down from Sheffield once or twice and slept on my floor. I realise now that I should have offered him my bed. Being an only child, it never occurred to me. Luckily he was an only child too, and I hope it never occurred to him either.

Ann and Peter were the twin oases in my self-imposed desert.

A lady opposite saw me working away and when we met in the street she asked me what I was writing. She was an actress, and she had a husband in the business, and a very young baby. She invited me over to tea. She was Phyllida Law, her husband was Eric Thompson, of *Magic Roundabout* fame, and the baby was Emma Thompson.

I also went sometimes, in those early days of the sixties, on Sunday evenings, in company with several other people many of whom I forget, to the flat of Sandy Wilson, creator of *The Boy Friend*. I met Robin Ray and Susan Stranks, and they befriended me and were wonderfully encouraging and generous. At Sandy Wilson's we planned a revue and had a lot of fun. Nothing came of it, but it did wonders for my confidence to hear people laughing at my jokes.

One Sunday morning Charles took Ann and me to a pub in St John's Wood, where he seemed to know everybody. Olivia Manning was there. I hadn't yet read anything of hers, though I later came to love her Balkan trilogy. I hardly spoke to her, but I did wonder what it would be like to be a successful writer surrounded by admirers. I was anxious for Ann to shine, to show everyone what an intelligent and wonderful young woman she was, but she went very quiet, either because my anxiety made her nervous, or because it made her angry.

My most extraordinary meeting was with Douglas Fairbanks Junior. Anne and Buttered Chapati had met him at a party and invited him for a drink the following evening. He was staying with the American comedienne, Bea Lilley, who lived in Hampstead. He probably wouldn't come, but, just in case he did, would I come and provide a little intellectual stimulation?! I think a friend of theirs from Leeds, Michael Landy, was probably also there.

Buttered Chapati and Anne had tidied the little room as best they could, but I could tell that they were very conscious of its limitations, and perhaps regretting the invitation. Time passed and we all grew increasingly nervous. Then, just when we'd decided he wasn't coming, he arrived, full of apologies.

We had drinks in the flat and moved on to a noisy pub nearby. I don't recall much detail after that. I imagine we ate somewhere, and it was well past eleven when Douglas Fairbanks Junior left us. By no glance or hint did he ever suggest that he was in an unusual environment. He bought his round and let us buy ours, conferring on us the dignity of equality. He laughed at my jokes, and unless he was a very good actor his laughter was genuine – but he was a very good actor, so I'll never know. I mention the evening because it was the most perfect example of being a gentleman that I have ever encountered.

And my plays? They were sent to all sorts of people, and they came back from all sorts of people. I was with David Conyers again now. He had recovered, and had asked me to return, and I had felt it only fair and loyal to do so.

Michael Codron wrote that he was very worried about me. He didn't think I'd found my voice. This conjured up a sweet scene. 'Can't you sleep, darling?' 'No, I'm worried.' 'What about, my pet?' 'David Nobbs. He hasn't found his voice.'

I received a very encouraging letter from Frederick Bradnum, Script Unit, Drama (Sound), BBC. He returned one play, 'Master of Latin', but had sent two, 'A Slow Poison' and 'Theodore' to the Controller, Third Programme. He said, 'We have, by the way, spoken to him about you and said that we think that you are, to say the least, worth encouraging, so your name is now in his mind.'

Nothing ever came of it, and quite rightly. They weren't bad, but they weren't good enough. I threw them all away long ago. I can't remember 'Theodore' at all.

Encouragement of this kind was enormously important, as I strove to create something worthwhile. Thank you, Frederick Bradnum, wherever you are.

Tottenham Hotspur began the 1960–61 season with eleven straight victories. I'd always had a sneaking fondness for the round ball, probably out of natural perversity, having gone to a rugger school. This enthusiasm had grown considerably in Sheffield. Now Charles, a rugger man, went with me to see Spurs play Birmingham City halfway through that run. Charles seemed too elegant and laid back for White Hart Lane, but he took to it like a duck to sliced bread. Spurs scored three brilliant, precise, intelligent goals in the first ten minutes, went on to win 6–0, and we were hooked. They did the league and cup double that winter, bringing enormous joy into my life at this time of struggle. Since then, they have given me forty years of completely avoidable angst.

Early in 1961, John 'Feet Up' Aarons and I went to Scotland in a Mini hired by John. We left London on a Monday morning, and wondered if we should call on William, who had now recovered so fully that he was back at Cambridge. We decided against it, as we had a long way to go.

We had a great time and I fell in love with the Highlands. As John drove back towards Inverness on the long journey home, a car overtook a lorry when there was no room to do so, and came straight for us. Both drivers braked fiercely, but the impact still came at quite a speed. Just before the impact John said, 'This is it, David' and I said 'Yes' and then the crash happened. The other car ended up on the verge, facing the same way as us. The other driver had blood on his face, which John wiped off with a handkerchief. We were entirely uninjured.

We returned to London to learn that William had killed himself with an overdose. His body had been discovered on the very morning that we had thought of visiting him. We would have been too late anyway, but it added to my feeling that I should have done more. I suppose you always think you should have done more. To be honest I suppose you always could do more. I think that in returning to Cambridge William went to the house where his demons lived. I believe that his intellectual brilliance created an unbearable feeling of apartness, even of inferiority, hard though that may be to grasp. I think he had the mind of a very mature man in the body of a very immature youth.

I miss William still. I can see him now, with his boyish, shy, lop-sided grin. His earnest face would break into laughter like the sun breaking through on a heavy autumn day. On many days, when we weren't around, the sun can't have broken through.

His mother offered me some of his clothes. I couldn't have worn them. She offered me some of his books too, and these I did take. Mollie has remained a firm friend and has entertained me royally in several elegant homes, but we haven't talked about William. We were born in reticent generations, in a reticent land.

My world fell apart on a Saturday afternoon. I had made a real effort to clean the place up for Ann, but she didn't notice. She was far too anxious about telling me that she had a boyfriend at Reading University and was leaving me.

I pleaded and begged and wept and grovelled. It must have been a disgusting sight, but Ann was very patient and even came to see me a couple more times to help me get over the shock. Thank you for that, and for having the courage to tell me in person, Ann, wherever you are. It did help.

We had never lived together but I had always assumed that one day we would come together for life. Had Ann felt like that? I was her first lover. She was still very young. Occasionally she could be strangely withdrawn. She told me that on occasions she felt uninhabited – a striking phrase. Sometimes uninhabited, often uninhibited. Did I strive hard enough to understand her? I mentioned earlier the morning when we met Olivia Manning. There had been other times when I'd wanted her to shine – when she met my colleagues in Sheffield, for instance. I'm sure she'd felt that she was on show. I'm sure that I put her under pressure. And what had I to offer that was so very special? Sex and love? A lot of men could offer those. I certainly had no money. I had a single bed in a grotty room. Curries and films were our luxuries. Big deal. Whole worlds awaited her. How could I have been so confident, so complacent?

Ann had never met my family, nor I hers. My family didn't know of her existence, hers didn't know of mine. Should we have been braver? Would things have worked out better if we'd been braver? Or would we just have crashed pointlessly into a wall of disapproval?

I think my commitment must have been completely unstated. Certainly we never talked about getting engaged. I don't know how deep a commitment she had for me. Great fondness, certainly, but love?

When I set out to write this autobiography I didn't think that I'd be asking so many questions. I do think, though, that for most of us life is the process of learning which questions to ask. To expect answers as well is somewhat optimistic.

Matters in the family didn't help me at this sad time. Both my grandmothers had died peacefully in their beds at great ages. I had been particularly upset at Granny Williams's funeral when people came back to 16, Eaton Crescent after the bilingual funeral, and had tea and bara brith, and chatted and even laughed. I hadn't yet understood that you had to grieve and that, when you had grieved, you had to assert together, before you went your several ways, that life must go on.

Now both my grandfathers died within a few days of each other and within a few days of Ann's bombshell. These were dark days of tears and sleeping pills.

I think my mother knew, from my demeanour at these funerals, that I had private grief of my own as well. On a weekend visit to Orpington, early one Saturday evening at dusk, I was foolish enough to wander along Ann's cul-de-sac and look up at the room where we'd spent Easter, as if my tears could charm her back. Nothing was said when I got home, but I think my mother understood a great deal. I felt a great warmth coming from her. We didn't speak. There was this whole secret lying between us, and yet we felt very close. It was a strange moment, in our dark and sombre hall.

One Saturday morning, Joe Hirsch knocked on my door and said, 'There's no reply from Rita and Anne. You think they killed themselves?'

Nothing would have surprised me just then, but sense prevailed, and I said, 'They probably had a late night.'

'I give them two hours.'

Luckily, they woke before that.

Buttered Chapati got married and went to Canada. I don't know what happened to Anne, or Izzy, or any other occupants of number 16.

I didn't stay long in Lymington Road. I couldn't bear it. My room was full of Ann's absence. I went to live in an even more extraordinary household in Lady Somerset Road, on the ill-defined border between Kentish Town and Tufnell Park. Charles had moved in on the first floor with his girlfriend (maybe already his wife) Shirley, a potter he'd met while working on the design and construction of a bridge on the Ross Spur motorway in Worcestershire. Charles had become a civil engineer, the most civil I ever met.

The owner of the house was an extraordinary, larger than life Dutchman named Tammo de Jongh, part artist, part landlord, part philosopher, part guru, part dictator.

Tammo and his disciple, Ken Carter, had created a Cosmology, which defined the human psyche entirely in terms of the four elements of earth, air, fire and water. They made an effectively contrasting pair,

Tammo loud and overpowering, Ken quiet, thoughtful, courteous and kind. We all lived by this Cosmology for a time. I mention it so briefly only because this is my story, not theirs.

I was in a ground floor flat with its own separate entrance, so I was of the house and not of it. The house itself was a bit like that. There was always talk of its being run as a community, but somehow it never happened. There were no communal meals, although we spent many hours in Tammo's room cum studio, at his feet metaphorically.

At first I shared the ground floor with a very silent young man whose name has been swept away by the fog that envelops much of this part of my life. He had once been catatonic, Tammo told me, and I didn't find it hard to believe. Eventually he moved upstairs and Barry Slater joined me. I was now in the same house as my two closest living friends from Cambridge.

Charles went off to work each morning in his immaculate suit, seeming so at odds with this strange house yet managing to be completely at ease in it, as far as I could tell. I envied his ability to be himself at all times and in all places.

I wouldn't say that Barry had come out of the closet because I don't know that there had ever been a closet. I think I had just been too naïve to realise earlier that he was gay. He didn't leave me in much doubt now. He had one or two very strange friends. I don't recall how he was earning his living at this stage – tutoring, perhaps. It would be many years before he found the academic career which would lead to the publication of several books and to his appointment as Doctor and ultimately a Professor of Philosophy at the University of Western Australia. He's extremely clever and I'm sure he would have been just as successful if he hadn't been to Cambridge, but I very much doubt if in that case he would ever have become coach to the Western Australian Croquet Team – a gloriously improbable achievement.

Other occupants of the house included a forthright, warm-hearted Scottish artist, Don, and his forthright, warm-hearted wife Doreen, and a very pretty girl called Paddy Dombey who got engaged to a rich architect while I was still making up my mind whether to ask her out.

*

I was at a very low ebb. Even with sleeping pills I wouldn't drop off until about two hours before I was due to wake up.

My savings had finally run out – I can't think how they lasted so long – and I looked for a job that wouldn't stretch me, so that I'd have energy to write in the evenings. I went to the Nu-Type Secretarial Agency and failed their typing test. This was rock bottom. However, Nu-Type didn't abandon me. They sent me to Smith's Advertising Agency in High Holborn as a temporary voucher clerk. I went for a week and stayed half a year.

I was leading a double life: in the evenings and at weekends, a member of a semi-artistic, semi-alternative, semi-literate, semi-community; by day, a commuting temp.

Every morning I caught the tube from Tufnell Park to Chancery Lane. Every lunchtime I ate with the office personnel in a steamy, cheery restaurant in Chancery Lane. Every evening I caught the tube from Chancery Lane to Tufnell Park. Every evening I was knackered. Often Charles and I would walk up Dartmouth Park Hill to a pub called the Lord Palmerston for a few pints and some games of shove ha'penny. I did no writing.

I did, however, learn a lot about offices and boring jobs. I must have been garnering further information for Perrin.

My colleagues were friendly and so was the boss of the department, Ralph. He soon decided that I was above the usual standard of voucher clerk, and every week he offered me a permanent post. Every week I turned him down.

At some stage Charles and Shirley bought a full-length narrow boat and moved away. At some stage Victor Spurber came back from Israel because he found it impossibly military and aggressive. At some stage he began attacking me verbally and spoilt it by apologising and explaining that his psychiatrist had told him to be more assertive. At some stage he went back to Israel again because he needed to assert his Jewishness. At some stage I managed to write a play set in a lunatic asylum in which the staff were madder than the patients. We read it as a community play. Tammo roared throughout, but he laughed because it fed his view of the world, not because he really appreciated the writing.

It did nothing to ease Michael Codron's worries.

At Christmas Smith's Advertising Agency decided that they would no longer pay the Nu-Type agency's weekly fee for my services. I must take a permanent post or depart.

In the course of the firm's Christmas party I was asked to leave by a member of the management as temps were not invited. Everyone in our department said that if I left, they'd take me to the pub and we'd have a better party. He backed down with a red face and a sullen expression. Suddenly I felt that it would be very pleasant to stay with these nice people and do a routine job and have no worries. Ambition was a sin of pride. Why should I feel that I was so special? In the morning I would apply for a permanent post.

But I didn't.

My next job was with the *St Pancras Chronicle*, a weekly newspaper with an office in Camden Town. There was a news editor, a chief sub, an elderly lady called Della who was the Marylebone Correspondent and wrote her stories on lavatory paper, and there was me.

The owner/editor was ancient, ailing and absent. I did as little work as possible. Once a month I covered the meeting of Camden Borough Council, and I made the stories from that last for the four weeks till the next meeting. I also covered Hampstead Borough Council, Hampstead Magistrates' Court and St Pancras Coroner's Court. I don't think I ever found one story on my own initiative.

I sat in cafés, and thought about my writing, and maybe even did a bit. One day while strolling up Tottenham Court Road, at the southern tip of my patch, I met a man who knew me. I knew that I knew him, but I couldn't place him. He suggested a pint. That was something I never refused. I assumed that a few shrewd questions would soon elicit his identity.

'What are you doing these days?'

'Still the same old thing.'

'Ah. Where are you living?'

'Still the same old place.'

'Ah . . . Er . . .?'

'Yes. Still with her.'

'Ah.'

The moment had long passed when I could have admitted that I had no idea who he was. Two pints later we parted, and I still hadn't placed him.

A year later we met again, and I was still none the wiser.

'Where was it we last met?' he asked.

'Tottenham Court Road,' I said. 'We went for a couple of pints.'

'What a memory you've got!' he said.

I found Camden Council fascinating. The Labour people were passionate and friendly. Councillor O'Connor, the Labour leader, was particularly charming, and I found that all my sympathy was with the feisty socialists. In particular I admired Councillor Peggy Duff, who looked rather like Margaret Rutherford and was a passionate supporter of CND. I'm sure my reports had a considerable socialist bias, but I doubt if anybody noticed.

Hampstead Council was very different. It was full of smooth Tories and Liberal novelists.

Hampstead Magistrates' Court didn't provide many very dramatic cases. One man gave his name as Jesus and his address as Everywhere, but I can't recall the charge or the sentence. There was a lot of shoplifting, a few minor thefts and motoring offences, and a large number of cases of non-payment of television licences.

One morning several Pakistani gentlemen appeared for not paying their licences. One of them, a Mr Bhutto, admitted his offence with great good cheer, accepted the verdict graciously, and left.

'Call Mr Ditto,' yelled the court official.

The cry of 'Call Mr Ditto' was repeated, but Mr Ditto never came. It was a second identical charge against Mr Bhutto, and he'd gone home. No wonder he'd looked cheerful.

On another, painful, occasion a police officer asked me to go on an identification parade. I think it was my flasher's mac that made them think me suitable. I wasn't a snappy dresser.

The officer explained that it was a case of flashing at a Spanish au pair girl on Hampstead Heath. So it *was* my mac.

They led a repellent individual out of the cells. He was shifty and unshaven and wearing a mac very like mine. They stood him next to me.

The au pair girl was led in. She had jet black hair and the look of a flamenco dancer. She moved slowly and gracefully along the line, looking us up and down, mainly down. It was all so inevitable. She pointed at me, just as I had known she would. I felt guilty, which was absurd.

They led the lucky miscreant back to his cell.

'We know it wasn't you,' said the officer, 'but just for the record we need your name.'

'Nobbs,' I said.

The laughter rang through the police station, but would I ever make people laugh on purpose?

One case in St Pancras Coroner's Court stood out. It was an inquest on a man who died of asphyxiation while strung up encased in armour. This man was the highly respected church organist of a Kentish village. Every Friday he visited London on some honourable pretext, and in fact got his bizarre thrills in an exotic brothel. Two coroners' courts, two identical deaths. Just how many exotic brothels were there in our land, and just how many men who couldn't get satisfaction without them, and just how many fatalities?

I didn't report any of this. The paper wasn't interested. The man didn't live in St Pancras.

At some stage during these years of fog a play of mine, *The Club*, was put on in a little theatre near Leicester Square, imaginatively named The Little Theatre. The play told the story of a foreign artist trying to get accepted into British society, in a Britain seen as a club with strict rules. I imagine I wrote this at Lady Somerset Road, under the influence of Tammo, who must have admired it hugely since it fed his view of the world.

It had good lines and amusing passages, but it was dreadfully didactic. There was, though, a bit of strength, a touch of theatrical effectiveness, which just about kept it afloat through its over-stated sermonising. I think now that it was so bad that the fact that both the audience stayed to the end was a great tribute to something in my writing.

I still sometimes saw Emmanuel Plotsky from the old Lymington Road days. He was good company and had a fund of funny stories, mainly about disastrous weddings, one of which had been his own. Manny was a would-be writer who didn't have the discipline to complete anything. He was a great friend of the jazz musician and novelist, Benny Green. Manny told me that Benny had put him in a novel, though he had respected his privacy by changing his name. He said it was typical of Benny Green's lack of inventive powers that he appeared in the book as Emmanuel Blinsky.

Manny was a member of a theatrical group which went around the pubs performing plays. He only had quite small parts as he really wasn't very good. One of the members, John Bardon (not to be confused with John Bowden or John Dowden), went on to have a very solid professional career. Manny invited me to a party the group were having. I don't recall a great deal about that party after all these years, but I do remember people asking eagerly, 'Is Mary coming?' It was clear that the party wouldn't be quite as successful without her as it would be with her, and she did indeed light it up when she arrived. Among her party attributes, which may or may not have been exhibited on this occasion, was an ability to play the piano and a knowledge of the words of a formidable number of songs.

I felt a strange sense of what I suppose I should call avant-vu about Mary, that I knew her before I had seen her. She was lively, witty, feisty and warm. I was attracted to her immediately – and she must have been attracted to me because we started to go out together fairly soon – but nothing happened that night to suggest that I had met my future wife.

Mary was a Channel Islander, a 'Guernsey Donkey'. Her father had been a driver and general factotum to a local bigwig. She'd been bright enough not only to win a scholarship to the best school on the island but to become head girl. She'd gone to Bristol University to read medicine but had left to get married. Her husband had given her three children, Dave, Chris and Kim, who have added far more to the richness of my life than I have room to tell, but he hadn't given her much else. He had left her and had never even sent a Christmas card to his three children since then.

I don't recall how Mary was earning her living at that time. I don't recall our first date. I don't recall the first time we slept together. I've never kept a diary. I had no idea that I'd ever be writing my autobiography.

So what *do* I recall?

I recall the first time I saw her act. She really was extremely good. She was playing a villain in a melodrama the pub group were doing. Afterwards a member of the audience bought all the cast a drink, except her. 'I'm not buying you one,' he said. 'You're horrid.' It's the nature of success, for a thespian.

I recall the first meal Mary cooked for me, at her house in Richmond. It was pancakes filled with spicy beef. I was to enjoy this dish greatly in the future, but not that first time. I adore spicy food, but this was ridiculous. She'd bought the very hottest chillies without realising. My nose ran. My eyes watered. Sweat broke out all over my scalp. 'It's delicious,' I insisted through my tears. 'A bit hot, but really delicious.' I ate every mouthful. Sometimes a man has to do what a man has to do.

The winter of 1962/3 was memorably severe and there was a huge snowfall in London on New Year's Eve. The piles of swept snow turned black and stayed for seven weeks, ugly little slag heaps at intervals along all the streets. Mary, a great party giver, threw a party and people had to stay till the next day because of all the snow. When I visited my parents in Orpington, the frost didn't melt all day from the inside of the sitting room windows, even though we had a coal fire blazing. But most of all I recall the ferocious blast of ice that hit my face as I crept out of Mary's house of a morning, having tip-toed down the stairs so as not to wake her innocent, sleeping children.

My eyes watered as I struggled blearily to Richmond Station, where I caught the tube. I had to change somewhere to catch the rickety, rackety North London line that would take me home to Kentish Town. The frost was caked on the windows of the train, and it was almost impossible to see the rosy sun rising over the dirty white snowy streets of North London. There was a cruelty, a merciless cold, in the blue of the sky on those wintry mornings, but there was a thrill to them too. The other passengers looked like respectable people on their way to their offices. I was a writer, going back to his flat, unshaven after a night with his lover. I began to feel like a real writer again.

It was all very well feeling like a real writer, but what was I going to write? I don't think I ever gave up hope entirely, but it was hope with no basis whatsoever. Nobody wanted my book or my plays. I had lost the great discipline that had once been my strength.

Then *That Was The Week, That Was* exploded on to our screens.

8 A TOUCH OF FROST

IT WAS YOUNG, vigorous, bold, iconoclastic. It criticised the Establishment fearlessly. It held public figures to account. From the vitality of the opening song to the almost manic intensity of David Frost as linkman, it attacked. *That Was The Week, That Was* was of my generation and it spoke for my generation, but – and I believe there's a lesson here for the makers of today's TV – it was sufficiently grounded in intelligence and truth to have a considerable appeal for older generations.

I enjoyed it from the start. I was thrilled by television as I had never been before.

Then it dawned on me that *TW3*'s topicality must make it an opportunity for me. The confidence of my Cambridge days had long gone. My belief in my talent had been buried deep by now – but I don't believe that I ever despaired that I wasn't good enough.

I began to read the papers every morning before going to the drab offices of the *St Pancras Chronicle*, with a view to finding possible ideas.

My first was for a monologue for David Frost, on the thesis that sport would be more interesting if it was scripted like theatre, and theatre would be more interesting if it was spontaneous like sport. I forget what sparked it off, and it seems extremely contrived to me now, but I was pretty pleased with it at the time, and phoned the *TW3* office from a public call box.

I was asked to post my item, but I insisted that it was too topical for that. At this point David Frost took the phone and uttered the line that I would hear so often in the next few years: 'David, super to talk to you.' I never relish admitting this, but he recognised my name from the Cambridge Footlights. The old boys' network.

He agreed to send a taxi, but where to? Hampstead Magistrates' Court. I swear I heard him blink. I explained that I wasn't appearing on some charge that would bring discredit to the BBC, and the first of several taxis was dispatched to the venue. The court officials could never get over the sending of a taxi for one envelope. There were mutterings about the waste of the licence fee, but speed was of the essence for such a topical show.

David asked me to ring him, the next day, and I did. 'David, super to talk to you, super sketch, I'm doing it on Saturday.'

I told everybody. Mary was sitting there in Richmond, waiting expectantly. My parents were filled with a mixture of pride and fear in Orpington. Auntie Kathleen and Uncle Charlie and cousin John were glued to their set in Yeldham.

David did just one line of my piece, in the middle of a link between sketches. It was a line about how silly it would be if Sir Laurence Olivier came on in a play as the nightwatchman for the last two minutes. It didn't make much sense, especially if you didn't know what a night-watchman was in cricket. I felt humiliated. One line!

Well, it was one more line than most people ever had on television, and by the next week I was feeling enthusiastic again. A large black taxi collected another small white envelope from Hampstead Magistrates' Court, and this time the whole sketch was done.

After that I had sketches performed pretty regularly. One of them was particularly successful. It was based on a comment made by Penelope Gilliatt, in the *Observer*, that English films seem to use cars instead of sex in a particularly British sort of symbolism. Lance Percival played the motorist. An unseen Millicent Martin played the car.

*

'I'm a nice car.'

'Yes. How many cylinders have you got?'

'Two.'

'Good. And you're only eighteen horsepower.'

'No. Please. Don't start.'

'What's wrong?'

'It's been so nice. Don't spoil everything.'

'Women!'

'I'm sorry. I can't help it.'

'Here. Have a sump oil.'

'You just want to get me tanked up, don't you? And then before I know where I am you'll be obtaining the power for automatic clutch operation by making use of the partial vacuum in the engine inlet manifold.'

'I just want to take you for a drive.'

'I'm sorry. But a girl's got so much to lose. She's never the same once she's been decarbonised.'

'Well, I'm off, then.'

'No, don't. Well, just a little ride. But not fast.' (HE SETS OFF) 'Be gentle with me. I haven't got shock absorbers.'

'Change gear.' (SHE CHANGES GEAR) 'Horn.' (SHE BLOWS THE HORN)

'I like that.' (SHE BLOWS THE HORN AGAIN)

'Double bend.'

'Do it again.'

'We'd be in the hedge.' (PAUSE). 'Let's double de-clutch, Mildred.'

'No . . . I . . . please. Be patient with me. I may later.'

'That's right. Keep yourself in a state of independent front-wheel suspension – a disadvantage of which is that the unsprung weight of the heavy beam axle is inconsistent with good road-holding.'

'I loved the way you said that.'

'Did you? You know you wouldn't look too bad if you used a bit more anti-freeze.'

'Do another double bend.'

'It's kinky.'

'It's not. I like other things.'

'Such as?'

'I don't like to say it.'

'Go on.'

(COYLY) 'I like it when you move the gear lever and close the switch, thus energising the solenoid and causing the left hand side of the piston to be exposed to the partial vacuum in the reservoir.'

'You've been driven by other men.'

'You've driven other women.'

'It's not the same thing.'

'Why are you stopping? I'm not going to a lay-by with a strange man.'

'I'm not stopping.'

'What are you doing?'

'Reversing.'

'Pervert.'

My mother and father were very proud and said that they'd enjoyed it. Thirty years later, my mother told me that she had at last realised that it was risqué!

Encouraged by my success, Peter Tinniswood sent in a sketch which was also accepted, and by the beginning of the second series he had left the *Sheffield Star*, I had left the *St Pancras Chronicle*, and we had rented a small, appallingly furnished flat in Narcissus(!) Road in West Hampstead.

Each week we rang Ned Sherrin with two ideas. Each week he said he liked one and wasn't interested in the other. Each week we wrote up both ideas and sent them by taxi. Each week Ned used the one he hadn't been interested in, and didn't use the one he'd liked the sound of. We were paid by the minute for any item that was used, and something of ours got into the show almost every week. We didn't earn enough to move out of our horrendous little flat, but we were able to contemplate unheard of luxuries like holidays.

I wouldn't describe either Peter or me as a naturally political being. Our particular sense of humour, along with the diffidence which made us feel like junior partners, led us away from the major issues of the day towards minor, less expected targets. We both had a strong left-wing bias, however, and much later, in 1966, we were at Hampstead Town Hall cheering with the great crowd when the Home Secretary, Henry Brooke, lost his seat in the General Election, a loss which was attributed in no small part to *TW3*'s brilliantly savage attack on him in the form of *This Is Your Life*, in which the guests were all people badly affected by his decisions, or the lack of them, as Home Secretary.

On Saturdays when Spurs were at home we would go to White Hart Lane, usually with Charles, have a few drinks at the Old Angel on Highgate Hill, and be on parade in front of our set in time to revel in our part in this prestigious show.

Among the other writers were Willis Hall and Keith Waterhouse – both vastly experienced and possessed of a maturity of style that our raw partnership couldn't emulate – Caryl Brahms, Herbert Kretzmer, Peter Lewis and Peter Dobereiner and, in company with David Nathan, the great Dennis Potter, who would become the most famous playwright in British television's golden age.

It was tremendously exciting, after all the years without reward, to make one's living as part of a team of such quality. Some of the cast were brilliant too, particularly Roy Kinnear, broad and bumbling, the only true actor in the team, and Willie Rushton, larger than life as his wonderful self, and Millicent Martin, who was very funny in sketches with Roy as well as singing the opening song brilliantly.

What was most exciting about the show, in retrospect, was its immediacy, although we took this for granted at the time, not having experience of any other way of working in television.

Once we had an idea on a Saturday morning and it was written, delivered, rehearsed, learnt, performed and transmitted that day. It was exhilarating. If I had submitted the idea today, I'd need two planning meetings, two script editors, a treatment, seven drafts of the script and three years later I'd be told that the idea had dated. Sometimes a taxi would arrive in Narcissus Road on a Saturday evening just for a couple of one liners, which would go out to the nation three hours later before anyone realised how bad they were.

We learnt a painful lesson with one of our sketches, a two-hander about opinion polls for Roy Kinnear and Millicent Martin. Roy's first line was 'I hardened against the Labour party during the night.' Collapse of studio audience, who then remained silent, searching for further double entendres, throughout our thoughtful piece about the excessive influence of opinion polls. You can't start with sex and then go on to politics. It has to be the other way round, as indeed it usually is with politicians.

Peter and I didn't go to any of the shows, although I dimly remember one end of series party, but I think that was for one of the sequels, not *TW3*. I had attributed this to our diffidence, but now I've read, in *That Was Satire, That Was*, a very thorough and entertaining tour of the satire boom by Humphrey Carpenter, that none of the writers went, and for a very simple reason. They weren't invited. A great strength of the show was that the writers weren't drawn from 'Showbiz' but almost entirely from journalism, although of course many of us transferred to 'Showbiz' as a result. I think it would have been nice to have been invited though.

One show I did occasionally attend was a Saturday morning radio programme, presented by David Frost, called *Frost At The Phonograph*. Everybody chipped in and there was a party-like atmosphere in the studio, which usually meant that the listeners felt excluded. Once I told David that I wouldn't be in the following week as I was visiting my parents. On a previous show I'd written a gag about the journalist, writer and professional sentimentalist Godfrey Winn, who had teamed up with Semprini to give a show of prose and music. 'Godfrey Winn and Semprini go together like tripe and onions,' I wrote. 'Semprini is of course the onions.' When I told my mother this, she said, 'You shouldn't make jokes about people like Godfrey Winn. They're very influential.' Unwisely, I related this to David.

The following Saturday I sat there with my mother – my father made himself busy, most programmes embarrassed him by this time – and, early in the programme, David said, 'We have a letter here from eight-year-old David Nobbs from Orpington, and he writes, "How do hedgehogs make love?" Very carefully, David, and so should you.' This was bad enough, but later I heard, 'And here's another letter from eight-year-old David Nobbs from Orpington. "I want to be a writer when I grow up. Have you any advice?' Yes, David. Don't write jokes about people like Godfrey Winn. They're very influential.' My mother went white and said, 'You told him!' and I felt torn between shame at betraying her confidence and shame at trusting David Frost.

The mention of making love very carefully reminds me of the time my mother found a French letter in my jacket pocket. She was upset and angry. There was nothing I could say in mitigation. Then she softened. 'Well at least it wasn't used,' she said.

Often I watched *TW3* with Mary. Our relationship was continuing although I don't think we were aware in the early days that it would lead to a real commitment.

Sometimes I went to Orpington to spend the weekend with my parents. They had no idea of the existence of Mary. How secretive I was, how compartmentalised my life. Many other people were just the same, though, in those days right at the beginning of what would be dubbed 'The Permissive Society'.

I was deeply embarrassed when I watched *TW3*'s *Which* Report on religion with my parents. This item, written by Robert Gillespie and Charles Lewsen, was a parody of a consumer guide – 'Of the dozens of products on the market we investigated the following six: Judaism, the Roman Catholic Church, the Protestant Church, Islam, Buddhism and Communism.' They applied three basic tests: a) What do you put into it? b) What do you get out of it? c) How much does it cost?

The BBC received a record 246 complaints about this sketch, but my parents admired it. My father in particular relished its wit and accuracy and laughed heartily. 'Don't be embarrassed,' he said. 'It was very witty and had a lot of truth. I wish you'd written it.' Not for the first time, I'd under-estimated my parents' breadth of understanding and sympathy.

I'm one of the few people who doesn't remember what he was doing when he heard that President Kennedy had been assassinated, but I was visiting my parents on the Saturday and I was very worried about what

TW3 would do, and whether the satire would seem heartless. In the event they mounted a gushing tribute. This made me deeply uneasy. I can't pretend that I had some kind of prescience about the character defects that were soon to be revealed. I just felt that satirists can't afford to gush. It's the role of the satirist to satirise, and to be silent where satire is deemed to be inappropriate. From that moment onwards, we looked as if we were all playing at being vicious.

The Motoring Correspondent of the *Sunday Express* threatened to sue *TW3* over a sketch Peter and I had written:

> This is a cut-away diagram of the working parts of the B.M.C. – The British Motoring Correspondent. (POINTS TO DIAGRAM OF A MAN) I drove this correspondent hard for three hours – and all I got out of it was a load of sycophantic regurgitated company hand-outs.
>
> It had the traditional gear – deerstalker hat and sheepskin jacket – but I did notice that the knees seemed a trifle worn. This can be explained by excessive crawling on them, to cadge free facility trips from the motor companies.
>
> Fuel consumption was reasonably economical – 15 gin and tonics per published paragraph – and it had a fairly satisfactory liquor-holding capacity.

You get the point. Ned asked us if we would write a letter denying that we had based our piece on this particular correspondent. We had never even heard of him, so our reply went something like this:

> We would like to assure the motoring correspondent of the *Sunday Express* that we have never read his column or indeed the newspaper in which it appears. Our aim in 'Mental Fatigue' was to create a fictional motoring correspondent who was lazy, greedy, corrupt and drunken, and we deeply regret if he has taken this personally.

We heard no more.

*

In November, 1963, during the run of the second series, the government announced that the programme would stop at the end of the year, because 1964 was an election year. There were many enemies of *TW3* in the BBC, a few controversial items had needed to be defended, and it's clear that this was an excuse, and a pretty thin one. That it shouldn't be on during an election campaign was fair enough, but during the whole of an election year? It was ridiculous, and Ned Sherrin asked us to write a piece about it. This we did, and it announced the cancellation, for various spurious reasons, of *Andy Pandy*, the *Weather Forecast, Victor Sylvester's Dancing Club, Sportsview*, the *Black and White Minstrel Show, Doctor Kildare* and the Welsh Programme *Yn Ein Barn Ni*. It was a great success at the time, but it reads pretty feebly now, and I will spare you it.

Eventually, a sequel to *TW3* emerged. It was called *Not So Much A Programme, More A Way Of Life*, and contained more interludes of chat between the sketches. This doomed it to a much slower pace and a much more ponderous feel than *TW3*. David began by sharing the role of front man with Willie Rushton and P.J. Kavanagh. However, this didn't really work, and soon Frost was back on his own. He's a man born to host a show. I wouldn't be surprised to learn that his first words were, 'Good evening and welcome.'

Peter and I continued to work on NSMAP – there's a doomed acronym for you – and we were still hacking away at the joke face in the final Sherrin satire show, *BBC 3*, which was hosted not by Frost but by Robert Robinson. This gave the impression that satire had become respectable.

Ned is reported to have regretted the title, *BBC 3*. It certainly didn't succeed with Auntie Louie. 'We can't get BBC 3 on our set,' she told me.

It was probably just as well that she couldn't, because, on 13 November, 1965, Kenneth Tynan became the first person to say 'fuck' on television. If he'd known how many times it would come to be used, in lazy sloppy sit-coms, without any semblance of wit, he might have hesitated.

Of all the things that Peter and I wrote, three little filmlets gave me most pleasure. These were directed by John Duncan, OWMA (of whom more anon). There was a sweet little film about pantomime horses out to pasture in the summer, a parody of Cowes and Henley called Royal Darts Week, and a film, during the week when an eagle called Goldie escaped from London Zoo, about a keeper escaping and refusing to come down from a tree.

Only one of our sketches ever really flopped, and that was the very last one – we were mocking Lord Willis, a writer who did a great deal for writers, so I think we deserved it. Because this was the last show, Robert Robinson gave us all verbal credits. After our thin little piece had finished, he announced – a touch acidly, I thought – 'That piece was penned by David Nobbs and Peter Tinniswood.' It was a sad ending to more than three years of exciting writing.

During those heady days of Satire, I met Peter Cook for the first time at the Establishment Club in Greek Street, Soho. The club, Peter's brain-child, was of course really the Anti-Establishment Club. I liked the fact that it was on premises that had previously been the Club Tropicana. Peter invited me to attend a satirical improvisation session upstairs. Peter Lewis and John Bird were also there. I was utterly over-awed by my hero, and by the sheer pace of his invention, and said hardly a thing. However, I did have two sketches in the next show at the Establishment. One, an absurdist parody of a quiz show, failed to take off, though Peter loved it. The other, a monologue that began, 'How do? My name is God, and I'm here tonight because I'm omnipresent' did make a few amusing points about the worship of Mammon.

I remember the Establishment Club as being more like a small theatre than a club. It escaped the tawdriness of Soho, but at some cost in atmosphere, I felt.

In the bar before the show one evening I chatted to a very pretty Hooray Henrietta, who was so impressed when I said I had material in the show that I felt she would have acceded to any request I might make, not that I had any intention of making any. She and her whole family walked out during John Bird's performance of my monologue and she gave me a fierce glare as she departed. That's the trouble with satire. If it's truly successful, the whole audience will walk out, unless you're preaching to the converted, which is pretty pointless.

I'm certain that I didn't live up to Peter Cook's hopes, and in any case there was very little scope for writers other than writer-performers in the world of Peter Cook. My involvement with him proved short-lived.

Not so my involvement with Frost. After *BBC 3*, David moved on to *The Frost Report*, produced by Jimmy Gilbert, OWMA. There was a great team of writers on this also. Tony Jay would send us a witty and thoughtful essay on the subject of the week, and we would create our little bits with scant relevance to his thesis. The sketches starred John Cleese, Ronnie Barker and Ronnie Corbett. The show sparked *Frost On Sunday* and, ultimately, *The Two Ronnies*. It was all seamless. I went from *TW3* to *The Two Ronnies* without ever having to seek the work.

Peter didn't want to continue in the Frost world, but I was commissioned to write for the shows David did at Rediffusion. Commissioned! I had regular work, albeit only as a jobbing writer.

Suddenly there was Frost almost every night. These programmes had the inspired titles of *Frost on Wednesday*, *Frost on Thursday*, *Frost on Friday* and *Frost on Sunday*. The first three were chat shows of a kind, but the word 'chat' doesn't even hint at the vitriol Frost could aspire to at times. Various writers were assigned to different days, and it was our job to create one-liners which David could introduce at the top of the show or in his introductions to his guests. I was given Thursdays, with two other writers, Peter Vincent and David McKellar. We became known as McVinnob. We would fire ideas at each other all day, then type them up and hand them to David, who would say, 'Super'. Some nights he would use nothing.

However, the trouble with writing gags for David was not so much the fear that he wouldn't use them as the fear that he would. We were satirists trying to be clever and naturally a lot of our thoughts were vicious and pejorative. We included them to show that we'd been working, even though they were, we thought, unusable. But nothing was unusable to David, who knew no fear and had no shame. Barry Cryer wrote a line about Sir Cyril Black, MP, a member of the hang 'em and flog 'em brigade. David introduced him with Barry's joke. 'And now,' he intoned in his intense, nasal voice, '. . . Sir Cyril, a man who listens to the Speaking Clock just to hear the words "at the third stroke".' It wasn't a line to put Sir Cyril at his ease and lull him into indiscretion.

David banged his jokes out with manic intensity. I wrote one about American Starfighter planes, which had been crashing in such numbers that they had all been grounded. 'Good evening,' barked David at the top of the show. 'Since the American Starfighter planes were grounded on Monday, only five have crashed.' So serious was he that the audience took it seriously. There wasn't a titter, just the silence of a whole audience of three hundred people thinking, 'That's interesting, isn't it, mother?'

David's presentation as a front man has serious limitations – it's relentlessly one-tone. There is no light and shade. There are no quiet moments. It shouldn't work, but it does, and when it's your jokes he's delivering you begin to be quite fond of it. He carries you with him on his torrent of words. His extraordinary, grating, aggressively classless accent actually captivates me, in a strange love-hate compulsion.

In the evenings, after our work was done, Peter Vincent and David McKellar and I would stand in the hospitality room and help to entertain the guests. The visiting celebrities must have had very little interest in this giggle of comedy writers making inane conversation, but only two, Hermione Gingold and Shelley Berman, were ever less than charming to me. George Brown, the Labour minister, was as charming as a newt, and two of my very favourite actors, Paul Newman, small but beautifully formed, and Peter Ustinov, large but beautifully spoken, were courtesy personified.

We would spend the evening sipping a brandy and apple juice concoction created by our hospitality room barman, Eric, and watching the show – or at least part of it. Sometimes it was just too embarrassing. Ian Davidson, who I think was script editor for all the shows, claimed that there was an embarrassment order in which people would leave the room, like a pecking order in hens, when David was being particularly shameless. Ian said that he was always the first to leave, but I wasn't far behind. We would stand in the corridor, sipping Eric's specials, and every so often the door would open and another embarrassed writer would slip out. After the show we would slip back in again and sip more specials; it was all slipping and sipping. David would come up to us and ask our opinion on the show and none of us would admit that we spent most of our time in the corridor. We didn't need to as these inquests were not thorough. The conversation would go:

David: 'Super show?'
Us: 'Super.'
David: 'Super.'

The most embarrassing show of all for us was David's famous demolition of Emil Savundra, the founder and mastermind of the Fire, Auto and Marine Insurance Company, which had collapsed. It was a riveting programme and Savundra deserved what he got, but so confident had he been of his ability to outwit David that he'd brought his wife and young daughter to the hospitality room to witness it. McVinnob were aware of this. Most people in the room weren't. Cries of 'Get him, David' and 'Nail the bastard' rang out. The corridor beckoned.

One of the shows was broadcast live from the foyer of the Aldwych Theatre after the first night of *US*, Peter Brook's powerful play about the Vietnam war. The play, a passionate critique of American imperialism, ended with the cast as refugees wandering blindly into the auditorium with paper bags over their heads. The idea was that the audience would help them. None of the celebrity audience moved a muscle as the actors blundered about. 'You just don't give a damn, do you?' shouted one actor. 'We know you're actors, darlings,' said Kenneth Tynan sweetly. Collapse of cheap gesture. I was sorry for the actors, who escaped having egg on their faces only by having paper bags on their faces. But I hope the ending was removed from subsequent performances. It was unworthy of a great production. The audience must be trusted to get the message. They can't be forced to prove it.

*

Frost on Sunday was a sketch show, again with Ronnie Barker and Ronnie Corbett and John Cleese. The writing team was formidable, and we all used to gather in a church hall to throw ideas around. The other two-thirds of McVinnob were there, plus Ian Davidson, Graham Chapman, John Cleese, Eric Idle, Michael Palin and Terry Jones. You will no doubt have recognised that I was privileged to sit round a table with the five men who, augmented only by the cartoonist Terry Gilliam, would later become *Monty Python's Flying Circus*. Did I note that they seemed like a future group? Well, not particularly, but they did share a wild, irreverent, surreal sense of humour. It was a joy to sit at that table. The repartee was brilliant and if ever there was a dull moment Terry Jones would enliven it by falling backwards off his chair in spectacular style.

Sadly, I can remember only one example from all that repartee. Somebody, improvising, began, 'The police are working on the theory . . .' and John Cleese interrupted with '. . . that they have been outwitted by the criminals.' Many a true word, etcetera.

I get asked a lot of awkward questions about what people are like, but I never mind when they ask, 'Is Michael Palin really as nice as he seems?' They're so pleased when I say that he is. Thank goodness someone is, in this vale of disillusionment. Terry Jones is the height of amiability too, but the only Python I saw purely socially, and that only rarely, was Graham Chapman.

Graham was wild, like me at parties in Sheffield but more so. When the BBC invited 'Mr and Mrs Chapman' to a reception to celebrate *The Frost Report* winning the Golden Rose at Montreux, Graham brought his boyfriend, looking as avant-garde and disreputable as possible, and wearing a name tag, 'Mrs Chapman'. I offered Graham a drink in the BBC Television Centre bar, and he said, 'Three pints, please', explaining that he drank three times as fast as everybody else.

I made the occasional contribution to these sessions, but they weren't really my bag. So many of the people were performers. Professionally I'm a solitary being. When I have a blank sheet of paper in front of me, my brain becomes excited and all things seem possible.

There was a time, in the middle of all these Frost programmes, when staleness set in and David called a meeting at his house. There was no doubt that it was a crisis meeting, but it was never called a crisis meeting. We all sat round a vast circular table, David came in, sat down, looked at us all gravely, even sorrowfully, and said, 'Thank you all for some absolutely super shows. We're meeting today to consider how we can make them even more absolutely super still.'

At the end of the final series of *The Frost Report*, David had taken over the Battersea Fun Fair for a party. This was flashy if you didn't like him, generous if you did. It was fun. Mary and I actually went on the Big Dipper while drinking a glass of wine. It didn't travel.

Mary and I went to two more of David's amazing parties. For one, he hired Alexandra Palace, and again there was a funfair. It was a vast, star-studded occasion and the guests included a very frail Judy Garland just weeks before her death. At some stage, and already with a few drinks under my belt, I had a misfortune with the zip of my trousers. These things happen to the best of us. I wandered through the gathering of the high and mighty, holding my trousers together, and approached a lady, who, though more than somewhat grand, looked to have a kind face. 'Do you happen to have a safety pin upon your person?' I enquired. It gives me no pleasure to relate that Barbara Cartland was not helpful.

At some stage my flies must have been secured. No doubt a friendly fairground operator came to the rescue. Anyway, there Mary and I were the next day, on the front page of the *Evening Standard*, in a dodgem car. The caption didn't mention us because there were far-better-known people in some of the other cars – Peter Cook and Dudley Moore, the Bishop of Southwark and – the reason for the picture making the front page – Stirling Moss.

The other great Frosticular bash was a sit-down meal at the White City, where I had seen the great Arthur Wint run the 440. This party had a somewhat sadistic streak. I had to run the Olympic steeplechase course between starter and main course, and consume a plate of cornflakes placed on top of the water jump.

*

David once rang me to say, 'Super to hear you. I'm doing some of your bofferoonies on the *Billy Cotton Band Show*. Do you want to be paid in money or champagne?' Not a difficult choice. A man has some style. I received a bottle of vintage Krug, and I didn't have to send my agent ten per cent. Many people would have just done the bofferoonies and hoped I wasn't watching. A bofferoony, incidentally, was David's word for a gag.

I can't conclude my memories of life with Frost without mentioning my breakfast with him. David Frost's celebrity breakfasts were famous. Prime Ministers and Archbishops valued the invitation. Imagine my pride when I was invited to breakfast with him alone. He had a proposition to put to me.

His Spanish housekeeper invited me into his house in Kensington and I sat examining my surroundings. This was my third visit. I'd been to the crisis meeting and also to a charming end of series party in the sitting room on the first floor. His house was pleasant, not unstylish in a rather modern way which contrasted quite successfully with its period exterior, but it was curiously impersonal, as if he'd rung an interior decorator and said, 'Furnish and decorate a house for me, please.'

After I'd waited for several minutes, his housekeeper informed me that David had just received a very important phone call from America. Would I mind breakfasting even more alone than expected? He would put the proposition to me on the way to the studio.

I minded very much, but what could I do? And what studio? I wasn't going to any studio.

I had a very leisurely breakfast, then David rushed in, said, 'Super to see you. Super,' and bundled me into his Rolls, which he proceeded to double park in the King's Road while he dashed into a wine merchant's to order wine for a party that evening. I hadn't been invited.

We set off again, towards a hideous tower block just north of the North Circular in Stonebridge Park, an area of North-West London that makes Neasden look glamorous.

At last the proposition came.

'I've got a book about Australian sportswomen. It needs some bofferoonies. Would you be interested in putting some bofferoonies in to jazz it up?'

'No.'

We had arrived. David walked into the studios. It took me three buses to get home.

Nice sausages, though.

9 NOBBS AND TINNISWOOD

THE SAD THING about the so-called Satire Boom is that it was so built up in the media that its total demise became inevitable. There should always be some outlet for topical satirical comedy. There is always a need to call our masters to account. It should be a tradition, not a trend. However, we live in a society dominated by trendiness and scornful of tradition, so Satire had to go, lock, stock and smoking barrel.

As Satire sank slowly into the sea, Peter and I were asked to write a situation comedy for Lance Percival. This was a wonderful opportunity, but Ned Sherrin warned us that a sit-com was a very different animal from a satirical sketch. Loftily, we felt that we didn't need this advice.

Our brief was that Lance was playing a young man – himself, in essence – who was footloose and fancy free. He could go anywhere, do anything. There would be no other regular characters. It's easy to see now that this was a recipe for disaster. It removed, before we even started, all possibility of the three great necessities for situation comedy – situation, conflict and character. Also, it was based on a complete misreading of Lance's not inconsiderable talent.

Lance had excelled on *TW3*, mixing genial improvised calypsos with

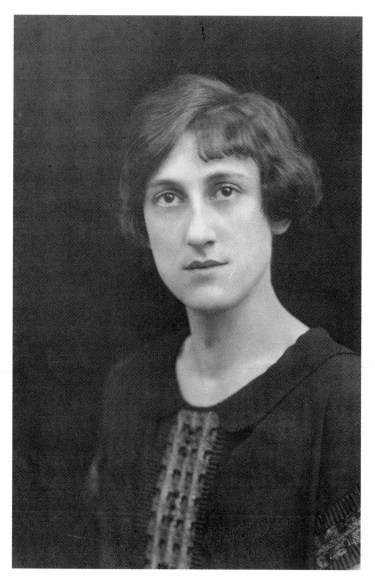

My Mother.

My mother at eighty.

My father in his early teaching days.

My father in his later years at the City of London School.

razor-sharp caricature where he was at his best, like a cartoon on legs. His Field Marshal Montgomery was a joy. I'd seen Monty do it himself, at Marlborough. He was good, but he wasn't as good as Lance. I think now that Lance could have played a whole ship of fools, but as himself, with that toothy grin which condemned him to being at least slightly vacuous and goofy, and without strong, regular supporting characters, he didn't stand a chance. Any possibility of stardom sank slowly into the sea, along with Satire.

It wasn't primarily our fault – we were presented with the concept, a concept that would have needed a Tati or a Chaplin, and would have been difficult even then, and we hadn't the clout to argue – but we weren't shrewd enough to see the dangers. I think we should have done better for Lance, and I feel very sad about it.

Our producer for *Lance At Large* was the legendary Dennis Main Wilson. I've been told, of about sixty-three people, that they were the original 'legend in his own lunchtime'. Dennis must have been at the top of the short list.

With his erect back and clipped speech he might have passed for a military man, had it not been for his enthusiasm and his two pairs of glasses. One pair sat on the bridge of his nose, the other pair – one containing beer, the other whisky – were in his hands. He was short, lined and dapper. He sailed on a tide of enthusiasm and alcohol, and was enormous fun to work with, but he didn't have a shred of caution in him, and we needed caution badly.

Our first script was well received, our second less so. Lance came in his Jaguar to discuss it. What must he have felt when he saw our spectacularly horrid flat and drank our milky coffee with skin floating on the top? He must have wondered if these two plonkers would destroy his career.

Nobody hung about in those days. We were into production before all the scripts were written. Peter and I visited Dennis's office and as we walked in the door he barked, 'The very men. Ayrshires or Black and White Friesians?'

We gawped.

'The cows that block the road in episode one. I'm on to the farmer now. Do you want Ayrshires or Black and White Friesians?'

Just cows, we thought. Dennis told us, when he came off the phone, that every detail counted, and of course he was right.

He took us under his wing and we sailed in the wake of his energy. He took us to a nightclub in Shepherd's Bush – sounds like a contradiction in terms – and bawled above the music, 'David, Peter, young minds, need to know, Christianity, bum steer?' On another occasion he asked us, 'Need to keep in touch, you're young, tell me, what books should I read?'

After *Lance At Large* I didn't see Dennis for ten years, but one day I walked into the BBC bar and there he was, a little thinner, a little more lined, beer in right hand, whisky in left – or was it the other way about? – looking as if he'd been standing there for all those ten years. A gleam came into his eyes as he saw me. He strode towards me. 'I read them,' he said.

Not long after that I came across him again and fell into drinking with him, as one did. I regret to say that he took off his jacket and attacked me, and we had to be separated. It's the nearest that I've come to a fight in my adult life. Dennis had said, 'My son doesn't want to join the BBC. Bring them up, train them, and what do you get? Betrayal.' I said, 'Dennis, you're being over-emotional. You can't run another person's life.' 'Nobody accuses me of being over-emotional,' he shouted.

One day, many years after *Lance At Large*, I met Dennis in a BBC corridor. 'The very man!' he said. 'New show. Terrific. Ground-breaking. Three minutes too long. Too close to it. Need a new pair of eyes.' He led me into an editing suite, and I watched his 'terrific, ground-breaking' show. He was often over-enthusiastic but not this time. It was the first episode of *Till Death Us Do Part* by the wonderful Johnny 'Real Writers don't have Briefcases' Speight.

'You don't need the scene in the estate agent's,' I said. 'It weakens the marvellous claustrophobic feel of Alf's world.'

'Done,' said Dennis. 'Cut. Gone. Thank you.'

That was how it was done, in the old days.

*

The transmission of *Lance At Large* was deeply embarrassing. The reviews were actually not too bad, but the public can be very blunt about TV, as if it's their property because it comes into their homes. 'What went wrong with your programme?' barked a forthright cousin twice removed, and at that moment I could have wished her three times removed. I skulked round West Hampstead, imagining that everyone was saying, 'That's the sap who wrote *Lance At Large*.' What must it have been like for Lance?

Peter and I struggled to become natural collaborators, but it wasn't in us. We were commissioned by Sid Colin, author of *On The House* and other hits, to write a satire (oh dear) on British holiday resorts seen as prison camps from which people had to escape. It was called *Mutiny At Bella Vista*. When he was Head of Comedy at the BBC Frank Muir said, 'God save me from good ideas,' and I know what he meant. This idea sounded good, though it doesn't now, but it was a straitjacket. It prohibited all surprise.

A much happier collaboration was *The Signalbox of Grandpa Hudson*. This was based on one of the plays I'd written in Lymington Road, one of those plays that had worried Michael Codron. Peter was able to identify its strengths and weaknesses and instigate an immensely effective rewrite. Thus strengthened, it was bought by ATV's prestigious *Armchair Theatre*. It was an odd-ball comedy, but it worked, and it proved an enormous boost to both of us. The cast included Ian McShane; Susan Farmer, who was married to him at the time; John Woodvine; a well-known old music hall comedian called Billy Russell; and Margery Withers.

John Woodvine was particularly dry and funny as a struggling taxidermist who specialised in dodos and great bustards. 'Is it my fault if all my species are going extinct on me?' he enquired. He told us that he hoped this role would lead to a lot more comedy parts, but it didn't really happen. His distinguished career has been largely in serious roles.

The main thrust of the play was that Grandpa Hudson, the Billy Russell character, was a railway fanatic, and people could only move from one part of the house to another when signalled. Talk about realism!

The recording took place over two hours of an evening at Teddington. A few years earlier it would have been done live. A few years later it would have been rehearsed and recorded scene by scene over two days. Nowadays it would probably be filmed on location over two weeks. Television has become steadily more professional, and steadily less spontaneous.

For this play we had our first ever script editor, Norman Bognor, later to become a best-selling novelist, damn him, not that I'm a jealous person.

The role of script editor in those days was less than it is today. A few suggested cuts, one or two proposed refinements, that was all. We sat proudly beside Norman in the control box as our piece sprang to life on the many screens all around us. Towards the end poor old Billy Russell, very funny but struggling with the lines, jumped two pages, cutting out much of the denouement.

To our astonishment Norman Bognor turned to us and said, 'Excellent. I don't think the cut mattered too much, do you?' We were too shocked to speak.

'Pity about the cut,' came the elegant, cultured voice of Basil Coleman, the director. 'We'll have to go again, Norman. It ruins the whole sense of the scene.'

'Oh yes,' said Norman, turning not a hair. 'It's absolutely essential.' Peter and I were far too relieved to be even remotely upset by this dramatic volte-face.

Peter and I achieved two other distinctions. We wrote the first comedy series ever to be on BBC Radio's Third Programme. We also wrote the last comedy series ever to be on BBC Radio's Third Programme. You've guessed it. It was the same one.

Hardluck Hall – shades of my beloved Thomas Love Peacock – was satirical. The names of some of the characters – Priscilla Houseproud, Sir Sidney Servall, Tom Ology, Robin Robot, Doreen Nylon – fill me with dismay now, but it was better than it sounds, exploited radio techniques inventively, and was great fun to do. A splendid cast, including Valentine Dyall, Hugh Burden and Stephen Moore, seemed to enjoy it hugely. Peter, of course, went on to do a lot of marvellous radio work. The producer, Richard Thomas, emigrated to New Zealand, but I don't think it was as a direct result of the series.

Peter and I didn't just write together and live together (in the platonic sense, folks) and watch Spurs and *Z Cars* together. We went on holidays together, we even had dysentery together. It was in Venice. Peter, the trendsetter, got it first. I, the copy-cat, soon felt queasy, and went to a café round the corner, where I said, in my strained Italian, to the fury of the lady of the house, 'I'll have the minestrone soup, and then order something else if I still feel all right after that.' Her reply was somewhat strained too.

Peter and I both lost a stone in less than a week, and I couldn't eat sardines for ten years.

We went back to Venice later, this time with Mary. With the money we'd made from *Lance At Large*, we were able at last to travel in something resembling style – first-class train, Rhine steamer and Europabus. We were leaving behind a fairly spectacular failure, but we ate fine meals and smoked large cigars and felt as if we had begun to make it.

In St Moritz we listened to a passionate argument between a group of Swiss men in a bar. I assumed it was a deep philosophical or political debate, but Peter, who spoke German, told us that they were discussing the best way to skin a tomato. Sometimes, it's better not to understand.

Mary had to fly home from Venice. The children were returning from boarding school (paid for by her ex-in-laws). This time Venice had been wonderful, and I was so very sad when she went.

The three of us also went to Denmark, where Peter ordered drinks in his fluent German in a bar near the border. As we left, the barmaid heard us talking in English, chased us down the street, and said, 'Come back. I thought you were German. I've over-charged you terribly.'

I referred earlier to the great relief I experienced in a public convenience in the Outer Hebrides. Peter and I had met the brother of the Lord Mayor of London in a pub in a tiny village on the island of Harris. He suffered from sleeping sickness and the Lord Mayor had banished him to this spot for the year of his Mayoralty, in order to avoid potential embarrassment. We drank three pints, and suddenly there was the last bus, and we didn't have time to go back in to relieve ourselves.

There are no trees in the Hebrides. The passengers all looked like fierce Protestants, and neither of us dared desecrate their homeland in full view before we boarded. Oh, the time it took for that bus to wind down to the little town of Tarbert. At one stage it took ten minutes to get a goat into the boot. The agony was appalling.

Occasionally we went on canal trips with Charles and Shirley – joyous, gentle times on their narrow boat. We saw Britain from a different angle and met wonderfully friendly people in canal-side pubs, but how I dreaded returning to that mean little flat in mean little Narcissus Road. The money from *Lance At Large* had been spent. The future was uncertain.

Then Peter and I had a vision of such fame and fortune that we would never need to live in mean little flats again. Two men offered us a most intriguing proposition. One of them was called Ken Levison. The other wasn't. Memory is selective.

We were commissioned, along with many others, to write a visual script, with no dialogue, for Fernandel, the legendary French comedian of international fame. The Anglo-French project, financed by Raymond Coty, was to be a worldwide silent series.

The other writers, including people far more experienced than us, struggled. We thrived on it. We revelled in our freedom from what is, paradoxically, the greatest strength of us both – our dialogue.

Only three scripts were accepted, and two of those were ours. Filming began on one of them. I flew over to Paris, stayed on the Champs-Elysées, ate oysters at Pruniers, sat in a darkened studio alongside Fernandel and Raymond Coty, and watched the rushes. I should think it's the worst experience anybody's had with rushes since Moses.

Fernandel should have been arrested for mugging. The direction proclaimed, 'A joke is coming, folks, and it's going to be really funny. Here it is. I say, that was pretty rib-tickling, wasn't it?' The lights came up, and the room was horribly silent. We all trooped out. Nobody spoke to me, but then nobody spoke to anybody else either. The series was cancelled that day.

The fact that I got oyster poisoning, and couldn't eat solid food for a month, only added to the gloom. I had to use my bag on the plane. The humiliation! I longed to hold up a sign that said, 'This is not air sickness, it's oyster poisoning. I am an experienced gourmet, wit and traveller.'

It was the end of the road for Peter and me. Starting a series without dialogue had brought home to us both the difficulty we had with dialogue in collaboration. We each had very distinct prose styles. Peter's, in particular, was wonderfully unique. He felt that to write together, except on silent films, involved too much sacrifice, too much compromise. I would try further collaborations, but I too would come to the same conclusion, a few years later. I am my own man, for better or for worse.

Besides, this was a disappointment too far. To have all that snatched from us – the collaboration couldn't take it.

We had lived in each other's pockets for too long. We had irritated each other considerably. Now we would be free to preserve our friendship and admire each other's work from afar.

That was the idea, anyway. It didn't work out quite like that.

10 Last Comedy Writer Before the M1

WHILE I WAS still sharing a flat with Peter, I heard from my old friend Geoffrey Strachan, now with Methuen, that they had accepted *The Itinerant Lodger* for publication.

This was a rare moment of pure joy, and I use the word 'pure' advisedly. This was nothing to do with money, or with fame. This struck at the very essence of what a writer is. One letter from a publisher, and I was no longer a pathetic, struggling figure, a fantasist. I was a writer.

The version Geoffrey saw had changed somewhat. I had a new agent, David Conyers having had another nervous breakdown. Jonathan Clowes had become an agent because a friend of his, Henry Chapman, had written a play for Joan Littlewood at Stratford East – an excellent play which I had seen, as it happened – and didn't feel that his agent had done him any favours. Jonathan asked him what an agent should do, and what his agent did, decided he could do better and became an agent himself. Now – probably because Jonathan was a friend of David Conyers, although neither of us can quite remember – he became my agent too. It was the best move of my professional life.

Jonathan liked *The Itinerant Lodger* but felt that it needed a bit of work. I would go round to his house in Torriano Avenue in Kentish Town to eat home-made soup – tinned ravioli wasn't nourishing my brain – and to discuss the rewrites chapter by chapter.

Torriano Avenue is a very short road, but I have connections with two houses in it. William's mother, Mollie, lived there for a while, in a supremely elegant cottage, after the death of her second husband. I house-minded for her once or twice. Did I mind house-minding? I loved it. I still hoped that one day I might cease to be a struggling writer and have an elegant home of my own.

I enjoyed every moment of my time with Geoffrey as he too made his detailed comments about my manuscript. I have never managed to send in a manuscript that didn't need improving, and I've always enjoyed the process of working with an editor on my text. We have a common aim – to improve the book. And Geoffrey, gentle cultured Geoffrey with such a fine mind, was the best possible person to work with.

Another great moment was the arrival of the proof copy. There it was, in print, my creation. The thrill of that moment is as great today as it ever was, and, if it should ever not be, it will be time to stop.

The actual publication day was something of an anti-climax. The traffic roared as if nothing special had happened. The commuters scurried to the tube stations utterly oblivious of my existence. How could it ever come to pass that anybody would buy my book?

That morning I bought the *Daily Telegraph* and found – oh joy of joys – that it was reviewed. It was 2 September, 1965. My joy didn't last long. Robert Baldick wrote:

> Every other page is graced with a send-up of the judiciary, a take-off of the clergy or a knock-down of the police, all executed in the well-tried manner familiar to the fireside viewer.
>
> The victim of these Establishment villains, the lodger of the title, is a pathetic, incompetent creature called Fletcher, Cooper, Simpson or whatever, who changes his name almost as often as his digs and his job.

As a bus-conductor, Fletcher insists on giving free rides to all and sundry, and is sacked. As a would-be postman, Cooper works out a points system to ensure a fairer distribution of mail, and is committed to an asylum. Simpson is arrested and convicted of a grotesque charge of uttering obscene documents, while Baker is hounded into bed by his landlady and has to organise the funeral of a fellow-lodger who has been lying dead upstairs for 17 years.

By rights this succession of comic incidents should induce a state of delicious hilarity. It wore me down, I fear, into a profound depression.

And this was the paper my mother read. Never mind Robert Baldick's profound depression, what about mine? It lasted all morning, until lunchtime, when a man rang from Lisbon to buy the film rights, on the strength of Robert Baldick's review. Such is showbiz.

Dennis Lewiston was a film cameraman who wished to become a director, and he felt that this might be his vehicle. He was happy for me to write the script, and paid me a modest but not unreasonable amount of his own money to do so. In addition he took me for some nice lunches, mainly to a restaurant in Marylebone where I ate dishes like sole veronique and coq au vin that are banned now that everything has to be on a bed of something else.

I was a starving writer, Dennis an established member of his profession, and halfway through the main course he would push his food aside and say, 'Right. To work.' I was determined to finish my food, and ploughed on.

Dennis told me that he was a great friend of Lynn Redgrave, and might well be able to persuade her to take the lead role. I pointed out, somewhat diffidently, through my coq au vin, that the lead role was a man. Dennis said that we could change his sex. I struggled with a recalcitrant shallot and pointed out that he had a sexual relationship with his landlady. Dennis said that we could make it a landlord. I mumbled through a wodge of mashed potato that the landlady had sexual feelings for the two dead airmen upstairs. Dennis said we could make them

Wrens. He was prepared to change the sex of everybody in the book because he knew Lynn Redgrave. I swallowed my doubts and my last piece of broccoli and agreed.

I'm not really mocking Dennis, whom I liked and who had faith in me. I'm mocking the film business, because I'm sure Dennis was right, and Lynn Redgrave did represent his only real chance of getting the thing made. It didn't happen, I've lost the script and have no idea how good or bad it was.

Actually other reviewers were somewhat kinder to *The Itinerant Lodger*. Norman Shrapnel in the *Guardian* wrote, 'You could call it a male Alice's adventures in Kafkaland, and as a first novel it earns good marks.'

In the *Sunday Telegraph*, John Higgins wrote, 'Mr Nobbs uses a wilder humour, reminding me of the nonsense world of N.F. Simpson's plays.' He ended, 'The truth, I suspect, is that One-way Pendulum humour soon leaves the writer out of breath.' (Did he mean 'the reader'? Well spotted, anyway. Bit of finding one's voice still to be done.)

The good old *St Pancras Chronicle* wrote, 'Resident of Hampstead, David Knobbs, journalist and script-writer, has had his first novel published . . .'

I had my first fan letter, too. My second letter, but my first fan letter.

The first letter had been addressed to David Nobbs, Writer, Lance At Large. It had contained no comments on the show, but asked if I was related to Cedric Nobbs, who lost a leg in a tractor accident in Southern Ireland in 1929. (I wasn't.)

This letter was far more exciting. It was from Dr Robert I. Zantho, Parisinkrt 43/b, Szeged, Hungary. He wrote:

> I have read your novel and found it very interesting indeed. I was somewhat puzzled about the frequent changes of names and identity of your hero/or anti-hero/-lodger, and I wonder about the possibility for the so much looked-for panacea for all mankind, but I think that together with Wilson-Simpson-Baker-Smith we are all looking for something such through all our life.

If I do not trouble you, I would much interested of your
literary ancestors: whom do you regard as a major influencing
factor to your writings. And – but perhaps this is a too
dilettant question: how would you characterize your hero in
a single sentence/ is he sane or insance? . . ./

The charm of the imperfect English just added to the thrill of knowing
that somebody so far away had read what I'd written. This letter was
very special.

Mary had by this time moved from Richmond to a spacious but rather
bleak flat on Cathcart Hill in Tufnell Park, up the road from my old
cosmological home in Lady Somerset Road. I had been continuing to
visit her and stay the night and creep out while her children were still
asleep, but they were now boarders at the Royal Russell School near
Croydon. I moved in. I had a bedroom of my own in the basement and
became lover in term-time and lodger, not very itinerant, in the
holidays. Somebody living opposite us, who knew my Auntie Dilys,
noticed, presumably having nothing better to do, that I slept with Mary
in the term-time. This news found its way to my parents, who were
disappointed in me all over again. It really was rotten luck.

Did such things matter in the sixties? To my parents, yes, and
therefore to me. And 'the sixties' were not my sixties. I didn't take
cannabis, or wear flowers in my hair, or go to pop festivals. I wrote.

By now, back in Wales Auntie Dilys, she of the inquisitive friends, had
moved to a flat in Sketty, Auntie Louie was in an old people's home, and
the house in Eaton Crescent had been sold after my Uncle Kenneth died
there, painfully and much too young, of cancer. When I heard of his
death I saw him vividly, at ten o'clock one Saturday morning, in the hall
of the Swansea house, suggesting we went for a drink at his local. I said
I'd go. 'Come on, then,' he said. I said, 'It's ten o'clock.' He said, 'My
local's in Cardiff. I wouldn't dare drink nearer home.' That was what it
was like, to be of chapel stock in Swansea. Should have gone for that
drink, David. No chance now.

It was a big year for me, 1968. First of all, I had my second novel published. *Ostrich Country* was the story of a young chef called Pegasus Baines who gets a job in a hotel in Suffolk and lusts after the unhappily married wife of the owner. He also has a girlfriend in London and he turns indecision into an art form.

The climax of the book is a meal served by Pegasus to a gathering of all the people who really care about him. I intended the meal to be bizarre and awful. The fish course is hake with rhubarb. The meat course is hare braised in honey and grated chocolate, stuffed with oysters wrapped in seaweed, and served on a bed of bananas and pimentos, with boiled potatoes and curried pumpkin. It sounds just like the sort of stuff that's served up in a hundred London restaurants these days.

I re-read *Ostrich Country* earlier this year. At first I was entranced. Reading one's own work many years later is a strange experience. One has changed, one hopes one has grown, but one is still the person who chose those particular words all those years ago, and so, inevitably, one finds much that one likes. I was captivated by its charm and energy and humour. It's a more realistic effort than *The Itinerant Lodger*, but with fantasy elements in the shape of Pegasus's dreams, in which he finds himself working in a nuclear power station and getting frozen for 375 years, and thawing out in 2363.

The extraordinary thing was that thirty-three years after publication I couldn't remember how the book ended. The sad thing was that I didn't really care. I became bored. I used to despise all the devices that writers use to keep the pages turning. I wanted to capture my readers with style and wit alone. I did capture quite a few, too. The book did fairly well with Methuen and Pan and I know that many readers hold it in high affection. Several people have suggested that there might be a film in it, but it has never happened.

(Since writing the above I have read *Ostrich Country* yet again, more carefully, and skipping the fantasies in which I was trying so hard to show that I was clever that I only succeeded in showing that I was stupid. Without these fantasies, I no longer got bored. So I'm still trying to get it accepted as a film. Where are you, Dennis Lewiston?)

*

Peter Tinniswood's first novel, the comic novel that I had persuaded him to write on the moors in 1959, came out in 1968. It was called *A Touch of Daniel* and Peter wrote in the copy he sent me: 'To David. Thank you for everything in helping me write this book.'

I was stunned by his work, thrilled by its effortless humour and its boldness. Also jealous. It seemed to me to be so much more accomplished than my own early work. It's recently been reprinted by Prion Books, and I had the honour of contributing a foreword. If you haven't read it, do so (the book, not my foreword).

Mary and I got engaged in 1968. You won't be surprised by now to learn that I recall nothing of the great moment. I doubt if I went down on one knee, partly because we still didn't have fitted carpets and partly because grand romantic gestures don't seem very appropriate when you're already living together. You find that you're happy and so you slip into marriage. We decided, now that the decision was made, to have the wedding as soon as possible – in November.

Mary assembled her three children and told them that she was going to remarry. We had assumed that they had seen through the lodger/lover routine, but they looked at her in astonishment and said, 'Who to?' When she told them it was to me, they were thunderstruck. I don't think they were displeased – just astonished. Clearly I hadn't struck them as a romantic or glamorous or mysterious figure. I had struck them as a lodger.

I feel that I can't have been the most wildly romantic of fiancés.

By this time I had of course introduced Mary to my parents. I think it was a huge shock to them that I was marrying a divorced woman. How can I get across to younger readers how vast a thing that still was to people of the culture and background of my parents?

I think I've made my love for my mother's Welsh family clear, but the narrowness of Welsh chapel folk in those days is hard to imagine now. Auntie Louie refused even to see me again. I had love to give and time to give it, but she preferred to sit alone in her old people's home in Sketty and purse her lips and send into oblivion the young man who once had been enthralled by her dreadful photos of her dreary holidays in Switzerland. My Auntie Dilys, round whose sun-soaked bedroom at the top of the narrow town house I had run my bus service, cut me out of her will.

The narrowness of my father's family was more tempered by worldliness, but I knew that even for my father this was not an ideal scenario.

I don't know if any woman can be the ideal wife of a mother's only son. I don't know what dreams my mother had for me, but she said, 'I suppose she's from a working class background.' I was stunned. I would never have described my mother as snobbish. She had snobbish friends whose snobbery she mildly mocked. If she had any snobbery herself, it was of a gentle kind, fuelled by fear of what the neighbours would think. She had an absurd desire that I should conform. Once she told me 'Peter Hall won't want you in the Royal Shakespeare Company if you have holes in your socks.'

I don't say that it would ever have been easy for my mother to accept that I was marrying a divorced woman from a working class background (with its unjustified and unspoken assumption that working class people were more likely to get divorced). I don't know that Mary's family would have considered themselves working class or any class. They were lovely respectable people of modest means. But I wasn't going to argue the case. There was no point in talking about it. The truth of the matter was that my mother was dismayed that I was taking on a ready-made family and wouldn't give her the little Nobbs grandchildren that she craved. Mary made it clear from the start that, having gone through the natural cycle of motherhood and having begun to see her three children growing up, she wouldn't consider beginning the cycle again. This was no problem to me. I became a father to them. I didn't think of them as 'not my own' any more than I thought of them as 'my own'. I don't believe in owning people.

Some people regarded me as unfortunate in never having my own children. Some thought I engineered it, so as to avoid broken nights and dirty nappies. It was, of course, pure chance, not a policy. The woman I fell for had three children and quite naturally didn't want any more, so that was that.

My mother could never entirely hide her feelings. She was Welsh, after all, even if she wasn't a gusher. I think Mary knew at least something of what my mother felt.

On 31 October, 1968, while working for Yorkshire Television, I went to Keighley to stay with Barry Slater (also of modest origins). Barry was now teaching at Bradford Grammar School and living with his mother. He drove us to Ripon, through the well-heeled, well-groomed country-side of North Yorkshire, on a lovely lingering late autumn evening. We ate a splendid dinner at a fine, plush restaurant called the Old Deanery, under the shadow of the no-nonsense cathedral. It was a splendid evening of good fellowship, and it turned out to be the nearest I would get to a stag night. I remained blissfully unaware that during that splendid evening, at another splendid evening in London, my father had collapsed and died.

Had I written my father's death in a script, I would have been told that it was sentimental and unbelievable. He had retired from teaching earlier that year, and was principal Guest of Honour at the John Carpenter Club Dinner in the school dining hall. I presume it was an all-male event, as my mother wasn't there. He made, by all accounts, a marvellous speech. Barely had he finished when, with the applause still ringing in his ears, he slumped in his chair and died.

On the death certificate the cause of death was given as a pulmonary embolism. I believe he died of emotion. A deeply unassuming man, he wouldn't have known how loved he was. The blood, surging proudly through, had found a weakness. A beautiful way to go, I suppose, but too soon, too soon.

I caught a train back to London, where my first task was to identify the body at a police station. I dreaded it. I hardly dared look.

My father didn't look dead. He seemed to have shrunk slightly, but to be at peace. I found it difficult to believe in the finality of his death, difficult to believe that if I reached out to touch his face he wouldn't open an eye and wink.

Twenty years later, I ended an episode of *A Bit Of A Do* with Rita's father collapsing and dying in her arms on the dance floor at a dentists' dinner dance. 'Dad!' cried Rita. 'Dad! You can't be dead. I haven't told you that I love you.'

This was an uncharacteristic line, potentially sentimental. Gwen Taylor played it with truth and feeling, not with sentimentality, and I wrote it with truth and feeling, not with sentimentality, because of course it was me, crying down the years, saying what I felt in that police station.

My father was a warm, kindly man. He was easily embarrassed and would leave the room at the first hint of a risqué story. Emotion embarrassed him. I don't have an idealised view of him. He could be selfish. He hardly ever took my mother on holiday until she practically made him do so. He didn't notice what she was wearing. When he came home, he didn't ask her anything about her day and didn't tell her anything about his. He spent a lot of evenings working on his text books. He was an Anglo-Saxon, she was Welsh, and he disappointed her in the little things of life. Yet, despite this, I would say that they were, in essence, a very happy couple.

None of my best work was done before my father died, and for that I am sad. It's not so much that I wanted his approval, as that I wanted him to feel proud of me. He would have enjoyed it so. I just hope that he saw enough to believe that I had what it took to survive in the life I'd chosen. I dread to think that he may have been totally disappointed in me, his only child.

His first teaching post had been at King Edward's School in Birmingham, and a tribute to him in their Chronicle of July, 1928, made an astonishing statement: 'His ambition has always been, as he told us, to become a literary man.'

He told them. He didn't tell me. I didn't discover that article till after his death, and I only had one hint of it in his life. One day – it must have been several years before his death, because it was in the breakfast room, and my parents moved to a bungalow quite a few years before he died – he showed me, very shyly, some pieces that he had sent to *Punch*. They'd been rejected, and I could see this had been an enormous disappointment to him. They were funny, accomplished pieces, on mathematical themes. I could see why they had been turned down, but I also thought that they were good enough not to have been. It was a rare moment between us, this close encounter of the breakfast room kind.

I'd like to end by quoting two extracts from the tribute to him printed in the January 1969 edition of the *Old Citizens' Gazette.*

> He had a delightful sense of humour. The very first words he spoke to a form are said to have been 'The name's Nobbs, no K.' And there is a story of his Marlborough days. The form he had to take could see him through the window coming across the Court: and when the look-out for the day cried, 'Cave, Nobbs!' the harmless but noisy schoolboy idiocies were hushed. But one day he entered the block by a route invisible from the window, strode to the classroom door, cried, 'Cave, Nobbs!' and gave them a few seconds to subside before he entered.

And

> There is much that I remember, after forty years, too intimate for the general eye. But I can tell of the patience and gentleness with which he measured little children for gas-masks in 1938; or the kindly wisdom with which as billeting master he solved triangles of which the sides were hostess, guest and parent; or the tact with which he prevented differences in Common Room policy from hardening into divisions. He was never hasty, nor flustered, nor aggressive, and never bore malice. For with his first class brain (with star) he had the rarer gift of wisdom. We shall not look upon his like again.

My mother faced widowhood with quiet but immense courage. She might have been daunted if she'd known that she was to have almost twenty-eight years of it.

Uncle Mac and his wife Auntie Dot came down from Scotland, and Auntie Dilys came from Swansea. I remember us all sitting round the dinner table in my parents' bungalow, and Mary being asked about her work. By now she was a child care officer in Hackney, her earlier jobs having included working in air traffic control at West Drayton and being secretary of the Amateur Fencing Association (epée etcetera, not garden). Mary gave a discreet, bowdlerised version of the problems of the children she encountered, but even this was sufficient to shock Dilys to the roots. 'You have to remember, Dilys, that our two families are quite exceptionally narrow,' said Uncle Mac.

My mother insisted that we should not postpone the wedding. I'm not sure if we were right to go ahead so soon, but we did. It was, inevitably, a sombre occasion. We were married in Finsbury Register Office, in Rosebery Avenue, near Sadlers Wells, but nobody was dancing. My three step-children came up from school for the day. Auntie Dilys came too, dropping her disapproval for the duration.

Our little reception, in our humble flat, went off 'as well as could be expected under the circumstances'. Auntie Dilys even went so far as to drink some champagne. Afterwards, we took the children to see *2001 – A Space Odyssey* and then packed them off back to school.

The following spring we had a short but sweet honeymoon by the banks of the exquisite Dordogne, not yet wildly over-run by Brits. We went by train, as we still had no car. At La Vielle Maison in Souillac the chef/patron came out in his chef's uniform to wave goodbye as we left. At the Beynac Hotel in Beynac nightingales sang, and the patronne found time every evening to ask what we'd done that day.

By that time my beloved Uncle Charlie had died. He'd caught a chill at my father's funeral and never really recovered. He was very much older than my father, while Auntie Kathleen was a few years younger than my mother. He died thirty-three years ago, and she survived until last year.

I must have been working very hard all this time, because my third novel was published in 1969. Again Geoffrey Strachan was my sympathetic, constructive and inventive editor. I can't sum the book up better than by quoting Geoffrey's succinct blurb for the jacket.

Why should up-and-coming, 32-year-old executive Robert Bellamy get himself the sack? What made him draw a caricature of the Exports Manager on the wall of the non-executive gents? Why is he his own worst enemy?

Is it because he nearly ran away from boarding school on his third day or because, when he was 14, his mother developed a fatal friendship for a man who looked like Hitler? Perhaps his sense of inadequacy stems from his once being mistaken for a draft of 350 men. Or from his failure long ago to do justice to the facilities at Mme Antoinette's Maison d'Amitie (Paris branch). Has he been too slow with Sonia, too fast with Frances?

Whatever the reason, one act of brinkmanship seems to lead to another. Robert finds himself involved in a series of embarrassing farewells and confusing interviews and an open-and-shut court case as he drifts towards the prospect of a stiflingly happy Christmas and an intolerably cheerful New Year.

This is a sharp and funny picture of a man at odds with society and himself, uncertain whether he is on the side of God or Mammon.

Note how I used my experience of my journey to Germany in National Service.

The scene at Mme Antoinette's Maison D'Amitie (Paris branch) upset my mother. I rang her one day and she was very brusque. I asked her what was wrong.

'You told me one can only write about what one knows.'

'Yes.'

'I've just read the scene in the brothel.'

She took some persuading, but in the end I think she believed that I had been talking nonsense, as young men will. Of course one can't only write about what one knows. There'd be no historical novels if that were true. One uses imagination, instinct and intelligence to create what one doesn't know.

Again, the book didn't do badly and again it was published in paperback by Pan. On the whole I was getting fairly widely reviewed, with a fair amount of praise and respect, as if I was an established novelist of stature. I didn't feel like that, and I don't think I got invited to literary parties. I certainly didn't go if I was invited. I thought of myself, artistically, as a lonely figure, hacking away at the word face.

I think now that *A Piece Of The Sky Is Missing* was a considerable advance on *Ostrich Country*, but that I'd gone to great pains to conceal the fact. I told the story in a most bewildering series of flashbacks and flashforwards. The concept, like the title, was taken from jigsaws. I was constructing a jigsaw of a man, and in jigsaws you don't start at the beginning and work through to the end. Perfectly valid, but how difficult to read! It was the sort of book that I'd abandon, if I was reading it, unless I could get through it in one or two sittings. Why couldn't I have been more straightforward, and, dare I say it, less flashy?

I think the answer to that lies in the fact that my primary source of income was television, and most of my television work at the time was, of necessity, as we will see in the next chapter, very conventional. My novels became my indulgence, my release from discipline and restraint.

Peter Tinniswood was married in the sixties too, to an Irish lady called Patsy, whom we knew as Puts. She was very Irish, and good fun, and in the next few years the four of us had some good, if boozy times.

My wedding took place under the dark shadow of personal tragedy, Peter's under the dark shadow of public tragedy. He had returned to journalism, on the *Western Mail*. The day before his wedding was the day of the Aberfan disaster. A great heap of slag and slurry hurtled down into the village of Aberfan in heavy rain, engulfing the little school and killing a large number of children. Peter spent his wedding eve covering the disaster. That was his stag night.

As the sixties drew to a close, I was settling into married life and being spared any further emotional roller coasters for a while.

I hadn't set the world on fire, but I had earned enough money to buy a house. We found one in Barnet High Street, near the point where it opened up on to the delights of Hadley Common. It seemed like a suitable place for a writer, being semi-detached on to a pub with a very unusual name – Ye Olde Monken Holt. The house was called Twixt, because it was between a pub and a Baptist chapel. It was a cottagey house, with a touch of character, built in the 1830s. It had a narrow frontage but went quite a way back. It had four bedrooms, a dining room of some charm, a study large enough for my needs, and a living room upstairs at the front, which you entered by descending two steps. Square bay windows gave just a touch of elegance. I was thrilled with it.

It didn't occur to me that I had escaped the suburbs only to go back to them. It didn't occur to me that I had turned my back on the world of the chapel only to move in next to one. I loved Twixt. So did Mary. So did the children.

I think my mother might have liked the house, but she wouldn't have been my mother if she hadn't found fault just a bit.

'You didn't tell me it was opposite a garage,' was her very first, flattening comment.

Garry Chambers wasn't too thrilled about my move either. Garry was a member of the writing team on *The Two Ronnies* and other shows. He was a master of the mordant one-liner.

'You've upset me,' he said, 'moving to Barnet.'

'Why, Garry?'

'I'm going to have to take down the board in my garden in Finchley.'

'Why? What does it say?'

'Last Comedy Writer Before the M1.'

11 Is Anybody Any Good At Maths?

ON OUR FIRST night in Twixt I hardly slept. The house rattled with every passing bus, and I was convinced that it wouldn't last the night, even though it had survived the preceding 150 years.

I had fitted carpets for the first time at the age of thirty-four. Those carpets gave me enormous joy. I padded around bare-foot in order to relish them. They were symbols of my prosperity. I didn't welcome this prosperity entirely for its own sake. I welcomed it because it proved to me that I hadn't been an unworldly fool in deciding to be a writer.

I settled down now to my version of adult life. I was a father in all respects except the actual. The children left boarding school and went to local state schools. I didn't have their real father to contend with, so I became like a real father to them, and they were like my real children to me.

We had family Sunday lunches, like most families in those far-off days, but ours had an extra little touch to them. On Sunday lunchtimes we would pop into the pub, join the suburban drinkers, and pop back in turn to put the vegetables on, so that lunch would be on the table cooked to perfection just one minute after we'd left the pub.

On the whole these were good, happy years, these years as head of my new family. There was always good food. Mary is a great cook and I'm not too bad and all the children and their friends appreciated our food. More than one of their friends wanted to run away from home to live with us.

Kingsley Amis lived not far away, across the common. I saw him with his family in a pub called the Two Brewers. I hadn't spoken to him in Marlborough. Here was my chance not to speak to him again. Well, what could I have said? 'Hello, my father taught you. Oh, incidentally, I'm a writer too!'? Naff.

By now Mary was head of a team of child care officers. Hackney was one of the two most deprived boroughs in England, and this was hard work at the cutting edge. There are no thanks for social workers when things go right, but all hell breaks loose when they go wrong. If I ever doubted the value of what I did, Mary would point out how desperately social workers needed a laugh in the evenings.

With Mary at work and the children at school I often had the house to myself, but frequently I would find myself next door (in the pub, not the chapel). Bank managers and financial consultants abounded. Fred Twilley, the landlord, said that they drank so freely and laughed so loudly because they were under the cosh at home. He dubbed them the Lunchtime Heroes. Victor Borge said that one of his relatives invented a cure for which there was no disease. I collected titles for which there were no programmes.

Fred had a feel for a phrase. Now that I was a landowner (0.11 acres) I bought a gadget for pruning the tops of the fruit trees in our tiny semi-walled garden. Fred promptly called me Percy Long-Prong.

We made good friends in the Monken Holt, including the local bookseller, David Muir, who revived my irrational obsession with Tottenham Hotspur, and Eric Stevens, who wrote news bulletins for ITN. Eric lived with Mary Punch, a forthright outspoken Irish journalist, in an elegant bookish first-floor flat overlooking Hadley Common. Whenever we arranged to go out with them, one of them would turn up the worse for wear and the other would be very apologetic and protective. They did this in turns, but seemed unaware of it.

Eric was a man of great modesty. I got him drunk on whisky on our patio one afternoon and he revealed in his cups that he had been a paramedic in the war, had been invalided, still had pain from the shrapnel in his head, and had been to Buckingham Palace twice to be decorated. He was horrified when he realised that he'd told me. It's such a pity that the boastful don't realise that the brave are always reticent.

Eric was to leave his mark on one of my best pieces of writing.

Talking of Buckingham Palace, there lived on the opposite side of the Baptist chapel a wholesale butcher from Smithfield. He had a pretty Swedish wife, and he painted the railings of his neo-Georgian house gold. Everybody called his cottage Buck House, and it wasn't because they were impressed.

The pub was voted *Evening Standard* Pub of the Year and got more crowded than ever, but we only once had any real disturbance when a coach outing erupted into shouting and fighting at one o'clock in the morning. Fred promised us a written apology from the guilty party, but we never heard from the Regional Crime Squad.

We were invited to a Sunday drinks party by a man called Keith, who lived in a big Georgian house across the common, beside the silted pond. The purpose of the party, Keith said, was to give a real sense of community to the north end of Barnet High Street.

I wasn't surprised that mine hosts Fred and Brenda hadn't been invited, but I did expect to see the butcher and his wife Inge. They hadn't been invited either. 'I understand he's in meat,' explained Keith in a low voice.

I looked forward to seeing our dear friends Eric and Mary. They hadn't been invited. 'I understand they're not married,' explained Keith in a low voice.

I did meet Keith's new neighbours and I told Keith that they seemed nice. 'Yes, they do,' he admitted rather sadly, but then he cheered up. 'But to be fair we don't know them very well yet.'

The suburbs are great places for comedy writers.

Many of our holidays were in Mary's native Guernsey, which I loved from the start. By the time I met her, her mother was a diminutive white-haired old lady, a lovely person. Her father had been a bit of a devil and lived now for his memories, but his memories were failing him.

I heard about legendary relatives including Auntie Annie, who ran the Divers' Arms in Alderney and took snuff, and Granny Thoumine, who had her first ride on a motorbike at the age of eighty.

Guernsey was a paradise for the children. They didn't need theme parks or museums. There were glorious beaches for swimming and rock pools for exploring. There were sea bass and bream to be caught. When the mackerel shoals came near, carts would go round with the cry, 'Mackerel. Fresh Mackerel.' Pity the poor people who have only had it peppered.

Dave was a most natural fisherman, fish gave up the ghost at the sight of him, but Chris did his bit too and caught a bream which would have won the visitors' prize for August, had we not found a better use for it. Mary's mother stuffed it and baked it.

We bought our first car, a dashing second-hand red Ford Corsair. Mary passed her driving test first time. I didn't. However, I had passed my test by the time of our first major outing which was an ambitious one. We went from Barnet to Alicante, via the heart of the Pyrenees.

The death of President Pompidou was announced on television while we were in a restaurant in Carcassone. The waiters were in tears. What British politician would inspire a waiter's tears?

We visited Mary's ex-in-laws, John and Kay, in their posh bungalow in a small resort between Campello and Villajoyosa, on the Costa Blanca. Mary got on better with her ex's parents than he did. John took us into the mountains to eat rabbit paella, we watched the fishing boats come in at Calpe, and I had experiences which must wait until I tell you about the television series that they inspired.

While my books were bringing in a certain amount of money, it was the television work that had enabled me to begin to live a moderately prosperous life.

Above all there was *The Two Ronnies*. I was script editor for the very first series, but my role was modest, as the Rons would invariably choose most of the material.

It was soon decided that the show would begin and end with the two Ronnies at a news desk, reading cod news items. I was opposed to this. I wanted them to have a more personal relationship as a duo, more in the Morecambe and Wise mould. They didn't want this, and hindsight shows that they were right.

I still wanted them to sign off with something personal. Perhaps they should just say 'goodnight' as themselves. Ronnie Barker said that he wouldn't feel comfortable even saying 'goodnight' as himself. In the ensuing discussion, the solution provided itself: Ronnie Corbett would say 'It's goodnight from me' and Ronnie B would say 'and it's goodnight from him'. This inability to be oneself at all in performance is what divides the comedian from the comic actor. I'm sure that neither Peter Sellers nor John Cleese would have felt happy saying 'goodnight' as themselves.

I was trying to turn the Rons into something they weren't. They were two actors, not a double act: two beautifully contrasting actors, both physically and stylistically. That they were both called Ronnie was an outrageous piece of good fortune. Would the show have been as successful if it had been called 'A Ronnie and a Nigel'?

The Two Ronnies provided me with a good regular income for years, a great deal of praise, and a fair amount of pleasure. It was an enormously popular show, always intelligent though never at the cutting edge. I felt that it could have been braver, and bolder, and less rigid in its format, and less reliant on tit and bum jokes, but then, as I will explain later, I was really wishing that I was writing for *Monty Python's Flying Circus*. It would be churlish of me, however, not to acknowledge that being involved with *The Two Ronnies* was one of the better experiences of my working life.

I ceased to be script editor after the first series – did I go or was I pushed? – but for many, many years I wrote sketches for the show, many of them with Peter Vincent. Peter's father was an air vice marshal, but I couldn't imagine anybody less military than Peter, and in the wonderfully classless world of comedy it didn't matter whether your father was a dustman or a duke. I no longer felt middle class, or any class. I just felt that I was me. It was one of the great attractions.

Peter, or PV as he is always known, is quirky, unpretentious, disorganised and always charming. I don't think he's ambitious enough to have made the most of his undoubted talents. Frankie Howerd once asked me, 'Is Peter Vincent a good writer?' 'Very,' I said. 'Why?' 'Well he dresses so like a good writer that I thought he possibly wasn't,' said Frankie, he of the devious mind.

The third member of McVinnob, David McKellar, had begun to disappear from view behind an increasing mass of unkempt hair and beard. Now he disappeared completely, to enter the world of corporate videos in the Midlands. We missed his energy and enthusiasm and the fertility of his ideas.

There were quite a few writers working on *The Two Ronnies*, but we weren't a team. We didn't have planning meetings. We didn't attend read-throughs or rehearsals. We ploughed our lonely furrows, and then came together on studio days.

The vast bulk of the studio day was taken up with a technical rehearsal. The various items in the show had been rehearsed and polished in a draughty church hall. Now they were performed for the first time in the sets, in front of the cameras, under the lights. It was an agonisingly slow process, with constant stops for technical adjustments.

The writers would straggle in during this process, and then there would be the dress rehearsal. It was far too late to change things. We were there to show our faces, to meet each other, and because it was a privilege to have our work so well performed and we might find out later that these had been some of the best moments of our working lives.

Garry Chambers would be there, and Barry Cryer OWMA, and Dick Vosburgh, Canadian, dry as a prairie, ingenious, splendidly cynical, a walking encyclopedia of showbiz knowledge, and looking, with his dark beard, rather as Peter Tinniswood might have looked if he'd eaten regularly.

I hope the other writers will forgive me, however, if I single out the late Spike Mullins. Spike wrote the monologues that RC performed in his chair, and wrote them so beautifully that it was impossible to imagine anyone else doing them (until David Renwick came along afterwards and was just as good). There was a wonderful contrast between the dryness of the material and the cheery sparkle with which Ronnie delivered it. I can still quote lines – 'My great uncle died at Custer's Last Stand. He wasn't taking part in it. He was camping nearby, and he went over to complain about the noise.'

But it's Spike the man of whom I wish to speak. Spike and his wife Mary lived near Slough, and Spike spoke in a dry white whine, which made his nuggets of wit wonderfully incongruous.

I remember a BBC Governor approaching us in the bar like a cold front from the Atlantic. He engaged us in deadly dutiful chat. 'Does it take you a long time to get here?' he queried like a minor royal.

'Well, yes,' said Spike. 'I live in Slouth. Well, I say "*in* Slough". Just outside really. There's a bus to the station every half hour, and a train to Paddington every twenty minutes, but they don't always coincide.'

'Oh, God, why did I ask?' was the silent subtext to the Governor's fixed smile.

'Two tubes Paddington to White City and you've still got a bit of a walk,' droned Spike mercilessly. 'Maybe two hours altogether from the house to here. Long time without a woman.'

'Yes, yes, jolly good, well, keep up the good work, ha ha, splendid,' said the unnerved Governor before beetling off to safer pastures as fast as his dark-suited legs could carry him.

I remember thinking, 'You'll never be able to say things like that, Nobbs, but supposing you wrote about a character who could!'

Ronnie Corbett received a simply wonderful sketch from a mystery writer, with the nom-de-plume of Gerald Wiley. Ronnie B had a part in it, but the starring role was for Ronnie C and it was written specially for him. But who was Gerald Wiley? Some thought it was Tom Stoppard, others plumped for Harold Pinter.

Ronnie C invited Gerald Wiley to meet the team for a meal in a Chinese restaurant near Rediffusion's studios. We all sat down to eat, and realised that there was no stranger there. Then Ronnie B stood up and announced that he was Gerald Wiley. Amid much hysteria, Ronnie C presented him, slightly sheepishly, with a set of expensive cut glasses which he'd bought for the famous writer.

Ronnie Barker wrote many fine sketches, including the famous 'Ironmonger's Shop' in which Ronnie C asks for a succession of items and Ronnie B misunderstands and brings the wrong object every time. The secret of this sketch was that it was played incredibly slowly. When one says that pace is vital in comedy, one means that the *right* pace is vital, not that everything should be performed at breakneck speed. Here the desperate attempts of two stupid men to understand each other needed to be stretched almost to breaking-point. The audience were on the edge of their seats, gleefully anticipating the next glorious cock-up.

Ronnie B did upset us, however, by ignoring the unwritten writers' code. Dick Vosburgh suffered particularly from this. Dick wrote very conceptual sketches. One of these was called 'Sketcherism Spoon' about Dr Spooner, who, not unnaturally, spoke in Spoonerisms. I quote:

WIFE: Do you feel like some breakfast?

SPOONER: Indood I dee. A suggestion to warm the hartles of my – cockles of my heart. I rather fancy some hot toatered bust, a rasher of strakey beacon, and some of that cereal that goes pap, snockle and crap.

Ronnie B wrote a sequel. Dick should have been asked to write the sequel. This was by no means a one-off occurrence, and it infringed the unwritten copyright to the idea and caused a considerable amount of resentment, especially as we were paid by the minute for what we wrote. Still, I would have cause to be grateful to Ronnie Barker later on, as we will see, so I mustn't labour the point.

One of my sketches was about a restaurant called the Complete Rook, where every dish in the menu was based on rook. This was appearing in one of the show's many repeats, and I wanted a permanent record of it, but I was going to Bristol for the weekend, so I set the video for Sunday, 7.15, BBC1. The clocks changed that weekend, and I got *Songs of Praise* instead. I watched it for several minutes before I realised it wasn't a *Two Ronnies* skit.

I do have a permanent record of my sketch 'Party Names'. It's in Swedish. It's about using mnemonics to remember people's names at a party, and of course it all goes wrong. At one point, Ronnie C says 'I'm Neil. Lien backwards,' and everybody says, 'Oh, all right' and they lean backwards. It's better when you see it, though not much, but the Swedes bought the sketch, and recorded it, and sent me a copy, and I've watched it without understanding a word, and suddenly all the Swedish actors lean backwards. In those moments of quiet repose that occur even in a life as packed as mine, I sometimes think, 'How could that joke possibly have worked in Swedish?'

During those years I also wrote for many of the top comedians – Tommy Cooper, Ken Dodd, Frankie Howerd, Dick Emery, Jimmy Tarbuck and, above all, Les Dawson. One job seemed to lead to another pretty seamlessly. Some of them I welcomed more than others. All of them interrupted my main work and prevented me developing as a novelist, but I had a family, and we needed to live. There was always a team of writers, and one's share of the final script fee was quite small, so one needed to move on to the next project.

A few writers (and a few actors) make a great deal of money. The rest are grossly underpaid, in my opinion, for the pleasure that they bring. I hope I've brought a lot of pleasure in my life but I'm surrounded by people far better off than me – lawyers, property developers, loss adjustors, accountants, dealers in fruit machines . . .

Enough of all that. Back to the comics.

Roy Hudd was the first comedian I wrote for. He did a quirky, rather lightweight series for Yorkshire Television. Roy hadn't developed a full comic persona, in fact I don't think he ever did, so this was very much a writers' show. It wasn't a huge success. Roy would later achieve his greatest successes as a marvellous actor.

With Dick Emery it was different. He had a small band of regular characters whom he played brilliantly. The writer wasn't required to be original. One was serving these characters, one was serving the comedian. One was, not to put too fine a point upon it, a hack, albeit a rather superior one.

My next stint was with the legendary Tommy Cooper. At the beginning of my first Cooper series, all the writers gathered in a small room in the entrails of the BBC, far far from daylight, and were addressed by Tommy's agent, who seemed about as funny as Liverpool Street Station.

'There are two things you need to know about Tommy,' he told us. 'He can't say the letter R. So if you're going to set a sketch in, say, Retford, set it instead in . . .' He thought for a long time, trying to dredge up a town without an R in it. '. . . in, say, Hull. And Tommy is very superstitious. He doesn't like the colour green. So, no green and no Rs.'

'Bang goes my Robin Hood sketch,' I said.

He glared at me. I'd have thought any evidence of humour on the part of the writers would have been welcome, but no.

It wasn't rewarding writing for Tommy, for two reasons. He didn't really need writers, he just needed the vaguest suggestion, which he would mangle brilliantly. And I didn't like him.

Almost everyone of my generation found Tommy Cooper sublimely funny in a way that defies logic and explanation. I saw him at Batley Variety Club and he took three minutes to find his way through the curtains. We just heard chuckles and saw bulges in the curtain. The audience were in hysterics before they'd even seen him. However, the good humour and inspired innocence of his act was just that, an act. Off-stage I found that all the vitality and charm left him. He seemed a selfish man who drank too much and showed no spark of warmth.

Knowing Tommy and being disillusioned about him made no difference when he went on stage. I enjoyed his act as much as ever. He was a comic genius. He was irresistible. You don't need to like Mozart to admire his music.

The heading for this chapter is a quote from Tommy. The scene is a pub. Tommy has insisted on taking everyone there. He has ordered pies without asking what anybody wants. Very generous, we feel, those of us who are new to the game. Then comes the killer phrase. 'Is anybody any good at maths?' I didn't let on about my father. I didn't want to be the one who had to divide the bill by seventeen.

Ken Dodd once used a much more promising phrase – 'What are you having, lads?' He'd insisted that all the writing team have a drink in a bar called the Captain's Cabin, near Piccadilly, after a radio recording. He didn't arrive till 10.59. He got out a piece of paper and wrote down all our drinks. He returned from the bar, at 11.02, with a single light ale.

'They'd closed,' he said. 'They let me have a drink as I hadn't had one all night.'

Stories like this abound, but I can't really grumble. He invited me to see his show in Bournemouth, and raid my hotel bill. I liked him.

He was virtually the same off stage as on. He just was Ken Dodd, comedian – eccentric, childlike. The fact that he was completely self-centred didn't matter, and I doubt if anyone could become a great comedian if he wasn't. It was a privilege to write for him. On television he's mildly amusing and a little childish. On the boards he's a giant. I was reduced to hysterics in Bournemouth by a picture he built up of a man falling into a vat of glue in a factory in Swindon. It was the first time I really understood the phrase, 'I laughed till my ribs ached.'

The only trouble with his theatre show is its length. By the time he's finished the buses have stopped, the boarding houses are locked, the night porters of hotels are slumbering. People sleeping in shop doorways might be genuine vagrants or they might be Ken Dodd's audience.

He's a great student of laughter, analysing his every performance and marking his laughs. I found him full of helpful advice.

'Never forget, David,' he said to me one day, 'the letter K is the funniest letter in the alphabet. Kettering, Kettle, Eskimo . . .'

For some impish reason I interrupted with 'String vest'.

'Exactly!' he said.

At the end of the first show of one series he had the whole audience covered in foam. He decided it hadn't worked, and tried the same sequence for each succeeding show, finally deciding on the last show it had worked. The BBC got a hefty bill from Diddy Foam Products in Knotty Ash.

No, it was impossible not to like Ken Dodd.

Of course one has to write in a different style for each comedian. There is a cautionary true tale of a writer, highly respected and very busy, who was commissioned to write sketches for Dick Emery and told his secretary to send in old Tommy Cooper sketches that hadn't been used, substituting Dick for Tommy throughout. It would never have worked, even if Dick hadn't read, at the end of the first sketch, the give-away of all time – 'Dick gives his characteristic laugh, and his fez falls off.'

That reminds me – this is typical of the conversation of comedy writers in what Barry Cryer calls our anecdotage, one story constantly reminds us of another – of the story of the writer in our modern era who used his global search facility on his word processor to change the name of a character in a book from David to Nigel throughout. When the book was published, he discovered that the hero now visited Florence and admired Michaelangelo's Nigel.

At some stage hereabouts I found myself writing for the *Jimmy Tarbuck Show*, and met a northern McVinnob consisting of Mike Craig, Laurie Kingsley and Ron McDonnell. Jimmy is a very clever and successful man but I can't pretend that I regard him as one of the great comedians. He's a teller of gags. I can't tell a gag to save my life. This didn't seem like a marriage made in heaven.

No comedian required a more individual style of writing than Frankie Howerd. Not all his oohs and aahs, his hesitations and digressions, had to be written, but some did if the piece was to work for him. I wrote a lot for Frankie, for radio, with David McKellar, but I also wrote for him on my own, and I had a problem. I couldn't capture his style unless I spoke it out loud.

One late afternoon, the children were back from school and raiding the kitchen for bread and jam and cornflakes and all the things children eat after school, and no doubt some of their friends were there too, and I became self-conscious about wandering round my study talking out loud like Frankie Howerd. Also, strangely, I sometimes found that I had to stand up to write his material. I didn't have to become a stand-up writer for any other stand-up comedian.

On this occasion I felt claustrophobic, I had to go out to continue my work, so I set off across Hadley Common. I wasn't writing anything down. I can keep whole routines in my head for half an hour or more. So there I was, wandering across the sward going, 'No, honestly, missus, I was flambergasted. My flamber had never been so gasted. Titter ye not, madam,' when I saw a police car sliding along beside me. Three officers got out and approached me.

'Excuse me, sir, but what exactly are you doing?'

My reply of 'Writing for Frankie Howerd' seemed strangely lacking in conviction. I often urge writers to join The Writers' Guild of Great Britain which does a lot of good work trying to improve the lot of a lot of writers. I had never been as glad of the guild's existence as that day when I was able to produce my membership card.

'Thank you, sir,' said one of the officers. 'I'm terribly sorry to have doubted you, but we've had reports of an escaped lunatic in the area.'

I have to say that I felt the police suspicions to be thoroughly justified. There were times in my career, writing for comedians, when I felt that the only difference between me and an escaped lunatic was that I hadn't escaped.

It's well known that Frankie was gay. Well it is now, anyway. He lived with his manservant, Dennis, but he was always trying things on. One day he asked David McKellar round on a Sunday, David rang me and round we both went to Frankie's house. He came to the door, and his face fell. 'I didn't mean both of you,' he said.

From time to time Frankie would develop an itch in an inaccessible place. Inaccessible to him, that is. Not to us, unfortunately. David was asked to rub ointment on the spot. I wasn't. By this time I was feeling a bit offended. Deeply relieved, but a bit offended.

We never found Frankie mean. Quite the reverse. 'There's always good champagne in the fridge,' he said mournfully when David McKellar and I first went to his exquisite little Georgian town house in Kensington. After one script conference he took us both, and Dennis, to

Le Coq Hardi and gave us a handsome dinner. We had to watch the first fifteen minutes of *Hawaii Five-O* first, because Frankie had one of those new-fangled video machines, and its capacity was forty-five minutes. He would watch the rest on his return home.

'I have a rule in restaurants,' he told us. 'We don't ever discuss showbiz, or we'll end up going blind.' He was a generous and delightful host.

Nevertheless, he was difficult to work with, because he was so neurotic. A letter he sent to David and me at the end of one series can stand as our epitaph for this talented, tormented soul: 'Thank you for the lovely scripts. I'm sorry I was so awful. I promise that next time I won't be, but I will be.'

Another gay comedian for whom I worked was Jimmy Edwards. The news that the beloved macho farmer, boozer and star of *Whack-O* and *Take It From Here* was gay came as a surprise to many people, and certainly to me, especially as I had been lunching *à deux* with him every week after the read-throughs of a show called *Sir Yellow*. This was a period piece about a cowardly knight. It also starred Melvyn Hayes and it wasn't good. I was the script editor and my job was to save it. I failed.

John Duncan, he of the *TW3* film fame, had become Head of Comedy at Yorkshire Television under the mercurial and erratic Donald Baverstock. A lot of storms come in from Wales, and Donald was one of them. That's a fact, not a criticism. He was passionate about television, and never bland or dull. John lived in Thorner, a village five miles from Leeds, but he would arrive by bus in his huge wellies, looking as if he'd crossed half of Antarctica, and carrying a briefcase full of bottles of beer, which clanked as he strode along the corridors of power. He was a great ideas man. He shouldn't have been an administrator. He should have been a loose cannon firing off exciting thoughts to lesser and duller men.

One of John's odder ideas was to employ me as a contracted script editor for a year. The least trendy dresser in television was given an office in Carnaby Street and my very own secretary, a delightful Lancashire lass called Sheila Murray. *Sir Yellow* was my first show. I don't believe it should have been made, but I wasn't asked. The sad thing was that the writer, Johnny Heywood, showed real flashes of talent, but was not yet ready to write a whole series on his own, and he disappeared from view, presumably in disillusionment at the reception of his series.

At the end of series party, in a posh Italian restaurant in Leeds, a table was booked for twenty-six, but twenty-eight turned up, and two bit players had to sit at a separate table. One of them said, loudly and unhappily, 'It's easy to see who're the least important people round here.' His name? Bob Hoskins.

I also worked on a sketch show called *Hey Brian*, featuring a young comedian called Brian Marshall. He was lovely, but a touch lightweight. Television is merciless to comedians who are a touch lightweight. Chefs, panellists, straight actors, gardening experts, quiz-masters, weather forecasters, chat show hosts, travel presenters, make-over consultants, they can be lightweight. Newsreaders and comedians can't. *Hey Brian* wasn't bad, but in comedy 'wasn't bad' is never good enough.

Michael Mills, Head of Comedy at the BBC, commissioned me to script edit a slightly off-beat sketch show with the devastatingly punchy title of *Some Matters Of Little Consequence*. It starred Kenneth Griffith, Frank Thornton and Sheila Staefel. I was instructed to include a regular item penned by one of Michael's BBC colleagues, in which two sparrows – or they may have been swallows, it was a long time ago – sat on a wire and discussed life.

McVinnob, still working as a team at that stage, wrote a fair bit of the show, and there were some amusing contributions from the highly talented and eccentric writer John Antrobus, who wrote the play *The Bed Sitting Room*, in which Spike Milligan turned into – what else? – a bed sitting room.

My little show was light and uneven, but I learnt a lot. I recall with particular pleasure Kenneth Griffith as a very eccentric bomb disposal expert. Imagine a sketch about a bomb disposal expert now. How horror pushes in the frontiers of comedy.

Another favourite was a one-line quickie, written by Peter Vincent, for which the director, Roger Race, built a sizeable section of a London sewer at Ealing Studios. The item began with a close up of some real rats (trained by Steve Race, no relation of Roger). The camera pulled out to reveal the splendid BBC sewer. The Cambridge eight rowed into the sewer and the puzzled cox enquired of a passing sewage worker, 'Excuse me, is this the right way to Mortlake?' No accountant would countenance such expenditure on one line today, but good comedy is not calculable in accountants' terms.

Roger Race had learnt his comedy under Dennis Main Wilson, and he really 'went for it'. Sadly, he learnt his drinking from Dennis too. One night he got in an underground train at White City and woke up three hours later to find the train still at White City, as he thought, only to learn that it had been to Ongar and back while he slept. He died much too young.

When a TV show is recorded in front of a studio audience, there is always a warm-up man to get the audience in the mood. Our warm-up man, Gordon Peters, told our audience, 'Morecambe and Wise are in the next studio. I bet you all wish you'd got tickets for that.'

When Duncan Wood became Head of Comedy, he asked me to edit the shows down from four to two. In that form, and without the talking swallows – or were they sparrows, it was a long time ago – they really weren't bad, and I felt that one day I might get things right.

But not yet.

Meanwhile, I watched things that were really good. I could see the gap between the good stuff and mine. I didn't need London Transport staff to shout 'Mind the gap' at me. I minded it terribly.

My fellow funsters from the Frost farragos were putting on *Monty Python's Flying Circus*, and I thought the vast bulk of it brilliant. I won't mention the best-known bits, just two of my favourite items. The first was the singing of insurance shanties. Those two words scream through laughter at the lack of romance and danger in so much of the modern world. The other was about a firm called 'Confuse-A-Cat', which was called in to cure a cat that was so immobile that it was . . . well . . . catatonic. The Confuse-A-Cat van arrives, a team of acrobats get out with ladders and all sorts of elaborate props and perform a mini-circus to the utterly unresponsive cat. At last the cat slopes off. The owner is delighted. It's thumbs-up for another successful job by Confuse-A-Cat.

Brilliant. Inspired. You don't agree? You think it's just silly? That's why it's so stupid to become a comedy writer. People never agree what's funny.

I couldn't write stuff like that, because the people I was writing for wouldn't have performed it. You can only really be silly when you're performing it yourself. Imagine a group of classical actors coming in to rehearse *The League of Gentlemen*: 'What's my motivation?' 'You're as mad as a hatter and it's funny, that's your motivation, matey?'

My next series was a McVinnob effort – a sit-com for Yorkshire Television called *Shine A Light*. The margin between success and failure in comedy can be very small. The show was a disaster, yet it was so nearly good.

We were all three good writers, and I think we wrote scripts that were very nearly very good. I have one great talent. I have a tremendous, awesome, frightening talent for hindsight. Not for nothing am I known as 'Mr Retrospect' in domino playing circles. I can see now that our great error was in having two lighthouse keepers, not three.

Yes, our series was set in a lighthouse, often held to be the perfect setting for a sit-com, since there is no escape. *Steptoe and Son* worked as a series about just two people because, apart from the brilliant scripts, it was a father and son relationship. The tension between two lighthouse keepers, however, is not in that class. It wasn't even a clear-cut master and servant relationship. Three men would have allowed for a much more varied scenario.

Our director, Bill Hays, was a theatre director of note, but there's always a risk when people of note turn to sit-coms. They believe they're slumming it. They don't realise that all the things that make great drama are the things that make great comedy. It has to be taken utterly seriously and it has to be played truthfully.

The casting was bad. It really consisted of two actors – Timothy Bateson and Tony Selby. Both were good, there was nothing wrong with the casting of either of them. What was bad was the casting of *both* of them *together*. There was no light and shade. There was no warmth. The fault had begun in the scripts, I freely admit, but the casting intensified it. Each could have been good with someone else, and preferably two someone elses. This is Mr Retrospect speaking, of course. I realised none of this at the time. I was only thirty-seven.

We weren't helped by our lighthouse. I don't know how the designer managed it, but it was round in the studio yet didn't look round on camera.

Things might still have gone modestly, rather than badly, had not Leeds United played Chelsea in the FA Cup. There were no penalty shoot outs in those days. Leeds and Chelsea slugged it out through three or perhaps even four replays, all televised live on the nights of our transmission. All the schedules were moved back till after the matches, all of which went to extra time.

You take your consolation where you can. It was good to feel that we had produced the best ever series about two boring old tits in a square lighthouse at midnight.

David McKellar, fine fellow, fine writer, went off in disillusionment. Peter Vincent and I tried again at Yorkshire with another sit-com, called *Keep It In The Family*. A bit over-wrought. A bit under-cast. Not great, not awful. An old pro, Jack Haig, kept trying to fit his comedy sneeze in. I wonder if Ibsen ever had that trouble: 'Ibbo, I've found a moment when my comedy sneeze could really liven up your doll's house.'

John *TW3* Duncan was supportive throughout my time at Yorkshire, but he wasn't right for his administrative role, and he left. His track record wasn't particularly stellar, but his last act was the best. He saw a play called *The Banana Box*, by Eric Chappell, and he commissioned a pilot of a sit-com based on it. John may have walked off into the distance in his wellies, his empties clanking in his briefcase, but he left Yorkshire Television a little leaving present. He left them *Rising Damp*.

I hope I can also claim that another fine idea of John's was to make me script editor for *Sez Les*, starring Les Dawson. Sixty-eight shows followed, sixty-eight very happy shows and, on the whole, I believe, sixty-eight pretty good ones. This was a truly happy experience. Forgive me if I list the main members, but I'd like the regrettably few who are still alive to know that they are not forgotten: David Mallet, director; Bill Hitchcock, producer; Barry Cryer, fellow writer; Bob McGowan, designer; Don Clayton, floor manager; Terry Knowles, stage manager; Brenda Fox, wardrobe, and Les himself, of course, supported by Roy Barraclough, Eli Woods, Julian Orchard, Norman Chappell and Kathy Staff.

Les, with his verbose monologues and gurner's face wasn't everybody's cup of tea, but for the vast number whose cup of tea he is, we did the business. Les wrote all his own monologues, Barry and I wrote the bulk of the sketches, and a lad called John 'oh, dear, here's another new one' Hudson wandered in from Lancashire, wrote perfect sketches that didn't need one word changing, and wandered off back to Lancashire to get a proper job.

Ideas were welcome from any source. More than once, Don Clayton wrote a quickie on the bus to the location, and we did it there and then. We sailed by the seat of our pants. There was a great deal of drinking at lunchtime, but great work was still done in the afternoons. One lunchtime, in the Labour Club across the way, Les fooled around, playing the piano out of tune. People laughed, it was in, though I have to say that I am so tone deaf that I didn't know why people found it funny.

John 'no need to remind you who this one is' Cleese admired Les and joined us for a few shows. Norman Murray, Les's agent, was impressed and said, 'Who is this boy?' I sat in the canteen with John, Les and Roy Barraclough. A cleaning lady approached, asked for the autographs of all three, then turned to me and said, 'Are you anybody?'

The awful thing is, I hesitated before answering.

Barry Cryer and I achieved one great first with John and Les. We wrote a Hamlet and gravedigger sketch which didn't get one laugh from the studio audience, not even a faint titter. To make John Cleese and Les Dawson unfunny together takes real class.

On a happier note, Les and John performed a sublime little quickie written by Barry. Les, in a filthy raincoat, enters a posh bookshop, asks, 'Got any dirty books?' John looks at him in disgust and disdain, a whole variety of scornful looks which we timed at 54 seconds, then says, 'Yeah. What kind of thing are you looking for?' Try that without the pause. There's no joke at all. The pause was the joke. Eat your heart out, Harold Pinter.

I have two favourite remarks that were said to comedians by members of the public. After Harry Secombe (I wrote for him too) had died a death in Bradford, a man went up to him and said, 'Tha were very good. I almost had to laugh.'

Les's favourite story was of a man who approached him in Sunderland and said, 'Are you open to constructive criticism?'

'Yes,' said Les.

'You're crap,' said the man.

Our producer, Bill Hitchcock, who once directed a film in Vienna and couldn't speak a word of German and called through a loud-hailer, before a scene involving the Lippizaner horses, 'Makken mit der klippen-kloppen', sadly died. Then David Mallet moved to pastures new, so we got a new director, Vernon Lawrence, a pink-faced uproarious former novice monk.

At Vernon's first show, Barry and I sat in the control box, on a row of seats far beneath the director and his assistants, so that we could be silly if we did it quietly. Sitting with us were David Mallet, who had come for old times' sake, Les's dear wife Meg, and Bob McGowan, our designer, a delightful man whose speech was so clipped that he made Dennis Main Wilson sound like Proust. If an idea wasn't right, Bob would say, 'Plughole.'

The show began with a pre-titles filmed quickie, written by Barry.

'I wouldn't have shot it like that,' said David.

'I didn't mean that,' complained Barry.

'He promised me he'd never wear that shirt again,' said Meg.

Bob didn't need any words at all that day. He drew me a picture of a parachutist approaching the ground with his parachute unopened.

That picture proved prophetic. Paul Fox, the new Head of Programmes and Duncan Wood, the new Head of Comedy, didn't have much time for *Sez Les*, although Duncan always said 'Great show, lads.

There's a large one at the bar for you,' and then stood beside us till we'd both bought him a large one back. They tried new things with Les – more prestigious things with Alan Plater and Simpson and Galton, real writers like what I had not yet become. The new things didn't work as well as our stuff, because Les was Les.

Bob McGowan died in Brisbane, far too young. Meg also died too young. Julian Orchard and Norman Chappell both went quite young, and now of course Les himself has gone. I feel lucky just to be here.

Les was prepared to try anything in *Sez Les*. He went into the ring with a professional wrestler. He played the piano in mid-air suspended on a Kirby wire. As Jock Cousteau, the world's foremost underwater bag-piper, he immersed himself completely in a tank of water, still playing the bagpipes, in front of the studio audience.

Yes, Les had short arms and long pockets – there is this streak of meanness in so many comics, as if they feel that they entertain us so much that we are in their debt. Yes, when Roy Barraclough went to stay at Les's new home in Lytham St Anne's, he had to pop out, ostensibly to buy cigarettes, actually to eat a cooked breakfast because he wasn't being fed. Yes, Les did promise us a trip to his house, which never came, so we had to rely on Roy's description – 'a veritable forest of onyx'. Yes, he didn't buy his round, and on the rare occasion when he did, he had trouble getting served – '*I* have no trouble,' said Don Clayton. 'They know me.'

But no matter. We had laughter aplenty, Les would let other actors have the tag of the sketch, and when Barry or I topped a gag of his in the bar he would slap his thigh with delight. He was a thoroughly nice man. Only a nice man could introduce a guest with the words, 'And now, somebody who until today I thought was a venereal disease – Labbe Siffre', and Labbe Siffre didn't mind.

It was great fun writing with Barry Cryer. The man's a walking compendium of funny stories, which might hide the fact that he's a sharp and intelligent observer of the human comedy. He's borne with great patience a lifetime of being mistaken for Barry Took, even after

Tookie's sad death. A few weeks ago Barry came to stay and I took him into the village pub. I heard one barmaid say to another, 'Mr Rushton's got one in.'

Barry was far better than I at coming up with amusing routines for chat between Les and his guests, and in our sketches and quickies he wrote with a fastidious feel for words that made nonsense of his disparaging description of himself as 'not a real writer – a bits and pieces man'.

I've mentioned my first fan letter. Now they were pouring in, one every five years:

'My father's name was Arthur Joseph Nobbs. One thing I did see in London about 10 years ago was a cleaning clothes shop, name on window Nobbs, closed every time I was able to get there.'

'I remember seeing a young boy's picture in the "Daily Mirror" some 12 years ago, he was working a plough somewhere in Somerset, his name was also Nobbs, this one I did nothing about, at the time, as I was putting some hours in work at the time.'

'May I ask for your co-operation? I am trying to trace the ancestors of my great-great-grandfather, Abraham Nobbs, who was a bookseller and stationer in Hungerford, Berkshire, about 160 years ago . . .'

It wouldn't be many years before I actually got a letter from someone stating that they had enjoyed something I'd written.

But not quite yet.

12 THE FALL AND RISE OF REGINALD PERRIN

I SLIT THE letter open eagerly. It was a rejection slip. It was the best bit of news I ever had.

I didn't realise until much later that it was good news. When I talk to writers' groups I always advise them not to be too depressed by rejection slips. You don't know if it's bad news till the end of the story.

I'd been asked to put forward an idea for a series of half hour plays on topical themes for BBC Pebble Mill. My idea had been a play about a businessman driven berserk by the pressures of the rat race and the absurdities of conspicuous capitalist consumption. I can't recall now how much of what eventually became *The Fall and Rise Of Reginald Perrin* was in my brief synopsis. I'm pretty sure that calling his mother-in-law a hippopotamus was.

The letter said that they weren't interested and reiterated that what they wanted was plays on topical themes, as if that wasn't what I'd sent.

If my idea had been accepted, that's all Reginald Perrin would ever have been – one half hour play.

I've identified various factors in my early life which may have contributed to the formation of the idea behind Reginald Perrin. There was an actual, immediate trigger too. I read an article in one of the Sunday supplements about Mortons' efforts to find a new jam, about the endless tastings, the endless market research, the endless questionnaires. I lost the article long ago, but I had felt a great sense of what those researchers must have felt, on bad days, endlessly asking if the jam was too fruity, not fruity enough, too bland, not bland enough, too blandly fruity, too fruitily bland, ad infinitum.

I remembered, too, a nauseous advert for a mortgage company: two smug parents in matching sweaters with two smug children in matching gear, all giving fixed smug smiles because they were safe. In my mind this was a key image for the world against which Reggie was rebelling.

I decided to use my half hour play as the basis for a novel. The book, in its early first version, was very close to the finished article right up to the moment when Reggie turns the river red with the world's largest loganberry slick. After that it went off the rails. It took Reggie to a mental home, and I began to get stuck.

My agent, Jonathan Clowes, lent me his house at Penhurst, deep in the unspoilt Sussex countryside. The only other person around was Henry Chapman, who had given up writing and was working for Jonathan as gardener and general factotum.

For four and a half days I wrote and wrote and wrote. I lived off tinned foods, so easy to prepare that they barely interrupted the flow. I was inspired. I slept each night for no more than six hours. There was nobody to bath for. There weren't even any curtains to pull. Jonathan didn't like curtains.

On the Friday evening Jonathan arrived with his wife, Enyd. In the morning he took me for a walk round the estate, and we had a typical conversation.

Jonathan is slim, bearded and quiet. He looks spiritual. One would not be surprised to find him seated at the Last Supper.

'The book's worked out really well,' I said.

'Good,' said Jonathan. He sounded absent-minded, but I had heard him sound just as other-worldly when saying that a proposed fee was half what he was expecting. 'Good. I think I'll extend that oak copse a little.'

'Good idea,' I said. 'I think I've been inspired this week.'

'Terrific,' he said. 'I think I might plant a few ash down the bottom there.'

When I got home I found that everything I'd written in Sussex was complete and utter rubbish. I managed, with great difficulty, to create some form of ending to the book, and I sent it off to Jonathan before going on a family holiday to Guernsey.

Jonathan sent me a telegram – the only telegram he ever sent me. It read, 'I didn't get where I am today without recognising a good book when I see one – J.C.' He already knew what was going to happen. I didn't get where I am today without being lucky in my agent.

It didn't mean that Jonathan thought that the end of the book worked, and neither of us was surprised when Geoffrey Strachan at Methuen said that he thought that the second half went off the rails. We told him that we agreed. Jonathan asked for a commission on the basis that I would do the work we all realised the book needed. Methuen refused. They wanted to see the finished article first.

I realised eventually that a mental home is the worst place to send a fictional character who is in any degree mental. If he was totally sane he could be locked in a mental home and there would be drama. If he was at all mental he must be in the normal world. The solution must lie in the confines of the world I'd created for him. It was now but a short step to finding the solution – that he returns to his wife in disguise and marries her again. I conceived the idea of his leaving his clothes on a beach and starting a new life. This would become known in the media as 'doing a Reggie'. This was flattering but rather disturbing. I'm not keen on being blamed for other people's tragic lives.

I'm often asked if I got the idea from John Stonehouse, the Labour MP who left his clothes on a beach in Australia to begin a new life. No, the book was written and delivered before he did it. So, did he get the idea from me? Highly unlikely, since he did it before the book was published.

I also pulled back on the extent of Reggie's abnormality. He mustn't be insane. There was nothing further to say about him if he had lost all contact with normality. In the first half of the book he was behaving abnormally in a normal situation. In the second half he was in an abnormal situation. He must want to behave normally.

The book now worked well, but Jonathan felt that Methuen hadn't shown enough faith in me, and we should send it elsewhere.

I forget how many publishers turned it down. A lot. One, Macmillans, actually asked to see me, and a Macmillan, who sounded like Peter Cook doing Harold, asked me that unanswerable question: 'You're a very clever young man, aren't you?' Young! I was almost forty. I think I made some ghastly non-committal English noise in the back of my throat.

'All this satire on the food industry is very funny, very sharp,' he said, 'but coming back to marry his wife is, of course, completely unbelievable. Agree to change that, and we'll give you a hundred pounds.'

I was angered by the paltry sum but even more angered by the patronising 'of course'. Mr Retrospect is deeply grateful to him. In that moment, I suddenly knew that I really believed in the second half of my book.

Jonathan sent it to several more publishers and never lost his optimism. 'Everything really good gets published in the end,' he said.

He was right. He usually is. Gollancz took it, and with enormous enthusiasm. The redoubtable Liz Calder, my editor there, remembers bursts of laughter coming from offices all over their building as people read the book. Liz was a great editor and I recall lovely lunches at Inigo Jones and Langan's Brasserie on publication days.

Gollancz were keen for me to get pre-publication quotes from well-known people whom I knew. I got a lovely one from Stan Barstow:

> I enjoyed it very much. It's funny, touching and deep, full of hilarious incident and very acute observation. Last but not least, I do simply admire the way he puts words on a page. I hope it will do well.'

This, from the great, the impeccable author of *A Kind Of Loving* and many other fine books was a huge thrill. The best writers can be wonderfully generous.

Ronnie Barker also wrote a lovely piece:

> Reggie Perrin is a sweaty, charming, paunchy, sad, hilarious man. He inhabits an intriguing, mundane world. A world in which everyone jogs along quite nicely and then, suddenly, nothing happens. But in a most exciting way. A world where the ordinary suddenly occurs when you least expect it. Our world. But, unlike most of us, Reggie sets out to change it. His failure to do so is completely successful.
>
> I laughed two hundred and eighty seven times and cried twice. I would love to play Reggie Perrin in a film. I still feel I *am* Reggie Perrin as I walk about. What a beautiful book.

I think that is particularly interesting, in view of what happened later.

Meanwhile, Ronnie went on to *The Book Programme* and read an extract – the scene where Reggie orders ravioli followed by ravioli followed by ravioli, and read it beautifully, as one would expect. (Many years later, incidentally, I saw a very prominent factory on the outskirts of Nice with a huge sign – Perrin's Ravioli. Perrin is quite a common name in France, Perrins make some excellent Chateauneuf-du-Pape. Had I unconsciously seen the name in connection with ravioli? Had the tins of ravioli I consumed in the house of Joe Hirsch been from Nice? I'll never know.)

The book came out to some good reviews and was named Book of the Week in the *Telegraph* supplement.

A few days after publication I went to John Lewis, never knowingly undersold, to look at slatted garden furniture, and there, also looking at slatted garden furniture, was a lady with my book in her hand. This was the first physical evidence of a reading public that I'd ever had. It was quite a thrill. I almost introduced myself, but decided it would be very naff.

More than one reviewer found the book embarrassing to read on public transport, as it induced great spurts of loud laughter. Imagine my joy when I saw someone reading it on the Northern Line. Any moment now, I thought, there'll be a great spurt. Was there hell as like? I watched him all the way to Edgware and his face never cracked. In fact, he grew gloomier and gloomier.

And I didn't even live in Edgware.

Now at last I began to get letters that weren't entirely devoted to asking if I was related to obscure people called Nobbs.

I can't resist quoting one:

> I have just finished reading your book *The Fall and Rise of Reginald Perrin*, and all I can say is that I have never read such an entertaining, true to life story, that hits so well on the peril of the middle class wage slaves. I am widely read for my age, having indulged in Shakespeare, Tolstoi, Solzhenitsyn, Daudet, and all the other great writers. But the only conclusion I can draw is that your genius tops them all.

You're allowed to be a bit over the top at fifteen!

Another letter showed just how much people can read into things. I wrote in the Epilogue to the book, 'The same gale caused a plastic bag to get caught round the exhaust of a Rentokil van in Matthew Arnold Avenue, Climthorpe.' This was no more than a piece of the detail I love so much. To me Rentokil is a funny name and so is Matthew Arnold Avenue. It was a piece of picture building. But a reader wrote:

> Who was going to be asphyxiated in the van? The Perrins live in Coleridge Close and so far I can't find any other reference to Matthew Arnold Avenue in the Poets' Estate. I feel so stupid but this just nags at me. Authors do sometimes leave solutions to their readers! But this just stumps me.

I must mention one more letter – from Peter Campbell, of Gillingham, Dorset. As his behaviour gets odder, Reggie starts using the wrong words for things. His favourite words are parsnip and earwig. Mr Campbell found, in James Joyce's poem 'The Ballad of Persse O'Reilly' the words parsnip, earwig and hippopotamuns [sic]. He wondered if any of the inspiration for Reggie came from the poem. Not consciously. I've read most of the great man, even *Finnegans Wake*, but I don't recall reading the poem. The most intriguing explanation would be that these are words which have a particular power for writers.

Mike Cox, Head of Drama at Granada, read the book, enthused, and made me an offer I couldn't refuse. He wanted to do Reggie's story as a two-parter, each part 90 or 120 minutes, starring Ronnie Barker.

I couldn't refuse the offer, but my agent could. Jonathan astonished me by saying, 'Oh no. No, you're going to see Jimmy Gilbert. It'll be a sit-com at the BBC.'

I couldn't believe my ears. My novel a sit-com! But Jonathan assured me that as a sit-com it would have a much longer life and create a much greater stir than any drama. So I went to see James Gilbert, Head of Comedy at the BBC.

I'd known Jimmy ever since *The Frost Report*. He had a quietly humorous, dignified air, and had never quite got over the fact that when he first employed me I didn't even have a television set.

He invited me to sit down. The chair in which I sat gave a mournful sigh, like a cross between a muffled fart and an elderly toad's sigh of satisfaction. An omen?

Jimmy had a reputation for indecisiveness, but one must take as one finds, and my Jimmy Gilbert was decisiveness personified. He'd commissioned a pilot script before I'd settled in the chair.

'Do you have anybody in mind for the part of Reggie?' he asked.

'Yes,' I said. 'Ronnie Barker.'

'Excellent,' he said. 'Very good. Leonard Rossiter it is.'

A lot of casting is political. The BBC already had as much Ronnie Barker as they could cope with – *The Two Ronnies*, *Open All Hours* and *Porridge*. Leonard Rossiter was a huge success on ITV with *Rising Damp*, and the BBC wanted a slice of the action, just as Mike Cox wanted to grab a slice of the Ronnie Barker action from the BBC.

I wasn't thrilled at first. I recalled that description of Ronnie Barker's: 'a sweaty, charming, paunchy . . .' Even as I write this passage I recall something I've never mentioned to a soul before because I'd completely forgotten it. In the early stages of bringing Reggie to life I used to picture my Member of Parliament for Barnet, Reginald Maudling. That was where the Reggie bit came from. As Reggie developed, I forgot this.

I was disappointed not to get Ronnie, but I soon became excited about Len. He was hilarious in *Rising Damp*, and I had seen that he was a great actor in *The Irresistible Rise of Arturo Ui*. Suddenly I felt that he might be irresistible in *The Fall and Rise Of Reginald Perrin*.

That title was James Gilbert's incidentally. It suggested the unexpectedness of Reggie's journey. It inspired Ronnie Hazlehurst's haunting signature tune and the opening credits, despite which many people including journalists still miss the point and call it 'The Rise and Fall . . .'

The hardback of the book had been called *The Death of Reginald Perrin*. I wasn't sad at the death of *The Death of* . . . I'd seen it in one bookshop in the murder mystery section.

I struggled a little with the pilot script. When I next arrived at the office of the Head of Funny Chairs his face was long and he'd recruited one or two allies, and their faces were long, and my chair's sigh had a tone of infinite regret.

Jimmy came straight to the point. 'None of us like your script,' he said. 'You've put all these jokes in. It isn't funny any more. Why have you put all these jokes in?'

'Because it's a sit-com.'

'Your book's funny. The lines in your book are funny. That's what I've commissioned.'

I think I've always had an underlying faith in my ability as a writer, but I've not always had sufficient faith in the quality of any particular piece of writing. I had to go away now and look at my novel and learn to believe in it.

My second draft went down well, and from that moment I was trusted utterly. No script editor, no committee, no interference from higher authority. Barely a word was changed during the three series that followed, unless, very occasionally, it was found not to work in rehearsal.

Len was working on *Rising Damp* at YTV at the same time as I was there with *Sez Les*, and we arranged to meet in the bar.

'Your book's the second best novel by a modern English writer that I've read this year,' he told me.

I thanked him profusely.

'The best was by your friend Peter Tinniswood.'

'Yes, he's wonderful, isn't he?'

Later Len told me that I'd disappointed him greatly by not being irritated at his putting Peter's book first.

Yorkshire Television had walk-throughs of scripts the day before the recording, so that all the technical staff could see the piece in full. Len invited me to see the walk-through of *Rising Damp*. I knew the director, Ronnie Baxter, and the floor manager, Mike Purcell, son of the great Irish actor Noel Purcell. They greeted me warmly. I sat in the seats that next day would hold the studio audience, and the walk-through began.

After a few minutes Ronnie asked Len, who was standing in a doorway, to move a little further to his right.

'Why?' asked Len. 'What's Rigsby's motivation for standing a little further to the right?'

'No motivation,' said Ronnie. 'It's just that I get a better picture that way.'

'Oh I forgot,' said Len. 'It isn't about comedy. It's about pretty pictures. Silly me. Well, I'll tell you what. I'll go and sit in the studio audience, and then you can get a really pretty picture of your doorway with no distractions.'

Len strode off the set, across the studio floor and up to the top tier of the empty seats.

'Carry on,' he called out.

There was a dreadful silence in the studio, then Len wandered down and sat beside me. There was a faintly manic gleam in his eyes.

'Going well, isn't it?' he said.

I think the truth was that Len didn't respect Ronnie. I worked with Ronnie many years later and found he could be blinkered with actors, but the fact was that he directed the sharpest, snappiest, most successful sit-com in ITV history, and he must have had something to do with that, and it was very wrong of Len to allow Ronnie's weakness to blind him to his strength.

Mike Purcell said, 'You're going to be working with that man? God help you.' I felt much the same.

I can feel a detour coming on, and before I indulge in it I must just say that in *Perrin* we never had scenes like that. On the whole it was a happy show. Len was a perfectionist and not always easy to work with, but I ended up being extremely fond of him.

The detour is a play called *Our Young Mr Wignall.* It was so intertwined with the beginnings of Reggie that I feel that I must deal with it here.

Mike Cox at Granada took his defeat over *Perrin* with good grace and asked me to do something else for him. I was thrilled. In those days the word Granada invoked either great drama or the Alhambra. Now it invokes a travel lodge or a motorway service station.

I came up with an idea about two fluffy-toy salesmen who visit Manchester on business. The eponymous younger man spends his evenings pursuing girls and getting nowhere. The older man, who is retiring, has a different lady every night, and doesn't let on to them or the younger man. The audience know all this, the characters don't, so it's a riot of dramatic irony, with the risk of predictability avoided by the quality of the comic detail.

I talked the basic idea through to Mike, who laughed and commissioned it. No synopsis, no script editor, no story conferences. Simplicity and trust.

Alan Dobie, an actor I admired greatly, played the older man. I was bitterly disappointed. He seemed to be sleep-walking through it. Then I saw the rushes. Brilliant. Albert Welling was excellent, too, as the younger man, and there were several beautiful cameos, notably from Brian Martin as a camp barman in the Hawaiian Bar and James Warrior as Mr Bristle, of the Glamorgan Surgical Appliances and Rubber Goods Company. James's off-stage name is Will. I hope you'll remember that, or there may be confusion later.

Another member of the cast, Linda Marchal, gave a very amusing performance but refused to say the phrase 'verbal diarrhoea' because she found it disgusting, which was surprising in view of some of the things she came out with when she became Linda La Plante.

Richard Martin directed with fine brio, Mike Cox oversaw it with watchful bonhomie. It was unalloyed joy, but not for the people of Bolton. The manager of the Pack Horse Hotel asked if he could keep the tacky Hawaiian set that we had used in what had previously been a pleasant Lancashire watering hole. For all I know it's Hawaiian to this day.

The play necessitated research into the way Lancastrians talked. The exact rhythms of speech are important to me. I sat in pubs in Manchester, Oldham, Bolton and Bury. In Bury I heard so many classic remarks I had to rush out to the loo to write them all down.

When I told the landlord I'd just come from Manchester, he said, 'Oh, Manchester! I don't use it,' with infinite scorn.

'I'm *actually* from London,' I said.

He brightened visibly. 'Oh, London,' he said. 'We used to go there back end, but she couldn't get Courvoisier.'

That remark lit up whole acres of their married life. That's one of the things I love about the North. People are so unselfconsciously revealing.

Attracted by the comment, 'If you threw a petrol bomb in Yates's Wine Lodge, somebody'd drink it' I went to the Yates's in Oxford Street in Manchester and heard the following Pinteresque exchange:

'I saw 'im yesterday.'

'Who?'

''im.'

'Oh. 'im. Where?'

'Down the bottom.'

'Aye, well, he would be.'

Our Young Mr Wignall would not have been as good if I had not done this somewhat unusual, and hugely enjoyable, research.

I was unable to go to the location filming of the pilot episode of *Perrin*, but all it involved was his journey to and from the station through

Coleridge Close, Tennyson Avenue and Wordsworth Drive. Hazel Holt in *The Stage* was very critical of all this walking and asked for a better ratio of ice cream to feet in future. I think she was wrong. You had to have something of the routine in order to make sense of Reggie's rebellion against it. She, to her great credit, thought she was wrong too, and wrote so at the end of the whole shooting match.

The bulk of the show would be recorded in the studio before an audience, and there were a few days of rehearsal in a church hall in Hammersmith. I was nervous and excited to be meeting Elizabeth Perrin and C.J. and Doc Morrissey and David Harris-Jones and Tony Webster for the first time. I might hate them all.

I didn't. The director, John Howard Davies, who had burst on to the scene as an impossibly beautiful Oliver Twist, and was never allowed to forget it (and now I'm not allowing him to forget it) had made a brilliant job of the casting.

John Barron was a wonderfully acerbic C.J., his essential niceness enabling him to play the awful man utterly ruthlessly and still retain a bit of our affection. John Horsley was sublime as Doc Morrissey. Every few months I watch his examination of Reggie in the first episode, so brilliant was the comic acting of them both. Bruce Bould and Trevor Adams were super and great as the sickening sycophants, while Sue Nichols was lovely as the object of Reggie's fantasies and fears.

Pauline Yates played the role of us looking at Reggie, much as we saw *Fawlty Towers* through Polly and *Hi-de-Hi* through Geoffrey Fairweather. If you don't realise how important an element of a comedy this can be, consider how much *Hi-de-Hi* lost when Simon Cadell left. Pauline was normality and had to be at least a little bit dull. She never seemed dull, and she was also splendid in the second series when the worm turned.

During the rehearsals of the pilot Len said to me, 'This is so strong that we don't have to try to be funny.' It was then that I began to have hopes about the series.

The pilot was deemed a success, the series was commissioned, I wrote it fast and with sudden confidence and relish. I was as faithful to the book as I could be – I didn't want to upset the author, these novelists can be temperamental – but I was ruthless where necessary. I felt that for a sit-com done in front of a studio audience I had to lose all traces of the book's incestuous relationship between Reggie's brother-in-law Jimmy and Reggie's daughter Linda.

The sublime Geoffrey Palmer as Jimmy and the sparkly Sally-Jane Spencer as Linda were cast by Gareth Gwenlan, relatively young and inexperienced, who took the hot seat of directing Len when John Howard Davies took his hot seat as Head of Comedy. Gareth also cast Tim Preece as the boring Tom, and Tim gave an object lesson on how to play boring without being boring.

When Gareth turned up for filming with a new car and new clothes and a new briefcase, John Hobbs, the vastly experienced, vastly amusing, vastly camp first assistant or second director, said, 'Who got a director's set for Christmas, then?'

Gareth won Len's confidence very quickly and there were never more than tiny disagreements between them.

The pre-series filming was extensive and important, and a complicated schedule saw the vast BBC caravan travelling around Dorset and Wiltshire in the summer of 1976. The sun blazed down on us and touched us with the golden glow of optimism.

The whole production unit turned up one day in a little Dorset village, and parked in its only street, to film one little fantasy scene of Reggie and Joan parked in an old car on the lawn of a suburban house.

A woman from one of the houses questioned me. What were all these people doing? I pointed out the costume department. No problem there. Len and Sue were in costume. I wasn't so lucky with the sound department. What were they doing? Nothing. There wasn't any sound in that scene. And what about the lighting department? It was bright sunshine and we didn't need any lighting. What were all those burly men doing? Nothing. Sometimes they had to build tracks. Sometimes we needed cranes or hoists or all sorts of equipment. We just didn't need any now. Who are all those people on the bus? Actors and extras. We don't need them this afternoon.

'They can whistle for their licence fee next year,' shouted the woman as the vast procession moved off.

If I'd told her that the real waste wasn't in this highly visible area but hidden away in the layers of management and in the expense of all the accountants hired to save money she'd have been even more angry.

We had a most enjoyable night's shoot at West Bay near Bridport. The lighting department came into its own creating moonlight for Reggie's famous walk into the sea.

Mary, Dave, Chris and Kim all came down to see some of the filming, and we had a wonderful time, half seaside holiday, half watching the filming, in blazing sunshine and temperatures in the mid-nineties.

One stifling Saturday evening the whole unit decided to go for drinks at a nearby hotel, not knowing that it was hosting the annual dinner dance of the East Dorset Bowls League that evening. Actors and technicians mingled with the bowlers, who were mainly quite elderly, and danced them off their feet. I don't believe that to this day some of the bowlers know that there were intruders at their do. I heard one woman say, 'Well, I have to hand it to Algy. This is the best the dinner dance has ever gone.'

I'm only human, and I felt a great joy, as the wagons rolled across the baked lands, to know that all this was happening because of me.

At Longleat, in the sumptuous safari park of the Marquis of Bath, we filmed the scene in which Reggie, fed up with a family outing to a safari park, sees three lions, stops the car, gets out and approaches the torpid beasts, saying, 'I've seen livelier lions in Trafalgar Square.' The lions advance towards him and he rushes back to the car.

As the scene was being filmed, a coach load of Welsh pensioners arrived and saw the three lions. The driver stopped the coach and all the pensioners crowded to the windows and began to take photographs. What they didn't know was that the lions were BBC props men in lion skins. Just as they were setting their cameras, there came a loud cry of 'Cut' and the BBC props men did what BBC props men do when they hear a cry of 'Cut'. They lit up. Plumes of smoke emerged from the mouths of the lions. There must be some very puzzling photos in yellowing albums in Pontardulais and Ammanford and Tredegar.

We moved on to Witney, where I saw Len behave like Reggie Perrin in real life. As he was booking into his hotel, the hotelier said, 'We close the door at 11.30 and we don't give a key.'

'Thank you so much for being considerate enough to tell me that before I walked upstairs,' said Len. 'Goodbye.'

He booked into a B&B across the green, returning to the crowded bar of our hotel only to invite us all, gleefully, for drinks in a pub across the green. The hotelier's face as we trooped out en masse was a study in fury and dismay.

The studio recordings went well. It's a strange business, recording a television show in front of an unrepresentative gathering of about two hundred people. The rhythm and pace of the show cannot but be influenced by the laughter of a group of people who can be stirred into a frenzy by the warm-up man or reduced to boredom by the delays and repetitions that occur when things go wrong.

Our warm-up man was Felix Bowness, an amiable soul with an infectious laugh. He played the jockey in *Hi-De-Hi*. It's a horrendous job. If the warm-up man isn't funny enough, it can kill the evening. If he's too funny, it can kill the show. If he's bluer than the show it's very dangerous. Felix pitched it just right.

Len was very good with the studio audience too. He would make a deliberate mistake very early on and move backwards to the beginning very fast as if rewinding himself. This would relax the audience, who tended to go tense at the commencement of recording.

The question of whether a show should have a studio audience is a vexed one. Len, the supreme comic actor, delighted in them. I did too. It puts writers and actors on their mettle. It forces you to be more than mildly amusing.

It can be dangerous, too. I have heard people say that they look for three laughs on every page. What unmitigated cobblers. The great Simpson and Galton could go two pages without a laugh, if the laugh at the end of them was good enough. Ditto John Sullivan or Clement and Le Fresnais, anyone who really understands the craft. There's no comedy worse than a sit-com with artificial laughs at regular intervals.

Before leaving the subject of studio audiences I must mention what promised to be my darkest hour. One week, after Felix had asked if there were any large parties in, I heard a loud 'Ja. We are from Hamburg. We are forty-four people from the steelworkers' union.' My heart sank. Any more large parties, asked Felix. 'Oh yes,' squeaked an unmistakably Japanese voice. 'There are fifty-six of us from Osaka shipyards.' My heart sank further. 'Aren't there any English groups in?' asked Felix. 'Oh yeah,' came a flat, dull English voice. 'There are sixty of us.' 'And who are you?' asked Felix. 'The Milton Keynes Funeral Directors' Association,' intoned the voice.

They turned out to be one of the very best audiences we ever had. So much for stereotypes.

The series became known for its catch-phrases, so while it was in some ways a complete original it was also in the mainstream of British comedy traditions. Good catch-phrases develop naturally. Those in *Perrin* are symbols of the repetitive nature of the world that is driving Reggie to distraction. The 'great' and 'super' of the two yes-men are an expression of their sycophancy. They are amusing in themselves, but what is really amusing about them is how they come to irritate Reggie.

Jimmy's 'Cock Up On The Catering Front' is an illustration that he's stuck in his past. He's proud of being *Major* James Anderson. He hankers after the old military certainties.

The most famous catchphrase was C.J.'s 'I didn't get where I am today . . .' The great thing about this was that it was infinitely variable, it was an open sesame to absurdity. 'I didn't get where I am today by wearing underpants decorated with Beethoven.' 'I didn't get where I am today by indulging in hanky-panky willy-nilly.' But the absurdity had at its core the truth about this boss figure. His life consisted of getting where he was today and letting you know it.

C.J. used a veritable barrage of clichés. He lived and thought in clichés, which he often got wrong. Round about this time I used to experiment with a particular cliché. I would drop it into the conversation at appropriate moments. It was 'What's grist to the mill is nose to the grindstone.' It is of course complete nonsense. Nobody ever challenged me. Nobody ever laughed. 'That's true,' people would say, or 'I suppose so,' or some such reply.

While on C.J. I must answer a question that you haven't asked. But people do. Does he represent J.C. in reverse? Not my agent, but Jesus. Is he an anti-Christ figure, the God of Mammon?

I don't know.

Come off it. You're the writer. You must know.

Well, let's say that I didn't think of it consciously. If I had I'd have abandoned it, for fear that the comedy would disappear beneath the significance, but it *is* a bit suspiciously neat. I have to say that I think the naughty old subconscious may have been at work there.

Reggie felt trapped in this world of catch-phrases. The only approach to a catch-phrase that I allowed him was his comment on his journey – eleven minutes late, blah blah blah. This was less a catchphrase than a simple expression of a fact, of another instance of his being trapped.

He was a man trying to find an individual way through a corporate world. It was implicit that he was without religious faith. He was searching for value, for moral certainty, and he was constricted by habit, routine, discipline and all the forces of conformity.

A great part of the appeal of his character came from the fact that he could say the things that someone like me cannot say, though I think them.

My favourite moment in the TV series (it doesn't occur in the same way in the book, the author had missed an opportunity, I had to improve his work quite often, you'd be surprised) sees Reggie arriving late for lunch at a conference of the British Fruit Association. Sir Elwyn Watkins, Chairman of the Watkins Commission on Pesticides, says 'You missed a very good little talk from Dr Hump. He touched mainly on the role of fruit in a competitive society. His thesis was, in a nutshell, that fruit should not be – indeed cannot be – less or indeed more competitive than the society for which – and indeed by which – it is produced.'

Reggie leant forward, looked Sir Elwyn straight in the eye, and said, 'Really? That *is* uninteresting.'

I can't sum up Len as a comedy actor better than I did in a book called

Leonard Rossiter, compiled by Robert Tanitch and published in 1985 by Robert Royce, with part of the proceeds going to the Malcolm Sargent Cancer Fund for Children, Len's favourite charity.

I believe that you cannot create great comedy without taking risks. Leonard Rossiter was a very fine comic actor, and he took very great risks indeed. Throughout every minute of all twenty-one episodes of *The Fall and Rise of Reginald Perrin* I felt that Len teetered on the verge of over-acting. Yet he never once went too far. That is comic genius.

I only accept three rules about comedy: (1) See above. (2) Rules are made to be broken. (3) Comedy disintegrates and disappears when you analyse it. I shall therefore take the great risk of breaking rule (3) and attempting to analyse Len's comedy. He was a brilliant technician and he created his best characters with such energy, clarity, consistency and truthfulness that he was able to use all his technical abilities to the full. I know of nobody who did better double-takes. He was brilliant at throwaways and visual jokes. His timing was faultless. His use of his body was excellent. He knew exactly where to put the inflexion for comic effect. He had above all the rare capacity to be extremely fast and extremely subtle at the same time. Yet none of these devices – artificial devices employed to promote laughter not illuminate character – interfered with his ability, in his best performances, to present a real human being whose plight could touch us deeply.

Len was, of course, much more than a comic actor, and I hope that the writer of the BBC news item saying that he would probably be best known for his television commercials will be transferred to television commercials when the BBC is forced to have them. I will remember Len not for his commercials, not for *Reggie Perrin*, not for *Rising Damp*, not even for *Arturo Ui*, but for his performance at the Mermaid in the one-man show written by John Wells about the painter Benjamin Haydon, who mistakenly believed himself to be a genius. I felt that all the human comedy, all the human tragedy, all the absurdity of mankind's pretensions were illuminated for us by Leonard. That is hyperbole, of course, but Len made me feel it. I was certain that night that I was seeing not just a very fine actor, but one of the all-time greats. Naturally, it being that sort of world, this seems to be one of the least remembered things that Len did.

So the shows went well, and our confidence grew, and after each show we went to one of the actors' houses and had a party. We kept something of the spirit of the summer of '76 going, and I think we all felt that we might never have quite such a summer again. Shortly after the end of the series John and Joan Barron gave a delightful dinner party, with superb wines, for Mary and me and for Len and his wife Gilly. As we left, John said, 'That was to thank you for the happiest working summer of my life.'

After the final show we had a party in a hospitality room at the BBC. Mary brought the food by car from Barnet, including a whole Wye salmon in aspic and a strawberry and lychee ripple, the star of Reggie's range of exotic ice creams. A great gastronomic joke to end a great summer.

But summer mellowed and ripened into autumn, and cold winds blew. Transmission approached. Nervousness increased. By now the series had assumed huge importance for me.

As it happened, *Our Young Mr Wignall* went out very close to *Perrin*, and went down extremely well. I missed the press showing, due to other commitments. The journalist Celia Brayfield, later to become a best-selling novelist – damn her, not that I'm bitter – told me that I had missed a great experience, the prolonged laughter of a group of hardened critics. Never mind. The greater pleasure is the knowledge of a job well done.

When *Perrin* began to go out, friends were complimentary, but friends usually are. I had no idea whether it was hitting the spot.

A travel agent who used the Monken Holt next to our house pleased me when he said, 'I loved the first show,' but rather spoilt it the next week by saying, 'I loved the show last night. To be honest I hadn't really enjoyed the first one.' Later he would say, 'I grew to love the series. To be honest I hadn't much gone for the first two or three.' Later still he said, 'I loved the second series. To be honest I didn't much like the first.'

Several people said that it grew on them, as if I had written a wart.

Then, round about episode four, it happened. I was in the foyer of the Dragonara Hotel in Leeds. Reception was on the second floor so all there was on the ground floor was a bare room and a lift. Three businessmen were waiting for the lift beside me.

'I'm going up the stairs,' said one. 'I didn't get where I am today by waiting for lifts.'

'Great,' said the second.

'Super,' said the third.

I wanted to dance. I knew in that moment that I had a hit.

I had a wonderful letter from James/Will Warrior, who had been so brilliant as Mr Bristle. Will's mother had had a phone call from Nancy Grifiths Cilaraenllwyd, who lived with her equally unpronounceable husband in a remote farm near Trapp, in the shadows of Carreg Cennen Castle. Nancy was a member of Trapp W.I., of which Will's mother was currently the President, and she was a distant relative of mine. I remember a wonderful childhood drive to her farm in mid-Wales, when she was still Nancy Williams.

Nancy rang Will's mother after *Our Young Mr Wignall*, and his mother asked her how she had enjoyed the play. Her reply linked the play with Perrin: 'Well now then Alice, there's a thing. I thought your son took his part well but I didn't like the play you see. That old Nobbs he's a bit vulgar you see. It's always old sex with him. It was the same with that Mr Perrin thing. Every time he mentioned his mother-in-law you saw a picture of a fat old sow. I think that's vulgar you see.'

I'm glad to say that I have hardly ever had any criticism of the hippo, on p.c. grounds or on any other. It was simply too extreme to be taken seriously in that way.

Detail is vital in comedy. Who can forget the wonderful exchange in *Dad's Army* where the German says, 'What's your name?' and Captain Mainwaring says, 'Don't tell him, Pike.' In the unsuccessful American

Sunbathing fatigues in Torquay, 1954. Left to right:
Colin Eales, me, Johnny Hannam, Pete Willis.

A Wild night out in Munster! John Bowden, me, David
Bird, David Pink and Mick Walls (I Think!).

A Lazy day in Cambridge. Sally Williams, Chris Rudd (right) and a friend
whom I Remember vividly except for his name.

The Old Post House, Broxwood – my home for twelve years.

Step-children and step-grandchildren at Broxwood. Left to right – Chris holding Auriel, Sarah, Talia holding Lee, Kayleigh, Dave holding Daniel, Joe, and Kim with Luke. Missing are John (back in France, working?) and Elsie (Excused – Not yet born).

Me and 'Reggie' – Leonard Rossiter.

EMPIRE, SHEFFIELD.
3RD APRIL 50.
CYNTHIA & GLADYS
~~JOHNNY LAWSON TRIO.~~
TONY FAYNE & DAVID EVANS
JOHNNY LAWSON TRIO.
6·46   R W.   9·1.
KAY CAVANDISH.
INTERVAL.
JOHNNY LAWSON TRIO.
DONALD B. STUART
FIVE SMITH BROS.
CHRIS SANDS.

Pages from Robb Wilton's notebook, listing his jokes and the bill at the Sheffield Empire on 3 April 1950 – a show watched by fifteen-year-old Henry Pratt in *Second From Last in the Sack Race*.

Relaxing during the filming of *Stalag Luft* – in Bellingham, Northumberland.

pilot it's 'Don't tell him, Henderson.' Barely funny at all. Too long a name. Well the point I'm making is that we had a brilliant chosen clip of a hippo. Another hippo might have been just mildly amusing. Our hippo was hilarious. It's just a shame there isn't a Bafta Award for Best Hippo.

One of the few things I disliked from the first series was the character of Reggie's son, Mark. This is not a criticism of the actor, who made a fine stab at it, but the character was surplus to dramatic requirements and, with his inept rhyming slang, just a little forced. I was straining for humour. It's so easy to get rid of a character. I did it in the second book in one sentence: 'They couldn't phone Mark, as he was touring Africa with a theatre group which was presenting *No Sex, Please, We're British* to an audience of bemused Katangans.

Ruthless coves, authors.

Everybody wanted a second series, but Len would only agree to it if I wrote a second book. He argued that the series had a depth and quality that came from its being adapted from a novel. He didn't want it to drift away into conventional sit-com-land. He was right, of course, and I settled down to write the unimaginatively titled *The Return of Reginald Perrin*. Lazy thinking, David.

I didn't find the book easy to write. I'd already told a complete story. Reggie tries to escape, finds the escape is not the answer, and returns. Could there be a valid sequel?

He ended the first book as Martin Wellbourne. Clearly he needed to return to his true identity. Clearly he couldn't remain at Sunshine Desserts. I'd said all I needed to say about that world. Just as clearly he couldn't settle down happily, so he needed to escape again, but what from? You can't write the same story twice. Well, sadly, some people can, but we won't go into that.

If his escape was to be different, he needed to escape with Elizabeth, not from her. He needed to do something absurd again, and this time, therefore, he needed to do it with Elizabeth.

I began to think of the book as if it was a musical composition, a series of variations on the theme of success and failure. It was much more interesting, much more telling as a critique on the consumer society if Reggie was escaping from success, not failure.

I had my shape. Reggie revealed, Reggie a very ordinary type of failure, doesn't go for failure, feels trapped in it, has an absurd idea, carries it out with Elizabeth, the absurd idea becomes a huge success, Reggie feels trapped by the huge success, attempts to destroy the huge success, can't, runs away, leaves his clothes on a beach with Elizabeth.

The only problem was – what absurd idea? Reggie's a businessman. It has to be a business project. He makes and/or sells something absurd.

I made lists of absurd things. They were amusing, but not amusing enough. The list grew longer. It took ages to find the solution, and I found it out of despair, because I couldn't think of any one thing amusing enough to build a series round.

He would make and sell all the items on my list. I had created the Grot Shop.

In comedy, if you start from the right port and are making for the right port, it will usually be plain sailing. So it proved. The publishers liked the book, Len liked the book, the series was commissioned, the scripts poured out, they were in some respects better than the novel, so that once again I wished I could go back and rewrite the book.

I'm the first to admit that the second book and series weren't the equal of the first, which had defined a despair that wasn't Reggie's alone but was present in the zeitgeist. I received quite a lot of letters from people in despair at their sense of being trapped in jobs that didn't satisfy them. Often they asked for advice. Some days I felt like Claire Rayner. I found my replies very difficult. I didn't want to be evasive and wimpish, but I couldn't offer life-changing advice on the basis of the information in one short letter.

There was no possibility of another such definitive theme. However, the Grot Shop idea was a marvellous vehicle for satire, scripts 3 to 7 were as funny as anything I've written before or since, and a wonderful time was had by all. The location filming took place mainly in Dorset again. This time we needed bad weather for a sequence about a disastrous holiday. We had the fire brigade standing by to provide rain. They weren't needed. We weren't very popular in our hotel as we came down to breakfast rubbing our hands and saying, 'Raining again! Terrific!'

The second series went down very well. The audience grew considerably. The audience appreciation index was high. What had been a cult show, albeit a large and popular cult, became a very successful mainstream comedy without lowering its standards.

One day, in a pub called the Windmill, across Hadley Common, I heard a really rather yobbish boy relate virtually the whole of the previous night's episode, which his mate had missed. My step-daughter, Kim, by this time reading philosophy at Keele University, reported that it was difficult to get anywhere near the TV room on *Perrin* nights.

The creation of items to be sold in the Grot Shops had been enormous fun, and had been something that others could happily contribute to. Mary, for instance, came up with the immortal 'elastic tow rope'. It was almost inevitable that somebody would approach me with the idea of actually making Grot items and opening Grot Shops. I was given a very nice lunch near Covent Garden, and we made lists of items that could feasibly be made and sold. I'm glad that the project never came to fruition. It would have undermined the satire.

I was anxious that the second series shouldn't be too linear and found fertile ground in the sub-plot about Jimmy's secret army. A little bit of this found its way into somebody's top fifty moments of TV comedy – number one was David Jason falling through the open flap on a bar counter. I was pleased to be there with the most verbose of all the entries. It's from a passage in which Jimmy is telling Reggie about his plans for his army.

REGGIE: Come on, Jimmy, who are you going to fight when the balloon goes up?

JIMMY: Forces of anarchy, wreckers of law and order.

REGGIE: I see.

JIMMY: Communists, maoists, trotskyists, neo-trotskyists, union leaders, communist union leaders.

REGGIE: I see.

JIMMY: Keg bitter, punk rock, glue sniffers, *Play For Today*, squatters, Clive Jenkins, Roy Jenkins, up Jenkins, up everybody's, Chinese restaurants, why do you think Windsor Castle is ringed with Chinese restaurants?

REGGIE: I see. Is that all?

JIMMY: Yes.

REGGIE: You know the sort of people you're going to attract, don't you, Jimmy? Thugs, bully boys, psychopaths, sacked policemen, security guards, sacked security guards, racialists, paki-bashers, queer-bashers, Chink-bashers, basher-bashers, anybody-bashers, rear admirals, queer admirals, vice-admirals, fascists, neo-fascists, crypto-fascists, loyalists, neo-loyalists, crypto-loyalists.

JIMMY: (ENCOURAGED) Really think so? I thought support might be hard to get.

The third series proceeded along the same principle of book first and then adaptation. Len was extremely enthusiastic about the book, and nobody had any doubt about the quality of the scripts. Mr Retrospect can see that it was significantly less good than the first two. Andrew Langley, writing in the *Bath and West Chronicle*, said that I should go away for a long holiday.

Had he but known it, I had already been away for a long holiday. With Mary's parents in declining health, we had spent three months in early summer in a lovely Guernsey granite farmhouse owned by an estate agent, who didn't live in it because it was too far from his work and his daughter's school. Guernsey is eight miles by five! Liz Calder and Gareth Gwenlan were among our visitors, and my mother and Auntie Kathleen made their first and, in my mother's case, last flight in order to spend a few days with us.

The estate agent decided to sell, and just before the end of our visit he phoned to say that prospective purchasers would visit that afternoon. He asked us to move a few pieces of furniture to hide damp patches. Don't buy a house off an estate agent, Mrs Worthington.

Mary's father died not long afterwards, and her mother died during the location filming of the third series. It was the end of an era, and cast a great pall over the beginning of the series.

When I returned to the filming I was told, 'Thank goodness you're here. We've a bit of a problem.'

The problem was that I had written 'Well at least we've got a nice day for it' and it was drizzling.

How about, '"Pity we haven't got a better day for it"?' I suggested.

'Brilliant. Thank God you were here.'

Little things went wrong. Some of the filming, done in my absence, seemed too perfunctory. Tim Preece was unavailable to play Tom, and we recast. It didn't work. Tim's performance had been so definitive that there was nowhere else to go.

The series lost me my best friend, Peter Tinniswood. Peter suddenly invoked the law and attempted to get an injunction against the BBC, preventing the transmission of the third series. The charge was plagiarism.

In his second novel, *Mog*, Peter had written the following opening paragraph.

> 'My plan is quite simple,' said Mrs Mortensen, who was Danish. 'I shall set up a small lunatic asylum in an ordinary suburban house in an ordinary suburban street.'

In *The Better World of Reginald Perrin* I had Reggie saying:

> I intend to set up a community, where middle-aged, middle-class people like us can learn to live in love and faith and trust.

And later, but still on the same page:

I'm sorry, old girl, but I want to live in an ordinary suburban house in an ordinary suburban street.

These words must have hit Peter with a blinding flash. He must have been absolutely convinced that he was being deliberately plagiarised. I can understand this. He was living through turbulent days. He had left Puts and the children and gone to live with an actress, Liz Goulding. He had told me he was contemplating this. He'd asked for my advice. I, still a happily married man, and very fond of Puts, had naturally argued against it. He had naturally ignored my advice.

I can't be sure what Peter was thinking. I didn't see him at the time. I can guess that at this troubling time I was a troubling figure to him, a figure from the life he'd abandoned, a figure who disapproved. He would look on my work with a jaundiced and vulnerable eye.

However, what could he actually claim that I had stolen? Ten words. It's impossible to claim that I stole the idea of a lunatic asylum, since my idea was not of a lunatic asylum, but of a community. The idea of setting things in a house was hardly individual enough to steal. Had I had Reggie buying his old house in Coleridge Close, there would have been no problem. Those ten words were the problem.

My contention was that those ten words proved not my guilty intent, but my innocence of intent. Had I ever made any conscious connection with *Mog*, I would not have been so foolish as to use the identical words.

Ironically, *Mog* had failed as a book, for me, precisely because, being set in a mental home, it had virtually no contact with the sane world outside it, no contrast between abnormality and normality. And now here was I making the same mistake and losing a friend for it.

A list of all the things I'd supposedly stolen from Peter winged its way to Twixt by fast courier. I spent an entire weekend going through everything we'd written and found a long list of things that I could claim, with at least equal credibility, that Peter had stolen from me. Some of the things he said I'd stolen from him were on my list of things which I said he'd stolen from me. It would have been comic to find two comedy writers arguing like that, if it hadn't been so sad.

Jonathan Clowes, agent for both of us, found me a top lawyer,

Michael Rubinstein, and the affair was swiftly defused, but Peter and I didn't speak for ten years and Peter left the agency because Jonathan had supported me. Jonathan had to support me, as I wasn't the one making waves.

I think it's a tribute to Peter and to me that we have managed, in the end, to become very good friends all over again.

I don't want to leave the subject of *Mog* on a sour note, so I must mention an astonishing book that Peter brought out in 1974. It's called *The Stirk of Stirk*. It's a prose poem, and the first chapter, the shortest that I know in English literature, tells its theme:

> Pay heed, for I am to tell of the adventures of
>   The Stirk of Stirk.
> With his two companions, the giant and the dwarf,
>   he tracked down Robin Hood.
> The giant was a Negro.
> The dwarf was no stranger to jeopardy.
> Oh the perils the three men faced.
> In the bitter winter.

Robin Hood turns out to be a very old, sick man. Maid Marion is a bashful young boy. The book is strange, spare, powerful, gripping and unlike anything else Peter has written. Its language glitters like the hard frost it describes. Its economy is exquisite. I could never write anything half as good.

It didn't do particularly well. It's that sort of world.

The third series of *Reggie Perrin* didn't do particularly well either. Not in its own right, anyway. It was a modest success only on the coat tails of the first two series. There were some good jokes and sequences, but it lacked tension. It was still a good TV sit-com by any standards and the audience figures were respectable, but it wasn't worthy of the first two series. Perhaps, like *Fawlty Towers*, we should have stopped at two.

Reggie Perrin helped turn Geoffrey Palmer into a star, but it ended Trevor Adams's acting career. After saying many great lines penned by

Shakespeare and others, his great line in Perrin was just that – 'Great'. People stopped him in the street and said, 'Great!' It irritated him greatly. He left showbiz and became a lawyer.

The programme lives on in all sorts of ways. My favourite is an Indian restaurant in Plymouth, called 'Veggie Perrins', run by a Gujurati, Bill Meswania, whose family moved to Kenya before he was born. The restaurant was the invention of a journalist in Plymouth, named Jon Massey, and it was opened by John Barron in 1995. I couldn't get there, but I went the following year, en route to France via Plymouth. I don't think any of the staff, except Bill, really understood what it was all about or who I was, but no matter, I like Indian vegetarian food.

Jon had all sorts of ideas including adopting a hippo at an ethically-sound zoo. He envisaged chains of Veggie Perrins across the land. It didn't happen. Bill was a restaurateur, not an ambitious businessman. I'm happy that the restaurant continues to exist and that even as I type I am drinking black coffee from a yellow mug that says, 'I didn't get where I am today by eating meat'.

There was a German translation of the first book, entitled *Mr Perrin Flippt aus*! and there is a Japanese version. The series still sells widely. In 1992 a horse was named Reggie Perrin. It hasn't set the race tracks alight. I've had letters from the Reginald Iolanthe Perrin Garden Cricket Society, a Reginald Perrin Appreciation Society in County Down, and several Reginald Perrin fan clubs. I received a letter from FREGG, the Free Range Egg Association, thanking me for my condemnation of intensive farming. Reggie inspired a sociological study of real-life management drop-outs at the University of Essex and figures in a book called *Understanding Executive Stress* produced at the University of Manchester. Richard Webber wrote a book about the series published in 1996 – and on time – by Virgin Books. It's been a question in Trivial Pursuit. Had I then become famous? Not quite.

I quote from three reviews:

David Hobbs is not a writer whose name commands instant recognition (*Burton Observer*)

Reginald Perrin . . . is David Potts's answer to Thoreau's piercing observation that most men lead lives of quiet desperation (Radio Orwell)

The Return of Reginald Perrin is every bit as good as David Dobbs's first book on the zany Reggie (*Linlithgow Journal*)

Nearly the last word on Reggie should go to a chapter in a book called *British Television Drama*, published by Palgrave. Chapter 12, by Chris Fox, was entitled 'The Emancipatory Strategies of Reginald Perrin'.

It must be stressed that this contextual approach makes no bold claims to discover the 'real' motivation behind David Nobbs's work: it is not, for example, suggested that, having digested volumes of Western Marxism, Nobbs penned Reginald Perrin in a bid to encourage the middle managers of the world to unite.

And

Rather than suggesting that Nobbs was aiming to do any more than articulate, in comic form, the existential crises of Middle England in the mid-1970s, this debate argues that his achievement was to produce a text which offers a window upon the dichotomies thrown up by the Enlightenment and by modernity. In short, it is proposed that Nobbs unwittingly offers the viewer a comic yet incisive representation of the contradictions inherent in capitalism.

This chapter was sent to me by Alan Plater with the comment, 'I'd love to know how much of this you were aware of.'

I think Chris Fox suggests my answer in the first extract. However, I have to admit that on reading the chapter, I soon found myself revising my initial view that the whole thing was absurd, and within minutes I was thinking, 'What does he mean – "unwittingly"?'

I can't resist quoting one more passage from the chapter, which I particularly enjoy because I've never before been tied in with the intellectual game of name dropping, and because it gives a bit of philosophical respectability to the third series, whose weakness was lack of conflict rather than lack of relevance.

> Just as Horkheimer and Adorno in their Dialectic of Enlightenment point out that there is a dark side to the Enlightenment, the growth of domination, so Reggie also realises that we are only using knowledge as a means to dominate, to shape human life into inhuman forms. As Horkheimer and Adorno note, capitalism makes the satisfaction of needs impossible by ensuring the sanctity of progress and forward thinking: one is never satisfied with what one has, one simply looks forward to what might have been. 'Perrins' offers an escape from all this in a therapy centre without therapists. This is a place where the disaffected can recover some of the values that have been corrupted by capitalism, as the 'Perrins' slogan suggests: 'Want to drop out, but don't like drop-outs? At Perrins, the drop-outs are just like you: they're more like drop-ins; so next time you feel like dropping out, why not drop-in?'

Of course he's justified in his use of 'unwittingly' in the second extract. I'm no Marxist. I am, however, a serious person as well as a humorous one, and I was serious in my critique of capitalist absurdity. The serious and the comic come together in Reggie's speech to the British Fruit Association Seminar in Bilberry Hall.

> Where was I? Oh yes. Progress. Growth. That's another one. Six per cent per year or whatever it is. More people driving more washing machines on bigger lorries down wider motorways. More scientists analysing the effects of more pesticides. More chemicals to cure the pollution caused by more chemicals. More boring speeches to fill up more boring

conferences. More luxury desserts, so that more and more people can enjoy a life increasingly superior to that lived by more and more other people. Are those our just desserts? Society functions best if I over-eat, so I buy too many slimming aids, so I fall ill, so I buy too many pills. We have to have a surfeit of dotes in order to sell our surfeit of antidotes. Well, it's got to stop.

And

You have a right to ask me what I believe in, I who am so anti-everything. I'll tell you. I believe in nihilism, in the sense that I believe in the absence of ism. I know that I don't know and I believe in not believing. For every man who believes something there's a man who believes the opposite. How many wars would be fought, how many men would have been tortured in this world, if nobody had ever believed in anything?

'But that would be awful,' I hear you cry. Well actually I don't, but that's what you would cry if you were listening. I deny it. Would the sun shine less brightly if there was no purpose in life? Would the nightingale sing less sweetly? Would we love each other less deeply? Man's the only species neurotic enough to need a purpose in life.

Reggie means all this seriously. I mean all this seriously. How do you incorporate that into a sit-com? You make him drunk. His audience doesn't listen. That speech, to me, was the crux of the whole thing.

The last word of all should go to Len himself. I once dared to tell him that I thought he was saying a line the wrong way. He made me say it my way. He said I was wrong, but he was so impressed by my fervour that he would do it my way. He did it my way. It got a big laugh.

In the bar, afterwards, I said, 'I was right, wasn't I?' He gleamed at me, and said, 'No, you were wrong, David, and so were the audience.'

At the end of the third series Len said to me, very quietly, 'I don't think we should ever work together again. Whatever we did would be compared to this, and I don't think we could ever top it.'

We remained on good terms, though not friends. We met on a couple of occasions when he was in plays in London. The first was when we went with Gareth Gwenlan to Greenwich to see a revival of David Turner's play *Semi-Detached*. Len had played Fred Midway in Coventry in 1962, but Laurence Olivier had got the part in the West End. Now Len returned and directed it as well. It also starred his lovely wife Gillian Raine, and Bruce 'Super' Bould and his real life wife Theresa (Tree), who had also come into *Reggie Perrin* as his fictional wife.

It was a difficult evening. Gareth made the mistake of asking Dennis Main Wilson the way to the theatre. Dennis was on the board of the theatre and in the middle of a driving ban. 'Take me. I'll show you,' he said. The problem was that Len hadn't seen eye to eye with Dennis since Dennis said to him at a BBC Entertainment Department party, 'Funniest man in England, Reg Varney.' At the same party, incidentally, Len said, 'If a bomb fell on this room tonight, what a gift it would be to British entertainment.'

We had a difficult time keeping Dennis and Len apart, and the evening wasn't helped by the fact that we disliked the production and Len's performance, although we thought that Gilly, Bruce and Tree were all good.

In the bar after the show, Len and Dennis were standing very close to each other in separate groups, and Len urged me to tell a story he liked about Dennis. I did so.

The story was told to me by Barry Cryer. One evening in the BBC Bar, bets were taken on how long it would be before Dennis mentioned *Till Death Us Do Part*. He was an expert at getting it into the conversation. When Dennis arrived, the conversation went:

BARRY: Those moon astronauts must have been brave.

DENNIS: We were very brave with *Till Death*.

Barry won the bet.

I told the story and everybody laughed. Dennis swung round and said, 'That sounded a good one. Can I have a repeat?' I only got out of it by saying, 'No, Dennis. There are too many repeats on the BBC already.' I would have hated to hurt that dear man. I never saw him again.

Later that evening Gareth and Mary and I went out to dinner in the Fulham Road with Len, Gilly, Bruce and Tree, and the air was thick with the absence of compliments.

I'm so glad that we saw Len again, in *The Immortal Haydon*, of which I have written earlier. We saw this with Vernon Lawrence. Afterwards, Mary and I were fulsome in our praise, but Len missed nothing and I could see him thinking, 'Oh, so they do praise things when they like them, so they really didn't like *Semi-Detached*.'

And then he went, during a performance of *Loot*. Len in a Joe Orton play! I had been looking forward to it keenly.

I was sad that he'd gone, but I wasn't shocked. The veins stood out and throbbed when he acted. Saliva sprayed the first three rows. The sweat poured off him. There was no safety net in Len's professional life. He was intense, dangerous, he gave his all. This may have had nothing to do with how he died, but it has everything to do with why I wasn't surprised.

Writing this has made me sadder than I was at the time. Writing this has made me realise how much I miss him – the man, for all his faults, as well as the performer.

13 And Now For Something Completely Different

Now at last I was free to write what I liked. I created a series which had the lowest audience figures ever recorded on BBC1 for a sit-com.

I hoped that by this time I had developed enough of a Nobbsian style to enable Michael Codron to sleep easily in his bed (in his bed, Nobbs! You amaze us. We quite thought he slept in a water tower) and I had no plans to reinvent myself as the Strindberg of the Northern Line. Nevertheless, my mantra for the next years would be the phrase immortalised by Monty Python, 'And now for something completely different'.

Perrin was the story of one man. My next series would be about a group. *Perrin* was about work. My next series would be about play. *Perrin* was set in suburban London. My next series would be set far from what my cousin John calls 'the maddening crowd'.

So when Jimmy Gilbert suggested that I write about British residents abroad, I leapt at it. It fulfilled the necessary criteria. Also, I knew the subject.

I thought back to that trip to Spain, in our racy red Corsair. On the first evening we were taken to a local bar, where every customer was English. There was much discussion of whose round it was, many offers of 'Have this one on me', many cries of 'No, no, it's my shout'. No money changed hands, and at the end of the evening the Spanish barman charged everybody individually for exactly what they had drunk.

These English exiles gave us stern warnings in their cups. 'Whatever you do, don't move to Spain. The Spanish don't know the word work. Manana rules. You need a plumber? No chance. You can't get a decent lawn to grow anywhere. Since Franco went it's not safe to walk the streets, and you hardly ever get any decent rain, and when it does rain it pours, they've never heard of drizzle.'

Next day we met all the same people at lunch. They were sober and it was Wednesday so it was shepherd's pie. 'So when are you moving out here?' they demanded. 'England's finished. The English don't know the meaning of the word work. You can whistle for a plumber. It's grey and drizzly all the time, you have to mow the bloody lawn every few days. And it isn't safe to walk the streets.'

And so I wrote about these people who had dreamt of living abroad and who went there and found that they were trapped. Mary came up with the perfect title – *The Sun Trap*. I even stole one of the characters we met on that trip – a woman who was so proud of all the money she had made running a mobile catering service for films on location that she kept the price tags on all her furniture.

Since the weather was so important to these people I created a retired weather forecaster with no dress sense. To my delight, Michael Fish commented during one of his weather forecasts that he didn't think he dressed that badly. So somebody watched.

Gareth Gwenlan directed, and he assembled a fine cast. There was Zena Walker, a lovely person and a very fine actress with a light comic touch. There was Donald Churchill, a good actor and a better writer and married to Pauline Yates. Graham Crowden, of blessed *One-Way Pendulum* memory, played a tactless retired diplomat with great energy. Joan Benham was excellent and elegant as his wife. Jo Rowbottom, an actress I'd long admired, played the lady with the price tags, and Derek

Waring was the weather forecaster. David Garth was an old news-paperman and Peter Schofield played the barman whose food ranged from 'steak and kidney pudding' on a Monday to 'fish and chips' on a Friday.

Our location filming was done in Nerja in December. We had lovely days in the sunshine, though when we queued for the one telephone in our rather basic hotel it was comic to hear everyone telling their partners at home how cold and grey it was. My room was a restorante for mosquitoes, and I was the only dish on the menu.

The unit was entitled to one day off, and voted to have it on the last day, when work was finished. Alas, at lunchtime the weather broke. A wall of fog approached Nerja like a convention of double glazing salesmen. There was nothing for it but to drink. Donald Churchill came into the bar I was in and said, excitedly, 'David, you must come to our bar. We're all in there sitting opposite us, and we're even better than we are!'

So I went round to the other bar, and there I saw a most extraordinary sight. Along one wall were our cast. Along the other wall were a group of British ex-pats who mirrored their characters almost exactly.

All the cast admired the scripts, I was a name and a success and they were thrilled to be in my series, and now here was that old tart Life Itself giving its seal of approval. I had got things right.

Well, getting things right isn't necessarily a recipe for success. Our studio recordings seemed to be going well, but so keen were the BBC to transmit their smash hit that it was on the screens before we'd finished recording.

There is a terrifying moment of truth when a show begins to transmit. The hype and the hope are over. You know within minutes if it's any good, and within minutes I knew that this wasn't.

I'd fallen into the oldest trap in the game. I'd written about bores and I'd failed to make the fact that they were boring interesting. I needed some more interesting characters to observe and be horrified by the bores. These people were so boring that they didn't even realise that their fellow bores were boring. Another dangerous element was that there wasn't a young person in sight. Even *Dad's Army* had Pike and the spiv.

I still hoped that in the end the truth of the series would outweigh its failings. No such luck. Our transmission time was immediately after *Points of View*. Episode Two was preceded by Barry Took asking what viewers thought of Episode One. 'Boring.' 'Repetitive.' 'Unfunny.' 'Drivel.' At the end of all that Barry said, and I felt that he said it with a touch of relish and I honestly didn't really blame him, 'You can see Episode Two of David Nobbs's new series immediately after this programme.'

It was brave face time. It was so hard to attend the remaining rehearsals and recordings. On the following *Points of View* there were letters of support for the series, but they came too late for team morale. I could hardly bear the unspoken disappointment of the actors.

The Sun Trap was littered with catch-phrases, but they didn't spring out of the characters as they had in Perrin. They didn't work. They sat there like over-anxious smiles.

When I teach about writing I say, 'Always be truthful.' The truth is, though, that Dame Truth is a fickle mistress. Truth only works if it is perceived as Truth.

Many people praised *Perrin* for the accuracy of its portrayal of life in Sunshine Desserts. The conversation would go rather like this:

'I didn't know you worked in the food industry.'

'I didn't.'

'But you must have done.'

'Why?'

'It's all so accurate.'

'I didn't know *you'd* worked in the food industry.'

'I haven't.'

'Then how do you know it's accurate?'

'Well, it must be like that.'

I had written about how I thought the food industry was, and this had coincided with how other people thought it was. In *The Sun Trap* I had written about how it was at that time, but it didn't coincide with how people thought it was.

People didn't recognise the types. It was a situation they didn't know. Our family and friends in Guernsey enjoyed the series. They knew the types. They knew the behaviour of the English ex-pats who lived there – their arrogance, their insularity, their insensitivity. I realised that I had written a series that would only really be popular abroad. I had written a television series for people who didn't have British television.

No wonder it had a low audience figure.

The series actually inspired a degree of hostility. It disturbed people's dreams about paradise in the sun. There's no doubt I'd have done better to write about sex-mad Spanish builders and plumbers who flooded people's houses.

However, I mustn't end up by blaming the audience for the fiasco. The scripts weren't good enough. Donald said more than he realised when he told me that 'We're all in the next bar and *we're even better than we are.*'

Nobbs 0, Life 1.

One of the great things about writing for television is that people only remember the good things. Hardly anybody remembers *The Sun Trap* now.

Among the people who didn't remember it was the BBC itself. They did the whole thing again and called it *Eldorado*. A lot more expense, same result.

Ah well. Onward and upward. What next?

I didn't take every job I was offered. I did turn down the chance to work on a sit-com about a group of fashion photographers, called 'Lovely On The Bum, Nigel', but I did accept another offer, and ended up involved in the most unhappy experience of my working life.

June Wyndham-Davis, a producer at Granada, commissioned me to write the opening episode of a series called *Send In The Girls* on the subject of using girls for promotional purposes in the world of commerce.

I had some very specific instructions from June. I was to take time to establish the girls' characters fully, and one of the characters, played by a very funny lady called Diana Davies, was to be seen making mysterious phone calls, the significance of which would be revealed later. Being a good boy and well brought up, I did these things.

We had a good cast, including the singer Annie Ross, Clive Swift, Dave Hill and my beloved James/Will Warrior, who played the Welsh proprietor of a German bierkeller in Manchester and proved that he was just as funny in lederhosen as out of them.

The filming in Manchester was fun, but when we moved to Whitby it all went wrong for me. We were booked into a private guest house entirely unsuitable for showbiz egos. The landlord proposed to close the bar at midnight. Disbelief! Uproar! Catastrophe! This nice man then asked us to tell him what we would be drinking, and he left the relevant bottles out for us to help ourselves.

At about five in the morning one of the young actresses decided to change her drink, reached in through the grille of the bar, and broke it. The landlord asked the guilty party to own up, and she didn't. I was so angry about the abuse of his trust that I sneaked on her. I won't make things worse by giving her name now! Anyway I was sent to Coventry by all the girls for the rest of the shoot.

Why did I feel the need to stay? To protect my piece against a director with no sense of humour.

The end of shoot party was held on the beach in a force nine gale. It had a punk theme. Several people including the producer had bolts through their noses. The rain poured. The gulls were swept away on the wind like tissues. I grew more miserable by the minute. In the middle of the night I found myself up to my knees in sea-water inside a Greek temple. I have hunted high and low since then, and no such temple exists.

I had the worst hangover of my life, and had to get out of my car on the way home, under the vast golf balls of the Fylingdales Early Warning System, in order to be sick. Several sheep gathered to watch. The sight of a depressed writer throwing up into a ditch was the most exciting thing that had happened to them for several months. I got back into my car and slept till five. Since I was hosting a dinner party in Barnet at eight o'clock I was understandably not popular with Mary.

Later June rang me to say that Brian Glover had written a very funny episode and his would go out first. Mine would go out last. She assured me that this was the second most important slot. I was furious, not because of a bruised ego but because I foresaw immediately what would happen. When my episode went out the first fifteen minutes were spent introducing people the audience already knew, intercut with Diana Davies making silent phone calls whose purpose had been revealed several times already. Naturally it was all extremely boring.

I was prepared to write *Send In The Girls* off to experience, but to my surprise John Temple, a producer at Granada, suggested that I do a sit-com on the same theme, though with completely different characters except for the indispensable James/Will as Mr Meredith, manager of the bierkeller.

I was happy to go along with John's idea. He was a very experienced old pro, quiet, pipe-smoking and cricket-loving. It was difficult to imagine that he had once been a stand-up comedian. We got on well and I found myself writing *The Glamour Girls*, based on two pro-motional girls and the agency that employed them.

The read-through of the pilot was on a Monday morning. I prepared for it in a rather unusual way, by driving my younger step-son Chris to catch a ferry. Nothing unusual in that, except that the ferry was to Greece and was leaving from Ancona, on Italy's Adriatic coast. Chris was in his twenties by now, and had been diagnosed with muscular dystrophy. One day he would probably be in a wheelchair. It was hardly spoiling him to drive him to Ancona. While on the subject of Chris I must say that to have him as a step-son was a strange experience. He reminded me so much of me, with his tempers and his wild humour, that I found it difficult to remember that he wasn't my own son.

On the way down we stayed in Rheims, Sirmione and Florence, but I drove back with only one stop. I covered 300 miles of German and Belgian motorway in three hours. I enjoyed this enormously, but when I stopped at a Belgian service station I found that I couldn't stop shaking.

After one day at home I left Barnet at 5.30 in the morning to drive up the M1 and M6 to Manchester. I beat the worst of the traffic, but I couldn't beat all the traffic that was also beating the worst of the traffic, so I was already pretty exhausted by the time I entered the rehearsal room for the read-through.

It was a horrendous experience. One of the actresses playing our two heroines was all PR and no trousers. The other one was professionally able, but had all the charm, on camera, of a rattlesnake with a grudge. The director, Gordon Fleming, told me that he didn't like writers to be present at rehearsals. He would welcome me at the Producer's Run, where he would astonish me. He did.

The rest of the day passed in a blur. In the evening there was a farewell party for somebody in Granada's bar, the Stables. I felt too tired to drink. Now that should have alarmed me.

James/Will Warrior and I went off to an Italian restaurant where I felt too tired to eat. I felt claustrophobic and began to sweat. I told Will I was going back to the hotel.

Outside the restaurant I reeled and fell, crashing full length on to the pavement. I stood up and fell again. For about ten minutes I tried to stand, and again and again I crashed down on to the pavement. There was nobody about on that cold Manchester night.

At last a young couple came by, hunched against the wind. I said to them, 'I'm not drunk. I'm ill. Inside the restaurant is a man called Will Warrior. Will you tell him David's very ill outside?'

Bless them, they did. Bless Will, he accepted the role of Stirling Moss on the spot, and I was at Salford Royal Hospital before you could say Gerry Robinson, should you for some strange reason wish to do so.

At Salford Royal attention was instant, which is just as well because they estimated that I was forty minutes from death. My blood pressure was too low to sustain life. I had steroids pumped into me, and I was placed in a bed. A doctor told me that I had Hodgson's Disease. I said I hoped Hodgson hadn't got mine. He groaned, but I began to feel better. My jokes might die, but I wouldn't.

They were lovely to me in Salford Royal. I had an EEC and was told my brain wasn't quite normal, but I knew that. I had an EEC and a TVR and discovered that I wasn't a member of the European community or a high speed train.

Granada sent a top executive and a bunch of flowers in that order. Mary hurried up from Barnet. Will came and told me that rehearsals were going well. His lie was welcome.

Note how I become frivolous when dealing with this serious event. It's the comedy writer's way. When people asked me what had been wrong I said I'd been rushed to hospital suffering from terminal bad casting. In fact I had clearly been suffering from what a doctor might describe as exhaustion or a panic attack, but a specialist with his greater income and prestige would call a vaso-vagal incident.

I received wonderful kindness in that crappy, peeling hospital. While I was in there Mrs Thatcher was elected to power. The whole hospital was in shock. People in their cosy homes exulted. People at the sharp end mourned.

Once I'd left hospital, Mary told me she had a rather greater problem than my little panic attack. She had cancer.

Under the circumstances, our little show didn't seem to matter very much. We had a small, cramped studio, as the main audience studio was still set up for the election special, and we had a very poor warm-up man. Then Gordon Fleming, a fine director of drama, did astonish me. During one of the few really funny lines in the piece he cut to two utterly irrelevant gays mincing down a staircase.

The show was lame. It was the perfect ending to a perfect week.

Mary was operated on in the Royal Free Hospital in Hampstead, but was told that she was not completely in the clear and would need further treatment. She asked for honest information on her chances. The registrar told her that she might, with luck, survive six years.

This was devastating news. I found tears streaming down my face as I told Eric and Mary in the Monken Holt. An ironic moment, since they both died of cancer long ago, and Mary is alive and free of the disease twenty-four years after the prediction. I do think people should be more careful before they play God.

It was no surprise that Granada didn't take up the option on *The Glamour Girls*. In fact, if anything it was a relief. It didn't seem to matter much, in the general scheme of things, that due to a cock-up on the communications front I found out about it not from Granada, but from Will. Jonathan was furious. Granada had been so keen for me to work for them, and now they were treating me in a very cavalier fashion. He phoned David Plowright, Head of Most Things at Granada, and David said that he would like me to go to see him, so that he could apologise.

Manchester is a long way to go for an apology, but I went. Brian Armstrong, the Head of Comedy, accompanied me to David Plowright's office. Brian's whole career had been in news, so they made him Head of Comedy. As I write this we have a Minister of Sport who can't answer simple sporting questions, a Minister of Transport who can't drive, a Head of Religious Broadcasting who doesn't believe in God, and not a single member of the board of Railtrack with any experience of railways. Granada were just ahead of their time, and Brian, to be fair, was better than some with a lifetime in comedy.

I told David Plowright that I didn't think I'd been given a fair chance due to the smallness of the studio, the inadequacy of the warm-up man, the unsuitability of the director and the miscasting of the principals. At each stage he asked Brian if it was true and Brian, squirming slightly, admitted that it was. I went away not only with an apology but with a firm commitment to make the series.

Mary and I decided that it was the right time to apply 'and now for something completely different' to our own lives. We had always planned a move to the country some day. Now we realised that there might not be as many days as we had expected.

We began to explore the County of Hereford. It's beautiful, relatively inexpensive, and has reasonable access to London and the north. It enabled me to live as close to my beloved Wales as I could without risking having one of its beloved inhabitants burning my house down when I was away.

One day, as we drove to look at a property north-west of Hereford, we both felt an uncanny sense of belonging among these low, wooded hills, these broad sloping valleys, these orchards and hop fields and sheep pastures, these quiet timbered villages. It was a grey, misty day when we first saw the Old Post House, in a tiny, exquisite hamlet that also contained the Old School House, the Old Forge, the Old Chapel and the Old Vicarage, to remind us of the times when it had been more than a sleepy collection of houses.

We left Barnet with some regret. We'd been happy there. We'd made good friends. Two of these friends, Richard Crisp and Rod Bacon, a two-man version of Joe Melia's 'What about the crispy bacon we used to get before the war?' did our removals for us. We took them to the local pub and they ordered Pernods. Not a good start to persuading the locals that we were just like them.

We moved on a glorious spring day. I looked at our little hamlet with delight. No more spotting of Kingsley Amis on the common and thinking what a gulf there still was between us. There were twelve houses in Broxwood. At last, I felt, I had a chance of being the best-known writer around. We went to the farm shop in an adjoining village and told them that we'd moved into the Old Post House. 'What do you do?' they asked bluntly. 'I'm a writer,' I said. 'Very appropriate,' came the response. 'During the war *Picture Post* had a photo of J.B. Priestley looking over your garden gate.'

The Old Post House is a traditional Herefordshire black and white house with quite a large garden with a view over open country to the back and orchards to the front. In the distance were the hills of Wales. I had a large panelled study upstairs and felt very happy there from the start. We were helped by the weather. March 1980 was a glorious month of gentle breezes and warm spring sunshine. We went to the Cheltenham Gold Cup on my forty-fifth birthday, and won nothing.

John Temple continued as producer of *The Glamour Girls*, but we had a new director, Malcolm Taylor, cheery and chubby and a lover of late nights.

Our two girls were Brigit Forsyth and Sally Watts. They were excellent. James/Will was as funny as ever as Mr Meredith, whose bierkeller was plagued by industrial action. In one episode his scantily clad waitresses were on a go-dressed. This is almost all I remember now of two series of dialogue.

In the pilot the owner of the agency had been Una Maclean. She'd been very professional as all fell into chaos around her, but it was obvious to me in retrospect (!) that the agency must be run by a man. The comedian Duggie Brown was cast in the role.

We had two very decent series, which were up against *Top Of The Pops* and narrowly beat it in the ratings, but this clash precluded all possibility of a spot in the Top Twenty, and the executives who decide these things did not regard it as a success.

Truth to tell, it wasn't. The series was simply too mild for its subject. It needed some clear satirical bite about sexual exploitation. Duggie Brown was good in the role that I'd written, but I'd written too gentle a role, and Duggie's niceness under-pinned the gentleness. In retr... well, you get the idea... Mr Garstang should have been a Rigsby type, awash with hypocrisy and unrequited desire.

It was also insufficiently peopled. There never seemed to be any other clients in the agency. It existed in Sitcomland.

One final memory of *The Glamour Girls*. One episode involved the girls parachuting for a publicity stunt. As they boarded the plane to take them up, they were supposed to look absolutely terrified. I shall never forget the look on Brigit Forsyth's face. She's a very good actress, but this wasn't acting.

Will, for plot reasons long forgotten, went up too, and the script had him landing on top of Blackpool Tower, where he hung, helplessly, swinging in the breeze. Of course the actors didn't really jump, but Will insisted on doing his own stunt. He is a most individual cocktail of a man – fat yet fit, fiery yet gentle. I felt distinctly queasy as I saw this lovely man harnessed up there in the service of my script.

Will felt more than a little miffed when Malcolm, who directed splendidly on the whole, shot it in such a way that it wasn't absolutely obvious that Will had done his own stunt. He cut from a long shot to a close up, exactly as he would have done if a double had been doing the stunt and the top of the tower had been built in the studio. Well, now the nation knows.

The Glamour Girls brought me just one letter:

> I am anxious to know if by any chance your parents lived in Calcutta during the year 1942 – namely, Cynthia and Arthur Nobbs. As I was there in the Army during the period, I met them, and I recall that they had a son named 'David'.

No mention of enjoying the programme.

The urge to write another novel was growing and becoming intolerable. I sat at my desk, with a blank sheet of paper in front of me, and repeated several times, 'And now for something completely different'.

My mind turned to Yorkshire. In my many visits to Yorkshire Television I'd often come across the forthright nature of Yorkshire folk. Two incidents in particular delighted me.

One day we were filming *Sez Les* near the Burley Road in Leeds, and Les asked me to go to the corner shop for cigarettes. A little old lady came in, and her conversation with me went as follows:

'What's to do in t'street?'

'They're filming.'

'Filming? Who's filming?'

'Yorkshire Television.'

'Yorkshire Television are filming in our street?'

'Yorkshire Television are filming in your street.'

'What are they filming?'

'*Sez Les*.'

'Yorkshire Television are filming *Sez Les* in our street?'

'Yorkshire Television are filming *Sez Les* in your street.'

'If I went down our street now, would I see him himself, Les Dawson, in our street?'

'If you went down your street now you'd see him himself, Les Dawson, in your street.'

'I don't like him.'

What splendid perversity.

I came across a similar quality a few days later, when I had occasion to complain about the beer in a pub near Hebden Bridge. It isn't easy for a Londoner to complain about the beer in a pub in Yorkshire. I approached the landlord diffidently and said, quietly, 'Landlord, I'm afraid this beer really isn't very good.' He looked at me with gentle sadness in the deep pools of his eyes and said, 'What's tha got to complain about? Tha never has to come in here again. I've had to drink the bugger for twenty-two years.'

Yes, I was sure; I wanted to write about Yorkshire. Many years later a friend overheard a conversation on the Ripon bus. It sums up so much of the no-nonsense Yorkshire attitude to life.

Two Yorkshire lasses were talking about the Royal Film Performance. One of them had been – not to the film, but to Leicester Square to see the stars arriving.

'Ooh!' said the other. 'Who did you see?'

'I saw that Tom Cruise. I saw that Nicole Kidman. Oh, and I saw that Brad Pitt.'

'Brad Pitt! You saw Brad Pitt! What was he like?'

The girl thought long and hard.

'He'd be nothing at a bus stop,' she said.

I wanted to write not about a Yorkshire Perrin, but about a working class lad born in the back-to-backs I remembered so vividly from my Sheffield days. I had the idea of writing about the times through which I had lived from the perspective of a character making a similar emotional journey to my own, but in very different circumstances. Right from the start I hoped that it would become a trilogy.

The first book would take Henry Pratt – for that was the name I gave my hero – up to the age of eighteen and his departure for National Service.

Liz Calder had moved on from Gollancz, and I was dealing with a very pleasant young lady named Victoria Petrie-Hay. She was very keen on the Pratt idea, but either she or a higher authority asked for three sample chapters.

Jonathan was quietly, softly, gently furious, as only he could be. Didn't they know I could write? Hadn't the three Perrin books done extremely well for them and for Penguin?

The answer, of course, was that they didn't know if I could write working class South Yorkshire. They didn't trust me to write something as completely different as that!

It's so much easier when writers write the same book over and over again. Why does Dick Francis spring to mind?

Not quite fair. He doesn't exactly write the same book every time –

but they're all about racing, they all have a psychopathic villain or villains, and most of them have a hero frozen by trauma who gradually unfreezes as he tackles and defeats his deranged opponent.

I mock with affection. I enjoy a Dick Francis. It's just the right length for the journey from York to London. Or it was until Railtrack got going. The other day I read the whole of *War and Peace* and looked up to discover we'd only got to Retford.

There is a serious point about one's readership here. We are entitled to write what we want, but our loyal readership is entitled to have expectations. Captain W.E. Johns stretched my loyalty with Worrals. Paul Theroux destroyed that of one lady in painful fashion. She went into a bookshop with his latest – I think it was called *Doctor Slaughter* – tore it into shreds with the strength given by manic fury, and screamed, 'How could he do this to me?'

I believe that we must try to take our readers with us on our journey to the centre of our talents. I wanted to take my Perrin readers to Yorkshire with me and, I hoped, pick up a few new friends along the way.

Methuen, still smarting from not having accepted the Perrin book, were eager to accept the idea of Pratt. I would be working with my old friend Geoffrey Strachan, and that was a real pleasure. Later, Geoffrey would suggest the title, taken from a reference in the book – *Second From Last In The Sack Race*. It is delightful, and I'm sure the book owed much of its success to it.

The story told of a boy born on the same day as me but in a back-to-back in the imaginary Yorkshire town of Thurmarsh, loosely based on Rotherham, the actual name being taken from the nearby mining communities of Thurcroft and Rawmarsh. I gave Henry my birthday in the interests of truth. It meant that I knew, from my own memories, just how aware he would have been of various world events, especially the Second World War, at every stage of his development.

Some critics thought that the whole book was autobiographical. As we've seen, Henry's first day at school was, and there was a close relationship between his public school days and mine. I even gave him that dreadful, shaming lie that embarrassed me so much at the

Ormerods. Uncle Teddy and Auntie Doris have their origins in Mary's ex-in-laws, John and Kay, but they grew into something different and, in Uncle Teddy's case, something altogether more ruthless. My mother thought that Cousin Hilda was based on her, but there were elements of my landlady in Sheffield there too. Like Reggie, she really isn't anybody I met, just as Henry isn't me, but has me-like qualities.

Having realised that I'd been too gentle in *The Glamour Girls*, I pulled no punches this time, creating what one critic called 'a bruising black comedy'.

Henry went to several different schools. He made an educational tour of the English class system. Frank Delaney wrote that he regretted the public school section as that had been done so often before, but it had to be there. I had experienced enormous class differences while going through Orpington and Marlborough and the Royal Signals and Cambridge and Sheffield and Rotherham, and at last I felt mature enough to write about them. Henry had to go from village school to elementary school to grammar school to public school where he was known as Oiky and where he learnt to moderate his accent so that when he went back to grammar school he was known as Snobby. That was the subject of the book.

I enjoyed doing the research. I revisited Sheffield and Rotherham, but so much had gone. Those wonderful old pubs with their rows of bells and their waiter service were no more. The pubs were brighter, louder, bleaker, tougher. I rang the *Star* and asked to speak to Len Doherty, but he wasn't there. Perhaps it was as well. I'm not sure that he would have wanted me to see him as he was then. It wouldn't be long before he hanged himself in his garage. He'd been badly injured when he was caught up in a terrorist bomb attack at Munich Airport on his way home from an assignment in Israel, and he had never recovered, mentally or physically. I remember him as an exciting drinking companion, a passionate romantic, and as a man who had the guts and energy to write three good novels as a miner. I cried, when I heard of his death, for the waste of a talent.

In Sheffield City Library I spent several happy hours knee-deep in

South Yorkshire dialect. I talked to people in pubs in Wharfedale about the war years. A perfectly respectable woman came into the bar, sank exhausted into a chair, and said, 'Ee, I'm right twined. I'm as twined as my arse.' I do find it sad that dialect is disappearing.

The highlights of my research occurred at the newspaper section of the British Library in Colindale. It was a magical place. You ordered your newspapers and magazines on a form, and a few minutes later a porter arrived, wheeling a trolley full of history. It was wonderful to sit at a table in that large, silent room, beside earnest men reading earnest tomes, and immerse myself in the *Beano* and the *Dandy*. One morning, when I was reading copies of the *Radio Times*, and remembering all those lovely children's programmes that had poured into my young mind, I completely forgot that I was supposed to be writing things down and had to go right back to the beginning. Gradually it's all being put on microfiche and for me that isn't the same. I adore paper. Paper is my friend and colleague. I hate machines. Machines are my enemies.

The book finally came flooding out. I did the research, wrote two drafts in longhand and then typed it all out, and it only took me fifty-eight days. I had to do it in that time. I needed to finish it before I went to Peru.

14 HENRY 'EE BY GUM I AM DAFT' PRATT

IT WAS A long flight from Lima, with several stops. As we drew nearer and nearer to Gatwick, I began to feel anxious.

I'm usually a bit anxious returning home after a holiday. My career has continued in my absence. There may be good news about projects, there may be bad news, there may just be a deafening silence. It isn't like coming back to a regular job, a proper job.

I thought back over the six weeks in Peru. We'd had a wonderful, amazing time, Mary and I. Kenneth Horne, in *Much Binding In The Marsh*, used to say, 'When I was in Sidi Birrani . . .' For the rest of my life I would be saying, 'When I was in Peru . . .'

The reason for our trip to Peru was John Medcalf. Signalman John Medcalf. Father John Medcalf. John 'Catholic Priest' Medcalf.

John had become a Catholic due to an experience in Graz Cathedral during his National Service. A roundabout route to Damascus. Later he had gone to Peru and taken Peruvian citizenship. He saw *The Fall and Rise of Reginald Perrin* in a bookshop in Lima and got back in touch. We'd corresponded. He'd visited us in Barnet.

I'd been a bit nervous, as I sat outside Ye Olde Monken Holt, with a pint of ye olde beste bitter, in the warm June sunshine, awaiting the arrival of my old mucker. A quarter of a century had passed. Would his visit be a success?

Then I'd seen him, shambling up the opposite pavement, a little thicker round the middle, his sandy hair a little grey, his clothes baggy and crumpled. A great cry of, 'I hope the Guinness is on, Nobby,' startled the Saturday shoppers, and I knew that everything would be all right.

Later he wrote to say that he would be returning to England in September 1982. If we didn't visit him before then it would be too late.

He had met us in Lima, and taken us on a tour of Peruvian highlights – to Arequipa, a beautiful Spanish city; then on the world's second highest railway to Lake Titicaca, the world's highest navigable lake; by train through the Andean altiplano to the lovely city of Cusco, with its Spanish houses built on ancient Inca foundations; and so, by train again, to fabled Machu Picchu, the Lost City of the Incas. We had travelled with him through his vast parish around the village of Banos del Inca, near Cajamarca, and had even attended an Indian wedding high in the mountains. We had flown to the Amazon and taken a thatched boat to a thatched jungle lodge. We had met amazing characters and seen great places. We had seen and smelt poverty on a scale that we'd never imagined.

What did it matter if Geoffrey Strachan didn't like my as yet untitled novel?

It mattered very much, I realised, for John Medcalf's story had had books at its centre. A Peruvian had approached him and said that he'd heard of a thing shaped like a brick from which you could learn things. This had inspired John to set up a rural library service in the north of Peru. Later he would be employed by the Sandinistas in Nicaragua to do the same. Books are valued in Central and South America. Books are classless. Books are about spreading knowledge, not keeping it to one-self. Books are about living and understanding, not about being bookish.

Peru was a wonderfully humorous country. No country which has a regular feature 'Pothole of the day' on the front page of its leading newspaper could be lacking in humour.

Our trip had revealed to me the universality of humour in all its glory.

I could be proud of my thing shaped like a brick. It had humour. It wasn't bookish. It might be enjoyed by people who had no wide experience of novels.

Geoffrey would like it. Geoffrey couldn't not like it. If he didn't, it didn't matter, I was still an immensely fortunate man, but he would.

He did.

Even he, though, didn't trust me entirely.

He sent the manuscript to a dialect expert, who found twenty-six errors. I couldn't believe it, until I discovered that he was from Oldham.

I explained that in the North of England there are things called 'The Pennines'. Yorkshire folk believe that the Italians named the Appenines after them. The dialect to the West of the Pennines is very different from that in the East.

They sent the manuscript to a dialect expert in Sheffield and he found just one error, which I modestly acknowledged.

I love dialect and deplore its inevitable decline. In Herefordshire everything was 'tidy job' and nothing was neuter. The man bringing the logs would say, 'Where do you want me to put him?' 'In that shed, please.' 'Tidy job.' If I said I was in London on Tuesday and got commissioned to write a sit-com, the reaction to this exciting news would be 'tidy job'.

In my village in Yorkshire there is a rare piece of dialect still extant. I play that great domino game of fives and threes in the Hare and Hounds every Tuesday ('What a glittering life you lead', I hear you exclaim) and the question, 'Whose turn is it to went?' is often heard. Even in the next village, two miles away, this is regarded as proof of our essential strangeness.

Apart from the little matter of dialect, Geoffrey and I were in complete agreement about the book and I enjoyed our detailed editorial sessions. No trouble is too great, as far as I am concerned, as one strives for the elusive perfection one craves.

Reviews were good and sales weren't bad either. It's a book that has gone on and on selling for the best part of twenty years. Thanks to J.K. Rowling Henry is definitely 'Second From Last in the Characters with the Initials HP Stakes' but my HP has given me and a lot of readers great pleasure. I'm proud of Henry Pratt.

One of my joys was hearing the book read on *A Book At Bedtime*. The adaptation, by Donald Bancroft, was splendid, and I wrote to tell him so. He replied that I was the first author ever to thank him, although he did admit that several had a very good excuse. They were dead.

Through Henry Pratt I met Jude Kelly, who later became artistic director of the splendid West Yorkshire Playhouse, and her husband Michael Birch. Jude The Not Obscure was running the Battersea Arts Centre at the time, and wanted to do a stage adaptation of the book. Did I want to adapt it, or would I let Michael do it?

I'd written all those stage plays, I'd adapted my work for television, but instinct told me that I wouldn't know how to distil this picaresque novel into a stage play. Michael's unique style of dress made him look like an avant-garde painter and decorator, but he lived and breathed theatre, and I felt safe in his hands.

Jude booked me to give a talk at the Battersea Arts Centre. I'd always avoided giving talks, and here I was making my debut in my late forties. I had no idea what to do, and planned a question and answer session. When I arrived I found that it was to be recorded for posterity by the National Sound Archive.

Three people turned up. I told them that I couldn't do what I'd planned with only three people, and invited them to join us for an informal discussion at the wine bar across the road. They refused. They'd come to hear a lecture in a draughty hall. Why should they be fobbed off with an intimate discussion with an author in a cosy wine bar?

There is to this day, I believe, no record in the National Sound Archive that I ever existed. I can't say I lose any sleep over it.

Maureen Duffy, that fine novelist and great campaigner for writers' causes, was appearing later in the same Battersea Arts Festival. She phoned me to ask how I had got on. I told her I'd cancelled because only three people had turned up. 'I've never had three,' she told me. 'Two, four, but not three.'

I soon learnt that you can never tell how big a draw you're going to be. My second solo appearance – or my first, since I cancelled the first – was at the Literary Society of the University of Kent in Canterbury. I'd been booked by a fan, David Clark, one of the select band of Nobbs groupies. I had a large audience, larger than David Lodge the previous week. Hurrah! David Clark basked in my glory, and my talk went down very well.

Afterwards I was taken to the canteen to meet other fans who hadn't been able to hear me because they had evening lectures, and then I found myself being driven to somebody's lodgings in the dark wilds of Kent for coffee. I sat on the bed in a little bed-sitter and students sat on the floor gazing up at me like nestling thrushes waiting to be fed. I obliged with stories of Saki, a great favourite of mine and theirs. How delightful it was to find that this sharp, glittering comic miniaturist was enjoying a revival among the young.

We returned to the University at half past two in the morning, to find my car locked in the compound, with my suitcase in the boot. I still hadn't booked into my hotel.

One of the students shinned over the gate, fetched the suitcase, lobbed it back over, climbed over himself and dropped athletically on his feet from a great height. 'He's John Buchan's grandson,' explained David.

A third public event around this time was an evening with Methuen authors in Newcastle: Sue Townsend, Henry Livings, Jeanette Winterson and me. It sounds like one of those 'Name the odd one out' questions.

There was a huge audience of Adrian Mole fans. All the questions from the audience were about Adrian Mole, which embarrassed Sue greatly. In the interval we all signed copies of our books. Sue told her queue, 'Don't all wait for me. Go and get *Second From Last In The Sack Race*, it's a better book about childhood than mine.' I mention that not to blow my own trumpet, but to record the amazing generosity of a fellow writer. I had the opportunity many years later to adapt Sue's *The Queen and I* for television. It contained many scenes of sublime brilliance, but I had to turn it down, with great reluctance, since events in the Royal Family changed so fast that it was impossible to keep up with them.

Michael Birch's adaptation of *Second From Last In The Sack Race* was a triumph, I thought. Three actors and two actresses played all the parts at Battersea. One of them was Tommy Cooper's son, a lovely and talented young man called Tom Henty, who was to die of alcoholic poisoning at a tragically young age. Another was black and, since the play featured a black member of the Paradise Lane Gang, I did ask Jude, who directed the play, if audiences out in the wilds would be sophisticated enough to realise that not all the characters he was playing were black. 'I think they should,' she replied drily. 'The fact that his first two roles are a parrot and Neville Chamberlain should give them a clue.'

The play toured some unusual venues up and down the country, and Jude told me it went down better the more working class the area was. This delighted me.

In Newcastle I had read out the scene in which Henry makes such a prodigious fart in class that he is elected to the Paradise Lane Gang on the strength of it. My next booking was at a public library in Nelson and I planned to read the same section. Five minutes before going on I took a peep at my audience. The average age was pushing seventy, and they were predominantly women. They weren't going to laugh at farting jokes, especially in a library. I planned a whole new programme in five minutes. It went all right, without being a total success, but afterwards the youngest person in the room, a lady in her forties, told me that she'd given her father *Second From Last* and had heard him laugh for the first time since his wife died. An evening that includes a moment like that can never be wasted time.

My plan was to write a non-Pratt novel, then a Pratt sequel, then another non-Pratt novel and then the final Pratt novel, and I managed to stick to this.

Pratt of the Argus was published in 1988 and *The Cucumber Man* in 1994. I'm unashamedly affectionate towards the Pratt trilogy. It was inevitable, I suppose, that when an omnibus version came out it should be entitled *The Complete Pratt*, although I was rather less than happy with the very first page of the book, which begins:

THE COMPLETE PRATT
David Nobbs was born in Orpington . . .

An omnibus edition of the Perrin trilogy also came out in the 1990s. That's typical. You wait fifty-five years for an omnibus edition, and then two come almost at once.

Second From Last took Henry through eighteen years. *Pratt of the Argus* picked him up at the age of twenty, after National Service, and took him through eighteen months. Once again the plot was entirely fictional, and the family history was entirely fictional, but his emotional life mirrored mine, and I used several of my experiences as incidents in the book. You will not be too surprised to learn that Henry's first word in print was 'Thives'.

The plot hinged on Henry's discovery of shenanigans involving irregularities in the council's planning department, irregularities which impinged on his emotional life and in particular on his love for Hilary. The book was a struggle and took eighteen months to write. I think Henry's personal story worked well, particularly in relation to Uncle Teddy, who sailed so close to the wind and eventually capsized, and Auntie Doris, who always made things worse by protesting about them. The actual plot, which becomes his one scoop, a scoop he may never be able to use, still seems over-complicated and fiddly to me, and its resolution necessitated bringing in several new characters towards the end, which is ungainly.

The book had some excellent reviews. Journalists loved its affectionate portrayal of provincial journalism in the days of clattering typewriters and booze. It did all right with the general public, too, as people found Henry a very sympathetic character.

The over-excitable would-be hard man, Colin Edgeley, is very closely based on Len Doherty. I hope some of the affection I felt for Len has come over in this memorial to him. Other characters are mainly composites or fictions, and Peter Tinniswood is conspicuous by his absence. I loved him too much to burden him with fictionalisation, even though we still weren't speaking.

Hilary – pale, loving, intense, passionate, loyal – was a complete invention, very clear to me physically, but not based on any known individual. Characters like her are created gradually, and suddenly become utterly real and visually complete. It's a miracle each time it happens.

Sometimes I get told that an element of my writing is exaggerated. One or two people thought that the art exhibition hung upside down was an exaggeration. As so often, the thing people find exaggerated was taken from real life. When I was at Cambridge an art exhibition was hung upside down due to a faulty marking on the crates, and received an enthusiastic review from at least one national newspaper.

Michael Birch, in his turn, found *Pratt Of The Argus* much more difficult to adapt.

By this time Jude Kelly was firmly established at the West Yorkshire Playhouse, where she revived *Second From Last . . .* to great effect. There was brilliantly chosen music, and there were slides of life in Britain between 1935 and 1953. These represented the historical background which I used so freely in the book. I loved them, but Jude and Michael felt eventually that they were a mistake, that it was the job of the play itself to invoke the atmosphere of those times. I'm glad, though, that they had the slides in that production, and there are pieces of music that I cannot hear again without the hairs standing up on the back of my neck.

There have been marvellous productions of the play in Oldham and Worcester, and Hereford and Harrogate, and in Bolton, and no doubt other splendid ones that I haven't been able to see.

The Hereford production was directed by Mary with an extremely talented amateur group, the Wye Players. With a large pool of amateurs to draw on, there was no need for doubling. The cast sat in the centre of the stage, watching the play, and stepped forward to do their bits as and when required, a Brechtian device that worked perfectly.

Second From Last exists in script form, published by Samuel French, as does *Pratt Of The Argus* in a new, revised version by Michael. It's a very clever piece of adaptation, and a rich and funny play, and it also worked very well at the West Yorkshire Playhouse.

The trilogy was completed in 1994 with the publication of *The Cucumber Man*, which took Henry's story from 1957 to the early 1990s. Henry was very real to me now; he was flexing his fictional muscles and deciding that he didn't want to be a writer like his creator. He could so easily have become one, with his journalistic background and his stand-up comedy at school. It would have been just too easy. The civil service, on the other hand, would be greatly at odds with his idealistic and quirky personality. It must be right for him, therefore, and I created as absurd an area of the bureaucracy as I could think of – the Cucumber Marketing Board. During the course of the writing Geoffrey introduced me to his cousin, Richard Melville, in order that I might glean information about the civil service. Richard told me that there had actually been, even though only briefly, a Cucumber and Tomato Marketing Board. This illustrated again how risky it is to compete with Real Life in the Absurdity Stakes. The meeting was fruitful and Richard convinced me that I was on the right lines.

The Cucumber Man is the story of Henry's desperately slow maturing, his battles against the sterility of bureaucracy, and his tortured search for personal happiness and success as husband, father and friend. Dogged by disaster, he is nevertheless one of life's great survivors, and so his destiny is a kind of triumph, albeit an unrecognised and unheralded one.

My Peruvian trip had its effect on *The Cucumber Man*. Henry is sent to the Cajamarca Valley by Overseas Aid to cover the Andes in cucumbers. I wrote to John Medcalf to ask whether cucumbers were known in Peru.

John replied from El Salvador. (His career after Peru took him to Hindhead, Nicaragua, Shoreham-by-Sea, El Salvador, Redhill and St Leonards.)

He wrote:

Cucumbers ('pepinos') are certainly known in Peru. Their despised status may be gathered from a popular phrase 'Me importa un pepino' 'I couldn't care a cucumber.' Shows how common or garden they are. The Peruvian variety is shorter and stubbier, usually part of a salad or a stew, never seen in sandwiches as far as I remember.

This news didn't spoil things. It added to the futility that Peru already had cucumbers before Henry introduced them, and didn't much like them.

A nice touch that I'd forgotten is that as Henry travels to London for his interview with Overseas Aid there is an article on Peru in the *Guardian* under the headline 'The Land Of the Soaring Condom'. Henry had trouble with condoms in *Second From Last . . .*, with misprints in *Pratt of the Argus* and with Peru in *The Cucumber Man*. This one joke ties the three books together rather exquisitely, in my opinion. I daresay nobody noticed, but it pleased me.

While on the subject of Peru I must mention that at John 'Catholic Priest' Medcalf's suggestion I became one of the sponsors of the Peru Support Group, replacing Graham Greene on his death.

John once asked Graham Greene to attend a Catholic conference in South America. He declined. Too old. So John asked him to write a speech for the conference. He declined again. Too old. But he suggested that John write his speech for him, and he would vet it. So John wrote the speech and sent it to Graham Greene. It began 'Distinguished delegates'. Graham Greene's only amendment was to cross out the word 'Distinguished'.

Sadly, John is now dead too. This marvellous, humble, humorous man died in his sleep in Santiago da Compostela in 2002. At his moving funeral in Redhill, a Peruvian woman said, 'We must carry on his work of comforting the afflicted and afflicting the comfortable.' I would have been proud to have said that in my first language.

Reviews of *The Cucumber Man* were hard to find, but in one of them, in the *Sunday Times*, the novelist Jonathan Coe ended his review, 'I think he is probably our best post-war comic novelist.' Poor Jonathan. 'Probably our best post-war comic novelist' has appeared on the jacket of every edition of every book since. Luckily he's become a friend and doesn't seem to mind.

Michael Birch did his stuff on this one too, and produced a lovely poignant play which again was produced at the West Yorkshire Playhouse, this time directed by Michael himself.

I was getting quite a few fan letters at this time. One or two are worth sharing.

One was a card to Henry and Hilary Pratt from a couple also married on 20 July, 1957. I found that very touching.

Another referred to the sadistic Sergeant Botney, who figured in the brief National Service passage in *Pratt Of The Argus*. The reader assumed that I was referring to a Sergeant Bott, who apparently terrorised 7 Troop at Catterick. I wasn't. Botney was Yentob backwards. I'd never met Alan Yentob, so there was nothing personal in it. It just seemed such an unlikely name that it was tempting to make it more likely by reversing it. I only discovered after publication that Botney was used by *Private Eye*.

There's no way that calling a sadistic sergeant Yentob backwards can be described as a good career move. I think I'm probably not very good at good career moves.

Two letters pointed out a mistake on page 213 of *Pratt of the Argus*. The sports reporter, Ben Watkinson, who is always about to go home to give the wife one, challenges Henry to name the four football league teams that begin and end with the same letter. There are actually five. I'd omitted Aston Villa. Both writers said they'd enjoyed the book, so I didn't get upset by their criticism.

There are two letters, widely different, which vie for my particular affection.

One began: 'I have just finished "Henry Pratt", a most delightful story. Now approaching 80, I have read more than a thousand novels. Yours is the first to mention wet dreams.' I felt tempted to reply that he really should try Jane Austen and the Brontë sisters, but of course I didn't. I respect anyone who's taken the trouble to write to me.

The second letter was from Mike Craig, writer, broadcaster and shrinking violet, whom I'd met on the *Jimmy Tarbuck Show*. In *Second From Last . . .*, Henry goes, on 4 April, 1950, to see the great, the immortal Robb 'The Day War Broke Out' Wilton at the Sheffield Empire. Mike sent me a photo-copy of Robb Wilton's notebook for the performance. On one side is the list of performers, and on the left side is his list of gags. It reads, 'Rope. 75 miles. Signpost. Walking streets. Prison. Flavours. Duchess. Know your face. Chivalry. Back answers. Car attendant.' What a wonderful memento.

Had I not gone to Peru, I doubt if I'd have canvassed for the Liberals in North Herefordshire, and if I hadn't, Henry's disastrous standing as Liberal candidate in Thurmarsh might never have happened.

My parents were Liberals at heart, and I am too. I can't believe the way people confuse moderation with weakness. I am passionately moderate. I loathe the far Left and the far Right.

I also believe that party politics are far less important than politicians think they are. I was in Italy in the middle of the seventh political crisis of that year, and the second of that week. The trains ran on time, the streets were clean, and the majority of the people seemed reasonably happy and prosperous. There certainly weren't any riots. There was nobody to riot against.

My main feeling about recent industrial history is how ridiculously reasonable the demands of the unions are when compared to the bonuses given to top management and above all to payments made to senior executives when they're sacked for being abysmal failures.

Anyway, there I was canvassing against Peter Temple-Morris, a Tory married to an Iranian and, in political terms, as wet as Henry's dreams. His stated policies, according to his manifesto, included the setting up of more 'anti-natal clinics'!

I called on hundreds of doorsteps. I only remember two of them. One man stood in front of his bungalow with his arms folded as I trudged up the path between his gnomes and said, aggressively, 'Now, then. What are you going to do about abortion?' I hummed and hawed and lost his vote if I'd ever had it.

Another man welcomed me, said he supported the Liberals, took several posters, promised his services on polling day and said, 'Oh yeah, I've always been a Liberal. Well, I lived in Dagenham, worked at Fords, you see, and it's full of blacks now.' It seemed hopeless even to begin to discuss the basic tenets of Liberal philosophy with him. I handed him the posters and accepted his offer of help. Politics corrupt, and absolute politics corrupt absolutely.

I enjoyed election day. I drove around the parish of Pembridge and found people who had never been to a polling station in their lives. As the day wore on, I found myself bringing people of steadily increasing frailty. Some of them only just made it to the polling station, gasping for breath, clinging to my arm. The silly thing is that I don't even know if all or even any of them voted Liberal.

We were beaten, not heavily but fairly easily. I think Jeremy Pincham, the urbane candidate, expected it, but I was devastated.

I don't believe I changed one person's mind with my canvassing. I don't think you can nowadays when there are so many debates on television. It's just a question of identifying your supporters and badgering them to vote on the day. It corrupted my view of Britain. A few days after the election, Mary and I went down to Tenby to stay with my mother and my Auntie Kathleen and their Scottish friend, Ella. I love the drive through the luscious Vale of Towy, but that day I found myself still sizing up every street in political terms. 'No point trying there.' 'That cul-de-sac looks promising.'

I've never helped at an election since. It's a waste of writing time.

Will there ever be a fourth Henry Pratt book? I don't think so. Too many of the main characters are dead. At the end of *The Cucumber Man* Henry appears to be content. Shouldn't he at last be allowed to remain so? Surely he can be spared the intrusion of that wretched author with his bag of disasters and humiliations?

'Are you self-important enough to want to be centre stage one last time, Henry?'

'Not any more, Nobby. You don't mind my calling you Nobby, do you?'

'No. I rather like it.'

'No, I think I'm past self-importance now. I've grown up. That means I'm not much use to a comedy writer any more. Goodbye, Nobby, and thank you.'

'Goodbye, Henry. Love to Hilary. Live a long time in peace, and die swiftly and painlessly in your bed.'

'You too, mate.'

15 TRICKY COVE, JOHNNY BLACKOUT

SOMEBODY AT TYNE-TEES Television once rang me and asked me if I was interested in writing a series for Manuel, of *Fawlty Towers* fame. I thought for a quarter of a second and said, 'No'.

'Oh. Why?'

'Because anybody trying to follow *Fawlty Towers* would be on a hiding to nothing, and because Manuel is a marvellous support character, not a lead. The funniest thing about him is how he infuriates Basil Fawlty.'

It's so easy to be clever about other people's ideas. It's so much harder about one's own. I did, with Jimmy from *Perrin*, something perilously close to what I was advising Tyne-Tees against. I loved the character so much. I loved Geoffrey Palmer's portrayal of him so much.

The idea was to pursue the secret right wing army theme. This soon brought me into conflict with the Head of Comedy, John Howard Davies. He grew more and more worried about the scripts, particularly when guns came into the picture.

'Guns aren't funny,' he told me. 'They kill people.'

'Jimmy's don't,' I pointed out. 'His ammunition doesn't fit.'

I couldn't convince John. The guns went, and so did the secret army.

Jimmy became a kind of conman trying to survive in a world that was beyond him.

At first John was happy with my efforts, but I knew in my heart that I was a fool to carry on.

By September, 1981, John was worried.

> I have now read both the scripts and I am terribly sorry to say that I am not convinced. The trouble is basically that I think that Jimmy is in danger, to me at least, of becoming two-dimensional. I found his peculiar and individualistic style too much to take other than in small doses.

I felt angry with John. He had forced me to emasculate the series and had then lost faith in it because it was emasculated. This blinded me to the validity of his comments about Jimmy's character. I became determined to make the thing work.

I was doing other writing, of course. I wrote a play for Nicholas Kent at the Oxford Playhouse. He told me it was the best one-act play he had ever read. Unfortunately it was a two-act play. I never did get the other act right. It was about Greenham Common, so very soon it was dated. Topical themes are dangerous. They become yesterday's themes before they become history.

I was approached by a film editor of great distinction, Jim Clark. Like Dennis Lewiston he wanted to move into direction, and he had an idea.

'I want to do a Holmes and Watson film for Ralph Richardson and John Gielgud. When can you come to London?'

'Tomorrow.'

I met Jim in his house in Kensington. I liked him, but I didn't like the idea, which was that Holmes and Watson were in wheelchairs, and some young Americans did all the leg work and reported back to them. I'm not saying it couldn't have worked, but it couldn't have worked for me. I could never have written those young Americans. I didn't believe in them.

Jim suggested another tack, which interested me far more – a film to pair Walter Matthau and Penelope Keith. I couldn't imagine anything better, unless it was Jack Lemmon and Gwen Taylor.

Jim presented me with the idea either of Penelope Keith as a Thatcher figure or Walter Matthau as a Reagan figure. I could see them both in those roles, and came up with a plot in which the Prime Minister and the President met for a crisis conference on a battleship somewhere, fell madly in love while he showed her his 'B' movies, and caused a political crisis in which everyone who was on the ship had to be eliminated. The reason for its rejection wasn't that it was preposterous, but that the chance of neither Thatcher nor Reagan being assassinated was very small.

I came up with three other ideas, one of which involved oil rigs and Scottish landowners. Jim liked this one, and suggested that we went on a tour of the rigs together. This was for January. I get bored with the idea of Tenerife but I'm not touring the oil rigs of the North Sea in January unless there's a real prospect of its leading to some writing, so I asked Jim if either Walter Matthau or Penelope Keith knew that an idea was being developed for them, and he said it was too early to involve them at this stage. I backed out. The prospect of the film being made was too remote, and in the early eighties almost everything written for television was still produced.

It's lucky I did pull out because Bill Forsyth's *Local Hero* must already have been in preparation, and it was uncannily similar to my idea.

I turned Jim down with regret, and I know he regretted it too. Quite soon he decided to stick with editing, and won an Oscar for *The Killing Fields*.

During the eighties I wrote some training films for Video Arts, of which John Cleese was a director. He starred in several of them, if you can be said to star in a training film. I didn't really enjoy these films, they were so very hard to get right, but Peter Robinson and Michael Peacock at Video Arts expressed great interest in the idea of the Jimmy spin-off, and *Fairly Secret Army* was born.

At some stage, before Leonard Rossiter's death, Jimmy had ceased to be Jimmy, and had become Major Harry Truscott. The reason for the change was that it had dawned on me that if he was Reggie's brother-in-law, people would wonder where Reggie was, and to introduce Reggie as a minor character would have upset the balance. Len wouldn't have been too thrilled either.

Up to this stage in my career Norman Bognor had been the only example I had come across of that dreaded breed, the script editor. For *Fairly Secret Army* I had my second script editor. A 21-year-old vegan Lesbian with a first in medieval literature at the University of Essex? No. John Cleese.

I yield to nobody in my admiration of John's talent. He always finds the right remark when the rest of us would be speechless. Mary and I were present at a Writers' Guild of Great Britain ceremony when one of the awards went to Salman Rushdie not long after the issuing of the fatwa. The Master of Ceremonies said that it was sad that Rushdie couldn't be there. 'Of course I'm here,' he said, entering theatrically, flanked by two burly bodyguards. He jumped on to a table, and spoke passionately about the power and importance of the written word. Then he exited rapidly to a prolonged standing ovation from the crowded room.

At last silence fell. John Cleese walked slowly to the podium to present the next prize. The silence grew deeper as several hundred people in evening dress thought, in unison, 'How will even John Cleese follow that?'

John looked at us gravely for quite a while, then said, 'Well, I was worried. I'd been told I had to follow Dennis Norden.'

Honesty compels me, though, to say that John failed me as a script editor. He liked the scripts too much. He liked Harry too much. He liked his verbal eccentricity, his deep sadness, his immovable prejudices, his utter incompetence. He didn't say, 'Come off it, Nobbsy, this is all very well, but where's the story? Not everybody's going to find a man hilarious just because he says, "Treacherous chaps, women".'

When the programme went out on Channel Four, it became a cult show. A cult show is a show which very few people watch, but which those few people like a great deal. There were many offices in Britain where people began to talk in Truscott-ese. 'Tricky blighter, Johnny Invoice' could be guaranteed to bring the house down. Unfortunately there were millions who were left cold by such things. For these people, there was no fall back, there were no fail safe devices.

We had a very good supporting cast in Jeremy Child, Diane Fletcher, Terence Alexander and Paul Chapman, who played my favourite of the characters, Peg-Leg Pogson, a mercenary soldier who claimed to have lost a leg in battle, but who in fact kept it strapped behind him when on duty.

The series divided the critics, as usual. Those who loved it almost always reviewed it in Truscott-ese.

Now I had another blackout, the only one I ever had that wasn't late at night. It was at lunchtime. We'd just had the readthrough of the scripts for the first series, and I must have been worrying fairly deeply. We went to a pub in Central London afterwards. I didn't fancy alcohol, which should have alerted everybody, and I began to feel very ill. My legs could barely sustain me. I went out for fresh air but it didn't work. Solicitous thespians broke my fall and laid me on the pavement as if I was a precious cargo. I imagine that the passengers on the buses crawling down the congested street saw Geoffrey Palmer and co bending over me and said, with contempt and envy, 'Drunk at 12.30. That's showbiz for you.'

I'd lost control of my bowels and my bladder. As the kind nurses in the Middlesex Hospital cleaned me up I felt deeply humiliated. It seemed like a flashforward to old age, but would I ever reach old age if this kind of thing went on?

The corridors of the Middlesex Hospital reminded me of those old Nazi bunkers underneath Ludwigshafen. I was wheeled to obscure rooms tucked away in distant corners, where I was put through all kinds of tests. As at Salford, I was treated with great kindness and care. As at Salford, nothing was found.

On my last night I was told, 'You're going home tomorrow, so tonight we're moving you next to the Indian. You have to be fairly fit for that, and nobody can stand more than one night.'

That wasn't racial prejudice. Nobody objected to the Indian because he was Indian. They objected to him because he was this particular garrulous and conceited person. He was charming, urbane and poshly spoken. His anecdotes were unstoppable. When he discovered that I was a writer, he launched into his memories of life with D.H. Lawrence.

'What arguments dear old D.H. and I used to have, David.'

'Really? Ah!'

'Frieda would bring us cocoa and say, "I bet you boys are going to be at it for hours."'

'"For hours"! Gosh!'

'Yes, and all night if dear old Ezra Pound looked in. I would challenge D.H. about his grasp of the psychology of women. Ezra would be really amused. "Dear boy, you're priceless," he would exclaim.'

'Gosh. Really? Ah.'

I goshed and reallyed and ahed myself into total exhaustion and almost wished that I could have another blackout.

It was impossible to tell how old the Indian was, and the awful thing is that it all just might possibly have been true and the poor man had spent thirty years trying to get people to believe him.

I was sent home, and told to rest and keep away from all the filming.

One evening Geoffrey Palmer rang me and said, 'How are you?'

'I'm fine.'

'We've all worried about you.'

'There's no need to. I'm fine.'

'Now you must relax. You're very precious to us all. You mustn't worry. You needn't worry. Everything's going wonderfully.'

'Great.'

'Do you think the back of my head's my funniest feature?'

'Of course not. Why?'

'The director seems to. He keeps shooting the back of my head when I'm saying my funniest lines.'

'Oh my God!'

'No, no. Don't worry. You mustn't. It'll all be terrific. Even the scene where he shoots the whole of your sparkling, intricate dialogue in long shot through trees will probably work.'

'What??? But this is dreadful!'

'No. It's fine. He's probably just clever. It'll be wonderful. Just relax. Everyone loves you and hopes you'll soon be better.'

Robert Young *was* clever and some of his direction was bold and fine, even brilliant at times, but the comedy did tend to get buried beneath the tricksiness at other times. Good comedy actually needs very straightforward direction and is therefore not very popular with ambitious directors.

For the second series there were changes. We had a new director, Roy Ward-Baker. He was immensely experienced, with a solid track record, and he did it all in a simple, straightforward way that was very effective.

We had a proper story this time. In fact at the end of my first month working on the scripts I still hadn't written a single word. I was too busy developing the story.

What I recall of it now is that Harry infiltrated a communist cell and slept with one of the members, played by the lovely Diana Weston, in order to discover all the secrets that she was in the habit of revealing while talking in her sleep.

I only said we had a proper story. I didn't say we had a believable story.

Some of the changes were forced upon me. Quite a long time had elapsed since the first series as Channel Four hadn't been able to decide whether it was worthwhile doing a second one. During this time the house where we had filmed the H.Q. of the Secret Army had been demolished. I had to write a scene in which the house exploded just as Harry approached it.

The longer people have delayed in making a commission, the quicker they want the commissioned programme to be produced. *FSA2* was no exception. As a result, some of the leading performers had other engagements and were only available on certain days. In the first episode, after the explosion, the injured Harry is visited in hospital by the Jeremy Child character. He complains that Peg-Leg Pogson hasn't been to see him, and is told that he's frightened of hospitals. I included this less because I thought it amusing than because Paul Chapman wasn't available on any of the days when we were filming in the hospital. In fact Paul and Jeremy could never be in the same scene throughout the whole series. Awkward blighter, Johnny Scheduling. Never quite got to grips with the cove.

Quite a dramatic incident occurred during the location work for the second series. We had promised to finish filming in a restaurant by 6 p.m. The head waiter attended to our every need, but we hadn't finished when the owner arrived shortly after six. He blew his top and tried to throw us out. We told him that we'd be finished by seven, and the crew would help set up the restaurant for the evening, and it was pointed out that we were paying good money.

'Money?' said the owner. 'What money?'

The head waiter went white. I have never seen the blood drain from anyone's face so quickly. He was sacked on the spot.

I once told Barry Cryer that I would believe I'd made it when the list of successes became as long as the list of failures. I don't think *Fairly Secret Army* can go in either category. It was itself, a bit of a freak, a brave attempt to turn a supporting character into a protagonist, a risky attempt to achieve success through absurdity of language. Bit of a minority interest, Johnny Language. Pity.

After all John Howard Davies's worries, I'm distressed to report that we had only one complaint in two series.

> I wish to complain about the portrayal of the Police Force in tonight's showing of an episode of *Fairly Secret Army*.
>
> Whilst I appreciate that this is a comedy programme, I was not amused by the police being shown as brutish, violent, destroyers of property and planters of evidence.
>
> It was particularly offensive that the officers shown carried the collar insignia of the Hertfordshire Constabulary, a small county force with an exemplary record of conduct.

I replied that I had never mentioned the Hertfordshire Constabulary and had not been responsible for the regrettable insignia. I was making the point that all forces, sadly, did not share the standards of his constabulary. I can pass the buck with the best of them.

*

I was now about to hit a patch where at last that list of successes began to threaten the list of failures. I was approaching the writing of *A Bit Of A Do*.

16 A Bit Of A Do

THE LONG AND rocky road that led to *A Bit Of A Do* began ten years before its transmission in a café in Covent Garden. I was early for an appointment with Victoria Petrie-Hay at Gollancz, so I wrote, over a cup of tea, the first scene of a play that I'd been thinking about. A professor of philosophy meets a darts groupie on a train. To her surprise, and his, he asks her out to dinner. To his surprise, and hers, she accepts.

The play must have been inspired by my step-daughter Kim. We visited her at Keele on several occasions. One weekend she said, 'It's no use coming on the Friday evening. Unfortunately it's my turn on the washing up roster at the Anarchists' Society.' She read philosophy and played darts in a pub in Tunstall. One elderly man, watching her, once said to me, 'That your daughter?' I nodded. 'You must be very proud of her,' he said. 'She throws a very consistent arrow.'

Yes, I was proud of her, and of her philosophy degree, and of her for signing on as a philosopher in the Job Centre in Stoke-on-Trent (no luck).

By this time all the children had fled the nest, although in Chris's case it would be more accurate to say that the nest had fled him. He stayed in our house in Barnet for several years after we moved to Herefordshire.

He was married by now, having met his Israeli wife Talia on the magic bus from Greece. Her first words to me, in Ye Olde Monken Holt, convinced me that we would hit it off. They were, 'Could I have a pint of Pedigree, please?' We were very conscious of Chris's muscular dystrophy, which was attacking him very slowly but so, so remorselessly. I won't say he had no bitterness, but on the whole he has faced this wretched illness with quite enormous courage.

Dave, the eldest, had married, divorced and married again. During the eighties he and his second wife, Sarah, spent an extended honeymoon serving food to 'The Convoy', as the New Age travellers were called. They were arrested, along with the rest of the travellers, at Nostell Priory, near Wakefield, and flung into Armley Jail. Dave was in a cell with eight people and one blanket which stank of urine.

Dave and Sarah were released on bail, but Dave had to report three times a day to Leominster police station. He was, after all, suspected of having possessed a two-pound bag of fine cocaine, which would probably have had a street value of several million pounds. Dave and Sarah assured us that it was self-raising flour, so they weren't too upset about things, but Mary and I had sleepless nights, so little faith did we have left in British justice. We imagined the stuff being spiked in the labs to give the police the convictions to justify the raid. Our relief when the lab report stated 'this would appear to be self-raising flour' was enormous.

We'd missed flower power but at least the family had dabbled in flour power.

How could the author of Reginald Perrin be upset by attempts to find an alternative life-style? I return to that picture of the smug family of Mr and Mrs Mortgage and their two little policies. Is that our ideal? How pathetic that our society should have felt so threatened by one convoy.

After the raid at Nostell Priory, incidentally, the police spent a lot of time asking questions about two characters, Horace and Boris, who had disappeared without trace during the raid. The police clearly thought they were drug dealers on a major scale. I wonder if they ever found out that they were the Convoy's pet geese.

It's time to return, by a roundabout route, to the play conceived in the café. The roundabout route is deliberate. It fits with *A Bit Of A Do*'s roundabout route to the screen.

In recent years that marvellous writer, human being and Hull City supporter Alan Plater and I have taught on residential courses at the Arvon Centre and twice at Ty Newydd, the only writers' centre in Wales, which is based in a picturesque house on the Lleyn Peninsula, the very house in which Lloyd George breathed his last, unaware that my grandfather had turned his portrait to the wall because he was wicked with women.

Neither Alan nor I are greatly into slogans or facile formulae for successful comedy. We teach (aided by Jimmy Perry, who comes all the way from London to discuss *Dad's Army* and his other great successes) through example and exploration, and find some wonderfully responsive students – what a lot of talent there is waiting to emerge, given half a chance. However, I do manage one slogan – 'Comedy is about reaction as much as about action' – and one simple formula – 'Action without tension doesn't work. Tension without action can work. Action with tension always works.'

I mention this because it's so relevant to *Cupid's Darts*. The first scene of the play lasted six minutes and had no action whatsoever. The philosopher and the darts groupie talk. Later they move on to a restaurant and talk a lot more. Then they go to a pub to play darts, and talk some more.

At the end she moves back to the darts players that she loves. The point of the piece is that he learns more from her than she does from him. She teaches him to live. There is no sub-plot except that he may lose his job. Dreadful, according to the people who teach writing by numbers. Rather surprising, then, that I got far more letters about this little play than about any other hour of television in my career. I even got a telegram from Lulu. (On the subject of sub-plots, I'm wondering if there was any sub-plot in *Brief Encounter*. Very minimal, if there was.)

Cupid's Darts worked so well with the audience because they became involved with the characters and wanted to know what happened to them, how their relationship developed.

I saw a production of *Brighton Rock* a few years ago at the usually excellent West Yorkshire Playhouse. I was bored. Action galore, drama galore, murder galore, no tension, because we hadn't learnt enough about the characters to care.

End of lecture.

No script can ever work if it isn't well acted. *Cupid's Darts* was supremely well acted by Robin Bailey and Lesley Ash, and indeed by everybody – there was a stunning portrayal of a snobbish bitch by Marjorie Bland.

Robin Bailey (Peter Tinniswood's Uncle Mort – another arm of coincidence) wasn't our first choice. I was told that Paul Schofield turned it down because he didn't do nude scenes, and Frank Finlay said it was a lovely play but he would be miscast, he wouldn't be able to make it work. How refreshing is honesty.

Lesley Ash was our first choice. David Cunliffe, the director, and I had auditioned her and three very competent actresses. She had only done seven minutes of TV comedy, she was jet-lagged, seemed dyslexic and read badly. David asked me who I favoured and I said, 'Lesley Ash.'

'But she was dreadful.'

'Awful.'

'Why then?'

'Because the others would be good, but she just might be magical. Why, who do you think?'

'Oh, Lesley Ash, of course.'

David told me later that he would never have dared cast her if I hadn't agreed. It would have been too big a risk. Knowing that he had the writer's approval, he could take that risk.

I've never heard a better reason for having a writer present at auditions. Needless to say, it hardly ever happens nowadays.

Herbert Kretzmer, who had written so many songs for *TW3*, asked if he could turn the play into a West End musical. I thought it was stretching a nice little Pygmalion-in-reverse idea beyond its capacity, but said nowt, and we met more than once in his London flat to discuss where the songs should come. Eventually Herbert rang me and said that some of his friends thought it was stretching a nice little Pygmalion-in-reverse idea beyond its capacity, and the idea was dropped. The poor man consoled himself by doing the lyrics for *Les Miserables* instead.

Enough of *Cupid's Darts*, a sweet little play which can never be repeated now because the discovery of Aids has swept away its innocence among other far more important victims. But it was this play, and its success, that won me the commission that became *A Bit Of A Do*.

David Cunliffe, who was now Head of Drama at Yorkshire, rang me and said he wanted to commission me to write anything I wanted.

I drove up the motorway to see him, and stopped at a transport café, this being the best way of avoiding Little Chefs without dying of starvation. At a table I saw two lorry drivers talking, and the whole plot of a play came into my mind in an instant. A lorry driver carrying dog food from Carmarthen to Hull meets a lorry driver carrying dog food from Hull to Carmarthen. Both men are married. Both men are seeking extra-marital adventure. Both men ask the other where they can find a good woman in Hull/Carmarthen. The answers are, respectively, the bingo and the Talk of the Towy nightclub. Both men meet each other's wives. Each tells the other of his conquest. Each man describes his wife in such unflattering terms, and his girlfriend in such romantic terms, that realisation never even threatens to dawn. We know. They don't. A feast of dramatic irony, the play to end at the moment when the four meet and realisation does dawn, leaving the audience to imagine how it all gets resolved rather than spelling it out. A whole play, conceived in a minute. Oh, if a writer's life was always like that!

Young writers should close their eyes before reading the next few paragraphs. They might tip them over into insanity.

'Right,' said David Cunliffe. 'Now I want something major from you. I loved *Cupid's Darts*. We must have faith in our good writers.'

'I had an idea for a play on the way up,' I said. I spelt it out.

'Yes, yes, very good, do that,' he said impatiently, as if swatting an irritating insect. 'But what I really want is six hours of television, on anything you want to write.'

I left David's office after ten minutes with a commission to do seven hours of television, six of which could be on any subject I chose.

I wrote the play quickly. It almost wrote itself. I posted it to Yorkshire Television. The following day I got a telegram from David.

> Thank you for Dogfood Dan stop it is absolutely smashing and very witty stop enjoyable and stylish stop would like to go into production immediately stop respectfully suggest Derick Bettent as director stop much love to you.

Within a couple of days Derick Bettent was phoning me to discuss the play. He turned out to be a Post Office misprint. His real name was Derek Bennett.

'David, I'm directing. We've no time to lose. It's a tight pre-production schedule.'

What?? This was three days after I'd delivered it. It turned out that my play had arrived on David Cunliffe's desk on the very day on which they'd been forced to abandon a play. They had a production scheduled, and no play. Sometimes you strike lucky.

This was the height of the Citizens' Band craze. I called the play *Dogfood Dan and the Carmarthen Cowboy* after the 'handles' of the two drivers. The drivers were splendidly played by Gareth Thomas and David Daker, a wonderful contrast between Welsh hwyl and Yorkshire grit, and their wives were appealingly played by Helen Cotterill and Diana Davies. The play caused no sensations but could definitely be chalked up on the success side of the ledger.

All too soon it was over and I found myself thinking about my marvellous commission from David Cunliffe. It was so unusual to be treated with such faith that for a while I found it daunting. Then the beginnngs of an idea presented themselves to me.

Pat Sandys, the eminent producer of *Cupid's Darts*, was looking for plays for a series called *Love and Marriage*. I had put forward three ideas that she liked – a play set at a dentists' dinner dance, the election of Miss Ball-Bearing 1983 and a play about a diamond wedding. The series didn't happen, or my ideas didn't. I realised, though, that all these ideas were set at functions, and I thought about a series in which each episode would be set at a different 'do', but featuring the same characters.

Life really is my inspiration. It was from our life in Herefordshire that *A Bit Of A Do* was born.

People in London often asked us, 'What do you find to do in the country?' They had no idea that the social life was far more hectic than in the capital. Functions came thick and fast.

Most people never get a chance to go to a dentists' dinner dance. I went to two. We had become friendly with our dentist, Karl Pigott, and his wife Beryl, hence the invitations. Dentists' dinner dances are odd events. You don't like to smile for fear somebody says that he can fit you in next Tuesday.

Through Karl and Beryl, Mary and I had joined the Vice-Presidents' Club of Hereford United ('Get a life, you sad bastard,' I hear you yell) and we went to most of their home matches with talented fellow novelist and script writer Alick Rowe.

Alick's friendship became invaluable to me during my time in Herefordshire. I've never wanted to move in literary circles, but I do start to feel starved if I can't have a good writers' discussion (and whinge) with somebody. Alick gave me all this and a great deal of laughter. Laughter between friends is one of my life's supreme pleasures.

It was natural, then, that we should all go to a charity horse-racing evening at the golf club to raise money for the retiring Hereford United goalkeeper – not David Icke, who had a hot line to God, but Tommy Hughes, who had a carpet-cleaning firm and whose wife was Karl's receptionist.

That same year we were invited to the Angling Club's Christmas party at the White Swan in Eardisland, a lovely village of black and white houses and part of what is now known as 'The Black and White Trail', because nobody is trusted any more to find an attraction unless it's listed and surrounded by signposts. In its golden age the White Swan was a splendid hostelry, run by a delightful extrovert called Richard Baldwin, who was no stranger to the grape or the grain. On Sundays in the lounge bar they used to have fancy dress. The genius of the idea was that you all had to come as the same person. If you haven't seen eighty-six Max Walls in a crowded bar, or eighty-one Biggles pouring out their banter, you are socially disadvantaged.

However, this particular Angling Club Christmas Party was not to be the pub's crowning glory. It was dogged by bad luck. It was bad luck that the entertainment failed to turn up. It was bad luck that an elderly villager stepped into the breach with his squeeze box. It was bad luck that only two of the five prize-winners turned up, and it was certainly bad luck that one of them had to leave because his mother died and his house was burgled in the course of the evening, so that the only prize-winner present was the man giving out the prizes, who gave one to himself.

A dentists' dinner dance, an angling club Christmas party and a charity horse-racing evening, and many of the same people at all three. I was nearly there.

I worked out a framework for the series, beginning with the character of Rita. I've never liked writing for specific actors, but here, for the first time, I found myself doing so. Gwen Taylor had been superb in one of Michael Palin and Terry Jones's *Ripping Yarns*. I saw her as I created Rita.

The framework would be that Rita's husband would leave her for a more glamorous woman, and in her loss she would ultimately thrive and marry somebody a great deal more glamorous. This required an actress who could play gauche and nervy at the start and find poise and confidence on the way. It required an actress who could look less and less dowdy and more and more attractive as the series progressed. Gwen would be perfect.

I decided to begin and end with a wedding. I would begin with Rita as mother of the groom and end with her as a bride. The first wedding would be a white wedding, the second a register office one.

In the end Rita's wedding had to wait. It proved too abrupt. Instead I had Liz, who left her dentist husband to be with Rita's husband Ted, marrying an old friend, and Rita turned up with a fairly glamorous younger man whom she would later marry. This was more believable. It was also the final punishment for Ted, who saw Liz leave him for someone of her own class, the bereaved solicitor Neville Badger.

I had five dos. The sixth would be what I'd called Miss Ball-Bearing 83. Now luck took a hand. I was invited to The Crowning of Miss Wyvern at the Chateau Impney. Radio Wyvern was our local commercial radio station, and Chateau Impney is a Chateau of the Loire which, for some inexplicable reason, is just outside Droitwich.

Here was my last function. I decided to call it 'The Crowning of Miss Frozen Chicken U.K.', because I wanted to get something ferocious about battery chickens into my scripts.

I couldn't get to the Chateau Impney, because of my collapse and my spell in the Middlesex Hospital, but I had a splendid informant who told me all I needed to know about randy judges, corruption and girls whose ambitions were to abolish world poverty while opening their own hairdressing salon. Dear informant, age has struck and I've forgotten who you are. Many apologies. You helped enormously.

Rita's husband needed to be rather pathetic. I called him Ted Simcock. He made fire irons, companion sets, door knockers, toasting forks, things that I hoped would be funny when Ted was pompous about them.

Liz, the posh lady for whom Ted falls, had to have a husband and he had to be a dentist, to facilitate invitations to the dentists' dinner dance.

Then I needed a chicken farmer, who would be plagued by ethical doubts when in his cups. I loathe the idea of battery farming. You know how wretched it is when you see those concentration camps which litter our otherwise beautiful land. So, I created Rodney Sillitoe, of Cock-A-Doodle Chickens. He needed to be a bit of a drunkard so that he could become maudlin about his chickens, but always drunk? That might be boring. I thought about our dear friends Eric and Mary, who got drunk alternately. I didn't think they would recognise that the idea came from them. In the event they'd have loved the chance. They both died before the series began.

I must mention two memories of dear, gentle, soft-spoken Eric. Both involve drink.

I can still see him pouring a glass of the Hirondelle white wine that was so ubiquitous in the seventies, taking a sip, and saying, 'M'm. One swallow doesn't make a summer.'

One lunchtime, in the pub, he said, 'I'm really worried about the thing I have to go to tonight. I think it'll be terribly boozy.'

'You are worried about something being boozy?' I exclaimed. 'What is it?'

'The inaugural meeting of the Irish-Finnish Journalists' Friendship Association.'

The more I wrote, the more I realised what a happy device I'd hit upon, in setting it entirely at functions. There were three great dramatic advantages. Firstly, people had to say important things quietly and carefully to avoid being overheard, especially as everyone was watching everyone else. Secondly, people would be reluctant to spell things out in public. Lines like 'We were so sorry when we heard' and 'We nearly didn't come, under the circumstances' could help to build enormous comic tension. Thirdly, a great deal would have happened in the intervals between the do's, and not everybody would know, so there were endless opportunities for putting one's foot in it.

What I had to be careful about was to keep it real, always real, so that the audience actually felt that they were there.

David Cunliffe phoned me, after he'd had all the scripts, and told me that Paul Fox loved them, and they were the most important drama productions lined up for the next year. He only had one request. Could I make one of the do's a barmitzvah?

I replied that I wasn't Jewish, had never been to a barmitzvah, felt unqualified to write about one, and in any case Jack Rosenthal's brilliant *Barmitzvah Boy* had immortalised the subject.

Next year David Cunliffe rang me again. Paul Fox still loved the scripts, it was to be the major drama production for next year, but he would still like me to add a barmitzvah. I said that I still wasn't Jewish and I still hadn't been to a barmitzvah. (I have now. Throughout much of the ceremony the men discussed Leeds United's midfield problems in low tones.)

I spoke to Geoffrey Strachan at Methuen and asked if they would be interested in *A Bit Of A Do* as my next novel. I'd never liked the idea of spin-offs from TV series but I felt forced into the position of turning the scripts into a novel because I simply wasn't prepared to waste the material.

When one adapts a novel one is cutting it back, distilling its essence, reducing and deepening it, as a chef does a sauce. I felt that I needed to follow the process in reverse, open it out, add a periphery for which there is no time on film. For example, on page 55 we read:

> At the very moment when Rita said, 'Who sent you?', Eva Blumenthal, in room 109, was gently rubbing unsalted Welsh butter over the genitals of her husband Fritz, in an effort to alleviate the corn chandler's pain.

No time for the Blumenthals on television. One creates them, uses them, obliterates them, and they never know.

I had several letters from David Cunliffe, regretting delays to the series. Advertising revenue had plummeted. Drama production had been decimated. All the letters revealed that the intended target of the series was Channel Four. This seems very odd to me now, but at the time I didn't care where it was put on, so long as it was somewhere.

David Benedictus at Channel Four clearly wanted the series, but was frustrated at the delays from Yorkshire. Then he left, and on 2 March, 1987, David Cunliffe was sent a very brief note by Peter Ansorge, the new Commissioning Editor, Channel Four.

He said that he had read both episodes and had enjoyed them, but they weren't a priority for him. I don't know why he had only read two episodes – perhaps he had only been sent two episodes – but I was more than a little upset that a letter which affected my career so seriously hadn't even been signed by the man himself.

He also said in his letter that he was looking for strong narrative links between episodes. This was exactly what my series had, but its glory was that they were subtle and not obvious.

I did what I always did when I received bad news about a script. I got it out of my system with an evening of food and drink, and settled

A Bit of a Tum. With Nicola Pagett, Paul Chapman, Michael Jayston, David Jason and Gwen Taylor on location in Knaresborough for *A Bit of a Do*.

Ice cold in Leeds. On location for *Rich Tea and Sympathy* with director David Reynolds and stars Denis Quilley and Patricia Hodge.

An act of faith. With Susan at the wedding of her daughter
Briget and Mark Granger.

My eighth step-grandchild, Max, comes second from last in the sack race at
Beckwithsaw School.

4 August 1998. Susan and I on our wedding day.

Peter Tinniswood. The Great man at breakfast in our garden during the brief North Yorkshire summer.

at my typewriter the next morning determined to create a new masterpiece.

The hardback edition of the book was published in 1986, and the paperback followed in 1987. Shortly after the publication of the paperback I found myself in Hull. No, I didn't, that suggests I'd been dumped there unconscious or stowed away on a cargo ship. I went to Hull happily, of my own free will, and visited Brown's, a bookshop of repute, and found no copies of the paperback.

There's a story of the poet Danny Abse's mother, on finding no copies of her son's book in a Cardiff store, exclaiming, 'But don't you know who he is? He's the Welsh Dylan Thomas.' My mother told me that she sometimes turned my books from spine on to face on, turning some lesser writer (in her eyes) like Nabokov or Naipaul from face to spine on, but she would never have complained that there were none of my books in stock, and nor normally would I. On this occasion, however, still feeling miffed at the rejection of the series, I felt outraged by its absence so soon after publication. I complained. The proprietor said, 'I've sold out. I put a dump bin by the door, being a great fan, and it sold even better than I expected. I've ordered more.'

I bought a copy of the local paper, and there it was at number four, just behind Jackie Collins.

The progress of the book came to the attention of Vernon Lawrence, now Head of Light Entertainment at Yorkshire, and he phoned me.

'The book's doing well, isn't it?'

'Pretty well.'

'Top ten?'

'Absolutely!' I didn't add 'For one week in Hull.'

'There are scripts, aren't there?'

'Yes.'

'Are they any good?'

Another of those unanswerable questions. I hummed and hawed, especially hawed, and he asked if he could see them without the Drama Department knowing.

Within a very few days he rang again and said that he loved the scripts and wanted to go ahead with the series. He only had two changes to suggest. (1) Could two events be set in each function room, to save expense? (2) Could it be set in Essex? The North was out of fashion. Answers (1) Yes. (2) Not on your nelly. All the rhythms are Yorkshire rhythms.

Vernon accepted defeat over Essex gracefully. He became executive producer, with David Reynolds as producer and director of three episodes.

It was tacitly assumed form the outset that this feeble little Channel Four discard was now a massive prime time ITV comedy drama.

The process of casting began. For Ted Simcock I produced a long list of the usual suspects, headed by John Thaw. Then David Reynolds rang and said that David Jason was keen to see the scripts. David as Ted? Impossible. Thirteen million viewers? Well maybe he could do it.

A small intimate luncheon was arranged, admission to Davids only – Jason, Reynolds and Nobbs. Ironically, I had to miss the meal because of a do – a funeral . . .

Reggie Jones, a friend from Ye Olde Monken Holt in Barnet, had died. It was a strange funeral. We were invited to the flat in Barnet, not to the crematorium. Even his widow, Barbara, didn't go to the crematorium. We sat in the flat and drank to his memory. I'd grown used to funerals over the years. I'd grown used to the pattern of grieving and then talking and laughing. Because we didn't go to any service, because we didn't express our shared grief, we felt that we hadn't earned the right to laugh and talk normally. It was a sad, stilted little affair.

I arrived at the restaurant in time for a brandy. Things seemed to have gone well, but there was a lot of 'I'll be in touch' and 'I'll talk to my agent'. By now, I'd got over the shock, and I really wanted David for the part.

For Liz Rodenhurst, his amour, we went for Nicola Pagett. I arrived at Yorkshire's London offices at the same time as she did and heard a receptionist, aged about twelve, ring the casting department and say, 'We've got a Miss Nicola Budget here for you.' We all got on well, and Miss Budget was offered the part, which was very exciting.

For Rita I made a list of Gwen Taylor. To my immense relief, she was available, willing and eager.

I sat with David Reynolds and Malcolm Drury, Yorkshire's Casting Director, throughout the auditions for the younger people. Nowadays companies don't have casting directors. They use casting specialists from outside. It's cheaper. I haven't had a sniff of the casting action for about ten years now, but who could be a better judge than the person who thought the characters up?

I felt a great surge of excitement when David Thewlis walked in, and we knew we had our almost gormless Paul Simcock, but all the young regulars were good – Sarah-Jane Holm, Wayne Foskett, Nigel Hastings and Karen Drury (no relation of Malcolm's).

Tim Wylton and Stephanie Cole were sublime as the Sillitoes, Paul Chapman was as good as ever as the dentist, and I had a moment of inspiration in suggesting Michael Jayston as the grieving solicitor.

Malcolm Hebden was very funny and also rather touching as the camp barman who spoke entirely in catch-phrases like 'One small Scottish wine coming up, thank you, sir, there aren't many of us left, there you go, tickety-boo.' Unusually for me, this character was based on a real person, a barman at Guernsey Airport whom I watched during a delay. He spoke entirely in catch-phrases for one hour and twenty-five minutes. I'm sure he had no idea that he was immortalised.

A Bit Of A Do was an enormously happy experience for me. I was present at virtually every moment of its production, and was encouraged to be so.

I only recall three problems with the cast, all of them purely professional.

From time to time Nicola Pagett asked us to let her soften her character, lest she be disliked. We pointed out that being disliked hadn't handicapped Larry Hagman or Joan Collins, but she would go away unconvinced. Then, when she got in front of the camera, she would forget everything she'd said and go for it ruthlessly and brilliantly. Nicola had a highly publicised breakdown a few years after our series. I wish her well as fervently as I can.

Gwen Taylor had a bit of a panic attack before the scene in which she had to sing a carol during the Angling Club Christmas Party. She didn't think she'd be able to sing it well enough. We pointed out that it was being sung by Rita Simcock, not Kathleen Ferrier. In the scene, Gwen was brilliant and it was a wonderfully moving moment.

Working with David Jason was a joy, but it nearly got off to a bad start. Towards the end of the rehearsals of the first episode, I watched what is called the Producer's Run (these comments refer to shows made in the studio. Most shows are made on location now). At the Producer's Run the technicians – cameramen, sound department, wardrobe, make-up and others – watch the show and work out exactly what's going to be needed from them. Hilarious laughter at a Producer's Run doesn't necessarily mean success. Glum faces don't inevitably presage a flop. I can't remember how this one went down because I was too worried by one aspect of it. When David Reynolds asked me if I had any notes, I said, 'Only one.' He couldn't believe it. Only one! 'Well, I've got a few others,' I said, 'but this one's so important I can't bother with the others. David Jason is sliding into Del Boy.'

After the technicians had left, David Reynolds watched another run of the show, and agreed with me. As the moment of truth drew closer, David Jason was unconsciously relying on old routines for comfort. Ted Simcock was disappearing before our eyes.

'I can't do anything now,' said David Reynolds, 'but I'll talk to David over the weekend.'

I don't know what he said, but he must have said something, because when we got to the studio Ted Simcock was firmly back in place. I think it reflects enormous credit on both David Reynolds (one of the real good guys of television) for confronting his star and on David Jason for taking his comments on board. From that moment onwards David's performance was nothing less than a joy. In lesser hands Ted could have been a bore. In David's he was an enjoyable bore, a delightfully pompous man, an unsympathetic character presented with enormous sympathy, but not with sentimentality.

Perhaps this is a good moment to speak about actors (and actresses) in general. Some writers dislike them. I most certainly do not. I have met very few who didn't respect the script and do their best for it. Hardly anyone has given a selfish performance in any of my work. I see us as colleagues. I see us as the exploited. We should stand firm, together, against the exploiters.

Writing cannot be described as a secure profession, but theirs is even more insecure. When a writer is rejected, he goes back to his desk and pours out his masterpiece. 'I'll show the bastards,' he thinks. If a rejected actor goes home and pours out his greatest ever performance, the men in the white coats will arrive.

A Bit Of A Do went out on Friday evenings at nine. The first show had an audience of just over fourteen million and after a slight drop it climbed to almost fifteen million, with only the soaps above it in the ratings. I found it extraordinary to know that so many people were watching something I'd written. I was unashamedly delighted to have a main-stream smash hit of these proportions. They may have come because of David Jason, but they stayed.

The first episode ended with a real comic bang as the wedding of Paul Simcock and Jenny Rodenhurst disintegrated in accusations and tears, with Betty Sillitoe hopelessly drunk, Elvis Simcock knocking out Simon Rodenhurst, the bride announcing that she was pregnant, Rita's father revealing that she was born out of wedlock, and Rita fainting from the horror of it all. Into the social carnage wandered Neville Badger, lost in his grief. 'I'm off now,' he said. 'It was just too soon. I just couldn't cope with the sight of so many people enjoying themselves.'

The more people told me that they were looking forward to episode two, the more worried I became. This was the one which ended with Rita's father dying in her arms on the dance floor, and Rita exclaiming, 'Dad! Dad! You can't be dead. I haven't told you that I love you' – hardly rib-tickling stuff. I needn't have worried. People loved that too.

Naturally Yorkshire wanted a second series, and Vernon asked me to write a short document for the management, outlining the story development. One page only. This was still not the age of vast synopses and treatments. People in power were still presumed to have some qualities of imagination and to be able to judge an idea's potential without having to wade through every semi-colon.

The document made almost no mention of Ted Simcock. It was for the management, not David Jason. Unfortunately, with astonishing naïvety, somebody showed it to David, who, thoroughly justifiably, asked, 'Am I in it or what?'

David didn't aspire to any more dominating a role than he'd had in the first series – it was to remain an ensemble piece – but, quite rightly, he wanted to know that he would have some interesting developments and challenges. David Reynolds and I had a hard job persuading him. Oh, the red wine we had to drink. How one suffers for one's art.

Persuade him we did, and we all had enormous fun making the second series which ended with Ted, who'd long ago lost the classy Liz and been desperately conned by the cynical Corinna Price-Rogerson, marrying a brassy young woman called Sandra and setting off in a caravanette to sell snacks from a lay-by off the A64, under the business name of Ted's Snax.

The first series had integrity in both senses of the word. It was truthful, and it was a whole. The second series couldn't quite match that. As with Reggie, I had written a story so complete that there was no further complete story to write. All I could do was to provide inventive variations on a theme. It was full of good things and often very funny, but it lacked the absolute rightness and reality of the first.

It was a blow to lose David Thewlis, who was ambitious and frightened of being type-cast. I wish he'd talked to me about his doubts. I would have told him that there could never be any more than two series. I would have asked him to trust me – never trust a man who says 'trust me'! – to explore his character in more depth. His loss was a major nuisance. He'd been so good that recasting was not an option. I had to lose Paul. To kill him off would have been disruptively tragic, so I sent him to prison, but the series missed him.

There had to be seven do's this time. Why? Because thirteen episodes were needed for foreign sales, thirteen weeks being a neat quarter of a year. You see what I mean about integrity at the highest level.

A list of the seven do's reveals that the concept was nearing exhaustion. Again, I began with a church wedding and ended with a civil one. This was pushing it. Couldn't do that again. It was absolutely natural to include a christening and a funeral, but the nature of the other three do's – 'The Grand Opening of Sillitoes', 'The Farewell Party' and, above all, 'The Inauguration of the Outer Inner Relief Road' – showed that I was already stretching things.

There just weren't enough feasible main-stream functions left for a third series, and in any case it would have been increasingly difficult to find reasons for this disparate and diverse group to continue to meet.

With the second series, because of the availability of actors, there was no time to write the book before the series. I took great care to turn *Fair Do's* into something more than a spin-off. I filled it out so that the town itself became a character. The book aspired to be a portrait of a society in a way the TV series could never be.

I am my own harshest critic. I don't believe that a writer can afford not to be. I have often squirmed while watching my stuff. Sometimes I've had to switch it off. Now, however, I could relax and watch with pride. I'm not ashamed to say that I revelled in it. Mary missed a few episodes because of rehearsals with the Wye Players. I would watch on my own and watch them again when she came home. The casting, the performances, the direction, the sets, the clothes, the music all came so close to what had been in my head. To watch this world, to believe in it, and to know that millions were enjoying it too – this was pure joy.

A Bit Of A Do is the only thing of mine to win awards. In 1989 it won the Royal Television Society's Drama Series Award. At the British Comedy Awards in 1990 it won the Top British Television Comedy Award and the Top British ITV and Channel Four T.V. Sit-Com Award. At the Tric Celebrity Awards it won the Mitsubishi Trophy for Sit-Com of the Year. It was never a sit-com, but who's complaining. It also won the Broadcasting Press Group's award for Best Entertainment Series.

At the 1990 Comedy Awards I was given a special award from the Writers' Guild of Great Britain. I was listening to the President, Alan Scott, praising some writer or other, and suddenly I saw all the cameras pointing at me. I almost died on the spot, but a minute or two later I was on the stage of the Palladium making a short and, I think, reasonably effective speech. The awful thing was that Mary wasn't there. David Reynolds had told me that I must go in case *A Bit Of A Do* won something, but he said it was going to be a rather long-winded and boring event. Somebody should have made sure that she was there – I suppose the thought was that if they insisted she came I would suspect something. I would never have suspected anything. Mary had supported me in all the years of struggle, and my moment of pride was considerably spoilt because of her absence.

I was thrilled to receive the praise of my peers but I realised that awards themselves don't mean much to me. I have photographs of them on the wall of my study, but I don't show them to people. They're there for me to look at when I'm struggling and need to be convinced that I'm funny.

I can't end this chapter on *A Bit Of A Do* without mentioning a few of the letters that came during this time.

8 April, 1981 One that I liked about Cupid's Darts
> I am writing to tell you how much I liked your play about the funny professor and the funny tart. I hope darts groupies are really like that, or at least some of them. Incidentally, what's it like being called Nobbs?

7 November 1986 An extract from a wonderful letter from the supremely generous Sue Townsend, about her mother
> She was very impressed that 'I HAD MET YOU' and wanted to know 'WHAT YOU WERE LIKE.' I told her that you were dapper and witty and had tons of je ne sais quoi – it seemed to please her.

Were you really speaking about me, Sue? Wow!

21 November 1986
> I know you will be relieved to hear that the unusual shape of

your left kidney appears to be due to a simple cyst. There is nothing to be done to this.

5 March 1989

My only criticism was Laurence's suicide at the end, I thought it unnecessary and it cast a sad note over a hilarious episode. By the way, can you tell me how tall Paul Chapman is? Either he's very big or everyone else is small!

In TV Times

I'm a Yorkshireman and capable of being critical of my county but I was offended by ITV's *A Bit Of A Do*, the allegedly fun-poking series based in Knaresborough. No pretence about a couple sympathetically weakening over the weeks or months towards an illicit relationship – just straight into a behind-the-bike-shed scene installed instead in a hotel bedroom. It was too crude even to titillate the Lower Fourth. The writer should be condemned to sleep in a wet pigsty, and his 'script' given to him as his pillow.

December 1989 Me to Jimmy Greaves

Dear Jimmy

I know that you have made several nice comments about my series A BIT OF A DO, and I feel that I must write to tell you that I can't imagine anyone whose praise I would relish more.

In my younger days I used to stand on the terraces at White Hart Lane, and for your debut match I got into the ground at 1.25 and stood behind the goal where you scored two in about five minutes in the first half. In later years I took to a seat and since 1980 when I moved here I've supported Hereford United. Well, nobody's life should be all pleasure.

Anyway, thank you for your nice comments and for all the pleasure you gave me at Tottenham. I'm a real football freak. I once sat next to Alan Gilzean in a restaurant in Cockfosters.

Far more exciting than meeting David Jason and Nicola Pagett.

December 1989 Jimmy Greaves to me

Thank you very much for your letter commenting upon my nice remarks about *A Bit Of A Do*. I can assure you I really did enjoy it.

May I say how surprised I am to learn that in your younger days you were a Tottenham Hotspur supporter and have enjoyed many a great game in that era.

It's interesting to know that one of your great pleasures in life has been that you once sat next to Alan Gilzean at a restaurant in Cockfosters and said it was far more exciting than meeting David Jason or Nicola Pagett. I can assure you that having shared many a bath with Alan Gilzean, meeting Nicola Pagett would be far more exciting for me!

I'd followed up the success of *Perrin* with a huge flop. Could I do better this time?

17 NEAR MISSES

PEEING THROUGH A catheter is a horrendous experience, far more painful than any rejection slip.

I had just undergone a prostate operation at an unusually early age. I was only approaching my fifty-second birthday. As I slowly recovered, I enjoyed listening to the other patients. The two in the beds on my left formed an unwitting double act.

'You remember that big fat antique dealer in Leominster with the orange wig?'

'Yes. Haven't seen him recently. What's happened to him?'

'Dead. You remember that little bald man on the cheese stall in Hereford market?'

'Yes. Haven't seen him either. Do you know anything about him?'

'Dead. You remember the tic-tac man with the high-pitched voice, always at Ludlow races?'

'Yes. He's another one I haven't seen for a while.'

'Dead. You remember that butcher with the loud voice and the squint, drank twelve pints of Guinness every night?'

'Yes. Haven't seen him either. Dead?'

'No. Moved to Kidderminster.'

It was a perfectly crafted joke, yet they saw nothing funny in it. Were they humourless anoraks or am I a heartless bastard? Answers on one side of the paper only, please.

The man in the bed opposite hated clerical gentlemen of every persuasion. 'They'll be streaming in soon, you'll see,' he told me.

A few minutes later a fresh-faced embarrassed young C of E vicar entered the ward nervously.

'It's started!' bellowed the man opposite. 'There'll be a stream of them now. Rabbis, priests, the lot, you wait.'

The clergyman fled as soon as he could.

Next to the clerophobe was a grumpy, disagreeable man. One of the nurses rang his wife and said she could fetch him, and the woman replied, 'If you send him I suppose I'll have to accept him, but I'm not fetching him.'

I told another patient of a visit I'd made to Birmingham, and he said, 'I'll never go there again. It's full of blacks.'

I couldn't let this pass without a fight. I made a passionate speech about racial equality. 'Do you actually know any blacks?' I asked.

'Only one,' he admitted. 'Our cashier. He's a wonderful man. He's the exception that proves the rule.'

You can't win, the way some people think, but what material! I was surrounded by sadness and danger and prejudice and all the rich absurdity of human life.

As I recuperated slowly, I was cheered up by a letter from Spike Mullins:

> I remember that Des O'Connor told me once that when his Father was going in for that operation he happened to mention the fact to Eli Woods who said, 'W – w – w – what are the s – s – s – symptoms?'
>
> And Des replied, 'Let's put it this way, he pisses like you talk.'

Eli Woods had stuttered his way through many Les Dawson sketches.

Back home I sat by the log fire and drank Hugh Brogan's marvellous biography of Arthur Ransome. Hugh had been in our college revue *Feet Up* and I remember now what the title signified. The programme showed a picture of a policeman with his feet up. The show was off-beat.

I wrote to tell Hugh how much I'd enjoyed the book, and he replied:

> Dear David
>
> . . . I was very gratified by your letter, and touched, and wanted to reply suitably – but how can I, when I cannot read your signature? I have so many friends called David – none of them living in Leominster, as far as I know – you see my difficulty? I really don't know how to get out of it, except by being frank . . . WHO ARE YOU? I really would like to know – one doesn't get such a letter every day. Oh dear oh dear

We made contact in the end, and I visited him when he was staying with friends in Kidderminster, where I saw no sign of the butcher with the loud voice and the squint.

This was not the first time my signature had caused problems. When Geoffrey Palmer was in Alan Bennett's play *Kafka's Dick* at the Royal Court, he told me that Alan was upset that it hadn't transferred to the West End and suggested I write to tell him how much I'd enjoyed it. It's a marvellous play, but I suspect that the title is a problem. Those who know Kafka will be stuffy about the use of 'Dick', those who are turned on by the use of 'Dick' will be turned off again by Kafka. This is probably why there's never been a play called Sartre's Bollocks.

Anyway, I wrote, and got a postcard back, thanking me for cheering him up at a low ebb. He ended, 'You live in a lovely part of the world. I can't quite decipher your signature. I've tried to reproduce it!'

Before the making of *A Bit Of A Do* I had two more sit-coms recorded by the BBC. The first was called *The Hello Goodbye Man* and was about a struggling salesman, played by Ian Lavender. The female lead was Mary Tamm, and among several good performances was yet another one by Paul Chapman. The Director was Alan J.W. Bell, of *Last Of The Summer Wine* fame. When I look back at the scripts I feel that they fell into a rather un-Nobbsian mode. They're neat and funny and quite sharp, but they lack the great quirkiness of humanity, the depth of character, the little touches that bring people to life. They just weren't as rich as the people I'd met in hospital.

On the day of the first recording it was obvious that Mary Tamm was very nervous, not having done much comedy and none with a studio audience. Alan asked me if I'd ask Ian Lavender to talk to her and soothe her nerves. I approached Ian in the bar with this aim in mind. He turned to me with an ashen face and said, 'I'm as funny as a grave, aren't I?'

I wondered whether to include that remark here. I liked Ian a lot and I don't know what he'll think if he reads it, but I decided that I must include it because it reveals, for people not involved in comedy, just how nerve-racking it can be. I've often thought I'm as funny as a grave. I can't believe there are many people in the comedy game who've never had such a feeling. You can fail to hit the spot in drama and never know, but if your first joke falls flat you have egg on your face and panic in your heart. Ian was being honest enough to admit what many people conceal.

And of course he *was* funny in *The Hello Goodbye Man*. Not as funny as he'd been in *Dad's Army*, because my scripts weren't as funny as Jimmy Perry and David Croft's. Mary Tamm grew into the part, and by the end of the series they were a sparky and likeable couple. Viewing figures were fair and Gareth Gwenlan, promoted now to the hot seat, commissioned a second series. Then Graeme Macdonald, Controller of BBC2, pulled the plug on it.

I don't kid myself that *The Hello Goodbye Man* would ever have grown into one of the great series, but it was a true sit-com and it would have improved with time. The characters would have become more rounded, richer. Ian himself told me that it took four series for *Dad's Army* to really take off. You're rarely given time now to grow to love the characters. Out they go, and in come another lot that you aren't given time to love.

My next sit-com was a reworking of my play *Dogfood Dan and the Carmarthan Cowboy*, taking six half-hour episodes to tell what the play told in fifty minutes. I knew that this was a risk, but I was very keen to find out what happened after the four characters had met in the scene which had formed the ending of the play.

Alan J.W. directed again, and the two lorry drivers were Peter Blake and David Storey, while their wives were Arbel Jones and Lizzie Mickery. Lizzie had been in *Our Young Mr Wignall*, and has gone on to not inconsiderable success as a writer. Arbel has become the sort of friend that you don't see for three years but with whom it takes seven seconds to get back on the old footing.

The one real plus about the series was that Mary and I worked together professionally for the first and, as it turned out, the last time.

In the sixties, after the pub group, Mary had done some fine work at the much-loved old left-wing Unity Theatre in Camden Town. She had appeared in more than one Brecht play including *The Good Woman of Setzuan*. Then, with the Wye Players in Hereford, she had found the opportunity to act and direct at a proper theatre, with a company which took its work seriously and had several actors at least as good as some professionals I'd worked with.

She decided to give a professional career a go. Alan had seen her in a play in a pub in West London and thought she'd be just right for the part of the waitress in three episodes, a small part that could pass by unnoticed but could be a very effective cameo. She went to London for an audition and I was so nervous on her behalf in rural Herefordshire that I had to have three large sherries in record time. She got the part and was excellent in it, and I didn't have to become a secret sherry drinker.

The audience figures weren't brilliant but the appreciation index rose ten points in the course of the series, and this is the kind of indicator that might point to future success. However, once again Graeme Macdonald didn't commission a second series. So, I never did discover what happened to the four characters after their fateful meeting.

Why have I tried so many sit-coms? Simple. I love them. I don't know how people can be so sniffy and snobby about a genre that has given us *Hancock*, *Steptoe and Son*, *Dad's Army*, *The Liver Birds*, *The Likely Lads*, *Rising Damp*, *Fawlty Towers*, *Blackadder*, *Porridge*, *Hi-de-Hi*, *One Foot in the Grave*, *Only Fools and Horses*, *Sergeant Bilko*, *M*A*S*H*, *Cheers* and *Frazier*, to name but a few.

I love the studio day, with its camera rehearsals and rising tension, the absurdity of the studio audience, the even greater absurdity of the warm-up man, the retakes, the buzz. It's addictive.

Mary went on to do two successful professional tours of *Stepping Out*, Richard Harris's play about a tap dancing class, in which she was superb as the pianist, and Jude Kelly cast her in two plays at the West Yorkshire Playhouse, including Andy de la Tour's sparkling NHS farce, *Safe in our Hands*. The performance that moved me most, though, was with the Wye Players in *84, Charing Cross Road*. I found this a very poignant piece of theatre, though I hated the film with Ann Bancroft. To open it up for film was to destroy it. I could hardly bear to watch the ending with Mary in the role. In real life our relationship had become more one between friends than lovers, but on the stage, on this occasion, I was deeply moved in a most personal way, beyond what I could now feel in my personal life.

I had had no experience of American television. I'd been invited to write the American version of *Perrin* but had declined. Having done the story for book and television I wanted to move on, and I trusted the land that produced *I Love Lucy*, *The Burns and Allen Show*, *Rowan and Martin's Laugh-In*, *Sergeant Bilko* and *M*A*S*H* to do a good professional job. I was wrong. They didn't set up the world that was driving Reggie crazy, thus turning him from a tragic figure into a zany fool at a stroke. It was no fault of Richard Mulligan, who was excellent in the role of Reggie Potter as he was called. I was embarrassed to see the show on Channel Four until I realised that it would reveal how much better *my* scripts were. It was sad, though, to see Reggie relegated so far down the list of successful characters called Potter.

Then the prospect of writing for America arose when I was invited to lunch at the Athenaeum Hotel in Piccadilly by an American producer named Buddy Bregman.

I met Buddy in the starchy, silent restaurant. 'David Nobbs!' he said. 'David Nobbs! I cannot believe that I am in the same room as the creator of Reginald Perrin. I cannot believe that I am sitting at the same table as the man who gave the world "I didn't get where I am today".' The wine waiter passed twice while he was saying all this. It was going to be that kind of lunch – the Perrier and grated carrot kind. Buddy seemed insulted that I'd been to South America but not to North America. 'You went to South America *first*?' He showed me a photo of his daughter. I said, 'She's a very beautiful girl, Buddy.' Luckily she was, but I'd have said so anyway. 'I can't tell you how much it pleases me to hear you say that, David,' said Buddy. 'That you, the author of Reggie Perrin, think my daughter is beautiful, I can't tell you how much that makes me swell with pride.'

As I scurried through the lobby to the street, after lunch, I heard a medley of voices behind me. One voice was unmissable above them all. 'Carla Lane!' it said. 'Carla Lane! I cannot believe that I am in the same room as the creator of *The Liver Birds*.'

That night, in the Cross Inn in Eardisland, one of the customers told me, 'I saw your programme last night, Dave. I watched him right through.' That was high praise, in Herefordshire. What a contrast. I don't need to tell you which I preferred.

I must record at this point that I have now been to North America. I've been to the weddings of both the lovely daughters of our friends the Colgroves in Maryland, and have visited Las Vegas and driven from there through Death Valley, Yosemite, San Francisco, Monterey, Carmel, Big Sur and the Mogave Desert. I met great generosity and good humour and enjoyed every single moment of it. Thought of ringing Buddy to tell him. Didn't.

At Yorkshire Television I followed *A Bit Of A Do* with a series called *Rich Tea And Sympathy*. It was about a biscuit manufacturer and his family, and the new woman in his life. We had a very good cast, with Denis Quilley and Patricia Hodge as the leads. Also in the show were Lionel Jeffries as Denis's crotchety father, Jean Alexander as Patricia's snooker-sodden mother, James/Will Warrior as a proud man of biscuits, Ray Lonnen as a rather unlikely policeman (he's become a good friend, sends wonderful postcards), a host of good youngsters, and one of the finest actresses in Britain, Anne Reid, who would be far better known than she is in any world whose judgement one could respect.

I was aiming at a light sophisticated romantic comedy in the mould of a Tracy/Hepburn relationship of mutual sparring and brittle affection. This kind of thing seemed to me to be a gap in British comedy.

I didn't bring it off. Maybe it's the kind of thing we Brits just can't manage.

The Quilley/Hodge relationship didn't quite gel. Denis Quilley is a marvellous actor, but his natural home is the stage, and he never seemed entirely at ease as the King of the Bourbons and the Hob-nobs. Patricia, in a better written part, had a wonderfully light touch, but they never quite seemed a couple.

The series wasn't by any means a failure, but it was being judged against *A Bit Of A Do*. The main fault wasn't with the casting, it was with the scripts. In *A Bit Of A Do* I'd managed to integrate a whole series of strands into a thrusting narrative that never lost its spine. *Rich Tea and Sympathy* lacked a spine. It was a series of disparate little areas. Some, like the sad, halting relationship between the James Warrior and Anne Reid characters, worked beautifully. Others, particularly those involving the young people, worked less well, and it was largely my fault. They were a middle-aged version of youth.

'How could I not have seen all this at the time?' enquires the master of retrospection.

Ray Lonnen's policeman character was addicted to Indian and Chinese restaurants, and it was a running joke that he always came across people in these restaurants who should not have been there, at least not with each other. One evening Ray and that episode's director, Michael Simpson, suggested I join them for dinner. I couldn't. I had a date with a lady called Susan. As I was a married man I didn't want to admit this, so I said I had a business meeting. Susan and I went to the Mandalay, an up-market Indian restaurant in Leeds – and who should come in but Ray and Michael? It was a scene identical to the one Ray was playing in the studio the next day.

This was my very first date with Susan, but it was not, I'm afraid, the very first date of my married life. Mary had come to most of my shows in the early days. Now we had begun to drift very slowly apart, or perhaps it would be more accurate to say that I had begun to drift very slowly away. I was no Casanova, but I wasn't a model husband either.

I think it was touch and go over a second series, but in the end the decision went against us. I probably accepted it too readily, because I could see the faults, but, my God, there were strengths there too, and maybe I should have fought a harder battle.

My next series was an adaptation of *Second From Last In The Sack Race*. It was made into a four-part TV series by Red Rooster, one of the so-called independent companies brought into being by Mrs Thatcher in her hatred of the major companies, which had had the cheek to ask her awkward questions about the General Belgrano. It was called *The Life And Times Of Henry Pratt*, and was produced by Jenny Reeks for Red Rooster and Sally Head for Granada. It was directed by Adrian Shergold. I wrote the scripts myself, using some of Michael Birch's stage adaptation in the process – with his permission, of course.

The whole series was an enormous pleasure for me, even though it was shot entirely on location, where it is very difficult for the writer to see what is happening on camera.

In the main the characters were very nicely cast, and Adrian is a talented director. I relished seeing my lovely Lorna Arrow and my horrible Geoffrey Porringer with his blackheads and the Lesbian teacher, Miss Candy, brought to life. It was a joy to see Alun Armstrong, whom I had long admired, as Uncle Teddy, and Maggie O'Neill as a gloriously quirky Auntie Doris. It was a thrill to see Stratford Johns, one of my heroes from *Z Cars* and *Softly Softly*, turning in a fine performance as the palindromic headmaster, Mr A.B. Noon, B.A. And the children! So much humour, so much character, so much talent. (Mary found the same when she directed the Youth Theatre in Hereford. Theatre is a wonderful training ground, encouraging imagination and teaching responsibility through being part of a team. One boy turned up to Mary's auditions with a prop – a stuffed gull. This lad from a council estate struck a dramatic pose, said 'Alas, poor Yorick' in fine style, looked down at his stuffed gull and said angrily, 'I asked for a skull.' Where does that come from? Where does it go? What became of him?

How many get the chance to carry on? How many, instead, will become financial advisers, or car salesmen, or drug addicts?)

I must express my gratitude to all those – grown-ups now – who played Henry so delightfully at his various ages. Thank you, Marcus Lamb, Andrew Nicholson, Robert Nicholson, Bryan Dick and Jack Deam.

I wasn't entirely happy with the series, however, despite all these strengths. I felt that it was under-cast at several vital points.

There was also a problem with the change of tone between the innocence of Henry's wartime evacuation to the countryside in the first episode and, in the second, the sordid reality of life in grimy post-war Thurmarsh with a father who'd lost an eye in the war. It was there in the script, but it was accentuated in the direction. Adrian lulled the audience with an episode that resembled a Hovis advert, then hit them hard in the second episode. Of course this is valid within an integral piece of work, but a week's gap rather invalidated it. The first episode became like an unrepresentative book jacket.

Directors love beautiful pictures, and Adrian was no exception. I think he put in too many pretty shots. Early on there is a scene where Henry's father takes him into the countryside for a treat. Henry is four. I quote from the book:

> They sat in a hollow with their backs against a rock, and ate their brawn butties.
>
> 'I hate brawn,' said Ezra. 'I hate gravy too. I like me food dry. It's more than me life's worth to tell her that. In life, Henry, tha has to eat a lot of gravy that tha doesn't want. There's going to be a war. That's what Reg Hammond reckons, any road. The world is changing. Think on, though, our Henry, before tha blames us for bringing thee into t'world. Remember this. Tha's English. Tha's Yorkshire. Tha could have been born Nepalese or Belgian or owt. Thank me for that, at least.'
>
> Henry was puzzled. His father had never talked to him like that before. And he was a sensitive child, aware of the fear and

unease around him, although he knew nothing about Hitler, and cared even less about the Sudetenland than all the hikers and cyclists.

'It's not going to be easy, lad,' said his father. 'But tha'll frame. Thy little mind's never still. Tha's got brains.'

Ezra handed Henry a last corner of brawn sandwich.

'Brains and brawn,' he said. 'Tha'll do. Tha'll do.'

They walked on, away from that hollow, which could have become a womb, given half a chance.

They walked along a track, across a featureless expanse of sheep-cropped, wind-stunted coarse grass. And Henry, sensitive, brainy young Henry, believed that he understood. His father was abandoning him, to fend for himself in the world. His father had encouraged him, told him that he could do it. His father, who had so recently told him to bugger off, was going home without him.

There's so much there that you cannot get into film. No small boy could show the false deductions that led to Henry's fears. In fact, nobody could. Nevertheless, the scene is a massive one, awakening us as well as Henry to the dangers of the times. Adrian shot it in three stages, walking beside a bicycle, looking over a high bridge on to a reservoir, and then with his father cycling with Henry in front of him on the bike. Only at the very end, on the bike, is Henry given brawn. There are no close ups, no chance of anything happening between Henry and his father, no sense of the importance of what his father is saying.

Nevertheless, the series was full of good things as well. It was rich, warm, funny, nostalgic, sad, comic and serious. I was proud of it.

My time in Herefordshire was drawing to a close. I look back on the twelve years I spent surrounded by its exquisite beauty with so many happy memories.

I hadn't realised what life would be like in the country. I hadn't realised that I would try to become a countryman. I went through a gardening phase, planted vegetables, double-dug, fertilised. Our first summer there I grew no less than twenty-one vegetables – eight potatoes, seven carrots, five sprouts and a cabbage.

I loved the country pubs. Sometimes Mary and I would put a casserole in the Rayburn and go to the White Swan in Eardisland for some good early evening craic – that marvellous Irish word. I played dominoes with farmers in the Rhydspence in Whitney-on-Wye, played bridge in the Swan in Kington, sometimes partnering the landlord's son and sometimes a man who set up the explosions in quarries. On Friday evenings I played darts for the Cross Inn in Eardisland. Girlfriends and wives would arrive at ten o'clock in those days before universal videos and relate the whole of the evening's episode of *Auf Wiedersehen, Pet.* I've seen the slow, remorseless decline of the pub games beloved of countrymen of limited means. The middle class people streaming out from the towns eat sun-dried tomatoes where once the darts board stood.

Cricket at Worcester, football at Hereford, theatre at Hereford and Worcester, and the beauty of Wales on one's doorstep. We made many good friends, especially among the Wye Players, and there always seemed to be at least one of my step-children living in Bristol. And there was always the occasional trip to London if we felt we needed a rest.

Food was just a bit of a problem. The only two top class restaurants were both more than forty miles away, though it was a joy in summer to drive through the smiling orchards and hop-fields and over the bare, whale-backed Malverns to the Croque-en-Bouche, or through the wild, deep border valleys to the Walnut Tree Inn at Llandewi Skirrid.

Towards the end of the eighties Mary and I became vegetarians, entirely out of our disgust at the treatment of animals. We had wonderful meals at home, but restaurants turn lack of imagination into an art form where vegetarian food is concerned. I felt that if I sat down for a morning I could create an appetising vegetarian meal for every day of the year without repetition. Restaurants simply don't try. I'm no longer a vegetarian, but it angers me when people dismiss it as faddish without knowing the reasons behind it. A man called Mr Pullee, proprietor of the Pen-y-Gwryd Hotel in Nantgwynant, wrote to the *Good Hotel Guide*, 'I would also ban vegetarians and similar faddish eaters.' Good God, Mr Pullee, is it faddish to wish to spare animals pain?

We were not entirely without literary friends, even during the time of the feud with Peter Tinniswood. We got to know that marvellous playwright Peter Nichols and his wife Thelma, who lived about thirty miles to the north, and the fiery, political, controversial, never boring vegan Gordon Newman and his partner Rebecca Hall, who lived about twenty miles to the south. In fact we invited them both to a lunchtime party in our garden, and Peter said to me, 'Gordon's a strange man. I told him where he was going wrong in his career, and he wasn't a bit grateful.' I made a mental note never to invite two writers to the same party again.

Peter was trying to write a novel and was frustrated by his lack of success. He seemed to think it against the laws of nature that he shouldn't be able to do it if I could. I would have given my left arm to write plays as good as Peter's. No use giving my right arm or I wouldn't be able to write anything.

I can't remember exactly when Peter Tinniswood and I ended our feud, but I know it was while I was still in Herefordshire, because he came to stay and we went to watch the cricket at Worcester. Over the years, bit by bit, ball by ball, pint by pint, joke by joke, we grew back into our true, deep friendship.

As one writer called Peter came back into my life, another, Peter Nichols, departed. I was at a huge literary thrash given by Methuen at Random House. I don't know what the collective noun for writers is – an anthology of writers, perhaps – but in this room there were writers galore, wives galore, editors galore. A woman approached me, a lovely, charming, smiling woman. I knew that I knew her, I knew that I liked her, but who was she?

'When did you come up to London?' she asked.

'Two days ago.'

'We came this morning. I hate coming up from the country on lovely days like this.'

I heard myself saying, 'What part of the country do you have to come up from?' The potential danger of the remark chilled me even as I said it.

'How strange that you don't remember, since you've been to our house twice,' said Thelma Nichols.

I'd felt a real rapport with Thelma, a good warm lass from Blackpill on my beloved Swansea Bay. My remark must have hit her like an avalanche. I made profuse apologies then and by post, but it was no use. I'm off Peter and Thelma's Christmas card list.

The death of Graham Chapman was a great shock to me, even though I knew how ill he was. I hadn't seen him much since those early Frost days, but towards the end of his life I came across him in the Old Angel pub in Highgate Village and wandered back to his large house nearby. If anywhere should have been called Liberty Hall it was this rambling mansion. It pulsated with warmth and indulgence. I drifted in very occasionally, and drifted out rather later than I intended.

I couldn't get to his memorial service. Instead I dressed up in very silly clothes in Scarborough and thought about him. I did send a letter, however, and it was read out at the service by his brother. I ended up with a passage in which I expressed something very sincere through comedy.

> I feel astounded by my good fortune. I could have been the ninth son of a struggling 17th century Bolivian waistcoat manufacturer. I could have run a small pyramid cleaning company in Ancient Egypt. I could have been a heron. I count myself extraordinarily lucky to have been born a human being, in Britain, towards the middle of the twentieth century, and thus to have experienced the great joy of *Monty Python*, and of Graham Chapman.

The birth of one's first grandchild is one of the great moments of maturity. Technically, Kayleigh is a step-grandchild, but the word 'step' can't detract from one's emotion and one's love. We were very proud of her. There had never been such a wonderful child. Well, she's still pretty good and doing really well at Shrewsbury Grammar School.

Mary and I have six other grandchildren, all of them lovely in very different ways. Kayleigh has a younger brother, Dan. Chris and Talia have two children, Aurielle and Lee. Kim resisted marriage, but that didn't stop her and her partner John – the first John for quite a while, I think – from having three children, Joe, Luke and Elsie.

Kim and John live in France, in a tiny village between the beautiful rivers Lot and Dordogne. John worked for a local builder, who regarded him as the son he never had, and took over the business when he retired. They lead a happy life in this rural idyll, fortified by the black wine of Cahors straight from the barrel.

None of my step-children have achieved what might be considered great worldly success, but I'm proud of them for being fine human beings and giving us the joy of our seven treasures, all different, all healthy, all intelligent, all full of character. I just hope we can conserve a world good enough for them.

A sad episode in my Herefordshire life was the death of Auntie Dilys in an old people's home in Kingsland, just a few miles away. Uncle Glandon, long retired as a surgeon at Shrewsbury General Hospital, lived in Bicton just outside Shrewsbury, and he found the home for my aunt. I hadn't seen her since my wedding day, but I visited her shortly after she entered the home, and stayed for about two hours. She had completely forgotten that I had done anything of which she disapproved. She thought she was in a hotel and was worried because she couldn't find her rail ticket home. Her mind had been going for some time and it had worried her that people would notice – 'Don't talk so much and nobody'd know,' my mother advised her. By now it was far gone. However many times I told her she was in a home and they'd look after her, she forgot. The conversation went round and round in a short loop, like the Muzak tape in a bad restaurant. I could cope with this, but I did feel slightly daunted at the thought of years and years of such visits to someone whose attitude to me hadn't really earned her my care. A few days later she died in her sleep. Oddly, I felt more sad than relieved.

Uncle Glandon was thoroughly urbane. When he and his second wife Dodo first came to lunch at Broxwood, my mother was a mass of nerves in far-away Chislehurst. 'You will make sure everything's done correctly, won't you?' she said. 'They're very particular.'

Mary laid on a very good meal. The main course was lamb – it was before our vegetarianism – and Glandon and Dodo asked if they could finish their gravy with their spoons, and dunk their bread in the gravy. 'We can't do that sort of thing with the rest of the family,' they said. 'They're so correct.'

Later that afternoon, my mother phoned.

'Well?' she said.

'What do you mean – "Well"?' I knew what she meant, of course, but I was narked.

'How did it go?'

'Oh, very well. They had a great time. They ate the gravy with their spoons, and dunked their bread in it.'

'They didn't!!'

I really don't think my dear mother believed me.

From time to time we would meet Glandon and Dodo in a pub halfway between our homes. Later, as they began to get more frail, we met at a pub very near to their house. By then these meetings were taut with dread as to what Dodo would say. She was tactless at the best of times, and now she was deaf as well.

One day she thundered, as we entered the bar, 'They get awful people in here in the evenings, but it's all right at lunchtime.' Later she said that they hadn't seemed very friendly. I'm not surprised.

On another occasion a very pretty Rastafarian girl came in. She had confidence and poise. There was character and vitality in her face. She had a truly magnificent Rastafarian hair-do.

'What on earth has that woman got on the top of her head?' bellowed Dodo.

Glandon died a few years after Dilys. Only my mother was left now from the old Swansea family, and had gone to live with Auntie Kathleen in Yeldham, where she was looked after most splendidly. My mother, the frail one, had grown out of her regular migraines and had survived. As she approached ninety she was slowly shrinking, as old people do, but her back was straight, her eyes were bright and her clothes were smart.

She was beginning to find it difficult to read, which was an enormous loss, but rescue was at hand in the form of snooker. She and Kay would stay up till two in the morning to see the end of one of the great matches. Even when we gave them a video recorder, they stayed up to watch the matches live.

I once phoned my mother from Dover to say we were back from a motoring holiday. My little trip came a bad second to the snooker.

'Good,' she said. 'I'm worried for Jimmy. He's started to rush his shots.'

'We had some lovely weather.'

'Good. I'm afraid Steve is going to grind him into the ground.'

Tennis was her other great love. It always had been. She often came to stay with us for the Wimbledon fortnight. We would leave her in front of the set from twelve till seven every day, and she used to be in heaven. Each year she had to move just a little closer to the set, in order to see the ball.

When there wasn't snooker or tennis, however, my mother was as keenly interested in other people as she had ever been. I felt that she and I had never been so close. I knew that she took secret pride in my career, and that made me all the more sad that my father hadn't lived to see me produce at least some worthwhile work.

My relationship with my mother would be put to the test, however, in August 1992, when I arrived in Yeldham with a car piled high with my possessions, and told her that I had left Mary.

18 THE NERVOUS NINETIES

MARY AND I had spent twenty-nine years together, six in sin and twenty-three in marriage. I had changed from being a lover to being a friend, albeit a very good friend. That would have sufficed for my parents and my grandparents. We are more demanding now.

Susan, who had been my companion in the Mandalay restaurant, had worked at Yorkshire Television as an extra on *A Bit Of A Do* and *Rich Tea And Sympathy*. Television extras are often mocked, and some of them deserve to be. They talk so grandly about their roles – 'When I worked with Larry Olivier . . .' But there are some from many different walks of life who do it for all sorts of reasons. One of our extras was a headmistress who did it to keep in touch with a different world. Susan did it to escape for a few hours from an unhappy marriage. She had spent more than thirty years working with her husband in their printing firm.

I was actually introduced to her by another of the extras, Sylvia Nelson, a vivacious Tynesider (I can't remember whether she's from North Shields or South Shields so I daren't call her a Geordie). Sylvia's husband, Terry, is the sanest psychiatrist I know (out of two).

I was attracted from the start to this lady with the stunning smile and the lovely green eyes, but it wasn't the first time I'd succumbed to a woman's charms – to be strictly accurate, it was the third – so there was no reason to think that this was particularly special. There was no blinding flash on my part and I was later disappointed to find that there hadn't been on Susan's either.

Our relationship blossomed slowly, but by the time Mary went off on her second tour of *Stepping Out* we were spending quite a lot of time together, and we went off to Western Scotland for a brief holiday. What lies I told from phone boxes beside lovely, lonely lochs. How could I have done it? Well, I did. The pleasure comes first. The lies, the awful phone calls, come later. Once you start to engage in deceit, it's all lies. I wasn't only lying to Mary. I was lying to Susan. She's no marriage-wrecker, and I found myself painting an exaggerated picture of a failed marriage to her.

I was lying to my mother as well, of course. That is how it is once you start. Never again. Never never again.

I didn't expect to be found out, although I suppose it was inevitable. I didn't know that when I was found out I would leave, and I suppose that was inevitable too. I knew myself too well – I knew that, if I stayed, I would be unhappy, and if I was unhappy I would not be rewarding to live with. I'm sure I'd have turned into a grumpy old man who'd have made Victor Meldrew seem like Mother Theresa.

Mary wanted me to stay with her until after her theatre tour had ended. I felt that I owed her this. It was not an easy time We were unhappy in Billingham and Swansea and Cambridge. I suppose I must still have been some kind of support.

The date of my departure was fixed – Tuesday, 11 August, 1992. The reason for the choice of date was that Dave and his family would be free then to stay with Mary and give her much-needed support and company. My departure was a great shock to all three of my step-children, and telling them was one of the hardest things I ever did.

There was a major complication, though. Susan's only child Briget (Susan's first husband couldn't spell) was marrying Mark Granger a few days before my scheduled departure. Mary didn't want me to go, but I had to. What kind of commitment would I be showing to Susan if I didn't go to her daughter's wedding?

They were married in Weeton Church, and the reception was at the Sandringham Hotel in Beckwithshaw, a stylish, flamboyant place of real originality and therefore, naturally, now closed.

It was bizarre. Suddenly I was a member of a whole new family, and the first time I met them I was in the role of father of the bride. When I add Chris's wedding and Kim's wedding (watch this space) and Dave's two weddings, I find that I have been to five weddings as a step-father and the real father hasn't been invited to any of them.

I met Susan's sister Patricia and her husband James. I met her eighty-year-old father Jack and his 82-year-old girlfriend Florence, who called him her toy-boy. I met her cousin Brian and his wife, Susan's ex's sister Marjorie. I met Mark's parents, Mary and Alan. I stood in the wedding photographs outside the church, smiling with my new instant relatives. Next day I went home.

It really was an enormous act of faith from the whole family, looking back on it. Had I bottled out of making the break and returning, the wedding photos would have been a fiasco – 'Who's that strange man in all the photos, Mummy?' 'We don't speak about him, dear.'

I did return. Well, I was in love, wasn't I? But was I? I thought I was in love with Susan. She thought she was in love with me. I don't believe now that we can have been, for love came later when we grew to know each other. Love blossomed daily with our happiness. I think we were very brave . . . perhaps a better word would be reckless . . . to do what we did before we really, truly knew each other.

On the last evening of my life with Mary we went out for a fine dinner together at the Three Cocks just over the Welsh border, and I don't think that anyone who saw us there would have been able to guess the situation.

Next morning . . . it all seems strange now . . . we had everything arranged in as civilised a way as we could. Mary went off shopping in her car. The moment she had gone, I hurriedly packed my car with the absolute essentials for my new life, just the bare essentials, so that I was gone before she returned.

How can I describe my emotions that day? My heart was as light as a lark, and as heavy as a tractor. It soared above the fields in joy and looked down on itself grinding through the mud in misery. It wasn't just guilt. I was leaving a whole world. I was leaving a city and county that I loved. I was leaving many good friends – Alick Rowe, the Wye Players, my colleagues at bridge and darts – and I would never see many of them again. I was leaving my step-children and my step-grandchildren. I would see them still. I would love them still. Nevertheless, I was leaving them.

And I knew that I would miss Mary too. I knew that I would be happy, I never doubted it, but I also knew that I would miss her. Life isn't simple, and contradictions and ambiguities were my soul mates that strange day.

I still think now, as I thought then, of how that day must have looked through the eyes of three women. Susan waiting, and wondering just a bit, surely, if I would really come. Mary . . . well, I wish I couldn't imagine her suffering, because she still loved me, God knows why. And my mother, doing the *Daily Telegraph* crossword, calm, unsuspecting, and ninety-one years old.

As I drove, I thought of my father. I've had no belief in life after death since I was eighteen, but my disbelief wavered on that extreme morning, and I wondered if my father was looking down and seeing me, and if my two strict grandfathers could see me too.

I parked my car, every corner crammed with the things I couldn't do without, in the car park of a pub. The condemned man ate a hearty bar lunch.

The condemned man? I felt like a condemned man as I hurtled towards my mother. I hadn't dared to tell her anything on the phone. I just didn't know how to break it. I thought of her parents, her brothers and sister, that strict but lovely family. I couldn't think of any way in which my mother could accept what I had done. I couldn't think of any words that I could use to tell her.

Well, I arrived at my aunt's house, I told my mother very directly, straight away, in words that I can't recall. She went white, she looked extremely small and frail. 'Oh, you haven't!' she gasped.

I didn't sleep well that night and I should imagine that my mother, who could worry for Wales at the best of times, didn't sleep at all.

She looked dreadful the next morning, with bags under her eyes, but she had retained her immense dignity. She'd thought long and hard in the long, hard reaches of the night. She'd accepted what had been done and what could not be undone. I suppose the real reason that I hadn't told her before was that I wanted my decision to be inevitable, and if I'd told her earlier I'd have been forced to endure her persuasions and reject her entreaties as I had rejected Mary's.

'Well,' she said. 'I hope you'll both be very happy.'

The press soon latched on to the situation and tried to dig up some dirt. I think it was because in *A Bit Of A Do* Ted Simcock left his wife and got his come-uppance. I think they wanted to portray me as a wicked hypocrite. Jonathan, my agent, said that he was surprised that they thought I had a sufficiently high profile. This was the only thing he ever said that upset me, in more than thirty years.

A reporter turned up at Broxwood, shortly after I had left, and found Mary gardening. He asked where Mrs Nobbs was. She leant on her fork, chewed, and told them in broad Herefordshire that she didn't rightly know when she'd be back. Maybe they didn't have it on their file that she was an actress. A cameo of that nature would have strained her nerve far more than her talent.

A few days into my new life I had to go to Suffolk to meet a writer called John Hadfield, and I stopped in Yeldham to spend a slightly more relaxed time with my poor mother. While I was there, a journalist paid an early morning call on Susan. The moment she opened the door, a lurking photographer unlurked himself and took a quick picture. Did they hope she'd look like a vamp, or ghastly and bleary in her unmade-up state? Impossible.

A short article did appear in the *Sunday People*, with no photograph, and that was the end of my life with the paparazzi.

Susan had a high-ceilinged Victorian flat in York Place in Harrogate. Our front garden was the Stray, the 200-acre open space that dominates the town. In the flat above us there lived a retired army officer, who once invited us up for drinks, discovered that we were going on holiday to Greece, and said, 'The only good Greek is a dead Greek.' Below us was an alcoholic caricaturist called Jerome Hirst. He produced delightful caricatures by day, was the lynch-pin of a lively group of drinkers in the Coach and Horses in the early evening, and then returned home to prepare his evening meal and to cook meat for his dog. Once, more drunk than usual, he left the dog meat on all night. The smell was foul, and the fire risk must have been considerable. After we'd moved, Jerome got cancer. The last time I saw him, in St Michael's Hospice, he was a shell. His last words to me were characteristic: 'You haven't cheered me up at all. Why don't you bugger off?' Dear Jerome, we miss you.

The flat was elegant, but I locked myself away down in a tiny inelegant office on the mezzanine floor, and wrote *The Cucumber Man*. Here I was leading a new life and meeting new people and making new friends, and every morning I would trot down a flight of stairs, with a mug of tea in my hand, to spend the day with some old friends of mine: Henry and Hilary, Diana, Auntie Doris and Uncle Teddy, Cousin Hilda and many others. What a joy. By now these characters from the Pratt trilogy were as real to me as the people in my real life. They were less real, it's true, in that they existed only in my head, but they were more real in another way, because I could see into their heads and knew their every thought. Sometimes my characters develop such a life of their own that, just occasionally, they refuse to do my bidding, refuse to accept their planned role in the narrative.

Another joy at this time was the transmission of *The Life And Times Of Henry Pratt*.

A few days before the first episode, Sally Head, the aptly-named Head of Drama at Granada, suddenly ordered the removal of the complete beginning of the show, in which a parrot imitates Henry's mother's cries of agony in childbirth, and is strangled by Henry's angry father. I'd not heard good reports about Sally, and this seemed like high-handed executive behaviour. I soon realised, though, that she was absolutely right. The sequence worked on the page. It worked even better in the theatre. It was essentially theatrical. Probed by the merciless eye of the camera it lacked reality. I'm certain that Sally acted not because she wanted to show how powerful she was but because she suddenly saw the truth about a programme she loved, and had the courage to act upon it.

On transmission day Sally gave a small launch party at the Groucho Club, that hotbed of media intrigue in Soho. She told us that this was one of the proudest days of her career, and would remain so whatever fate the series met.

Later that day, Jerome from downstairs left me the most spare and elegant review I ever received: 'D. α+++. J.'

The series did well. It gained decent audiences, and much praise and prestige. However, a new institution had been thrust upon ITV. It was called the Network Centre, and it was responsible for all ITV drama and comedy commissions, including those from the so-called independents. Its first head was Vernon Lawrence. Nothing in the media is as disastrous as having friends in high places. They prove their integrity by shitting on you from a great height. I'd written two scripts for the second series, based on *Pratt Of The Argus*, when the Network Centre turned it down in favour of a programme set in the same period which consistently got two million less viewers than we had.

Vernon is great company and has done me far more good than harm over the years. He loves being liked – well, don't most of us? – and I think he was utterly unprepared for the hostility his position earned him. Alan Plater spoke memorably at a Writers' Guild Awards Ceremony of 'Vernon Lawrence and the Temple of Doom'. He didn't stay long.

Our rejection may have been because new brooms sweep clean, but a more sinister explanation was rumoured. The theory was that the Network Centre wanted revenge on Sally Head/Granada for something she/they had done earlier. I know not if it is true. I hope not. I don't want my livelihood threatened for reasons like that.

I'll tell you one thing, though. I have been ruthless in admitting my failures. Well, this was not a failure. It was not rejected on merit.

It was Sally Head herself who phoned to give me the bad news. You see nothing unusual in that? Then you aren't in television. When bad news is to be delivered, people are on holiday, underlings are called in, they 'rang you and got no reply' when you know you were in. The excuses are legion, and you get told in a letter. Sally's voice broke as she told me that it was one of the saddest days of her career.

Jenny Reeks cared too. She's one of the people I respect most in the whole media circus. I enjoyed working with her enormously. Unfortunately, from my point of view, she joined the very Network Centre that had turned down our series, so she's on the other side of the fence now.

I sought comfort at weekends in house-hunting in the villages north of Harrogate. It was such an enjoyable process that for many months it didn't seem to matter if it was unproductive. Then depression set in.

Eventually, after more than a year of complications and setbacks, we found a house that suited us: an extended limestone cottage, formerly a kiln-worker's cottage, in an idyllic setting in a quiet valley with a paddock and a stream in front and a nature reserve full of rare orchids at the back. It's eerily silent except for the bleating of the lambs, the whooshing of the wind, the roaring of the bending trees, the volleys of gunshot at everything that moves, the monotonous mating call of those pheasants that survive the above, the explosions of the bird scarers, the cawing of the unscared rooks, the drumming of woodpeckers, the groaning of throaty tractors, the whine of sad microlites, the sighing of hot air balloons and the screams of low-flying Tornadoes. At night owls screech, toads belch, frogs fart, lambs moan, stoats rustle, vixens gasp orgasmically and power lines hum. Only people who live in towns think the countryside is quiet.

Here we lead a happy life, rich in friendships. We play a lot of bridge, mainly because we meet such very nice people. We entertain a lot. Susan is a very good cook, I am a fairly good cook, we love having visitors, and I think they love visiting. Never for a moment do I wish that I was nearer the centre of things. Indeed, when I get despatches from the centre of things, I wonder if we should move further away.

Real pubs are in sad decline but I'm still lucky enough to have two locals that I enjoy. The Hare and Hounds in my village is where I play dominoes. The Lamb and Flag in the next village is more for talk. There's more fun to be had in Trevor's back passage (this is part of the pub, I hasten to add) on a good night than from a whole series of some modern sit-coms.

While we were still hunting for our dream home, Yorkshire Television filmed a TV play of mine, *Stalag Luft*.

The idea seemed not entirely dissimilar to an episode of *Ripping Yarns*, and I felt I owed Michael Palin and Terry Jones the courtesy of asking their approval before I did it. I still have Terry's reply, which begins: 'Laughed my socks off at the Prison camp idea – I think it's smashing and of course I don't mind your using it.' His letter was dated 9 August, 1981. I finally got round to writing the script in 1993.

The story was simple. British prisoners plan the biggest escape ever – of everybody. The Germans, being the dregs of their armed forces, realise that they can't stop them and ask if they can come too. At first the British dismiss this idea, but then they realise that the Germans would be useful – they don't need uniforms or forged passports, they speak German, they know their way about. The British agree. The escape begins. The British don't trust the Germans so they make them go first. When the Germans have gone and they have the camp to themselves they wonder if it's worth escaping, so they spend the rest of the war there. At the end of the war the commander, Big F, is given the Iron Cross by Hitler in recognition of the fact that this is the only camp from which nobody has escaped.

However, their problems aren't over when they have the camp to themselves. They need men to volunteer to be Germans, in order to deal with visiting tradespeople and SS inspections. More people volunteer to be Germans than they need, and a few of them are just as vicious as the worst Nazis have been. I was thinking here of the great gap between the nobility of British troops in war films and all the cruelty I saw in Catterick.

We had a great cast, headed by – in alphabetical order, in case I want to work with them again – Stephen Fry, Nicholas Lyndhurst and Geoffrey Palmer. Adrian Shergold directed again, and did some brilliant things. A night shoot at an old army camp in Bellingham in Northumberland, when the American tanks rolled in at the end of the war, was a wonderful long sequence which had to be done in one take. There were quite a few German tourists camping at Bellingham. I think the filming must have puzzled them considerably.

The finished film lacked just one thing – pace. Those old war films went like the clappers. Kenneth More didn't think; he spoke and moved about. Nowadays so much is read into everything that it's impossible to go fast. Many people thought that at two hours *Stalag Luft* was half an hour too long. I don't disagree, but the real problem was that there was half an hour's good material left on the cutting room floor.

On the whole I've had a good ride from the critics. Sometimes they've been kinder than the audiences. *Stalag Luft* divided them as never before:

> *Stalag Luft*'s plot would have delighted Jonathan Swift . . . Nobbs's script was often funny, but never sacrificed the satire for the humour (*Daily Mail*)

> This lampoon of Colditz is limp, lacklustre and lacking in intelligence (*Daily Telegraph*)

> It was typical David Nobbs – his words were witty, thoughtful and neatly observed . . . I'll never be able to watch *The Great Escape* with a straight face (*Sunday Mirror*)

> After two bum-numbing hours I wanted to tunnel through my living room floor (*News Of The World*)

> A triumphant combination of witty words, faultless comic ensemble action and lightly controlled direction. Had it been 20 minutes shorter it might have been a classic (*Evening Standard*)

> Long before the end I was longing for the credits to roll so, like the POWs, I could finally be set free (*Scottish Daily Record*)

> The only complaint about this hilarious show is that it's a one-off (*Sun*)

All very silly (*Daily Express*)

I will praise it for its unhurried confidence (*Independent*)

There is a thin line separating farce from comedy, and it's a line writers cross at their peril. David Nobbs zigzagged to and fro across the line like a pub drunk, but it was a measure of his mastery of his craft that, although he stumbled several times, he never fell (*Daily Telegraph* again – different writer)

There is something deeply lazy about setting a comedy drama in a WWII prisoner of war camp (*Independent* again – different writer)

Mr Retrospect, he say that I took far too long to set the whole thing up. At the risk of upsetting other writers, I must say that I think a good script editor, one who knew what he or she was doing, might have helped enormously here.

Apart from that, which of the reviewers were right? All of them. Or, to put it another way, none of them. You can argue constructively about all sorts of aspects of comedy, and it's valuable, but it will only take you so far. In the end, when you answer the question, 'Is it funny?' you're beyond logical argument and value judgements. You're alone with your funny-bone. That's the peril of trying to be funny, and the reason why I still do it.

The only review I objected to came from Cosmo Landesman in the *Sunday Times*:

We got jokes that would have made Tony Blackburn blush with shame. 'I like tits myself,' said one soldier. 'I'm a leg and arse man myself,' his friend replies. The soldier continues, 'Blue tits, grey tits . . .' Recovered yet?

I loathe jokes like that. I'm a member of the Royal Society for the Protection of Birds from Bad Jokes. I know about birds and I said 'great tits' not 'grey tits'. But could I really have made that joke? I played the tape to check, and yes, there it is. Oh but wait. The whole point of the sequence was the contempt on the face of the recipient, a not very bright gardener. 'I hate remarks like that about living things,' he says. All right, maybe it misfired, but that was the whole point of the sequence. It was an anti-joke, to wipe the stupid smiles off the faces of those who'd thought it funny. Shame on you for your carelessness, Cosmo Landesman of the *Sunday Times.*

I had one very angry letter about *Stalag Luft,* from a retired squadron leader. He found it all very insulting to real life prisoners. I can't remember how I responded but I took time and care over my reply, and the gentleman apologised for his anger, and I felt a little ashamed, because I admired him for that anger.

My first project in my new home was *The Legacy of Reginald Perrin.* I felt that it was an enormous risk to do a *Perrin* series without Leonard Rossiter, but a writer's life isn't exactly strewn with physical danger and if we didn't take any creative risks it would be a sad story indeed.

I knew that I had a good idea – a rebellion of pensioners marching to take over the Government – a protest against the overwhelming youth culture of the age. I feel very strongly about this. It's so stupid to worship youth over experience. The only way for any of us to avoid old age is to die young. Youth culture means that we condemn ourselves to moving away from what is desirable towards what is dreaded. If we worshipped experience, we'd spend our lives moving towards our ideal. We'd all be much happier.

I can't bring myself to regret the television project. It was such a delight to meet so many old friends, including Gareth Gwenlan and the old cast, with the delightful addition of Patricia Hodge.

We assembled in a conference room at the BBC and read all the scripts in a day. Without Leonard the atmosphere was like a school common room when the headmaster's safely out of the way at a conference.

My theme got buried beneath the nostalgia of meeting all those old friends again and reliving the glory days. I relied too much on the old characters and the old catch-phrases. It was self-indulgent and a lot of people lost patience with it long before we got to what I still think was a splendid climax, though not one to which television techniques quite did justice, despite all the technological progress and digital tricks.

I think it was a mistake to write the novel. It was all right, a pleasant read, reasonably kindly received by the critics. I just about got away with it. But that's not the message I'd like to see on my gravestone: 'Here lies David Nobbs. He just about got away with it.' I realised that a project which I had felt to be a risk was actually the easy option. My theme would have been so much more effective if I'd explored it through new characters.

Through the writing of the novel I came across Peter Nichols again at another publishing party. He was cool, but polite. It was also my first meeting with Michael Frayn since my Cambridge days. He was polite, but cool.

I decided to leave while I was losing, and went to get my coat. Michael and Peter were just getting their coats too, so I hung back, feeling about three feet tall. After they'd gone out into the cold Kensington air I put my coat on as slowly as I could, so as not to seem to be trailing them, and I heard, through the open door, a brief and devastating exchange.

'Who *is* that man?' asked Michael Frayn.

'That's David Nobbs,' said Peter Nichols. 'We used to know him in Shropshire.'

'Oh my God!!' exclaimed Michael.

Michael hurried back and was most apologetic and told me how much he'd admired *A Bit Of A Do*, and Peter looked on from a corner of the mews, waiting for him and not wishing to speak to me.

Dear Peter and Thelma, should you by any chance read this, please forgive me.

I'd spent a great deal of my writing life adapting my own books for television, but I'd never adapted anyone else's work. I'd turned down an offer during the eighties, however. It was for Captain Marryat's classic, *Mr Midshipman Easy*. I quote from the letter:

There is, it seems to me, both a compatibility of humour and style; also other rare qualities vividly remembered from *Cupid's Darts*.

Cupid's Darts to *Mr Midshipman Easy*! Couldn't see it myself. Now, during the nineties, I was offered quite a few adaptations, and I soon felt like the poor man's Andrew Davies.

The first one was a delightful book by John Hadfield, called *Love On A Branch Line*. It was a story set in the 1950s about a civil servant who is sent to a stately home in Norfolk to close down a government agency which had been set up in the 1940s, to analyse statistics from foreign publications, and forgotten about ever since. He meets the delightfully eccentric Lord and Lady Flamborough and their three lovely daughters, all of whom fall for him. Sex, nudity and steam trains! Throw in some jazz, a few prancing peacocks and a vision of Arcadian England as it never quite was, and you have a most appealing cocktail.

John Hadfield had been the first director of the National Book League. For twenty-one years he had edited *The Saturday Book*, a highly successful annual devoted to the arts; he had produced anthologies; but *Love On A Branch Line* was his only novel, his pride and joy, his baby.

As I drove down to Woodbridge, less than a week after beginning my new life in Harrogate, I found myself following a bright red sports car being driven very fast and thought, 'That's a TV person and we're going to be friends.' It was Jacqueline Davis, our producer, and Susan and I have indeed become great friends with Jacqui, and with John Reynolds, one of the executive producers, and his wife Sheelah.

John Hadfield was in his eighties and frail. I think he was fairly suspicious of me that day. Little did he know that the great principle with which I approach an adaptation is to be utterly faithful to the original unless there is an overwhelming reason not to be.

We repaired to a nearby restaurant for lunch.

'The set menu looks very appealing,' said John Reynolds hopefully.

'Lobster!' exclaimed John Hadfield surprisingly firmly. 'That sounds good.' This was his chance of glory after a long period of relative obscurity. He wasn't going to be fobbed off with any set menu.

I was commissioned to turn the book into a four-part series, and was able to be splendidly faithful to much of the letter as well as to all its spirit. I reduced the whimsy to acceptable levels and found a different solution to the only weakness in the plot. In the book the civil servant, Jasper, receives a telegram announcing that the unit is to be closed down forthwith. This is a very unsatisfactory deus ex machina. In my version Jasper closed the unit down because he discovered that the secretary, Miss Mounsey, with whom he is falling in love, has made up every single statistic.

To my great joy I received a letter from John Hadfield in which he stated:

> My real problems, however, didn't really hit me until page 10 of Episode 4, when you introduced an entirely new (and quite brilliant) element into the main story, making Miss Mounsey a key figure in the story, and completely reshaping the climax – or rather, the reason for the climax. This worried me considerably when I re-read the whole thing on Sunday evening, because it was not what I had planned when I originally wrote the book! But by yesterday morning, after a further reading, I had to give you credit for an entirely original and very constructive *improvement* to the plot, for which, now, I am genuinely grateful.

Nothing in my career has given me more pleasure than the pleasure my adaptation gave John Hadfield.

The show was beautifully designed by Eileen Diss, and a splendid cast was assembled. I was thrilled to get Michael Maloney as Jasper. I'd seen his enchanting and deeply original performance in *Truly, Madly, Deeply*, and he didn't fail us here. Leslie Phillips and Maria Aitken were wonderful as the Flamboroughs, David Haig was brilliant as the alcoholic wastrel Lionel, and Abigail Cruttenden, Cathryn Harrison and Charlotte Williams were delightful as the daughters.

I had a touch of nostalgia from the cast as well as from the story. Joe

Melia took me back to Cambridge days, Graham Crowden to *The Sun Trap*, Stephen Moore to *Hardluck Hall* and Gillian Raine, Len's widow, to those post-*Perrin* parties.

The Flamborough Hall scenes were filmed at Oxburgh Hall in Norfolk, the very setting that had inspired John Hadfield in the first place. It's a most delightful mellow brick Tudor house surrounded by a moat, a drawbridge and an exquisite parterre.

The Lord of the Manor, Henry Paston-Bedingfield, far from being sniffy about our intrusion into this pure medieval world with our ugly vans and cumbersome lights and endless cables snaking over the manicured gravel, proved stage-struck, and he and his wife were thrilled to take part as extras. He didn't even mind if you sat in his private and rather up-market folding chair, though he would make a point. 'That's my chair,' I heard him say, 'but you're most welcome to sit on it. And that's my *Times* you're reading, but you're most welcome to continue to read it.'

We had a very enjoyable time both at Oxburgh Hall and in the time-warp feudal village of Heydon, where the fête scenes were filmed. You think it indulgent for the writer to spend happy days at the filming? Not so. A crisis befell the script. Lady Flamborough had come across Jasper kissing all three of her daughters. Now she invited him to feed a pea-hen. The script required the pea-hen to accept a piece of lettuce eagerly. 'All the girls seem to fancy you,' was Lady Flamborough's line.

The pea-hen refused to oblige. The line would have to be changed. Everyone looked at me expectantly – director, assistant director, second assistant director, cameraman, lighting man, sound man, make-up artist, producer, executive producer, Maria Aitken, Susan, pea-hen.

'How about, "*She* doesn't seem to fancy you"?' I said.

'Brilliant.'

There are moments, just occasionally, when it all seems very easy.

The shows were a delight. The reviews were excellent. Friends and colleagues were ecstatic. The viewing figures, though, were no more than respectable. This was too gentle and too stylish to be an absolute smash hit. The Theatre of Comedy were anxious to do a second series and I was commissioned to produce a short treatment. John Hadfield had begun another novel which involved some of the same characters, but it was set in and around Fleet Street, and this was clearly wrong for us.

I created a story-line which was much more in keeping with the original. Lord Flamborough discovers that he is dying of cancer. He leaves his private railway line to Jasper on one strict condition – that Jasper acts as moral guardian to all three potentially wayward daughters. Since Jasper is deeply attracted to all three, and all three are deeply attracted to him, it's a recipe for delight, danger and confusion. In the end, perhaps Lord Flamborough, a tough old bird, would defeat his cancer. Or perhaps not. When one starts writing a story one must leave some loose ends. It's through them that it breathes.

John Reynolds and I went to see Alan Yentob, head of BBC1, to discuss this treatment. He told us politely, respectfully, but very firmly, that *Love On A Branch Line* was too gentle for his taste. I couldn't help wondering if he'd read *Pratt Of The Argus* and come across Sergeant Botney.

I had contradictory feelings about this decision, as about so much. A second series, without the rich original of John Hadfield's novel, might have stretched things too far, might have done little more than repeat its theme. On the other hand, I despair of an environment in which it is not possible to have a success with gentle humour and charm.

What a great title *Love On A Branch Line* was. The title of my next adaptation was pithier, plainer, snappier. It was *Cuts*.

Cuts was a novella by Malcolm Bradbury, a minor work in his canon, but delightful for all that. It was his revenge on the TV industry for an unhappy experience that he endured over an abortive project. The book contains a romance between two characters, Cynthia Hyde-Lemon, who is pretty unpleasant, and Joscelyn Pride, who is unpleasant and not at all pretty. I was told, after accepting the job, that these were two real people who had upset Malcolm. I didn't want to know anything about this. It might have inhibited my bile, and I hoped, of course, that they wouldn't recognise themselves. Judge then of my horror when I discovered that a pot of yoghurt would feature in all the scenes between them, yoghurt having apparently played a significant part in their amour. Perhaps this was another bad career move!

The programme was a delight to make, and we had a splendid cast headed, in alphabetical order again, by Peter Davison, Nigel Planer, Donald Sinden and Timothy West.

Cuts was built around the attempt to make a major television series – epic, tragic, cheap – which will give *Eldorado* Television a renewal of its franchise. The director was Martyn Friend, who had also directed *Love On A Branch Line*. He was easy to work with, unburdened with egotism, good with actors and highly competent. Despite these drawbacks he seemed to be having a very successful career. He did a grand job on both projects.

I only had one difficult moment with him. Malcolm had written a scene about industrial companies sponsoring crisis-hit university departments, and had included 'The Durex Chair of French Letters'. Martyn thought this unbelievable. It is, but it's also glorious. I refused to cut it out. I felt that if I did I would never be able to look Malcolm Bradbury in the eye. We came to a kind of compromise, in that it was done, but as a joke.

Sadly, I never did look Malcolm Bradbury in the eye. He came up for a day's filming, and everybody found him as delightful as I had hoped, but my mother was taken seriously ill and I couldn't be there. We were also scheduled to meet at the Dartington Festival, Ways With Words, where I was to deliver the Writers' Guild lecture, but my mother died, and I had to postpone it until the following year. Now of course he has gone, much too young.

I've not found it necessary to 'do a Hitchcock' throughout my career – the sight of myself walking across the screen diminishes my sense of the programme's reality – but I couldn't resist making an appearance in *Cuts*.

The hero, or anti-hero, Henry Babbacombe, is called in to write the series. As he sits waiting for his interview the door of the Head of Development opens and she ejects a writer with the words:

Your scripts lack movement, tension, texture, style, shape and content. They're a rare combination of verbal diarrhoea and visual constipation. Now shove off and stop pestering us.

The part of the hapless scribe just had to be mine.

Cuts was a savage satire on the television industry – very entertaining but somewhat inward looking. I was surprised that Vernon and the Network Centre commissioned it. I think they must have been too, because they put the programme out on ITV on New Year's Eve when most people were partying, in the hope, I presume, that few people would watch it and even fewer would review it.

I didn't meet the author of my next adaptation either. It was *Vanity Fair* for the West Yorkshire Playhouse. I found it utterly daunting at first to have to condense this great book into two and a half hours, but when I got into it I found it much easier than expected and one of the great joys of my working life. The book shines with Thackeray's discovery of just how good he was, yet it's never self-indulgent except around the time when Becky Sharp was giving her ghastly soirées, when he yields to temptation and mocks the gits, twits and shits of the day.

The play was produced at the Courtyard, the smaller of the two Playhouse theatres, by Michael Birch. It was a community play, performed by amateurs, and it was a very avant-garde production with men in women's roles and vice versa, and with mime and dance. It wasn't your classic costume drama, and some people didn't like it, but I knew that I did when I felt so sad that it was over.

I had no ulterior motive in accepting this modestly paid job. It was enough for me that it had its brief burst of life in Leeds. However, my agent approached the National and the RSC, and we received nice replies but no real interest.

Trevor Nunn wrote:

Having worked for a while on *Vanity Fair* when my colleagues and I were looking for a successor to *Nicholas Nickleby* I am both intrigued and cautious. I shall certainly look at David's adaptation when I get to it on my reading list, with genuine interest, but I shall be aware that I concluded more than ten years ago that there were structural problems inimical to the novel that were insoluble dramatically. But thank you for sending me the material.

Sadly, I never learnt any more about these problems, leaving me wondering whether I'm so clever that I solved all the problems instinctively or so stupid that I failed to solve them and didn't realise it, even when I saw the play being performed.

I turned down, due to pressure of work, an offer by Frank Muir to adapt his novel *The Walpole Orange*, and he sent me a letter in which he expressed his disappointment and said: 'I have always admired your gift of making books funnier on television than they were as books.' Since my first six adaptations were of my own books, this is a deliciously double-edged compliment.

My final adaptation of the 1990s was of a book called *Kingdom Swann*, by Miles Gibson, but since its filming and transmission occurred in the next century, I'll leave it until my final chapter.

Throughout the 1990s my career as a public speaker grew despite my best efforts to prevent it doing so. Gradually I got sucked into the literary lunch circuit.

A few writers, usually four, make a speech after a luncheon and then sign copies of their books. There are two agony points: (1) The speech. (2) The signing. I don't mind (1), I'm fairly good at it, but doing well at (1) doesn't guarantee that you'll sign as many copies as the gushing, nervous girl who writes romances and the good-looking man who wrote about travelling through Patagonia on a mule. Your queue is so short that you sign very slowly, and chat a lot, in the hope that it will grow longer.

My first literary lunch was in Solihull. It was meant to have an athletics theme, but something had gone wrong along the way. My fellow speakers were the Olympic javelin thrower, Tessa Sanderson, the Olympic hurdler, David Hemery, and the Olympic news reader, Trevor

Macdonald. Having made my living as a professional writer for twenty-five years at this point, I rashly stated that if I sold less copies than 'Javelins Were My Life' or whatever Tessa's book was called, I'd give up. No reflection on Tessa, who seemed lovely. Anyway, I sold forty-two hardbacks, thought that was normal, and have never got remotely near it again. It did mean that I could continue my career.

Another hazard of the literary lunch is the top table. At one, in the Majestic Hotel in Harrogate, I sat next to a majestic lady who, on discovering that I hailed from London, said, 'We'll be visiting London a lot next year. Our daughter's coming out.' I longed to say, 'Really? What was she in for?' but of course I didn't. I'm not Reggie. Nowadays, when I tell people this tale, I have to modernise it. After the majestic lady has said, 'My daughter's coming out', I now long to say, 'Were you aware she's Lesbian?'

A third literary lunch, at the Devonshire Arms in Bolton Abbey, led to an invitation to speak at a business function. Flushed with claret and success, I accepted. It turned out to be the Christmas party of the Yorkshire branch of the Institute of Quarrymen at the Penguin Hotel, Wetherby. It was daunting. As Les Dawson would have put it, 'They had faces like bags of spanners. The men weren't much better.' See how I use Les as protection for a politically incorrect joke in these hazardous times at the joke face.

There was no stage, so I was level with my audience. My first two jokes fell on quarried ground. The sweat ran down my back in rivulets. Every fibre of my being told me to speed up and get off. That is fatal. I slowed down, and I got them. I made them laugh, by God, but I thought, 'Do I need this?' Afterwards, I certainly didn't feel like buying anyone a drink. Well, I'd entertained them, hadn't I? One performance, and I'd gone a long way to understanding why so many comedians are mean.

In Cleethorpes I shared a floor with Edwina Currie, who was . . . well, let's say there were no major surprises. At the luncheon (it's never just a lunch) they introduced us individually, with a tune. I was escorted by a local beauty, probably a former Miss Grimsby, to the strains of the *Perrin* signature tune specially arranged for the occasion, for no fee, by

Ronnie Hazlehurst. Edwina Currie arrived half an hour late, perhaps because she couldn't find a signature tune respectable enough for Cleethorpes.

Twice I've shared a platform with Victoria Wood. I've done literary festivals in places that didn't know literature existed. I've talked to the Harrogate Chamber of Commerce and the Harrogate Business Circle. I've sat at round tables and talked to Rotary Clubs and I've sat at Rotary tables and talked to round clubs. I've talked to Women's Institutes and ladies' circles and in libraries up and down the land.

My least successful public appearance was at Austick's Bookshop in Leeds. Gordon Newman and Rebecca Hall invited me to help publicise her very moving anthology of writings about vegetarianism. They felt that I might help to swell the crowds, and they believed that I was still a vegetarian. I wasn't. Susan and I sail on the Good Ship Organic. We dance to a free range tune. I believe, or I persuade myself that I believe, that I am likely to do more good that way, helping to fight battles that can be won rather than ones that never will triumph.

Anyway, it appeared that my presence had helped to swell the crowd. Not spectacularly. Just one person turned up. Embarrassingly, he turned up to see me.

He congratulated me on my books, said he found them very useful. The adjective surprised me.

'Useful? In what way?'

'Well, with my exams.'

'Exactly what exams are those?'

'My sociology exams.'

'Ah. Well not really "ah" actually. I don't understand. How do my books help you with your sociology exams?'

'You are Colin Nobbs, the writer on sociology, aren't you?'

The public appearance that I found most difficult was at Whitemoor High Security Prison, near March in Cambridgeshire, where I had to address the Long Termers/Lifers Group for two and a half hours. This had come about because a prisoner wrote to me to say that there were five Nobbs fans in the group. Flattery will get me anywhere.

It took me half an hour to get through security and the stringent precautions didn't exactly relax me. Then I was taken to an ante-room where it was explained that I would have to wait until all the prisoners who were at risk from other prisoners – sex offenders and child abusers etcetera – had been moved. This also failed to relax me.

Eventually I was taken to a room where there were sixteen long termers/lifers and one lady who described herself as an educational co-ordinator. If my view on sit-com provoked a riot, we'd be helpless.

My fan approached me immediately and apologised. The other four fans had been transferred and replaced by four Cypriots, none of whom had heard of me.

Oh how I struggled that interminable afternoon. Every tale I thought up seemed inappropriate to prison life. The Cypriot contingent looked particularly unimpressed.

When at last I asked for questions the first three were not encouraging.

First Prisoner: 'Why did they make such a bad film out of Tom Wolfe's brilliant book, *The Bonfire of the Vanities?*'

DN: 'I can't comment. I haven't read the book or seen the film.'

Second Prisoner (Cypriot): 'Which Cypriot writers do you admire?'

DN: 'I don't admire any.' (Shock and horror on Cypriot faces. Riot impending?) 'This is because I haven't read any.'

Third Prisoner: 'Have you ever met Prunella Scales?'

DN: (Warily)   'Why do you ask?'

Third Prisoner: 'Because I'm going to marry her.'

DN: 'Her husband, Timothy West, might have something to say about that.'

Third Prisoner: 'I could deal with that.'

I didn't dare ask any of them what they were in for. I felt it would probably be a breach of etiquette. One of them told me, in the fruity voice of a luvvie, that he had trod the boards with Mike and Bernie Winters. I longed to ask him about his crime.

By the end I was a wet rag. Luckily Susan was there to drive me to Yorkshire, having had an enjoyable afternoon looking round Ely Cathedral. I'll tell you how stressed I was. We went for tea at the nearest Little Chef, and I enjoyed it.

During the afternoon the prisoners had promised/threatened to send me material for a series about what prison was really like. Nothing materialised, but my letter of thanks from the prison staff contained an interesting paragraph.

> From your own experience of getting into Whitemoor and then having spent the afternoon with some prison staff and inmates, you'll hopefully understand if we say that prison contains a wealth of humour. Or, at least a great deal of the absurd and the incongruous. But most of it can't easily be presented to the general public for a variety of reasons – *not least* [those two words were their italics] the likelihood of libel suits then being issued left, right and centre! With fact often being more crazy, if not stranger, than fiction.

I think I can recognise a veiled threat when I see one.

Part of this book was actually written when I was a guest lecturer on the *Saga Rose*, talking on the only subject on which I'm the world's greatest expert – me. Cruising is one of the perks. I got no fee, but a free three-week Mediterranean cruise for two people wasn't to be sneezed at.

I had to do six talks of forty-five minutes each. Since they were all to the same audience, they all had to be different. Four and a half hours of material! Still, I seemed to go down well. After my first talk I had to move from the cinema to the Grand Ballroom because of the crowds.

I don't do jokes. Can't remember them, and, on the rare occasions when I do remember them, can't tell them. I love to find comedy in the little things of life, and the audiences seemed to share this love.

There was the waitress in the Grand Hotel in Eastbourne, for instance. I called her over and told her that the potatoes were completely inedible. She gave us a sunny smile and said, 'I know. A lot of people have said that,' and walked away cheerfully.

In the Queen's Hotel in Leeds my fried egg at breakfast had clearly been kept under a hot-plate in the kitchen. It had a greeny blue glaze, as if it was a pottery egg. I complained. 'Sir!' thundered the waiter, 'I have served in this hotel, man and boy, for thirty-two years, and I've never had a complaint before.' 'Well now you've had two,' said the man at the next table. 'You can take my egg back and all.'

In the same hotel Barry Cryer and the cast of YTV's popular old show *Jokers' Wild*, unable to sweeten their cornflakes with sugar lumps, asked for a sugar shaker. Their waiter shook his head. 'You might find a few London way,' he said scornfully, as if sugar shakers were the final proof of metropolitan decadence.

By the end of the cruise people were feeding me with material. A member of the crew told me that one couple, finding a strong wind blowing up the gangway, asked if they could disembark on the other side. When it was pointed out that this would entail falling into the harbour, they said, 'Well, couldn't you at least turn the ship round?'

A girl who worked in the spa told us that she got so fed up with the question, 'Do you sleep on the ship?' that she said to one woman, 'No. We get taken off to the nearest port every night by helicopter.' The woman in question must have told most of the ship this news, because in the questionnaires at the end of the cruise fourteen people complained that the noise of the helicopters had kept them awake.

I was continuing to get letters from the general public, many with a familiar theme:

> 'I was living in Westerham, Kent, until '73, and was on several committees with a Mrs Kathleen Nobbs . . .'

> 'Nobbs was my maiden name . . . As far as I can gather, my Grandfather, head-master at Shaftesbury Grammar School and my father all came from Dorset . . . Apparently we are descended from the Tolpuddle Martyrs.'

> 'I am writing to you because you have my maiden name, Nobbs, and as it is so rare . . .'

> 'I served in the services with someone of the same name as yours . . . I was posted to 1 OTB signals in Catterick as a

wireless operator between March 45 and June 45. It's during that period that we may have met. Later I was posted to Tonbridge, then to Palestine, with 3 British Infantry Division.' (The triangular div. sign appeared on the tailboard of the Army Three Tonner in the Henry Pratt series.)

'During World War II I served with a Sub Lt Nobbs RNVR, who too came from Orpington.'

'50 years ago I shared a "billet" with a friend named Valerie Naomi Nobbs. She had an older brother named David.'

'Are you the David Nobbs who lived in a Caravan Site at Kings Langley, Herts in the 1950s? If you are, then you know me as I lived in Eddy Pritchard's house, he was a lecherous old man, tight-fisted and totally unprincipled where married women are concerned. I divorced my wife in 1963. I now live in Sheltered Housing but at peace. Your new series is great, keep them coming.'

I like that last one, and I like the picture I get of a world crawling with David Nobbses. I replied rather sadly to all the letters, knowing that I was spreading disappointment. Perhaps it would have been kinder to pretend to be them all.

The nineties also showed me continuing to reveal my talent for passing out.

One of these collapses occurred very early in the decade. Mary and I had driven up from Herefordshire with Alick Rowe to see the first night of *Second From Last In The Sack Race* at the West Yorkshire Playhouse. We'd been about twenty cars behind a dreadful accident, in which a lorry ploughed into six vehicles and killed six people. We'd been stuck on the M42 for about three hours. All that, plus the first night, added up to tension. Then there were all the drinks in the bar – you were wonderful, darling – and I passed out shortly after midnight in the Shabab Restaurant.

My next collapse occurred after the recording of an episode of *The Legacy of Reginald Perrin*. The audience had been less than ecstatic, the cast felt flat. I had massive cheering up to do while probably admitting to myself at some subconscious level that we weren't going to repeat our triumphs of the seventies. Susan and I slid off to an Indian restaurant in Shepherd's Bush, and I slid off on to the floor.

Later during the 1990s I became active in the Writers' Guild of Great Britain, and I found myself being volunteered for an extraordinarily unpleasant task. A commission of three undertook a two-day enquiry to determine whether our Deputy General Secretary should be dismissed for simply not doing his job. He was a man of some charm, and he had good ideas, but he just didn't carry them out. We recommended that he be sacked. We had no alternative, but it wasn't an easy thing to do, especially just before Christmas. Afterwards I had three pints in a pub near King's Cross, and a gin and tonic on the train. Susan drove from York to meet me and we stopped to sample the delights of the Shahi Raj Restaurant in Boroughbridge. Then I felt an attack of passing out coming on. Susan got me into the car, did her Michael Schumacher impression, and rang our neighbour Louise, a doctor. She drove across two fields at ninety miles an hour, terrifying several sheep and two owls, took one look at me, pumped something into me, and I revived.

I saw specialists in York and Leeds and they ascribed the incidents to stress.

I was puzzled by the frequent appearances of Indian restaurants in the drama. Was I allergic to fenugreek? Did I have cumin poisoning? Would I ever be able to eat a dhansak again?

Our doctor, Rosemary Livingston, explained everything with common sense and clarity. The stress came at the end of a long day, when I would always eat in an Indian restaurant because they were the only ones still open. The blood pressure drops with the stress, the body just doesn't want to know any more. Digesting food takes blood. The pressure drops still further. Digesting spicy food takes even more blood. Not enough blood to go round. One passes out.

*

I've mentioned Susan's daughter's wedding. During the 1990s I went to two other weddings which were very important to me.

The first, in 1997, was my step-daughter Kim's. She and her Geordie partner John had been living together in France for many years. Indeed, their eldest son, Joe, had caused me the worst moment of my life to date. I suppose he was six or seven at the time, and I went canoeing with him and John's brother Tim on the beautiful but swollen River Cele. There'd been a lot of rain, and I think we were all a bit reckless. Our canoe overturned and I went under the rushing waters. I surfaced to see the canoe speeding away upside down, and nobody else in sight. Then Tim surfaced. It was probably only five or ten seconds till Joe surfaced too, but it seemed an eternity. I almost died of relief when I saw him.

I grabbed hold of Joe, but found that I couldn't clamber out without letting go of him. Tim chased the canoe, righted it and sped off to get help. I held Joe with one hand and a tree with the other and we waited. All was calm now, but those dreadful few seconds before Joe surfaced haunt me still.

Anyway, at the age of forty Kim had finally mellowed into acceptance of marriage. I was doubtful about going, as Mary would be there, but Kim was adamant that she wanted me, and in the event Mary and I got on perfectly well. I didn't find the situation awkward and I hope she didn't.

The wedding was held in the tiny office of the Mayor of Senaillac-Lauzes on the Causse de Gramat. The Mayor described it as the happiest event of his term of office. The reception was in the village hall and everyone in the admittedly tiny village was invited. The speeches were in English and French, and their French neighbour thanked them and their English friends for bringing life and vitality to their dying village. The following evening the French gave a party for the English. Never had the entente seemed more cordiale.

We can hate French politicians, who protect their national interests so much more fervently than do ours, but I can't abide the traditional English hostility to the people of France. I have never met anything but warmth and friendliness from them.

*

I also felt that it was only right and proper that I should be at the second wedding. It was, after all, my own.

My divorce came through in the summer of 1998 and we wanted to get married as soon as possible. My cousin John, though, is a farmer, and if we married before the last week in October he would be unable to come, and by this time in our lives we were so close that he would have to be there.

Susan and I decided, therefore, to get married very quietly, and have a reception the following spring. We also decided to marry in secret, reasoning that if all our friends knew we were getting married, they'd wonder why they hadn't been invited. So we sent cards off, on our wedding day, announcing that we were now married and an invitation would follow.

The unfortunate side effect of this was that it inhibited Susan's hen night and my stag night. Nowadays people go for stag fortnights in Amsterdam and hen weeks in Dublin. Ours were not so extravagant. At this stage Susan was taking her father's girlfriend Florence and her Auntie Ann who wasn't a real auntie to an Indian restaurant once a week. It was a trip they all enjoyed. Fortunately, that week it fell on her hen night, although, since the wedding was secret, she couldn't tell them that that was what it was. And if some people's hen nights are a little more frenzied than a meal in an Indian restaurant with two companions whose combined age was a hundred and seventy-two, so what? We aren't ageist, and she had a lovely evening giving pleasure to people she loved.

My stag night took place in the Hare and Hounds and the Lamb and Flag. I met one or two people I knew and I bought one or two of them a drink and one or two of them bought me a drink, as was only right and proper on my stag night. The only problem was that I also couldn't tell anyone that it was a special occasion. 'Only a half, thanks,' or 'Mineral water, please, I'm driving' don't quite create that unique stag night atmosphere.

One of them even said, 'No, thanks, I'm off home. I have to be up early', and I couldn't say 'What? On my stag night? You miserable swine', and so he went home, and so quite soon did everyone else, and therefore so did I.

At least I was able to write this up for my weekly column on the *Yorkshire Evening Post* – a brief return to journalism in a job found for me by Willis Hall, and one which I was beginning to find a rather tiresome interruption to my other work. I was delighted when Willis and I and every other freelance writer was sacked as an economy measure by the paper's new owners.

The wedding itself was at Harrogate Register Office. We had only two guests, Briget and Mark. They accompanied us on the first part of our honeymoon, which was a night in a hotel in the Dales. Naturally, though, we wanted to be on our own for the rest of our honeymoon, which was lunch in a pub in the Dales.

The following May, however, we had a splendid dinner for about ninety people in the thirteenth-century Merchant Taylors' Hall in York, complete with an inspirational jazz band. It was wonderful to have old friends like Charles and Shirley Barham and Anthony and Paula Lynch there. Ant had long ago given up selling slotted angles and had become a GP. Charles had long ago given up building concrete bridges and had become a potter with Shirley.

Sadly, Barry Slater couldn't get there from Australia, Peter Tinniswood was too ill to come, Auntie Kathleen was too immobile to come, and it didn't seem appropriate to invite my step-children.

However, as many of Susan's family as we could cram in were there: Briget, my beloved fourth step-child and her husband Mark (through them I had an eighth step-grandchild, Max, as characterful and rewarding as the others – there must be some hope for a world that can still produce children like these); Susan's sister Patricia, her husband James, and their two sons Ashley and Jonathan, and Jonathan's partner Louise; Florence, approaching ninety, with her toy-boy, Susan's father Jack; Susan's cousin Brian and his wife, Susan's ex's sister Marjorie, their daughters Christine and Diane with their husbands, Kevin and Gordon; and Auntie Ann who wasn't a real Auntie and who began the dancing, aged all of eighty-five, by dragging Jack on to the floor.

What could I produce against this tangled web? My cousin John, his daughter Shirley and her husband Mark.

I didn't feel outnumbered. They were all my friends now.

What have Lord Moynihan, Ivy Benson, formation dancing, the Victoria and Albert Museum, the Millennium of AD 1000, sex changes, Michael Innes's novels, noise pollution, proliferation of chefs on television, the generation gap, and village football got in common?

I've written about them all, and the projects have been shelved.

Almost everything I'd written between 1963 and 1990 had been published or performed. I'd read the delicious stories of P.G. Wodehouse and Scott Fitzgerald about the frustrations of being a writer in Hollywood, but they had seemed like tales from a distant world. It was distant no longer. The goalposts had been moved by the creation of all those independent production companies. They all have to have projects, so there are more and more programmes in development than ever before, but, at the same time, because other programmes are so much cheaper to make, less and less drama is being made. As a result, writers work more and more on projects that will never happen. They get paid, but they don't get any foreign sales and repeats or, far more important, any satisfaction.

How can writers be expected to have a burning commitment under the circumstances? Inevitably, they will hold back in order to avoid the worst pain of disappointment and rejection.

I've spoken warmly of Jonathan, my agent. More than ten years ago he cut back his list of clients and moved to France with his second wife Ann, who had worked for him for many years. We have been several times to their lovely home outside Angouleme – from a council house in the Borough of Camden to a Cistercian Abbey in France, not a bad journey and all on ten per cents. I tend to deal more with Ann now than with Jonathan. Like him she is a fine judge of a piece of work. Like him she relies more on persuasion than on confrontation, so they are the right agents for me, but they have become more than agents, they are friends. I'm sure I would have found it difficult at times, without their friendship and support and advice and encouragement, not to get discouraged, even though I'm nothing if not a fighter.

I never did become discouraged. Onward and upward. To battle.

At least my first piece of work to see the light of day in the new millennium was a resounding success.

19 GOING GENTLY

SUSAN AND I had been living together for many months before my mother felt able to cope with meeting her. What went through her mind in those months I could only guess. Did she think back to her kind and stern, wise and narrow father, the principles by which he lived, the shock he would have felt at my behaviour? How did she manage to come to terms with it to such an extent that, on the day they met, her opening words were, 'This is the moment I've been waiting for'?

The tableau in the house in Harrogate stands before me as clearly as if it happened this morning. Susan at the top of the stairs, very nervous. Me at the bottom of the stairs, very nervous. John and Auntie Kay behind my mother, also rather nervous. My mother, frail and erect and as smart as a peacock, pausing to gather her breath, to be seen at her best. How essential to a decent life is a touch of vanity. My mother didn't look nervous at all, but John told me later that on the journey up from Essex she had been shaking.

Once that hurdle had been surmounted, things went well and, as John said to me on my next and Susan's first visit to Yeldham, as we traipsed the ploughed winter fields in our wellies, 'It's given her some excitement. It's been something to live for.'

We visited Yeldham fairly frequently and my mother soon grew to love Susan. Also, to our great joy, she was still strong enough to come and stay with us in our cottage in our secret enchanted valley. I don't know how much of the view she could see, she pretended to see more than she could.

We tried to find places to visit that she might not know from her holidays in Yorkshire. One day we chose a pub in a tiny village on the edge of the exquisite Howardian Hills. 'Last time I came here I sat in that big chair in the corner,' she said.

We went to Filey, where a shoe shop has a splendid sign that says 'Cobblers to the gentry'. Filey! It's the comedy writers' town. The name is funny, whereas Scarborough, Whitby and Bridlington aren't. It has known its fashionable days, but now there were minibuses full of unfortunate children, and old people spending a week in respite homes.

Elderly people gaze at the sea as if it will give them added years of life. Rain was coming that day, and the light was eerie. The sky was a pale sickly yellow, the sea was almost white and utterly flat. Sea, sky and sand seemed to merge into one, and from the over-emphatic way in which my mother spoke, I'm convinced that, on her last visit to the sea, she couldn't see it.

My mother was very proud of her teeth, which were all her own, and of how much better they were than those of her more famous contemporary, the Queen Mother. The last time we took her out to dinner, she ordered sirloin steak and had no problem with it.

On the subject of parents and teeth, I was swimming with my father in Caswell Bay on the Gower Peninsula when his dentures fell out. He stood stock still in the water, took bearings on two headlands in his mind, returned when the tide went out and retrieved his teeth from the sand. Moral – maths can be useful. Second moral – if you've got false teeth, don't swim at low tide.

I was in the middle of my annual visit to Shrewsbury to see Dave and Sarah and Kayleigh and Daniel when Susan rang to say my mother had been taken to hospital. I don't think I can do better in describing the next fortnight than to quote from the article I wrote for the *Sunday*

Telegraph magazine in connection with the promotion of my novel, *Going Gently.*

I have only ever seen one person die. It was my mother. I found it a profoundly beautiful experience. I hope that doesn't sound heartless. Let me explain.

My mother, Gwen, was not far short of her 95th birthday when she was taken to hospital during hot August weather. Until that day, although she was becoming quite frail and was gradually losing her sight and hearing, she had remained mentally active, doing the *Daily Telegraph* crossword (and not their quick one) every day.

I hurried down to Essex to my Aunt Kathleen's house, where my mother had lived so happily for the past few years. The message from the hospital was that my mother had been suffering from dehydration and might have had a slight stroke. She was a little better that morning. My aunt told me that for the past few days my mother, most unusually, hadn't bothered to get dressed, but otherwise had been in good form. After my aunt's usual magnificent Sunday lunch I drove over to Colchester Hospital with my cousin John, who is like a brother to me as we are both only children.

The hospital is set in parkland and was uncannily peaceful in the Sunday afternoon heat. There was even the distant sound of leather upon willow. A cliché of an English afternoon . . . until I saw my mother.

I'd expected a bright if tired smile, a false alarm, a speedy recovery now that she was being given liquids. I saw a spry, frail old lady, very lined, very tired, hardly conscious. I knew immediately that she would not come home again. I was shocked. I didn't meet my cousin's eyes, lest I saw in them the confirmation of my fears.

The woman in the next bed came over, looked at my mother, and said, 'Oh bless his little cotton socks. Isn't he a lovely baby? How much does he weigh?'

'Seven pounds five ounces,' I said. 'Oh bless him,' she said. I felt embarrassed at my connivance in her illusion, in the presence of my cousin, who, being a farmer, is presumably sensible. But I saw no point in disabusing her of her illusion, which gave her happiness of a sort.

My mother was believed to be in no immediate danger. I returned to Yorkshire, knowing that I could be summoned back at any moment. The following weekend I went down with Susan. We sat for hours at my mother's bedside. We talked to each other, and to her. She didn't speak, and we had no idea whether she knew who we were or could hear what we were saying.

On the Saturday, the woman in the next bed wasn't touching lunch. 'You must eat,' admonished the nurse. 'I can't afford it,' the woman whispered in shame. 'Bless you, you don't have to pay,' said the nurse. 'You're in hospital.' 'Oh, am I? Sorry,' said the woman, who had thin, bruised arms. But she still didn't eat.

The next day my mother seemed exactly the same, but suddenly we realised that she was going to speak. We leant forward. Her voice was weak but clear, as she spoke her last words to us. 'Can you think of another word for stateless?' she asked. I felt happy to know that, wherever she was, there were crosswords there. 'Refugee?' suggested Susan, and my mother gave a nod.

That evening we told her that we'd see her the following weekend. We hoped that she had understood, as she had seemed to understand 'refugee'. I squeezed her hand. She squeezed mine. I hope she knew that it was mine.

The following Friday, at 1 a.m., a kind nurse rang to say my mother's condition was giving concern. We hurried down to Essex first thing in the morning. She looked older and smaller than ever. Her head was shaking and she was making clicking noises. The nurse told us that these were minor strokes, that she was unaware of them, that she wasn't suffering. I hope that was so.

By this time I knew that I wanted her to die, because there could be no way back to any real quality of life.

'How's the little one?' asked the woman in the next bed.

'Doing well,' I said.

'Bless his little cotton socks,' she said.

My mother wasn't expected to last the night, so I slept at the hospital. But there was no change, nor the next day. She clicked constantly and seemed far, far away.

When the woman in the next bed again refused her lunch, whispering that she couldn't afford it, I offered to pay for it. She began to eat with the air of a woman who once had perfect table manners, and thanked me so profusely that I began to feel a fraud for not paying.

That evening the nurses felt it was safe for me to go to my aunt's house, 15 miles away. 'She's putting up a magnificent fight,' one of them said. I slept fitfully, expecting a phone call at any moment. It came during breakfast.

I hurried to the hospital. Everything had changed. There was no more shaking of the head, no more clicking. Just quiet, gentle breathing, and peace.

Susan came over in the mid-morning. We sat in silence, watching my mother fade away. Her breathing grew slower, quieter, gentler. And then it began to happen, the phenomenon for which I was not at all prepared. The lines began to disappear from my mother's face. If worrying had been an Olympic event my dear, dear mother would have represented Wales. Now all her worries had melted away, and with them went the lines on her face. She looked years younger . . . thirty, forty years at least. Her skin was smooth and fine. She looked, I thought, quite beautiful.

Her breathing grew slower, fainter, slower, fainter. I thought she had gone. Then she breathed again, a barely detectable movement. And then she didn't breathe at all ever again. 'How's the little one?' asked the woman in the next bed, as if aware at some level that something had occurred. 'Sleeping,' I said in a shaky voice.

A nurse took us to a rest room and gave us a cup of tea. So British. So welcome. My legs were shaking. I was feeling deep sorrow and deep shock. Sorrow that what I wanted to happen had happened. Shock that what I knew would happen had happened.

The longer people live, the more their death surprises us. We have come to think of them as immortal.

We went back to my aunt's and were just in time for Sunday lunch. This was typical of my mother. She hated to be a nuisance.

You think that flippant? I don't mean it to be. You see, I now think that my mother did put up a magnificent fight – to die. That was why she hadn't dressed in the last few days. She'd been preparing herself. She dehydrated herself. It wasn't that she was unhappy, but her sight was failing, her hearing was failing, she saw that I was happy with Susan, her time had come. Her constitution was so strong that it was hard to die through sheer willpower, but she managed it beautifully in the end.

There followed a description of my father's death. Then I continued:

I've never made fiction out of my father's death. If I did, I would be accused of sensationalism, sentimentality and over-dramatisation. Fiction has more rigorous rules than life.

I've never made fiction out of my mother's death either. I have written a novel which could probably not have been written if I hadn't seen her die, but the woman in it is not in any respect my mother. I could not, knowingly, make fiction out of her.

So here I am, an only child, both parents dead, I'm now at the head of the queue, awaiting the summons. I hope it doesn't come yet awhile, but I no longer fear it. How can I, when I've seen the faces of both my dead parents at peace, after such contrasting deaths?

I fear dying, of course. I fear pain and humiliation. I fear deafness and blindness and most of all I fear a stroke. I fear becoming as mad as the woman who believed that my mother was a new-born baby. But I don't fear death. I believe that, until I saw my mother die, I did fear it.

The witnessing of my mother's death hasn't changed my religious views. I was confirmed in the Church of England, but lost my faith several decades ago, finding evidence of benevolent purpose in this world scanty. I'm an agnostic, but the word doesn't begin to express my sense of wonder at the existence of existence, at the fact that anything is.

One moment my mother was breathing, and she was warm. The next moment she wasn't, and soon she would be cold. It doesn't take much of a leap to imagine this in reverse. How powerful is breath. What a miracle is life.

The nature of my birth was out of my hands, but if I die half as beautifully as my mother, I shall be content.

My mother hadn't wanted a funeral. She hadn't wanted anyone to grieve. What she'd wanted was a Memorial Service at her beloved St John's Church in Orpington. I spoke to a couple of her friends who still worshipped there, and their view was that it was too late, she'd outlived most of her friends, she'd been away in Essex too long, and a decently attended Memorial Service was no longer viable.

So we had a funeral after all, in the United Reform Church in the pretty village of Castle Hedingham, watched over by its Norman keep.

I gave the address. I was determined, in honour of my mother's wishes, that there should be a laugh or two.

I spoke of how, when I was about eleven and furious, I told her I was leaving home.

'All right,' she said calmly. 'I'll just write out some lists that'll help you.'

I stood in the kitchen, with the unused servants' bells, trying to keep my courage and my anger going. My mother soon returned with two lists she'd written out.

'That's a list of instructions of how your various clothes need washing,' she told me, 'and that's a suggested list of some simple meals and how to cook them.'

I looked at the lists in helpless horror.

'I'm going to give you one last chance,' I growled.

I spoke also of her tact, of how on the prom in Swansea (there was never a promenade, just a prom) a Jewish lady came to sit beside us. I was about eight at the time. Neither my mother nor I were inadequate in the nasal department, and the lady jumped to conclusions. 'Are you staying with Gentiles?' she enquired. 'Yes, we are,' said my mother, 'and we find them very nice.'

I forgot to tell the story of the visitor with the large nose, when I was small. My mother warned me not to laugh at it, not to look at it, above all not to comment on it. I was as good as gold. She handed him a cup of coffee and said, 'Do you take sugar with your nose?'

I kept going almost to the end, then I caught sight of her coffin lying there, and I had to stop with a sob. She would have regretted that sob.

I don't know how long after that it was when I conceived the idea of *Going Gently*. Not far short of two years, I would think. I really would like to assure you that I didn't sit at my mother's bedside and think, 'Hey up! There's a book in this.'

The thought that nagged me was, how much had she understood of all the things we said in the hospital? Had she even known who we were?

I had wanted, for a very long time, to write a book with a woman as the central character. I also fancied, as the millennium approached, writing a book that spanned the twentieth century.

It was but a small step from there to the idea of a woman in hospital, unable to speak but who, despite appearances, could understand what was going on. She would have to understand what was going on, or there would be no novel – a woman looking back over her ninety-nine years from the beginning of the century, living her life again.

What sort of woman? A woman of left-wing sympathies. Why? 1) I wanted her to have some ideals and I have yet to be convinced that anybody on the right is not motivated mainly by self-interest. 2) If she didn't have left-wing sympathies, she would have a private ward to herself, which would have made the hospital scenes some of the dullest ever written. Practicality and idealism joined hands.

The most dramatic change that occurred to me after I lost my mother was that I found my Welshness. I'd never lost it entirely, had always supported Glamorgan at cricket, but now it burst out. Now I felt great surges of emotion at the singing before rugby matches in Cardiff. Now I exulted when Wales denied England the Grand Slam. We visited Central and North Wales with our German friend, Gerlinde, and I rejoiced at her and Susan's discovery of its amazing beauty. North Wales is spectacular, but with a tendency to grimness. South Wales is dramatic and lively and awash with chatter and music and generosity and sin. Mid-Wales is the landscape of dreams.

So my heroine would be Welsh.

Geoffrey and Susan Strachan were coming to stay, and I decided that I'd write a draft of the first chapter of the book and read it to Geoffrey. He liked it. He could see its potential.

In the end, to my great sadness, Geoffrey had nothing to do with the book because Methuen negotiated their independence from the great publishing monolith that was Random House. I had a two-book contract of which *Going Gently* was the second, and Random House refused to release me, along with a few others including Sue Townsend and Leslie Thomas. It was flattering, but distressing. I found myself farmed out to William Heinemann.

I was very lucky. I had already met Lynne Drew, the editorial director who would be my Geoffrey Strachan at Heinemann, and I liked and respected her. She didn't go through the book in quite such detail as Geoffrey, but her comments were extremely helpful and constructive. The publicity arranged by Karen Gibbings was as good as, perhaps better than, any I'd experienced before. I was consulted over jacket design and in fact gave the thumbs down to several, there was never any argument about it, and in the end they came up with a jacket that everybody liked.

Now Lynne has moved on and I have another new editor, Kirsty Fowkes. Surely my luck must have run out? But no. Her notes have been absolutely splendid, forcing me to be less evasive at certain key moments in the narrative. Tricky coves, autobiographies. Need a good editor.

When I hear of the experiences of other writers I feel that I'm a very lucky man.

But back to the gestation of *Going Gently*. If I go into it in more detail than some of my other works, it's partly because it's more recent, but mainly because I do believe that it's the best thing I've written, and because it brings my life full circle.

Once I'd decided that Kate would be Welsh, the rest of her background fell into place. My mother's immediate family were all dead (though there might be a few distant cousins wandering round mid-Wales saying, 'It's all sex with that old Nobbs') so there was nobody to be upset if I just put them in the book.

I placed utterly fictional Kate firmly in the bosom of my mother's family in Swansea. Annie was Auntie Louie, who wasn't a real auntie (does every family have one?). Oliver was Uncle Glandon in every respect, down to all the details of his life story. Bernard was Uncle Kenneth, ditto. In Bernard's brave and untimely death the scene is invented, but the death is Kenneth's, and I would like to think he approached death with Bernard's courage. One thing I didn't manage to fit in was his habit, after every joke he made, of saying, 'Joke. Joke over,' though I'm sure he wouldn't mind lending this to another character. He wasn't a petty man.

Enid (pronounced with the short Welsh e, not as *Ee*nid) began as Auntie Dilys but developed ideas of her own about who she was.

Apart from one or two of the journalists in *Pratt Of The Argus*, I think that *Going Gently* is the only work I've written in which I have used one of my friends as the inspiration for a character. Daniel Begelman, the Jewish artist, owes much to dear Victor Spurber, my old companion in sailing disaster. I've a soft spot for Daniel, so I hope Victor will be pleased, should he ever find out.

I wonder what my mother would have thought of Kate – bold, witty, sexy, generous, married six times, yet essentially a moral woman. That was the challenge I set myself: to create a woman who could be married several times and yet was moral enough for me to feel that there was just a chance that my mother would have approved of her.

The construction of the book was extremely simple. Every other chapter was set in the hospital in the present. The chapters in between saw Kate relive her eventful life in strict chronological order. The confusion of the flashbacks in *A Piece Of The Sky Is Missing* has been replaced by a construction that is crystal clear. I've also learnt a bit over the years about how to get people to keep turning the pages – devices which I would have despised in my earlier days, when I came over all puritanical about narrative.

After I'd written the first draft I visited South Wales to do my research. That is always my method. Until I've written a draft I don't know what I need to know. Now my enquiries could be quite specific. I went to the Archives Department of Swansea City Hall and found that my grandparents' home – 16, Eaton Crescent – existed in 1900 but was on the edge of the town (it wasn't a city then). Why not have them actually living in 16, Eaton Crescent, the house that had been so magical to me? I felt that it would give my writing a real edge.

Susan and I stood outside the house on a warm, wet Welsh afternoon. The first spears of rain were shooting in on the strengthening wind. It looked in good repair and I sensed that it was still a family home. I didn't want to go in. Too much would have changed. I stood and looked at the bay windows of the parlour and my grandparents' bedroom, and the two smaller windows of Auntie Dilys's bedroom. I heard the laughter of people long gone. Tears streamed down my face.

I don't feel uneasy about using the Williams family in that way. Let a short quote from the book serve as their epitaph.

> What fun they had enjoyed, in their smart new three-storey gabled terraced house on the edge of the spreading town. How could they have had such fun in a house where no swear-word was ever uttered, no sexual function was ever

mentioned, no naked thigh was ever seen, no alcohol was ever consumed unless you'd fainted first, no naughty joke was ever heard, no food was ever praised, and laverbread was eaten every morning? But what fun they had, except on Sundays. What charades they played, what quizzes they held in the cheery back room with the armchairs drawn up higgledy-piggledy round the cramped little coal fire, the sombre knitted texts on the walls, the shiny mahogany dining table.

For the hospital sequences I included the sad deluded woman who had been in the next bed to my mother, and peopled the ward with more sad women, friendless Hilda, windy Glenda, swearing Delilah and gin-swigging Lily, who thought she was on a cruise. Sadness and laughter, bedfellows on Ward 3C of Whetstone General Hospital.

I do believe that all the reviews of *Going Gently* were good, and that was certainly a first. A few critics didn't like the detective element, although that was what some readers picked out to praise to me. I think the critics thought it was there because I didn't trust my story to be gripping enough without it. It was actually there because it gave Kate a reason to go back over her life, a need to go back over her life, and because it represented the ultimate irony. People assumed that she was ga-ga. It was therefore necessary, in dramatic terms, for her to be as far from ga-ga as could be. What would demonstrate that better than her solving a murder that had baffled the police? I also liked the concept that she succeeded because she could ask no questions, because she could sift through no evidence.

The murder element may have been too perfunctory, but it was meant to be at least slightly perfunctory, as I didn't want the book to become a detective story. It needed to be there, but it couldn't be too important.

Despite that, I think now that it could and should have been better done. So there's the spur that will motivate me to write my next novel – my search for the elusive and impossible goal of perfection.

What particularly pleased me about the critical reception of the book was that nobody had anything derogatory to say about my creation of Kate, and only one of the many readers with whom I discussed the book found her unconvincing as a woman. My approach to writing about women is actually very simple. I certainly don't read books about the psychology of women. I use a lifetime's observation of women, allied to a lifetime's experience of people and their emotions. Women feel lonely when they're on their own. They feel depressed when things go badly. They need affection and love. In other words, in many of the basic human needs, they are exactly like men. What the two sexes have in common is vastly greater than the differences between them. I think that the vast bulk of men's comments about the essential oddity and unpredictability of women, about the strange way in which they are supposed to think – the 'odd chaps, women' of the Jimmies and Harries of this world – are quarried out of ignorance and prejudice and, above all, fear.

There's still an imaginative leap to be made, but if we can't make imaginative leaps we shouldn't be novelists.

Humour has been at the heart of all my writing, and I'd like to think that there's still plenty of humour in *Going Gently*, but it's a passage with no humour in it that has struck people in a way that has astonished me. Several people have used a passage from page 381 at the funeral of a loved one. I find that very moving. I am deeply honoured.

They are the words I gave Kate for a television programme that she made about death. Let them stand as the way I hope to be brave enough to follow, when I face what will one day come.

> We are all born once. We all die once. That is the end of the equality meted out by this world. Let us not fear this thing. We cannot avoid the fear of painful illness, but we must not fear death itself. It is not only inevitable, but desirable. Eternal life would be appalling. The value of life lies in its brevity. Relish the miracle of life every day. Make the most of it, both for yourselves and for others. If you live as long as I have, and are lucky enough to have as rich a social life as I

have had, you'll go to many funerals. Don't fear them. Don't fear other people's death. Hard though it is, don't grieve for your loss, but think of their peace and give thanks for their life which lives on in you. Nothing ends with your death, except unimportant little you. Life is a relay race. Pass the baton.

20 THE END OF THE BEGINNING

MY FIRST MAJOR project of the new millennium was the adaptation of a novel called *Kingdom Swann*, by Miles Gibson. Principal Films wanted me to turn this into a one-off TV film. It's the only book that I've ever read while cruising through the Suez Canal, and that odd fact sets the tone for what I found an odd experience.

The eponymous hero was a painter in late-Victorian England, whose work had fallen out of fashion. He took up photography, and his photography was exploited as pornography by his crafty cockney assistant, Cromwell Marsh. The book is full of the hypocrisy of late-Victorian and Edwardian England. It has vivid depictions of the poverty of East End London. It's strange and dark and at times savage, told in short, staccato scenes written with a poet's touch and a painter's eye. It contains a great deal of nudity and even necrophilia, and ends in a spectacular way with a stately home being bombed by a Zeppelin in the First World War.

I enjoyed the book very much, but had reservations about the thirty or so pages preceding the climax. However, I felt that I'd be able to deal with this and still be faithful to the book's spirit.

My first draft was not a success. Sarah Boote at Principal, a young lady with startlingly coloured hair, complained that I'd included whole sections of the book virtually unaltered. I got the impression that she thought she'd been short-changed.

I'd included whole sections of the book because I liked them and I try to preserve as much of what I like as is possible when I adapt a book. This is probably very naïve.

I won't go through the whole laborious process of how *Kingdom Swann* slowly became *Gentlemen's Relish*. Suffice it to say that about halfway through, as I struggled with successive drafts as you do these days (largely, I believe, because technology makes it possible), and as I fought in vain to keep the dark savagery of the original and the uncompromising tragedy of the ending, Sarah said to me, 'What we're trying to do is a *When Harry Met Sally* of Edwardian England.' I don't know how long Sarah had known that that was what we were trying to do, but I hadn't known it until that moment.

Martyn Auty was brought in as producer and we began to make some kind of progress together. I've touched on all my abortive projects in the nineties. I fully expected this to be another one. I felt tired and depressed and lacking in creative energy.

Martyn came to our house and we sat at the kitchen table and worked out a scenario for the end of the film. It was getting less and less like the original, but it would work. Martyn offered to write it up and I was very grateful. I still didn't expect the film to be made.

Then, suddenly, Billy Connolly loved the script and Sarah Lancashire loved the script and the production was scheduled and I received a letter from Martyn stating that in view of all his work on it, he would like a credit reading 'Co-written and produced by Martyn Auty'. I didn't like this wording one bit, but a more accurate version like 'additional material by . . .' would have involved an absurdly long credit or two credits for Martyn, so in the end I decided that I couldn't really argue in view of what had happened, and wrote it off to my extreme youth and inexperience. I was, after all, only sixty-four at the time.

I never felt entirely happy working on the script, and I don't feel I worked at anything like my best, but the thing got made, and for that I am extremely grateful to Sarah Boote and to Martyn.

*

I arrived at the read-through with some trepidation. The beginning of the script had been altered beyond recognition to enable the director, Douglas McKinnon, to show a great deal of period flavour without spending very much money, and the ending was a shared effort and unashamedly sentimental.

Billy Connolly loved every minute of it. There had been worries that he would be upstaged by the Cromwell Marsh character, played with relish by Douglas Henshall as a latter-day Michael Caine. It was clear that Billy, a generous man, wasn't remotely worried about being upstaged. He roared at Douglas's every laugh. Of course he had nothing to prove as a comedian and was more concerned with his reputation as a straight actor, if reputation meant anything to him. He played it absolutely straight.

Filming began in a rambling old house owned by a rambling old Russian princess who could occasionally be seen rambling around the rambling old house. It began under the shadow of the tanker drivers' strike. Clearly, if this was not resolved, the film would not be completed, since even the most resourceful production manager couldn't conjure petrol out of thin air, and it's almost certain that the two stars would never have been available at the same time again.

I went to a couple of days of the filming but I could see that creative input was not expected of me – there was Martyn Auty sitting at a table on the lawn in front of the house, doing rewrites. I'm just not used to that, but I could do nothing about it because we were going to America in a few days for one of the weddings and our Californian trip, and if I demanded to be involved in all the rewrites I wouldn't be able to go.

When I look back on all this, I'm shocked at how my attitude to my craft had changed. Here was a major TV film with major stars, and I was happy to leave it and go on holiday. I could have cancelled the holiday and just gone for the wedding, but I didn't. The old commitment wasn't there. Not a word had changed throughout all my television series without my permission. Now I was in the world of the film on location, where the writer is a nuisance to be placated.

The tanker drivers' strike ended, the film was completed and Susan

and I took our seats alongside the BBC's Head of Comedy, Geoffrey
Perkins, at the press showing at Bafta in Piccadilly. It wasn't the film of
the book, the opening gave no clue to the naughtiness that would
follow, and I thought Sarah Lancashire was sentimental as the housekeeper. However, I could see that it would be popular, and the finished
article was more faithful to my script than I had feared.

There was laughter but not, I felt, enough. At the end there was total
silence. I squirmed. I was convinced that I had just witnessed a complete
fiasco. Then the applause rang out, not frenzied, but warm and quite
prolonged, and then we were all in the bar and people were saying that
I must be very proud, and I still didn't know if I was or not.

The film went out on New Year's Day in a prime slot on BBC1, and
did well, and there's no doubt that it has had a revitalising effect on my
work and career. I still feel uneasy about the morality of it. We were
showing pornography in order to condemn the hypocrisy while
knowing perfectly well that we were getting a prime slot because of it,
which was itself hypocritical. Writer has moral scruples in the twenty-
first century! Well, I think the creator of Reginald Iolanthe Perrin has
the right to be just a little eccentric.

I'll quote from just two of the reviews.

It was funny, charming, beautifully performed, and never
shortchanged the development of its characters in the
interests of escalating farce (*Daily Telegraph*)

Gentlemen's Relish was the biggest load of crap I've seen
dumped on British Television for many a long year
(*Independent on Sunday* – Will Self)

The truth, my dears, is probably rather boringly halfway between the
two, but it all adds to the fun.

At the present time I'm working on several projects which seem to me
far more exciting than some of the vain efforts of the nineties, and I'm
working with renewed confidence and with my professional appetite
revived. I won't say any more about them as I'm superstitious about

work in progress. If they happen, you'll know about them. If they don't, it's best that you don't.

I will mention just one of them, because it's enabled me to work with two of the good guys. I'm adapting Jonathan Coe's wonderfully angry novel *What A Carve Up*, attempting to find New Labour horrors instead of his Thatcherite ones. He gave me a copy of his latest book, *The Rotters' Club*, with the inscription: 'To David, who has inspired me almost more than any other living writer'. That is a wonderful thing to be told. If I have inspired just one younger writer, I've done my job – I've passed the baton. I like Jonathan a lot. His real life mildness contrasts with his literary anger, and I do love his very English use of adverbs . . . '*almost* more than any other living writer' along with '*probably* our best post-war comic novelist'!

I must also mention my script editor on this project, Hilary Norrish. I've had more and more script editors as time goes by, more good than bad, but Hil's the best – energetic, inspiring, intelligent, creative, critical but respectful and – above all – fun. We must all have fun, folks. There is no chance of good comedy without it.

My long-standing friendships seem more and more important with time. Charles Barham, the ex-civil engineer, has retired from his pottery. Anthony Lynch, he of the slotted angles, has retired as a GP. I still see them both and they are still happily married to Shirley and Paula. Not so my old cricket chum, Tony Robinson. It's his turn for a difficult divorce. Barry Slater, mellow in his maturity, is an occasional but very welcome visitor from Oz, still bursting with philosophical work that I can't understand. Dave and Sarah and Kim and John seem happy. Chris, separated from his wife, now needs a wheelchair, and has a young Malaysian dental student girlfriend. He is one great example of guts and spirit as I approach old age. (My birth certificate tells me that I'm sixty-seven, so I've filed it under F for Fiction.)

I have some other wonderful examples of the human spirit to inspire me. I'll quote just three.

A year or two ago we gave a little Sunday lunch party. One of the guests, Tim, a man in his early eighties but still carrying himself as straight as an obelisk, walked down to us through the nature reserve, but got a lift back home, many hours later, and found one of his sons in his house. The son had phoned, got no reply, phoned a neighbour who said that Tim's car was in the drive, and had got worried.

'So you walked straight in!' exclaimed Tim, appalled. 'I suppose it never occurred to you that I might have been with a woman.'

Tim, like Eric Stevens of my Barnet days, was a war hero. Like Eric he would never admit it, unless perhaps he was very drunk. What must men like this think of the empty hype and egotistical blather of the people nominated as personalities by the media?

The next quote was told me by my old friend Will/James Warrior.

A great lover of canals, he bought an old pilot boat off an 85-year-old lady.

'I suppose there comes a time when you have to give up,' he commented.

'Do you mind?' she cried. 'My new boyfriend's a flying enthusiast. He's going to teach me to fly, so there won't be any time for boats.'

The third example is my old friend Peter Tinniswood, who lost a heroic fight against cancer in January 2003, aged sixty-six. When his voice box had to be removed, did he give up in despair? No. In his own words, with fine irony and courage, he 'found my voice again.' His writer's voice. His true, sublime, unique comic voice. Great radio plays streamed out, and so did wonderful letters to his friends. I quote a few snippets from mine.

About the dreadful dental problems related to his condition
> The ghastly climax was played out in Guys Dental School with a trainee Australian bimbo, obsessed with showing off her arse and tits to the students and a supercilious supervisor with all the charm, charisma and expertise of a carrier bag.

About this autobiography
> Your book came when I was at my lowest. And it sent my spirits soaring.
>
> Can you write another one before I have my piles seen to?

On death

I keep thinking of the time I bumped into Gwyn Thomas in St Mary Street, Cardiff. I asked him how he was doing and he said, 'Peter, my boy, I'm suffering from so many afflictions it's an embarrassment to know which one to die from.'

A wonderfully witty writer, Gwyn Thomas.

On health

I'm still taking my cod liver oil tablets. They're doing me a power of good. The trouble is I've developed an urgent desire to migrate to the Grand Banks of Newfoundland.

On rugby football

I thought the Rugby World Cup was awful. The game is a complete mess. It wasn't meant to be played in that way with enormous great hulks crashing into each other mindlessly and wingers prowling aimlessly with the wit and enterprise of condemned traffic bollards.

On sport

I've just heard Tim Henman has fallen out of bed trying to scratch his right ear. As a result he's gone up three places in the world rankings.

On writing

I've been commissioned to do a Tom Stoppard play for the telly. It's provisionally called 'Rosenkrantz and Guildenstern Are Dead – Or At Least They Were Last Time We Had A Meeting But Don't Quote Me On That One In Case I Get A Bollocking From Network For Not Thinking Of A Snappier Title That Would Persuade David Jason To Show An Interest'.

Wonderful to have found such a friend. Even more wonderful to have found him again. He lives on in memory.

Back to Will/James Warrior. Last summer Susan and I were drinking red wine on his deck while dusk slid mistily over the River Soar, and I asked a couple of his neighbours how they had met.

'I worked for him,' she said.

'Oh, what did you do?' I asked.

'I was fired,' she said.

'Oh, I'm sorry,' I said. 'Why were you fired?'

'That's my job,' she said. 'Being fired. From cannons. Across rivers.'

I had a great moment of doubt about my autobiography that evening. Why should people be interested in a man who sits on his backside and makes things up, when people do such extraordinary things even in this age of standardisation and soap-watching?

I decided that there was reason enough, not because of me, but because of the sweet spirit of comedy.

Was there a single person of good will in this world who didn't welcome the millennium with at least some fragile hope? Was there a person with any concern for life outside their own ego who didn't welcome the end of a century scarred by two horrendous world wars, and crave something better for mankind?

Wasn't that the very worst aspect of the tragedy of 11 September, 2001? All those hopes seemed to be dashed in one hour in New York.

I used to listen to Radio Four every morning as I prepared for work. I gave up when the student rebels in Tiananmen Square were killed. I felt guilty about giving up. I don't now. What can I do by way of political comment that could matter a jot? But supposing I can bring some brief joy through laughter? Infinitely more important.

Where does that dreadful event leave comedy? In the forefront, I say. The great Peter Cook complained that Britain was sinking giggling into the sea. The great John Cleese has become disillusioned with comedy. Maybe if one is not so great one can go on longer. I believe that comedy is more important than it has ever been. I worry about today's comedy, though. It seems to be getting cruder and cruder. Charm and subtlety are lost. The double entendre has been replaced by the single entendre.

We've moved from an age in which it was impossible to say 'fuck' on television to an age when it's obligatory. I have no objection to the word. I tell two true stories to which it is essential. A man in Ye Olde Monken Holt said to me, 'You wouldn't like my brother, Dave. He's a fucking uncouth bastard.' And the aforementioned Richard Baldwin in the White Swan in Eardisland asked a brilliant Irish cowherd called Eric to moderate his language as it was upsetting two tourists. Eric was genuinely contrite, turned to them and said, 'I'm so sorry. I didn't fucking see you.'

The sacred rule of three demands another true story which needs a swear-word. This one involves a milder word, but it was said by the six-year-old innkeeper in a school nativity play. Joseph asked him if there was room at the inn. 'Piss off,' came the response. 'I wanted to be Joseph.'

Many sit-coms use swear-words till it's tedious. That is deeply lazy. They also seem to think that lavatories, bodily functions and vomiting are hilarious, regardless of context. That is deeply childish.

Hilda in *Going Gently*, who didn't want to be released from hospital because her life in it was better than her life at home, had some words to say about modern television:

> I read that they want programmes with street cred. I don't know what street cred is. I live in a grove. I don't know whether there is such a thing as grove cred. They make programmes for young people and what's the point, they're at their clubs taking their drugs. The only decent thing an old lady in her own home can watch is the *Antiques Road Show*, and I expect quite soon they'll have suggestive jugs on that.

At the BBC in particular there is an obsession with television that's at the cutting edge, because television is at the centre of television people's lives. But millions of people are at the cutting edge every day. Teachers, doctors, nurses, social workers, police, paramedics, prison warders, bouncers, to name but a few, see life in the raw every day and want to leave these realities behind and have a bit of entertainment. And the executives know this, and constantly ask for feelgood fiction, even though it's at odds with their desire to be at the cutting edge. And oh how they neglect the middle-aged and the elderly, these hard young men and women in the BBC. Watch the armies of shaven-headed, militant, politically correct, black-leathered foot soldiers arrive every morning, and shudder.

But even they are preferable to 'the suits'. Artists tend to be very rude about accountants. This is because artists like to pretend that they aren't businessmen, but of course they are, unless they're giving their work away free. We don't like to admit that we need accountants.

My accountant, Stanley Rosenthal, spoke wise words to me when I joined him. 'I won't ever tell you how to run your life,' he said. 'Your life is yours. I will tell you how best, while you lead the life you choose, to manage your money.' It is not thus in today's media. All too often today, the accountants run the show. Walk along the silent corridors where the men in suits hang out. Stop to listen. You will hear a faint whooshing sound. What is it? It's the sound of tails wagging dogs.

I mustn't end on too negative a note. Good programmes still get made. Good books still get published. There is a basic, inextinguishable human need for stories. I ain't finished yet.

I still have energy and health, but who knows what's round the corner? The summer before last, after two very hectic days, including making a speech at the Lords Taverners Eve of Headingley Test Dinner (quite stressful) and spending a day in the sunshine watching England bat (very stressful), I had the latest of my blackouts, at a lovely fish restaurant, the Drum and Monkey, in Harrogate. As I was taken out on a stretcher by paramedics, I felt a dreadful urge to say to the shocked customers, 'Don't have the fish soup', but I know that it wasn't funny, and I have to stop putting myself in positions of stress.

Susan is a member of Greenpeace and she has a Greenpeace card saying: 'Boycott Esso', which is always in the window of one of our cars. The other day we almost ran out of petrol and needed to stop at the first garage. It was an Esso garage. We began to fill up. Suddenly we saw the sign, 'Boycott Esso'. We whipped it out of sight and salved our consciences slightly by only getting ten-pounds-worth.

That story seems to sum up my life. However much I try to be serious about politics, comedy wins in the end.

But isn't it right that it should? Isn't that my role?

My ambition isn't really to achieve one perfect work. That is unattainable. It is to write just one thing, before I die, that is purely, sweetly comic, that doesn't seek the power of its own point of view, but is content to entertain. I find myself moving, often, in the opposite direction. *Going Gently* represented a move towards significance. I have plans for another novel which will take me further down that road. A humorous writer should be ambitious, tackle major themes, progress, develop, intensify. He should also be pure, innocent, simple, an entertainer. I face quite a task, reconciling these two contradictory pulls.

Plenty to do, then, even though I've said I mustn't do too much.

The sun is breaking through the clouds. Buds are softening the outlines of the great trees on the horizon. A great spotted woodpecker is feeding from the nuts at the front of the house. There are great tits and blue tits and long-tailed tits and marsh tits and none of them know that they are being watched by a writer who hates feeble, stale sexist jokes about them.

I sit at my desk, looking out over the deserted valley. I stare at a blank sheet of paper. I'm free to put any words I choose on this paper. Nobody can stop me. The whole world is mine to rearrange. And the amazing thing is, people pay me to do this. It can't be true. It must be a dream. Surely I didn't really get where I am today?

ACKNOWLEDGEMENTS

First of all I must mention the many good friends who have not found their way into this book. You are not forgotten. You are appreciated. Sadly, a list of splendid dinner parties, holidays and sessions in the pub would not have been of great interest to the general reader.

I owe a particular debt of thanks to my editor, Kirsty Fowkes, who made me dig deeper and be less reticent at many important points in the narrative. Whatever you think of this book, you would have liked it less without her efforts on my behalf.

I'm grateful to Palgrave and Chris Fox for allowing me to quote from Chapter 12 of *British Television Drama* about 'the emancipatory strategies of Reginald Perrin'.

My thanks go to Liz Calder, Jonathan Clowes and Ann Evans, Barry Cryer, Allan Kassell, Geoffrey Strachan and James Warrior, who refreshed my memory on some of the incidents about which I was particularly vague.

A big thank you also to those who allowed me to quote from their writings and/or letters – High Brogan, Jimmy Greaves, Sue Townsend and Dick Vosburgh – and to Liz Goulding and Mary Mullins on behalf of their much-missed husbands, Peter Tinniswood and Spike Mullins.

The origins of some of the early photos are lost in the mists of time, but I'm grateful to those who cheerfully permitted me to use some of the more recent ones – Barry Henson for the photo of my second wedding, Peter Conway for Susan's daughter's wedding, and Yorkshire Television of the pictures on location for *A Bit Of A Do*, *Rich Tea And Sympathy* and *Stalag Luft*, and to Paul Chapman, Patricia Hodge, David Jason, Michael Jayston, Denis Quilley, David Reynolds and Gwen Taylor for agreeing to be seen once more in my company.